Quicken® 2014
THE OFFICIAL GUIDE

Bobbi SANDBERG

New York   Chicago   San Francisco
Athens   London   Madrid   Mexico City
Milan   New Delhi   Singapore   Sydney   Toronto

Cataloging-in-Publication Data is on file with the Library of Congress

McGraw-Hill Education books are available at special quantity discounts to use as premiums and sales promotions, or for use in corporate training programs. To contact a representative, please visit the Contact Us pages at www.mhprofessional.com.

Quicken® 2014 The Official Guide

1 2 3 4 5 6 7 8 9 0   QFR QFR   1 0 9 8 7 6 5 4 3

ISBN   978-0-07-182606-8
MHID   0-07-182606-8

Sponsoring Editor	**Proofreader**
Roger Stewart	Paul Tyler
Editorial Supervisor	**Indexer**
Patty Mon	Jack Lewis
Project Manager	**Production Supervisor**
Patricia Wallenburg	George Anderson
Acquisitions Coordinator	**Composition**
Amanda Russell	TypeWriting
Technical Editor	**Art Director, Cover**
Mary Higgins	Jeff Weeks
Copy Editor	
Lisa McCoy	

This book is dedicated to seven of the most wonderful people on the planet. In chronological order: Sam, Royce, Joseph, Helene, Carissa, Gabe, and Colette. Each of you is a gift, and I am always amazed at your caring selves, intelligent understanding, and your talents and skills.

None of you will ever know how much you are appreciated and admired.

Also, for the always helpful attitude, friendly information, and willing assistance, a special thanks to Anne Bobinac and the team at Whidbey Island Bank! We are fortunate to have you folks in our world.

And, of course, to my kids, the parents of the seven most wonderful people on the planet, and, as ever and always, to Sandy.

Contents

Part One   Learning Quicken Basics

Part Two   Banking

Part Four   Understanding Your Financial Position

Part Five   Designing Your Financial Future

Part Six   Appendixes

Acknowledgments

This book, like most others, is the end product of a lot of hard work by many people. Among them are

- Roger Stewart, acquisitions editor at McGraw-Hill Education, for his attitude, great sense of humor and understanding, knowledgeable suggestions, and positive outlook! He is erudite, amiable, and expert at this challenge. THANK YOU, Roger, for being you!
- The folks at Intuit, especially Dale Knievel for his kindness and patience when answering all our questions and his willingness to find the best information during a time of terrific pressure at his "place"! He and his team are the *best*!
- The support team at McGraw-Hill Education, which includes a very special Patty Mon, the finest editorial supervisor around. Patty is beyond helpful, always considerate and thoughtful, and just "there" for any questions, and always cheerful. The amazing Amanda Russell; generous, right on top of each step of the process, and always supportive, fun, and kind. Patty Wallenburg, the project manager, someone who has become dear and not just because of her can-do attitude, constant good humor, accomplished professionalism, warm understanding, and overall support. There are not enough words to describe the joy when one gets to work with these three ladies. And thank you seems not nearly enough.
- The technical editor, Mary Higgins, is the best in the galaxy. Her skills, suggestions, support, and ability improve each word of the manuscript. Thank you for all that you do.
- Lisa McCoy, the most adroit copy editor, is such an important part of the team. Her talent is amazing and I so appreciate all she does.
- Paul Tyler, proofreader, and wonderful indexer, Jack Lewis, who always make any publication better with their knowledge and talents!
- AND, to George and Jeff, a thank you seems barely enough for all you do. Suffice it to say you are greatly appreciated for your skill, talent, and professionalism.

Introduction

Choosing Quicken Personal Finance Software to organize your finances was a great decision. Quicken has all the tools you need to manage your personal finances. Its well-designed, intuitive interface makes it easy to use. And its online and automation features make entering transactions and paying bills a snap. But if that isn't enough, Quicken also offers features that can help you learn more about financial opportunities which can save you time and money—two things that often seem in short supply.

This introduction tells you a little about the book, so you know what to expect in the chapters to come.

About This Book

This book tells you how to get the most out of Quicken. It starts by explaining the basics—the common, everyday tasks that you need to know just to use the program. It then goes beyond the basics to show you how to use Quicken to save time, save money, and make smart financial decisions. Along the way, it shows you most of Quicken's features, including many that you probably didn't even know existed. You'll find yourself using Quicken far more than you ever dreamed you would.

Assumptions

This book makes a few assumptions about your knowledge of your computer, Windows, Quicken, and financial management. These assumptions give you a starting point, making it possible to skip over the things that you are assumed to already know.

What You Should Know About Your Computer and Windows

To use this book (or Quicken 2014, for that matter), you should have a general understanding of how to use your computer and Windows. You don't need to be an expert. As you'll see, Quicken uses many standard and intuitive interface elements, making it easy to use—even if you're a complete computer novice.

At a bare minimum, you should know how to turn your computer on and off and how to use your mouse. You should also know how to perform basic Windows tasks, such as starting and exiting programs, using menus and dialog boxes (called just *dialogs* in this book), and entering and editing text.

If you're not sure how to do these things or would like to brush up on them, get *Windows 7 QuickSteps* or *Windows 8 QuickSteps* from McGraw-Hill Education. This resource will provide all the information you need to get started.

What You Should Know About Quicken and Financial Management

You don't need to know much about either Quicken or financial management to get the most out of this book; it assumes that both are new to you.

This doesn't mean that this book is just for raw beginners. It provides plenty of useful information for seasoned Quicken users—especially those of you who have used previous versions of Quicken—and for people who have been managing their finances with other tools, such as Microsoft Money (welcome to Quicken!) or pencil and paper (welcome!).

Because the book assumes that all this is new to you, it makes a special effort to explain Quicken procedures as well as the financial concepts and terms on which they depend. New concepts and terms first appear in italic type. By understanding these things, not only can you better understand how to use Quicken, but you also can communicate more effectively with finance professionals, such as bankers, stockbrokers, and financial advisors.

Quicken Updates

One of the terrific things about computing in 2014 is our Internet connectivity and capability. Quicken's team, like all program developers, is working to improve the software throughout the year, not just when a new version is released. That means that Quicken can send small changes to their program each time you update the program. Because of this, you may see illustrations in this book that differ from the ones you see on the screen. The procedures haven't changed, only small changes have been made to make the program more user-friendly.

Organization

This book is logically organized into six parts, each with at least two chapters. Each part covers either general Quicken setup information or one of Quicken's financial centers. Within each part, the chapters start with the most basic concepts and procedures, most of which involve specific Quicken tasks, and then work their way up to more advanced topics, many of which are based on finance-related concepts that Quicken makes easy to master.

It is not necessary to read this book from beginning to end. Skip around as desired. Although the book is organized for cover-to-cover reading, not all of its information may apply to you. For example, if you're not the least bit interested in investing, skip the chapters in the Investing part. It's as simple as that. When you're ready for the information that you skipped, it'll be waiting for you.

Here's a brief summary of the book's organization and contents.

Part One: Learning Quicken Basics

This part of the book introduces Quicken's interface and features, and helps you set up Quicken for managing your finances. This section introduces you to the new Quicken Mobile app and its features. If you're new to Quicken, the first two chapters in this part of the book may prove helpful.

Part One has two chapters:

- **Chapter 1:** Getting to Know Quicken by Working with Accounts, Categories, and Tags
- **Chapter 2:** Getting Up and Running with Quicken Mobile

Part Two: Banking

This part of the book explains how to use Quicken to record financial transactions in bank and credit card accounts. One chapter concentrates on the basics, while another goes beyond the basics to discuss online features available within Quicken. This part of the book also explains how to automate many transaction entry tasks, reconcile accounts, and use Quicken's extensive reporting features.

There are three chapters in Part Two:

- **Chapter 3:** Recording Bank and Credit Card Transactions
- **Chapter 4:** Using Online Banking Features
- **Chapter 5:** Reconciling Your Accounts and Examining Your Banking Activity

Part Three: Managing Your Investment Accounts

This part of the book explains how you can use Quicken and Quicken.com to keep track of your investment portfolio and get information to help you make smart investment decisions. The first chapter covers the basics of Quicken's investment tracking features, while the other two chapters provide information about online investment tracking and research tools. You'll see how the features available at Quicken.com can help you evaluate your investment position.

There are three chapters in Part Three:

- **Chapter 6:** Entering Your Investment Transactions
- **Chapter 7:** Using Transaction Download and Research Tools
- **Chapter 8:** Evaluating Your Position

Part Four: Understanding Your Financial Position

This part of the book concentrates on assets and liabilities, including your home and car and related loans. It explains how you can track these items in Quicken and provides tips for minimizing related expenses.

There are two chapters in Part Four:

- **Chapter 9:** Monitoring Assets and Loans
- **Chapter 10:** Keeping Tabs on Your Net Worth

Part Five: Designing Your Financial Future

This part of the book tells you how you can take advantage of Quicken's built-in planning tools to plan for your retirement and other major events in your life. As you'll learn in this part of the book, whether you want financial security in your retirement years or to save up for the down payment on a house or college education for your children, Quicken can help you. It includes information on using Quicken's financial calculators and provides a wealth of tips for saving money and reducing debt.

There are three chapters in Part Five:

- **Chapter 11:** Planning Your Future with Financial Calculators
- **Chapter 12:** Reducing Debt and Saving Money
- **Chapter 13:** Planning for Tax Time

Part Six: Appendixes

And, to help you even more, two appendixes offer additional information you might find useful when working with Quicken:

- **Appendix A:** Managing Quicken Files
- **Appendix B:** Customizing Quicken

Conventions

All how-to books—especially computer books—have certain conventions for communicating information. Here's a brief summary of the conventions used throughout this book.

Menu Commands

Quicken, like most other Windows programs, makes commands accessible on the menu bar at the top of the application window. Throughout this book, you are told which menu commands to choose to open a window or dialog, or to complete a task. The following format is used to indicate menu commands: Menu | Submenu (if applicable) | Command.

Keystrokes

Keystrokes are the keys you must press to complete a task. There are two kinds of keystrokes.

- **Keyboard shortcuts** are combinations of keys you press to complete a task more quickly. For example, the shortcut for "clicking" a Cancel button may be to press the ESC key. When instructing you to press a key, the name of the key is in small caps, like this: ESC. If you must press two or more keys simultaneously, they are separated with a hyphen, like this: CTRL-P. Many of Quicken's keyboard shortcuts are explained in Chapter 1.
- **Literal text** is text that you must type in exactly as it appears in the book. Although this book doesn't contain many instances of literal text, there are a few. Literal text to be typed is in boldface type, like this: **Checking Acct**. If literal text includes a variable—text you must substitute when you type—the variable is included in bold-italic type, like this: ***Payee Name***.

Icons

Icons are used to flag specific types of information.

Sidebars

This book includes "In My Experience" sidebars. These sidebars are meant to put a specific Quicken feature into perspective by either telling you how it is used or offering suggestions on how you can use it. You'll learn a lot from these sidebars, but like all sidebars, they're not required reading.

About the Author

Bobbi Sandberg has long been involved with computers, accounting, and writing. She is a retired accountant currently filling her time as a trainer, technical writer, and small-business consultant. As a Quicken user since the program launched in the 1980s and a Quicken teacher since its inception, she knows the questions users ask and gives easy-to-understand explanations of each step within the program. She teaches at several venues, offering step-by-step instruction in a variety of computer applications. Her extensive background, coupled with her ability to explain complex concepts in plain language, has made her a popular instructor, consultant, writer, and speaker. She has authored and co-authored more than a dozen computer books, including *Quicken 2011 The Official Guide*, *Quicken 2012 The Official Guide*, and *Quicken 2013 The Official Guide*.

About the Technical Editor

Mary Higgins is a long-time Quicken user, having used each version since 1999. She enjoys pushing the limits of what the software is intended to do—clicking every button, navigating every menu path, reading the help files, etc. She reads and posts on the Quicken forums and finds it interesting to see how others are using Quicken and the different approaches to resolving issues.

Learning Quicken Basics

This part of the book introduces Quicken Personal Finance Software's interface and features. It begins by explaining how to install Quicken and showing you the elements of its user interface, including some of Quicken's online features. There is an entire chapter telling you all about Quicken's accounts, categories, and tags. Finally, it explains Quicken's mobile app and how you can access your financial information from your smartphone or other mobile device. The chapters are

Getting to Know Quicken by Working with Accounts, Categories, and Tags

In This Chapter:

- *Exploring Quicken's uses*
- *Installing Quicken from a CD*
- *Starting Quicken*
- *Exploring the Quicken window*
- *Understanding other Quicken features*
- *Finding help in Quicken*
- *Understanding online financial services*
- *Reviewing account types*
- *Creating your first account*
- *Setting up other banking accounts*
- *Setting Up One Step Update*
- *Understanding the Password Vault*
- *Working with the Account List window*
- *Establishing categories and subcategories*
- *Working with the Category List window*
- *Using tags*

I f you're brand new to Quicken Personal Finance Software, get your relationship with Quicken off to a good start by properly installing it and learning a little more about how you can interact with it. Although the information provided in this section is especially useful to new Quicken users, some of it also applies to users who are upgrading. In the next section, you'll learn about data files, accounts, and some of the many other features inside this software.

What Is Quicken?

On its face, Quicken is a computerized checkbook. It enables you to balance your accounts and organize, manage, and generate reports for your finances. However, as you explore Quicken, you'll learn that it's much more. It's a complete personal finance software package—a tool for taking control of your finances. Quicken makes it easy to know what you have, how you are doing financially, and what you could do to strengthen your financial situation.

Exploring Quicken's Uses

While many use Quicken only to manage their bank and credit card accounts, Quicken can help you manage investment accounts as well as help you organize other data, such as the purchase price of your possessions and the outstanding balances on your loans. It can even store a copy of the warranty that came with your purchases. With Quicken's online features, much of your data entry can be automated. Online banking enables you to keep track of bank account transactions and balances, and to pay bills without writing checks or sticking on stamps.

With all financial information stored in Quicken's data file, you can generate net worth reports to see where you stand today. You can also use a variety of financial planners to make financial decisions for the future. Quicken's tax features, including export into TurboTax and the Deduction Finder, can make tax time easier on you and your bank accounts.

Quicken Editions

Intuit offers several editions of Quicken 2014 for Windows for managing personal finances: Starter, Deluxe, and Premier. The features in each edition are shown in Table 1-1.

This book covers Quicken Deluxe and Premier Editions. Although much of its information also applies to Quicken Starter, this book covers many features that are not included in the Starter edition and a handful not included in the Deluxe edition. If you're a Quicken Starter or Deluxe user, consider upgrading to Quicken Premier so you can take advantage of the powerful features it has to offer.

What You Can Do	Quicken Starter	Quicken Deluxe	Quicken Premier
Track bank accounts and credit cards	x	x	x
Use online services	x	x	x
Categorize transactions	x	x	x
Financial Alerts		x	x
Create a budget		x	x
Manage investments		x	x
Tax planning		x	x

Table 1-1 • Quicken Edition Features

One more thing—Intuit also offers two additional Quicken editions. If you're a small-business owner, Quicken Home & Business can handle all of your personal and basic business financial needs, including the business expenses you need to track for your tax return's Schedule C. If you manage one or more rental properties, Quicken Rental Property Manager can handle transactions and other information for tenants, rental income, and related expenses that you need to track for your tax return's Schedule E. As you can see, Intuit has you covered with a Quicken product for all facets of your financial life.

System Requirements

Quicken 2014 is designed to work with Windows 7 and 8 and both 32- and 64-bit machines. You'll find no problem either if you install Quicken 2014 on a machine that runs Windows Vista or Windows XP SP2 and later. You'll need at least 1 gigabyte (GB) of random access memory (RAM) and a minimum of 450 megabytes (MB) of free space on your hard drive. Your monitor should have a minimum resolution of 1024×768. If you are installing from a CD, you'll need a CD/DVD drive. You need Internet access for working online and receiving program updates. You also need a printer for printing reports and graphs.

Getting Started

Ready to get started? This section explains how to install, start, and register Quicken.

Installing Quicken from a CD

Quicken uses a standard Windows setup program that should be familiar to you if you've installed other Windows programs. Insert the Quicken 2014 CD into your CD or DVD drive. A dialog should appear, asking if you want to install the program to your hard drive. If so, click Yes to start the Quicken installer.

The installer displays a series of dialogs with information and options for installing Quicken. Read the information in the Welcome screen as seen next. When asked to agree to a software license agreement, select the I Agree To The Terms Of The License Agreement And Acknowledge Receipt Of The Quicken Privacy Statement option, and click Next to continue. (Unless you select this option, you will not be able to click Next nor install the software.)

IN MY EXPERIENCE

If you have downloaded your program, simply locate the downloaded file and double-click to open it. The InstallShield Wizard begins to install your program and proceeds as noted here. However, you might consider saving a copy of your downloaded program onto an external device, such as a CD or external hard drive, just in case your internal hard drive has any problems in the future.

Keep a copy of your e-mail verification of purchase in the same location. It's much easier for Intuit to verify your information in case of any issues when you can provide purchase information and verification. Consider using Quicken's Attachment feature to keep all of your purchase information right in Quicken. See Chapter 3 to learn how to attach data to your Quicken transactions.

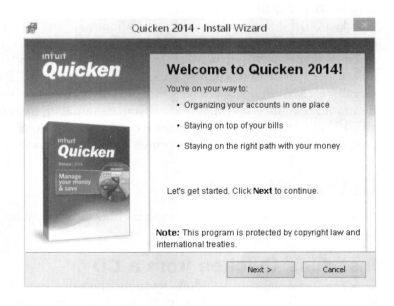

Click the Quicken Privacy Statement link to open and read this important document in a web browser window. Close the browser window when you're finished to return to the installer. You may clear the anonymous usage message check box if you choose. This option allows Quicken to collect information about how you use the program so that Intuit can make the program even more user-friendly. Click Next in the Install Wizard window.

In the Destination Folder screen, the installer tells you where Quicken will be installed—normally C:\Program Files\Quicken. You can click the Change button and use the screen that appears to change the installation location. To keep the recommended, default location, just click Next.

In the Ready To Install The Program screen, the installer displays a summary of what it will do. If this is a first-time Quicken installation, all it will do is install Quicken 2014 and any updates to the program. However, if you're upgrading from a previous year's version, the installer will begin by uninstalling whatever version is currently installed. (Only one version of Quicken can be installed on your computer at a time.) Only the Quicken program files will be deleted; your data files will remain intact so you can use them with Quicken 2014. Click Install.

For upgraders, the data file you most recently used in a previous version is converted to the Quicken 2014 format with a copy of the previous version's data file placed in a folder called Q*xx*Files, where *xx* shows the version year.

Wait while the installer uninstalls the previous version of Quicken (if necessary), installs the Quicken 2014 program files, and downloads any updates to your hard disk, as seen here.

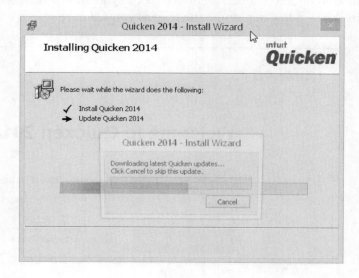

When Quicken is installed, you see a message that the installation is complete. By default, this is set to start Quicken as soon as you click the Finish button. Should you want to start Quicken later, clear the Start Quicken check box. Either way, click Finish.

If you have chosen to launch Quicken 2014, Quicken should start after you select Finish. Skip ahead to the section titled "Creating a Quicken File." If Quicken does not start automatically, follow the instructions in the next section to start it.

Starting Quicken

You can start Quicken in several different ways. Here are some of the most common methods.

- **Opening Quicken with the Desktop Shortcut or Windows 8 Tile**   The Quicken installer places a Quicken 2014 shortcut icon on the desktop of your Windows 7 (or earlier Windows versions). Double-click this shortcut to open Quicken. In Windows 8, a tile appears with the other installed programs. Click the tile once to open Quicken.
- **Open Quicken from the Task Bar**   In Windows 7 (and earlier) use the Start button on the Windows task bar to start Quicken and other Quicken components. Choose Start | All Programs | Quicken 2014 | Quicken 2014 to start Quicken.

If you have not used Quicken before, or if you installed Quicken 2014 on a new computer, you see the welcome message shown here. The choices you make in this window determine the screens you see next.

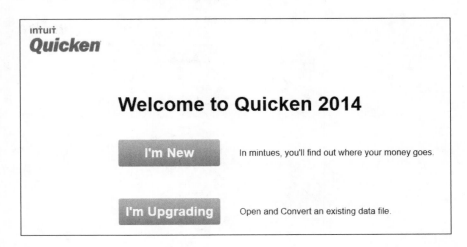

Some Quicken users are confused by this screen. They click the I'm New button when they aren't really new users, and then they can't figure out how to go back and convert their files from the previous version. To convert those files, just use File | Open Quicken File and navigate to the location where your files from the previous version of Quicken are stored.

New User Startup

If you are new to Quicken, click the I'm New button to create your Intuit ID. You use this ID information to connect with Quicken for updates, alerts, and to download information to either your desktop or mobile device. This is a two-step process. The first step is completing your personal identification information as seen here.

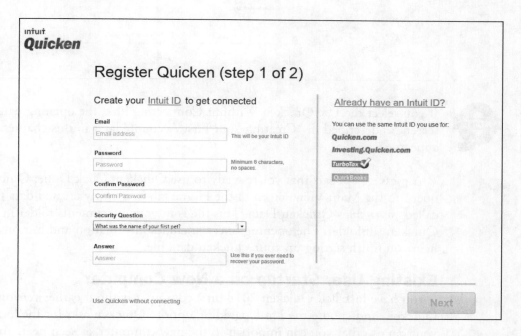

Quicken recommends that you create your Intuit ID at this time to ensure you receive all important updates and other information, even if you do not choose to download your transactions or use the Quicken Mobile App.

When you have completed step 1, click the Next button to complete your registration in step 2, as seen next.

intuit
Quicken

Register Quicken (step 2 of 2)

Tell us about yourself

| First Name* | *Required | Where did you buy Quicken?* |
| | Select... |

| Last Name* | What other methods have you used to manage your personal finances? |
| Last Name |

Check all that apply.

| Address* |
| Address | ☐ Quicken |
| | ☐ Online Banking |

| City* | State* | ☐ Spreadsheet/Track by hand |
| City | | ☐ Microsoft Money |

Zip*	Mobile Number	☐ Mint.com
Zip Code	Number	☐ Other
		☐ Not using any method

Learn more about our privacy policy and contact preferences.   Next

If you select the Use Quicken Without Connecting link, the opening data screen, as described in "Creating Your First Account" later in this chapter, appears.

A message appears that you're ready to use Quicken. Click Done. Quicken opens to the Main View screen of the Home tab in a newly created data file called *yourname*'s Quicken Data. This file is in your Documents folder in a Quicken subfolder. The opening screen includes information and buttons that help you finish setting up your Quicken data file.

Existing User Startup on a New Computer

If you have installed Quicken 2014 on a computer without earlier versions of Quicken, and choose the I'm Upgrading option, Quicken asks for the location of your data so that you can import it to the new computer, as seen next. Your earlier file can be restored from another computer on a home (or business) network, an external hard drive, DVD, CD, or Quicken's online backup. This process converts the data file named in the dialog to the Quicken 2014 format and saves the original file in C:\Users\ *yourname*\Documents\Quicken\Q*xx*Files. The path for the saved copy of the original file may vary depending on the previous version from which you are upgrading.

intuit
Quicken

Select your exisiting data file to get started

▓ Open a data file located on this computer
☐ Restore a data file I've backed up to a CD, to a disk, or online
☐ Start over and create a new data file

How do I move a data file from another computer?   Get Started

Converting a Data File as Part of an Upgrade

If you have updated Quicken on a computer with an earlier version of Quicken, the installation process converts your previous data for use with Quicken 2014. This process converts the data file named in the dialog to the Quicken 2014 format and saves the original file in C:\Users*yourname*\\Documents\\Quicken\\Q*xx*Files. The path for the saved copy of the original file varies depending on the previous version from which you are upgrading.

If you are upgrading from a previous version of Quicken, you may not see the registration screens until you download or update for the first time in Quicken 2014.

The Quicken Interface

Quicken's interface is designed to be intuitive and easy to use. If you are starting Quicken from scratch, after you have installed and created your Intuit ID, Quicken opens to the Quicken Home page shown in the next illustration. This interface puts the information and tools you need to manage your finances right within mouse pointer reach. You never have to dig through multiple dialogs and menus to get to the commands you need most. You'll see more about using this Home page later in this chapter.

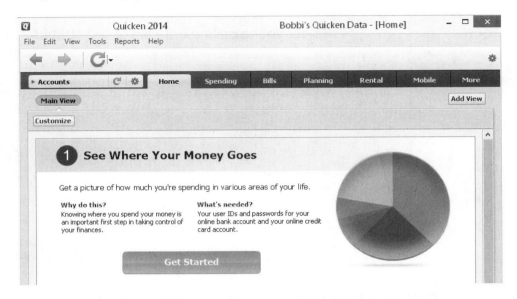

This section tells you about the components of the Quicken interface and explains how each feature can help you manage your financial life.

Exploring the Quicken Window

The main Quicken window gives you access to most of Quicken's features and your financial information. We'll look at each section separately.

Account Bar

The Account Bar lists each of your Quicken accounts on the left side of the main Quicken window, as shown on the following page. At the top of the Account Bar is a link to the All Transactions register, which shows the transactions for all of your accounts (with the exception of your Investing accounts) in one register. However, it does show transactions from linked investment cash accounts.

There are three main sections to the Account Bar: Banking, Investing, and Property & Debt. If the Account Bar is not displayed, you can display it by clicking the small right-pointing arrow at the left of the word "Accounts," as seen here.

If you can't see all of the accounts in the Account Bar, use the scroll bar on the right side of the Account Bar to scroll through its contents. You can also click the downward or right-pointing arrow next to a section heading on the Account Bar to hide or display, respectively, the list of accounts beneath it.

By default, account balances, rounded to the nearest dollar, appear in the Account Bar; however, you can right-click anywhere in the Account Bar to open a context menu. Choose Show Amounts to display the amounts, and clear the check mark to hide amounts from view. (Hiding amounts makes the Account Bar narrower so more information appears in the window to the right.) This contextual menu offers additional options for the display of the Account Bar, such as displaying cents in the amounts. You can also change the width of the Account Bar by dragging its right border.

The account names in the Account Bar are links to that account's register. You can customize the Account Bar to move accounts from one section to another or to hide an account's name from the Account Bar as discussed later in this chapter. Click View | Account Bar to open a menu with which you can choose where the Account Bar physically appears in your Quicken window, as seen next.

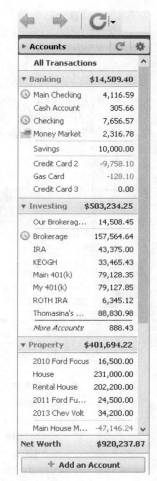

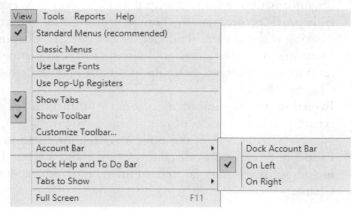

Tabs

Tabs, as seen below, help you navigate through Quicken. Some tabs, such as the Spending and Investing tabs, provide information about your financial status, as well as links and buttons for accessing Quicken features. Other tabs have views, such as the Main View of the Home tab, that enable you to view and customize Quicken settings for your financial situation. Use the Tabs To Show option from View in the Quicken menu to specify which tabs to display or hide from view. Some tabs are available only in the Premier or higher editions of Quicken.

 Many Quicken users choose to display all of the tabs until they find which features they use the most. For example, the Budgeting feature of Quicken is included in the Planning tab. Consider exploring the features available in each of the Quicken tabs before you decide to turn off its display.

A tab exists for each major area of Quicken:

- **Home** displays customizable views of your Quicken data. See Chapter 5 and Appendix B to learn more about how to work with and customize the Home tab views
- **Spending** provides information about your income and expenditures for all accounts, only a single account of your choosing, for all dates, or for a custom date that you choose. You can use the drop-down lists to customize the information in both graphical and list formats as explained in Chapter 5.
- **Bills** provides information about your upcoming bills and offers tools for working with bills and reminders as discussed in Chapter 4.
- **Planning** gives you access to Quicken's financial planners, as well as the assumptions you need to set up to use the planners effectively, as discussed in Chapter 11.
- **Investing** provides information about your investment and retirement accounts and any stocks or mutual funds you've asked Quicken to watch for you. See Chapters 6, 7, and 8 for investing information.
- **Property & Debt** provides information about asset and debt accounts, including your home, car, related loans, and auto expenses, as discussed in Chapters 9 and 10.

- **Mobile & Alerts** helps you set up your Quicken Cloud ID to work with the Quicken Mobile App. See Chapter 2 for information.
- **Tips & Tutorials** displays information about additional Quicken services.

The buttons in each tab indicate the current view or other options within each tab section. If there's more than one button or a menu in either of these areas, you can click a button or choose a menu command to switch to another view or account.

After you have created your first account in your Quicken data file, you will see a small button at the top right of your Home tab that reads View Guidance. This button appears on several of your tabs and can also be accessed through the Help menu. See "View Guidance" later in this chapter for more information.

Understanding Other Quicken Features

Quicken uses other windows to display information, depending on what you want to see or what task you are trying to perform.

- **List Windows**   A list window shows a list of information about related things, such as accounts, categories, tags, or scheduled transactions. You can use a list window to perform tasks with items in the list.
- **Report Windows**   Quicken's report windows enable you to create reports about your financial matters. You have the option to change date ranges, create comparisons, and customize reports. You can also use options and buttons at the top of the window to work with, customize, and save reports. You learn about all of these in Chapter 5.

Quicken offers a number of ways to access its features and commands, including standard Microsoft Windows elements, such as menus and dialogs, and Quicken elements, such as the Toolbar, the Action gear icons, and links and buttons within Quicken windows.

- **Menus**   Quicken has two ways to display menus. The recommended Standard display shows six items on the menu bar, as seen here. If you choose Classic Menus, you have an additional seven from which to choose. You can choose commands from the menus as follows:
  - Click the menu name to display the menu. If necessary, click the name

of the submenu you want, and then click the name of the command you want.

- Press the shortcut key combination for the menu command that you want. A command's shortcut key, if it has one, shows to the right of the command name on the menu. See an extensive list of Quicken's shortcut keys in Appendix A.

- **Shortcut Menus** Shortcut menus (which are sometimes referred to as context or context-sensitive menus) can be displayed throughout Quicken. Point to the item for which you want to display a shortcut menu and click the right mouse button. The menu, which includes only those commands applicable to the item, appears at the mouse pointer.

IN MY EXPERIENCE

There are two other menu items that affect how you see information in Quicken.

- Use Large Fonts makes the font much larger. This option enlarges the standard Quicken fonts in every tab, as well as in registers and on-screen reports. The downside of this option is that while the font is larger, you will see less information on each screen and some of the windows may be cut off. Also, the menu bar fonts stay the normal size.
- The Use Pop-up Registers option displays a selected register (or registers) as a pop-up on top of the regular Quicken window. The downside to using pop-up registers is that you cannot set your Quicken Preferences to open to a specific account's register if you use pop-up registers.

- **Dialogs** Like other Windows applications, Quicken uses dialogs to communicate with you. Some dialogs display a simple message, while others include text boxes, option buttons, check boxes, and drop-down lists you can use to enter information.
- **Toolbar** The Quicken Toolbar is a row of buttons along the top of the Quicken window, just beneath the standard menu bar, that gives you access to other navigation techniques and features. The Quicken Toolbar appears by default, but can be turned off and customized. Learn how to customize it in Appendix B. The default Toolbar contains three icons and a search box, and the Customize Toolbar gear icon.
  - **Back** (an arrow pointing left) displays the previously opened window.
  - **Forward** (an arrow pointing right) displays the window you were looking at before you clicked the Back button. This button is only available if you clicked the Back button to view a previously viewed window, otherwise it is grayed out.

- **One Step Update** (the blue curling arrow that points to the right) opens the One Step Update menu, so with your Internet connection you can update all of your online information at once.
- **Customize Toolbar** (the small gear icon) at the end of the Quicken Toolbar allows you to make changes and additions to the Quicken Toolbar. Learn more about customizing the Toolbar in Appendix B.
- **Search** is a global search feature you can use to search for transactions entered into Quicken. Just enter the search criteria in the field, and press ENTER. If you do not see the global search field, click the Customize Toolbar gear icon at the right of the Toolbar, then in the Customize Toolbar dialog that opens, click the check box to the left of Show Global Search. Then, click Done to close the Customize Toolbar dialog.
- **Filters**   Filters are a row of textual buttons and menus that appear just above the contents of many Quicken windows. Most filter items, which vary from window to window, are drop-down lists. Click the downward-pointing arrows to access the list.
- **View Guidance**   After you have used Quicken for a time, you may notice a button at the upper right of your Home and Spending tabs called View Guidance. This button opens a series of Qcards that explain specifics about that tab. See an example of a Qcard in the Spending tab here.

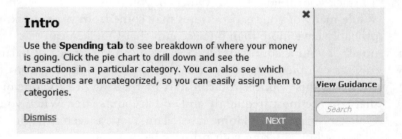

Finding Help in Quicken

In addition to the question mark icon in many Quicken windows and the Help button in some dialogs, Quicken includes an extensive Onscreen Help system to provide more information about using Quicken while you work. You can access most Help options from the Help menu, which is shown here.

Quicken's Onscreen Help uses a familiar Windows Help interface. You can use it to browse or search Help topics or display Help information about a specific window. These days, any decent software program offers on-screen help. So what's the big deal about Quicken's? Quicken's Onscreen Help is especially, well, helpful. It covers every program feature and provides step-by-step instructions for performing many tasks. Clickable links make it easy to jump right to a topic you want to learn more about. And as you'll discover while using Quicken, Help is available throughout the program—not just in the Quicken Help windows.

Understanding Online Financial Services

If you're interested in keeping track of your finances with the least amount of data entry, you should be considering Quicken's online features such as Transaction Download and Online Payment. However, you can't use them until you've set up an account with a participating financial institution and applied for the online account services you want to use. Learn more about online financial services in Chapter 4.

Accounts

To track your finances with Quicken, you must create at least one account. While many of your expenditures may come from your checking account, you probably have more than one account that Quicken can track for you. By setting up all of your accounts in Quicken, you can keep track of balances and activity to get a complete picture of your financial situation. You don't have to add all of your accounts at once. You can start by tracking just the one or two accounts that you use most frequently and add accounts later. When you first open Quicken, you see the Home tab's Main View, as seen in Figure 1-1, where you get started by entering your primary bank account.

In Quicken, a data file holds all of the information about all of your Quicken accounts. Quicken accounts can be checking, savings, credit card, investing, property, and debt accounts. When would you want more than one data file? For example, you may need two data files if you use Quicken to organize both your own finances as well as the finances of a community group for which you are serving as treasurer. Each of these data files would have its own separate set of bank, credit, and asset accounts.

Figure 1-1 • Quicken's Main View makes getting started easy and efficient.

Reviewing Account Types

This part of the chapter explains a bit more about Quicken's accounts and how you can create and modify your accounts. As discussed earlier, an account is a record of what you either own or owe. Quicken offers various kinds of accounts for different purposes. A link for each account you set up in Quicken appears in one of the three sections of the Account Bar. You can choose to hide accounts from the Account Bar, as discussed later in this chapter. Table 1-2 summarizes the accounts and how they are organized within Quicken.

- **What You Own**   In accounting jargon, what you own are assets. In Quicken, an asset is one type of account; several other types exist as well.
  - **Spending & Savings**   These checking, credit cards, savings, and cash accounts display in the Banking section of the Account Bar.

Account Type	Account Bar Section	Asset or Liability
Checking	Banking	Asset
Savings	Banking	Asset
Credit Card	Banking	Liability
Cash	Banking	Asset
Standard Brokerage	Investing	Asset
IRA or Keogh Plan	Investing	Asset
401(k) or 403(b)	Investing	Asset
529 Plan	Investing	Asset
House	Property & Debt	Asset
Vehicle	Property & Debt	Asset
Other Asset	Property & Debt	Asset
Debt	Property & Debt	Liability

Table 1-2 • Overview of Quicken Account Types

- **Investment** Your investment accounts display in the Account Bar's Investing section and are for tracking the stocks, bonds, and mutual funds in your portfolio that are not in retirement accounts.
- **Retirement** While also included in the Investing section, these accounts track investments in retirement accounts. Quicken distinguishes between different types of retirement accounts. One type includes individual retirement accounts (IRAs) or Keogh Plans, another combines 401(k) or 403(b) accounts, and most 529 Plans are included in this section.
- **Asset** Your asset accounts display in the Property & Debt section of the Account Bar. You use this type of account for tracking items that you own. Quicken distinguishes among three different types of asset accounts: House, Vehicle, and Other Asset.
- **What You Owe** The accounting term for what you owe (your debts) is liabilities. Quicken offers two kinds of accounts for amounts you owe.
  - **Credit Card** Credit cards will normally appear in the Banking section, and this is the best location for them. However, those cards that you have designated as Liability accounts display in the Property & Debt section. See the section on "Account Intent" later in this chapter to see how to show your cards in this section of the Account Bar.
  - **Debt** Debt (liability) accounts appear in the Property & Debt section. This section is for tracking loans, mortgages, and other liabilities. While it is possible to include credit cards in this section, most users opt to show their credit card accounts in the Banking section of the Account Bar.

If you are using either the Home & Business or Rental Property Manager editions of Quicken, you can also enter special business accounts such as Accounts Payable and Accounts Receivable.

After you have installed Quicken, its opening window offers easy access to features you use to configure your Quicken data file, as seen in Figure 1-1. The Home tab's Main View includes several areas. This part of the chapter provides a tour of each area and explains how you can use it to set up a Quicken data file.

Creating Your First Account

To begin using Quicken, you must tell the program what bank and credit cards you wish to track. In the See Where Your Money Goes snapshot, click the Get Started button to begin. If you don't see the Get Started button, you can still add new accounts. See "Setting Up Other Banking Accounts" next. During this process, Quicken may go online to download an up-to-date list of participating financial institutions.

The Add Your Primary Checking Account dialog box appears, as seen next. (If this is not the first account you are entering in Quicken, the dialog will say "Add Checking Account." This is true even if you have entered a "primary" account and then deleted it. You see the Primary Checking Account dialog only

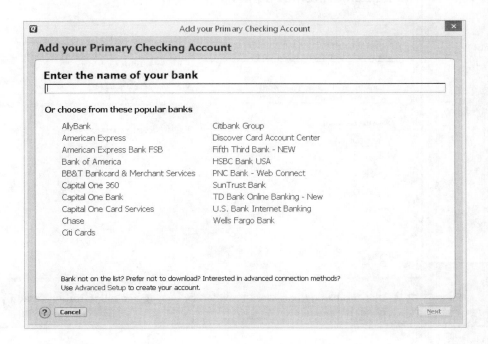

when you are setting up a data file for the first time.) Choose the name of your bank from the displayed list, or type its name in the Enter The Name Of Your Bank field. If your bank's name does not appear on this first group of names, when you type the first letters of your bank's name, a new list appears with a list of those institutions that begin with the letters you typed.

Note the Advanced Setup link at the bottom of the window. Use this if you do not want to download your information or if your bank offers more than one type of downloading service. See the section "Use Advanced Setup to Create a Manual-Entry Account" later in this chapter for more information.

Click Next to continue. Depending on your financial institution, you may see a dialog displaying connection services available for that financial institution. If so, make your choice and click Next. In the dialog that appears, as seen in Figure 1-2, Quicken prompts you to enter your user name and password as provided by your bank. (Should you want to save this password in the Quicken Password Vault, click Save This Password. See "Setting Up the Password Vault" later in this chapter for more information.) Click Connect to continue.

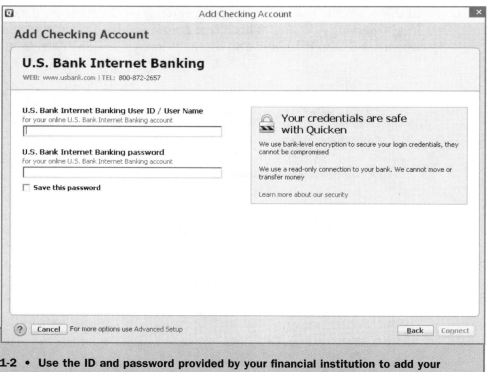

Figure 1-2 • Use the ID and password provided by your financial institution to add your checking account.

As you enter your user ID and password, Quicken will warn you if your CAPS LOCK key is on.

The Quicken Update Status message appears as Quicken connects to your financial institution. (If there are additional passwords or security phrases required by your bank, you are prompted to enter them. Do so and click OK or Next, depending on the prompt.) You may be prompted to create an Intuit ID, also called your Quicken Cloud ID, or enter your Intuit ID here.

If you have more than one account that uses the user ID and password you entered, all of the accounts may be downloaded. If you have not yet set up any accounts, in Quicken each account will be called by the account name shown on your bank's records. You may change the name to something more descriptive if you choose. If you have already entered some accounts, Quicken prompts you to add, link, or ignore each of the downloaded accounts. See "Using Downloaded Accounts" later in this chapter. After changing the account name(s) and selecting Add/Link/Ignore, click Next.

After the download is complete, your account (or accounts if you have more than one at that bank) shows on an Accounts Added list. Click Finish to return to the Home tab's Main View. Each downloaded account appears in the Account Bar, with the nickname you entered, as shown here at right. You may change the account names if you choose. See "Working with the Account List Window" later in this chapter.

▼ Accounts	⟳	⚙
All Transactions		
▼ Banking		$14,063
House Checking		7,563
Savings		6,549
House Credit Card		-49
Net Worth		$14,063
✦ Add an Account		

Setting Up Other Banking Accounts

After you have created your primary checking account, you can create additional new accounts with the Add An Account button that appears at the bottom of your Account Bar. No matter what type of account you create, Quicken steps you through the creation process, prompting you to enter information about the account, such as its name and balance. In this section, you'll learn how to use the Add Account dialog to set up new accounts.

Adding New Accounts

Quicken calls its default method of adding accounts "Simple Setup." This process begins by opening the Add Account dialog. You can open this dialog in several ways, as listed here:

1. Click Add An Account from the bottom of the Account Bar.
2. Choose Tools | Add Account.
3. Press CTRL-A to open the Account List. Click the Add An Account button at the bottom-right corner of the window.

 You can also open the Account List by choosing Tools | Account List.

The Add Account dialog begins by asking what type of account you want to create. From there its options change, depending on the account type and whether you want to set it up for available online account services.

Creating a Spending and Saving Account

This section covers how to enter Spending and Saving accounts, such as Checking, Credit Card, Savings, and Cash accounts. You will learn how to enter Investing and Retirement accounts in Chapter 6 and Property, Assets, and Debt accounts in Chapter 9.

Using one of the methods discussed earlier, open the Add Account dialog. Then select the type of account you want to create. If you choose Checking, Credit Card, or Savings, the Add (type of account) Account dialog screen opens, as seen next. You'll notice that the dialog is similar to the screen you saw when you entered your primary account. The only difference is that instead of Add Primary Checking Account, it says Add (type of account).

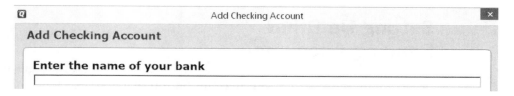

Choose a bank from the list or enter the first few letters of your bank or credit union's name. A second list appears. For most of us, our bank's name will be on the list. Click the name of your bank and click Next. If your bank's name is not on the list, you can still create an account and enter your transactions manually. Click Advanced Setup at the bottom of the window. See "Use Advanced Setup to Create a Manual-Entry Account" later in this chapter.

Enter your user ID and password in the appropriate fields and click Connect. The Quicken Update Status dialog appears showing that Quicken is receiving information from your financial institution.

 As you connect to your financial institution, you may be prompted for additional information. To ensure you type the correct information, you can select the Show Characters check box.

After the information is downloaded, the Account Added window appears with the name of your account. Click Add Another Account or click Finish to close the window.

Using Downloaded Accounts

If your user name and password connect to more than one account at a specific financial institution, all of the accounts may be downloaded when you connect. If you have already created accounts in Quicken, you will see a dialog from which you can perform an action for each of the downloaded accounts.

- **Add**   Use Add to create a new Quicken account with this information. You may rename the account to something more useful to you.
- **Link**   The Link option is used to identify a current Quicken account and combine the information in the download with that account. Make sure you have chosen the correct account.

 If you do not link an account correctly, you can correct it later. See Chapter 4 for more information.

- **Ignore**   If you choose to ignore this downloadable account, the information will not be downloaded into Quicken.

Review each choice before you continue to ensure you have connected the correct Quicken account with each downloaded account. Figure 1-3 shows an example of the dialog. After you have made your choices, click Next. You'll see the Account Added screen listing only the accounts you set as Add or Link.

 You may have noticed one of Quicken's features. As you opened the Add Account dialog, the Quicken window from which you started dims. You will never be confused about which dialog or window you're working on with this feature. You can adjust or even turn off the dimming. Click Edit | Preferences | Startup | Quicken Colors | Dim Disabled Windows.

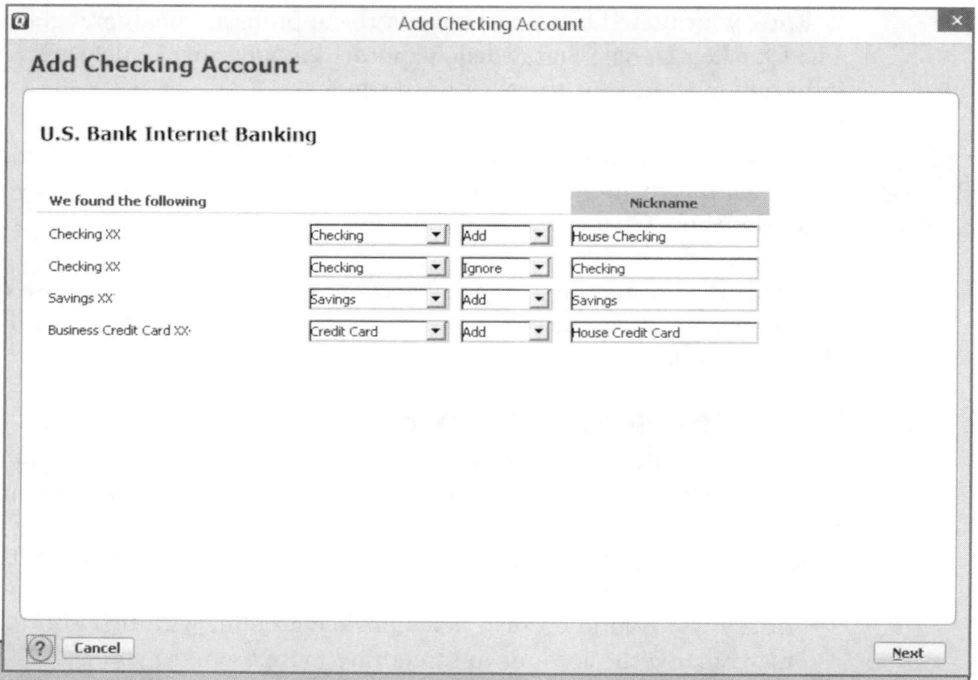

Figure 1-3 • Ensure you connect each downloaded account with the correct Quicken account.

Use Advanced Setup to Create a Manual-Entry Account

As mentioned earlier, if you prefer to enter transactions manually, you can use the Advanced Setup option. This option also allows you to select the downloading method. To access Advanced Setup, from the Add <type of account> dialog, click Advanced Setup at the bottom of the dialog.

Using One Step Update and the Password Vault

Many of Quicken's online features use One Step Update to update information and download transactions from your financial institutions. However, that's not all One Step Update can do. This feature makes it possible to handle many of your connection chores at once. When used in conjunction with the Password Vault feature, you can click a few buttons, enter a single password, and take a break while Quicken updates portfolio and account information for you. You can even schedule updates to occur automatically when Quicken isn't running.

The idea behind One Step Update is to use one command to handle multiple online activities. This eliminates the need to use update commands in a variety of locations throughout Quicken. One command does it all.

Setting Up One Step Update

Choose Tools | One Step Update or click the Update button (the blue right-curling arrow) in the Account Bar. If a dialog appears asking if you want to set up the Password Vault, click No for now. You'll see how to use this feature later in this chapter, in the section titled "Entering the Password Vault." The One Step Update Settings dialog appears, as seen in Figure 1-4. It lists all of the items that can be updated. Check marks appear for each item that will be updated when you connect. You can click the check boxes to toggle the check marks

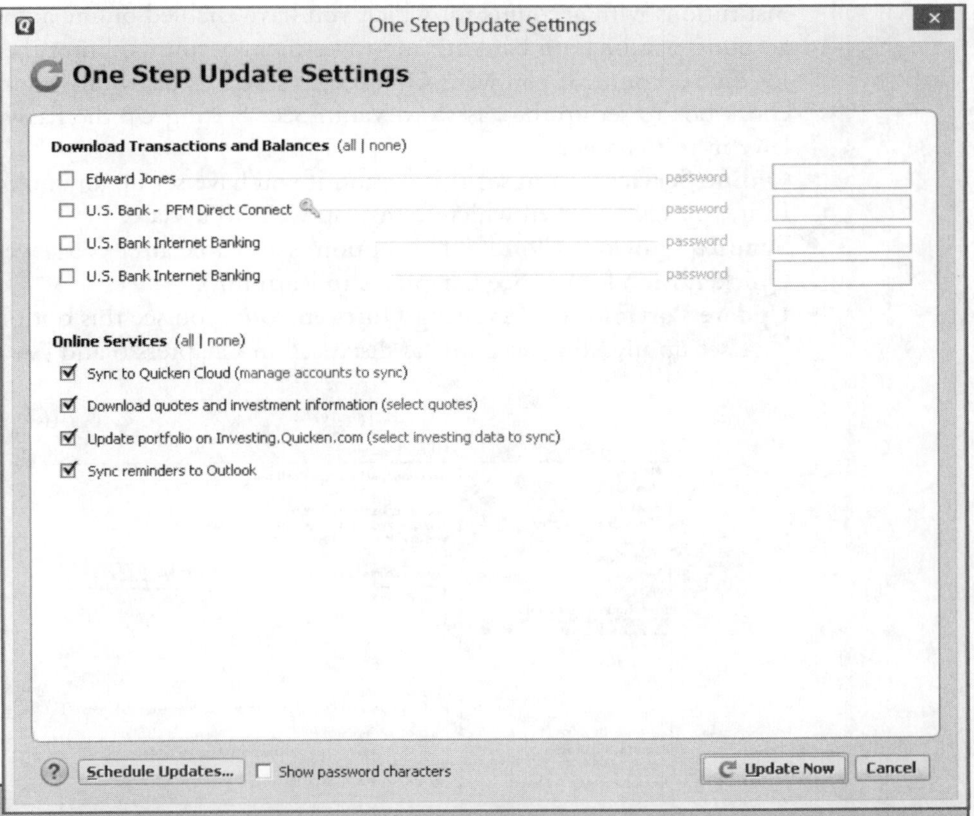

Figure 1-4 • Use One Step Update to download transactions.

there. If you have not added your Intuit ID to the Password Vault, you may be prompted to enter your Intuit ID when you click One Step Update.

 You may see a small key symbol next to some of your passwords. Click that key symbol to change the password for that financial institution.

 If you use your Outlook calendar to "remind" you, make sure to run a One Step Update each time you make changes in the Bill And Reminders dialog. Otherwise, the changes you made in Quicken are not updated in Outlook. Conversely, if you make changes in Outlook, remember to make the same change in Quicken. One Step Update works from Quicken to Outlook, not from Outlook to Quicken.

- **Download Transactions and Balances** Listed in this area are the financial institutions with accounts for which you have enabled online access. These accounts can be both banking and investment accounts. Enter the password for each account. If you want Quicken to save this password, click the Save check box to set up the Password Vault. See "Setting Up the Password Vault" later in this chapter.
- **Online Services** You see this section if you have set up any online services. In it, you tell Quicken which items you want to update.
- **Sync To Quicken Cloud** This option is available after you have set up the Quicken Mobile app. See Chapter 2 to learn how.
- **Update Portfolio on Investing.Quicken.com** You see this option once you have set up investing accounts as discussed in Chapters 6 and 7.

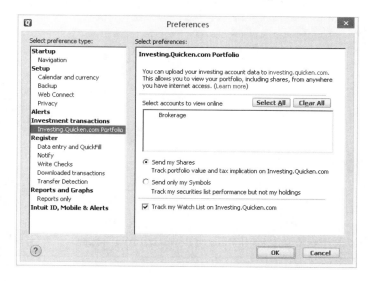

- **Sync Reminders To Outlook**   If you use Microsoft Outlook, you can synchronize your reminders with your Outlook calendar. These reminders will appear in your Outlook calendar as "All Day Events."

Click the Update Now button to perform the One Step Update. When the update is complete, the One Step Update Summary dialog appears. This summarizes the activity for the update. Small green circles appear to the left of each successfully updated financial institution. You can click the link showing the number of accounts updated to get a pop-up showing the accounts. You can then click the account shown in the pop-up to open that account's register or click the Close button at the bottom of the window to dismiss the One Step Update Summary.

The One Step Update Summary dialog does not appear if you have previously told Quicken to display the summary only when there is an error.

Scheduling Updates

You can schedule updates to occur when you're not using Quicken. Then, when you start Quicken, your data file is already updated with information from your financial institutions, and, if you've disabled automatic acceptance of downloaded transactions, ready to review and accept into your account registers. Your Investing.Quicken.com information can also be automatically updated based on information in your Quicken data file. To set up a schedule, choose Tools | Schedule Updates. The Schedule Updates dialog appears, as seen next. You can set options in each area of the dialog. When you have finished, click OK.

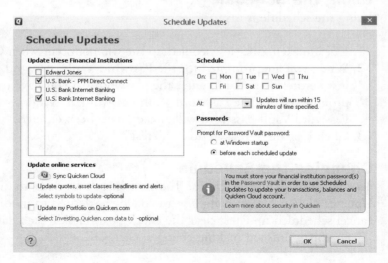

You will not see the Sync Quicken Cloud check box if you have not yet set up the Mobile feature.

These are each of the options.

- **Update These Financial Institutions**   The update area lists all of the items in the One Step Update dialog discussed earlier in this chapter. Click to toggle check marks beside each item you want to include in the schedule.
- **Schedule**   The Schedule area determines when the updates will occur. Select the check boxes for each day of the week you want the updates to occur, and then choose a time from the At drop-down list. Since your computer must be running for the updates to take place, set options for when you know your computer will be turned on. Updates will not occur, however, if Quicken is running; this ensures that the automated feature does not interrupt your work with Quicken.
- **Passwords**   Security options enable you to indicate when your computer should prompt you for the Password Vault password. (The Password Vault feature must be set up and used in conjunction with scheduled updates.) You have two options:
  - **At Windows Startup**   Choosing this option displays the Password Vault Password dialog when you start Windows.
  - **Before Each Scheduled Update**   This option displays the Password Vault Password dialog just before each update.
- **Update Online Services**   Choose the items you want to update.

Using the Schedule

Using the schedule is easy.

1. Exit Quicken, since a scheduled update will not occur when Quicken is running.
2. When you are prompted for the Password Vault password (which happens just before the update), enter the password. (If you have told Quicken to prompt you for the Password Vault password at Windows Startup, your Password Vault password will already have been entered.)
3. Click Update. Quicken does the rest.

Changing the Schedule

To change the schedule, choose Tools | Schedule Updates to display the Schedule Updates dialog. Make changes in the dialog as desired to modify settings. To cancel scheduled updates, clear the check boxes beside each day of the week. When you're finished making changes, click OK.

Do take the time to read the link about Quicken's security features that is available in the Schedule Updates dialog.

Understanding the Password Vault

Many Quicken users find it a nuisance to have to type in each password each time they use the One Step Update feature, especially if they connect to more than one or two financial institutions. Quicken's Password Vault feature enables you to store all your financial institution passwords in one central location. The passwords are protected with a single password. When you use One Step Update, you enter just one password to access all financial institutions. You must have Online Account Access or Online Payment set up with at least one institution to use the Password Vault feature.

Setting Up the Password Vault

Choose Tools | Online Center | Password Vault or Tools | Password Vault | Set Up New Password Vault. The Password Vault Setup dialog appears as seen next. It provides some introductory information. Click Next to display the first window of the Password Vault Setup.

Follow the instructions in each tab to choose financial institutions and enter corresponding passwords. You'll enter each password twice because the characters you type do not appear on screen; this is a secure way of making sure you enter the same thing both times.

When you've finished, select the No option if you have no other passwords to enter. Select Yes if you have other accounts you wish to include in the Password

Vault. Enter as many as you choose, and when all have been entered, click No when asked whether you want to enter additional passwords. Click Next to continue. You are prompted to enter a password, and re-enter it, to protect the Password Vault. Enter it in each box and click Next.

When you click Next, the Summary tab of the Password Vault Setup window appears. It displays a list of your financial institutions and indicates whether a password has been stored for each one.

You can use buttons in this dialog to change or delete a selected password, print all passwords, or change the Vault password. When you've finished working with the window's contents, click Done. Quicken creates the Password Vault.

Secure passwords traditionally have at least eight characters, combining both uppercase and lowercase letters, numbers, and symbols.

If you choose to print your passwords, do not leave the printed list in plain sight or affix it to your monitor.

Using and Editing the Password Vault

Simply choose Tools | One Step Update or click the Update Accounts button in the Account Bar. You will no longer be prompted for any passwords. Simply continue using One Step Update in the usual way, but with one difference: You

---

IN MY EXPERIENCE

Sometimes it's hard to remember what passwords are for what purpose. Just to review them:

- **Data File Password**   This is the password, if any, you have created using File | Set Password For This Data File. You'll need to enter this password when you open the Quicken data file. You can't do scheduled updates for a data file where you have set a data file password.
- **Vault Password**   You set and use this password when working with the Password Vault. All of your financial institutions' login information is stored safely within the Password Vault.
- **Login Information**   These are the user names, passwords, and PINs given to you by your financial institution so that you can access and/or download the information from their server into Quicken. You enter the login information when you run One Step Update or Update Now and you have not added the financial institution to the Password Vault.

In order for Scheduled Updates to function, you must have your login information stored in the Password Vault for each of the financial institutions you want to update. Also, both your computer and your Internet access must be on; however, Quicken must be closed to run the Scheduled Update.

don't have to enter passwords for any of the financial institutions for which a password has been entered in the Password Vault.

You can modify it to change passwords or add passwords for other financial institutions. Choose Tools | Password Vault | Add Or Edit Passwords. In the Edit Password Vault dialog that appears, click the Change Vault Password button to change the password to your Password Vault. Click Change Password to change the passwords for any account. Click Delete Password to delete an account's password. When you've finished, click Done.

Working with the Account List Window

You can view a list of all of your accounts at any time. Choose Tools | Account List or press CTRL-A. The Account List window appears (see Figure 1-5). This

Figure 1-5 • The Account List displays information about all of your accounts.

window displays a list of all accounts organized by type. If you want to see just one group of accounts—for example, your Banking accounts—click that group's name in the column to the left of the list. If you have entered only one type of account, such as banking accounts, there will be no pane at the left side of the Account List window.

You can click the small gear icon to the right of the blue curly arrow at the top of the Account Bar to open the Account List.

Account Intent

The Account Intent section lets you tell Quicken how you plan on using this account. For example, you might have a savings account that you actually are using as an additional retirement account. (However, you might want to check with your financial advisor to see if this is a wise use of your money.) To let Quicken know how you intend this account to be used, choose a value from the drop-down lists. These choices determine how the account will display in both the Account Bar and other lists and reports. Once you have made all of your modifications for this account, click OK to close the Account Details dialog and return to the Account List.

Viewing Account Information

By default, Quicken displays each account in the Account List window (refer to Figure 1-5) by the account name (grouped by account type), transaction download settings, and the current balance. If you have told Quicken to hide any of your accounts, you can opt to display them in the list by clicking the Show Hidden Accounts check box at the bottom-left corner of the list. Add informational columns to the list by choosing commands from the Options button at the bottom-left corner of the Account List window, as shown here. Just select a command on the menu to toggle the display of information on or off. This makes it possible for you to customize the appearance of the list and the information shown. See "Working with Accounts" later in this chapter for more information.

Select an account on the Account List, and click Edit to open the Account Details

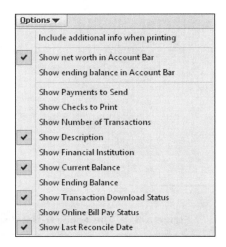

dialog seen next. From this dialog you can change the name of an account, enter additional account information, tell Quicken how to display the account, and modify the account's online services. Move between the tabs by clicking the tab with which you want to work.

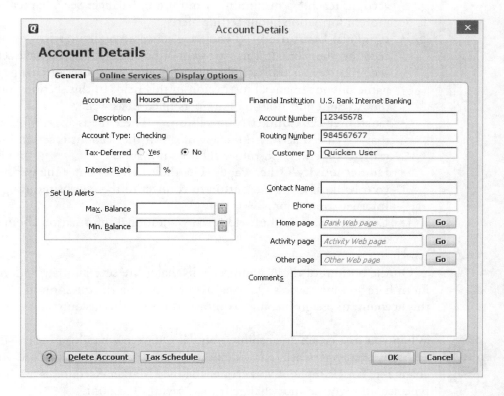

- **General Tab**   The General tab displays basic information about the account that you can view or edit. From this dialog you can enter information such as the interest rate you receive on this account and the account number, and you can create a link to the bank's home page. There are a number of options, of which only the account name is required. Not all of the options mentioned here will be available for all types of accounts:
  - **Account Name**   By default, this is the name you (or the bank) entered when creating the account. You can change it here if you choose.
  - **Description**   Add any additional information to further identify this account in this field.
  - **Account Type**   This field cannot be changed. It is the type of account you established when you first created the account.

- **Tax Deferred**   Click Yes to tell Quicken this is a tax-deferred account; click No if it is not.
- **Interest Rate**   Enter the rate of interest, if any, for this account.
- **Set Up Alerts**   Use this section to ask Quicken to alert you if this account reaches a maximum or minimum balance. See Chapter 6 for more information about setting alerts.
- **Financial Institution**   If you have activated online services for this account, the name in this field cannot be changed. If you have set this account to enter transactions manually, you may enter or change the name of your financial institution in this field. In this section you may see the Account and Routing Numbers filled in as well.
- **Customer ID/Contact Name/Phone**   These fields appear for accounts that have been activated for download. If the account is set up for manual transaction entry, Customer ID does not appear.
- **Home/Activity/Other Page**   Use these fields to enter the website(s) for your bank. Use the Go button to connect to these websites using your Internet connection.
- **Comments**   Use this field for any additional information about this account.

On the bottom of the Account Details dialog are several other option buttons. From here you may access Quicken help by clicking the question mark, delete this account, or assign income tax information for this account.

When you first create an account, you tell Quicken what "type" it is—that is, Checking, Savings, Cash, and so on. Once this type of account is set, you cannot change it. For example, if you create a Money Market Account as a "checking" type account, you cannot change it to a "savings" account.

The Delete Account button opens the Delete Account dialog. If you really want to delete an account, you must confirm the removal through this dialog. Purposely, Quicken does not make this process easy. You must type **yes** into the dialog and click OK to delete the account. If you have scheduled bills or deposits for this account, they must be removed before you can delete it. See Chapter 4 for more information about scheduling transactions. Remember that when you delete an account, you permanently remove all of its transactions from your Quicken data file. To get the account out of sight without actually deleting it and its data, consider hiding it instead, as described in "Display Options Tab" later in this chapter. The Display Options in Quicken 2014 are quite different from those in Quicken 2012 or earlier versions, so if you are upgrading, review them carefully. If you are upgrading from Quicken 2013, you will not see a difference.

- **Tax Schedule Information**   If the account has income tax implications click the Tax Schedule button to use the optional Tax Schedule Information dialog. As always, if you have any questions about the tax status of an account, check with your tax professional.
- **Online Services Tab**   This tab allows you to modify the settings in each account for your institution's online services. If your financial institution offers the ability to use Quicken's One Step Update or Online Bill Payment, you can set those options here. You can also set up Quicken Bill Payment through this dialog. See Chapter 4 for more information about the online services offered by many financial institutions.
- **Display Options Tab**   Use this tab to tell Quicken how you want to display this account, as seen next. You may keep the account separate, hide it in the transaction entry list, or hide the account name in both the Account Bar and in the Account List, as seen in Table 1-3. You may also tell Quicken to close the account entirely, which sets the balance of the account to zero and stops any downloads you've set up.

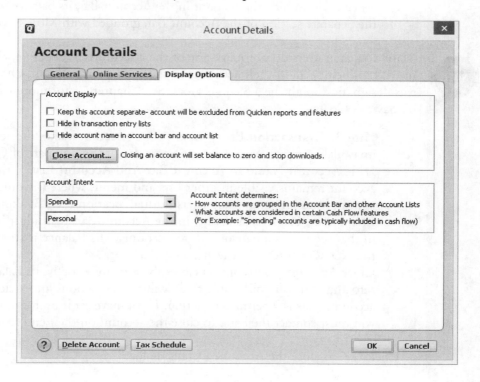

Keep Account Separate	Hide in Account Name and Account Bar	Account Shows
		Directly in Banking, Investing, or Property & Debt section
	X	In More under Banking, Investing, or Property & Debt section
X		Directly in Separate at the bottom of the Account Bar
X	X	In More under Separate at the bottom of the Account Bar

Table 1-3 • Account Display Options

- **Keep This Account Separate**   When this check box is selected, Quicken prevents the account from being displayed in lists, menus, and reports. This choice removes the account from view in its regular location on the Account Bar. The account is available in the Separate account section of the Account Bar, which includes the balances of all accounts you have marked with this display choice. Its balance is included in this Separate accounts section, as well as the Net Worth total at the bottom of the Account Bar. If you have also chosen to hide the account in the Account Bar, its balance will show in the Separate section of the Account Bar, grouped with More Accounts.

Many Quicken users do not mark any of their accounts as Separate, choosing instead to include all of their accounts in the appropriate section. One use for this designation might be a Savings Goal. See Chapter 12 for more information on Savings Goals.

- **Hide In Transaction Entry Lists**   The selection makes the account unavailable when you are entering transactions in any part of Quicken.
- **Hide Account Name In Account Bar And Account List**   Although the account remains visible in other lists and menus where it would normally appear, it no longer appears in its normal location (i.e., Banking, Investment, Property & Debt) in the Account Bar. Instead, it is grouped in that section as a part of "More Accounts." Its balance is still included in the Net Worth total in the Account Bar.
- **Close Account**   This option closes the account entirely. Its balance is set to zero and you will not be able to download transactions into a closed account. This is a permanent action. If you have set it up for online services, you must contact the bank to close the account on their end as well.

Click OK to close the Account Details dialog.

Manage Hidden Accounts

To set options or make changes to the display status of your accounts, click Tools | Manage Hidden Accounts. A useful dialog, as seen below, is displayed. From this dialog you can select how each account is to be displayed within Quicken. If you have many accounts, consider using this dialog rather than using the Account Details dialog in each account.

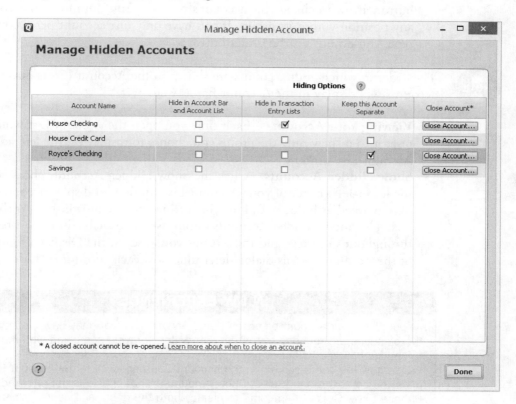

Working with Accounts

You can use options in the Account List window to reorganize accounts so they appear where you want them in the Account Bar.

- **Changing the Order of Accounts** By default, accounts are shown in alphabetical order in your Account List until you first move an account. As you first add accounts, they automatically sort themselves alphabetically. If you later decide to change the order and then add more accounts, the newly added accounts are inserted at the bottom of the section. To change the order in which accounts appear in the Account List window and Account Bar, select an account by clicking the line in which the name appears. Note that you must click somewhere on the account's line other than the name of the account or the Edit button. When you click the account name, the account's register opens. Clicking the Edit button opens the Account Details dialog. To move the account within its group, click the up or down Order button arrow to change the account's position. You can move an account to any position within its group. If you have only one account per account type, you do not see the Order button.

 The order in which your accounts are shown in the Account List is how the accounts will display in the Account Bar as well.

- **Viewing Your Accounts**   Each time you open the Account List, you can reset it to display only the group you choose to display on the left side of the Account List window.
- **Show Hidden Accounts**   Click the Show Hidden Accounts check box at the lower-left corner of your Account List window to display accounts you have marked as hidden. To hide them from the Account List, clear the check box. The Show Hidden Accounts option is also available in many areas throughout Quicken, and the settings you've set in the Display Options tab of the Account Details dialog determine how each account is "hidden."

IN MY EXPERIENCE

As you view your account balances in the Account List you may have noticed that the balances are rounded to the nearest dollar. To avoid confusion, you may want to change how the balances are displayed in the Account Bar.

To show the cents column in the Account Bar, right-click in the Account Bar to open the context menu. Select Show Amounts if that choice is not checked. Choose Show Cents In Amounts to display both the dollar and cents balances for each account. Now the totals in the Account Bar match the totals in the Current Balance column in the Account List.

After you have made a selection, the Account Bar context menu closes automatically.

- **Help Icon**   Clicking the small question mark at the lower-left corner of the Account List opens Quicken Help to the section on managing your accounts.
- **Printing the Account List**   Click the Printer icon at the bottom of the Account List window to print your list. The Print dialog appears. Click

Preview to see how your list will appear. Click Close to close the preview window. Click Print to print the list. See "Using the Account List Options" next to learn more about printing details in your list.

Using the Account List Options

The Options menu, seen earlier, offers you several ways to display the accounts in your Account List:

- **Include Additional Info When Printing**   When you choose this option, each time you print the Account List it will include all of the options you've chosen in the Options menu. Unfortunately, you need to reset this option each time you open the Account List, as the selection disappears once you close the Account List.
- **Show Net Worth In Account Bar**   The Net Worth number that displays in the Account Bar is the sum of the current balances of all of your entered transactions on each of your non-hidden accounts. This option tells Quicken to display that sum labeled as Net Worth in the Account Bar.
- **Show Ending Balance In Account Bar**   As mentioned above, the Net Worth balance on the Account Bar is the sum of today's balance of each of your non-hidden accounts. The Ending Balance takes into account the bills or deposits you have entered for future dates.
- **Show Payments To Send/Checks To Print/Number Of Transactions/ Description/Financial Institution**   These options create new columns in the Account List that display the selected information. If you have chosen to include the additional information when printing, these columns will appear on your printed Account List report.
- **Show Current/Ending Balance**   This is similar to Show Net Worth/Ending Balance In Account Bar, but it refers to the Account List. You may display both the Current and Ending Balances in the Account List.
- **Show Transaction Download Status/Show Online Bill Pay Status**   These options appear if you have activated any of your accounts for online services.
- **Show Last Reconcile Date**   Choosing to display this column in the Account List shows the last time an account was reconciled.

You may only choose one option at a time in the Options menu. Each time you make a selection, the menu closes and you must reopen it to make another selection.

- **Add An Account**   On the bottom-right corner of the Account List is the Add An Account button. Choose this button to open the Add Account dialog.

- **Done**   When you have made all of your adjustments and are through with the Account List, click Done to close the dialog.

Categories

When you create a data file, Quicken automatically creates dozens of commonly used categories. Although these categories might completely meet your needs, at times you may want to add, remove, or modify a category to fine-tune Quicken for your use.

Establishing Categories and Subcategories

Quicken starts with two category types. Income includes but is not limited to receipts such as your salary, commissions, interest income, dividend income, child support, gifts received, and tips. The other type is Expense, some examples of which are insurance, groceries, rent, interest expense, bank fees, finance charges, charitable donations, and clothing.

A subcategory is a subset or part of a category. It must be the same type of category as its parent category. For example, you may use the Auto category to track expenses to operate your car. Within that category, however, you might use one of the subcategories to record specific expenses, such as auto insurance, fuel, and repairs. Subcategories make it easy to keep income and expenses organized into manageable categories, while providing the transaction detail you might want or need.

Working with the Category List Window

You can view a list of all of your categories at any time. Choose Tools | Category List, or press CTRL-SHIFT-C. The Category List window appears as in Figure 1-6. Depending on which edition of Quicken you are using, the category groups may be different. For example in Figure 1-6, the user has included business categories in their Quicken Home and Business edition.

In this section, you'll learn how to use the Category List window to display, add, modify, delete, and perform other tasks with categories.

If you have added an Investment account, you may notice a group of categories with an underscore before their name. These are special categories used by Quicken for such transactions as computing realized gains on investing accounts. They do not exist until you create your first investment account and are then hidden.

You can also choose commands to determine what information appears with the category names in the Category List window. Click the Action gear icon seen

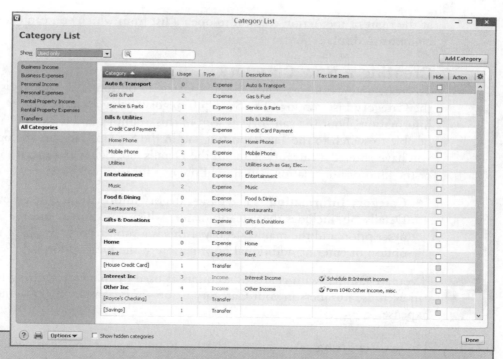

Figure 1-6 • **The Category List shows the categories in your Quicken data file with which you can classify your transactions.**

IN MY EXPERIENCE

Categories? Subcategories? Sounds confusing and like a lot of work? It is truly not much work, and using categories is well worth the time you spend doing it.

To use this wonderful feature, when you enter a transaction in Quicken, you'll classify it using one of your predefined categories. The next time you enter a transaction for the same payee, Quicken automatically assumes the transaction will use the same category, so Quicken enters it for you. And often you don't have to type the entire category and subcategory, usually just the first few letters. For example, type "Au" and the Auto category displays. Type a colon (:) and an "S" and your category and subcategory are entered as Auto:Service.

So don't leave the category field blank when entering your transactions. That extra step results in more complete reports and a clearer understanding of your finances.

at the right of the Action column to open a list from which you can choose what columns to display.

Creating a New Category

To create a new category, click the Add Category button at the upper right of the Category List window. The Set Up Category dialog appears. Enter information about the category, as seen in this example, and click OK. You won't be able to switch to the Tax Reporting tab in the Set Up Category dialog until you have entered a category name in the Details tab. Below is a quick summary of the kind of information you should provide for each category.

- **Category Information** The basic category information, entered in the Details tab, includes the category name, which is required, and the description and the main category if this is a subcategory. You have the option of entering additional information in the Description field.

 If you are familiar with charts of accounts as used by many accounting folk, you can even use numbers in your Category name—for example, 61000–Auto Expense.

- **Tax Reporting** You can use the Tax Reporting options, seen next, to specify whether a category is tax-related and, if so, what tax form and even the tax line item on which it appears. This can be a real time-saver at tax time by enabling you to organize your income and expenditures as they appear on tax forms. You learn more about using Quicken at tax time in Chapter 13. You are not required to enter anything in this area.

 When you have set a tax line and tax form for your categories, you can display a small red circle with a check by each transaction by choosing the gear icon and checking Tax-related. The tax information symbol will only show for transactions that are tax-related, not for all transactions.

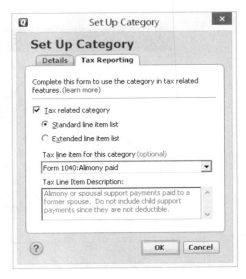

Click OK to close the Set Up Category dialog and return to the Category List.

Adding Multiple Categories at Once

Quicken makes it easy to add multiple related categories at the same time. Click the Options button at the bottom of the Category List window and choose Manage Categories to open the Manage Categories dialog as shown next.

Select an option from the Available Categories drop-down list at the top of the dialog. In the Category list on the left, click to add a green check mark beside each category you want to add. When you click Add, the selected categories appear in the Categories To Add list. Click OK to add the categories and close the dialog.

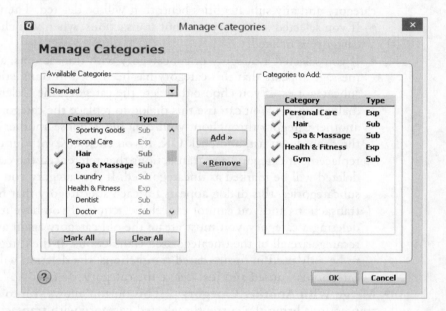

Category Groups

See Chapter 12 for a detailed explanation of category groups.

Editing, Deleting, and Merging Categories

You use the Category List window to edit, delete, or merge categories. Select the name of the category with which you want to work. The Action options arrow displays in the Action column on the right side of the window.

Before making any changes, back up your Quicken data file. That way, if you don't like the changes you've made, you can quickly go back to the file's state before you made the changes. See Appendix A for information on backing up Quicken data files.

- **Edit** Click a category to display the Action arrow. Click the arrow to see several options. Edit displays the Set Up Category dialog (shown earlier) for the selected category. You can use this to make just about any change to a category. You can even "promote" a subcategory to a category by clearing the Subcategory Of: field.
- **Delete** When you choose to eliminate a category, first ensure you have a current backup. Then, select the category to display the Action arrow in the Action column. Choosing Delete displays different dialogs, depending on the category that is selected. Quicken begins by warning you that the category and any subcategories beneath it will be deleted. Then
  - If you selected a category without transactions, when you click OK, the category is deleted.
  - If you selected a category or subcategory with transactions, a warning message appears that this category has been used in transactions or has subcategories. If you choose to delete the category, the Delete Category dialog appears. You can use this dialog to replace the category with another category throughout your data file. Choose another category from the drop-down list, and click OK. If you click OK without choosing a replacement category, any transactions that referenced the category you deleted will be marked as uncategorized. If the category you deleted has subcategories, this dialog appears for each subcategory that has transactions and you cannot cancel the action. If you have made an error deleting a category, you must create the old category again and recategorize all of the uncategorized transactions. If the category happens to be only used in future-dated transactions, the deletion will act like the category is unused and just delete the category.
- **Merge With Another Category** This button allows you to merge transactions using the currently selected category with transactions using another category. This, in effect, recategorizes all of the transactions for the selected category. Clicking Merge With Another Category displays the Merge Category dialog. Choose the category to which you want to merge from the drop-down list. If you want to delete the category you selected, turn on the check box—this makes the dialog work the same way as the Delete Category dialog. Click OK to perform the merge. One thing to keep in mind: if the category you selected is not used in any transactions, you do not see an option to merge the category. You can simply edit or delete it.

The Merge option is a bit of a misnomer. The process actually recategorizes the transaction to the new ("merged") category. You can only delete or merge one category at a time. Deleting and merging categories does not work when more than one category is selected.

Tags

A tag is an optional identifier used to specify what a transaction applies to. For example, if you want to keep track of all the money you spent for your last vacation, no matter the category, you can create a tag named Vacation. Then each expense you incur, whether categorized as Clothing, Auto Maintenance, Dining Out, or whatever, can be "tagged" as part of that Vacation tag. Because Quicken can produce reports based on categories, tags, or both, tags offer an additional dimension for tracking and reporting information.

Using Tags

Using tags is completely optional. It's not necessary to set them up or use them at all. In fact, many Quicken users, including a few at Intuit, don't take advantage of this feature. It's your decision. Quicken maintains a list of all the tags you create. You can display the Tag List window by choosing Tools | Tag List, or by pressing CTRL-L. An example of a Tag List with a couple of tags is shown here.

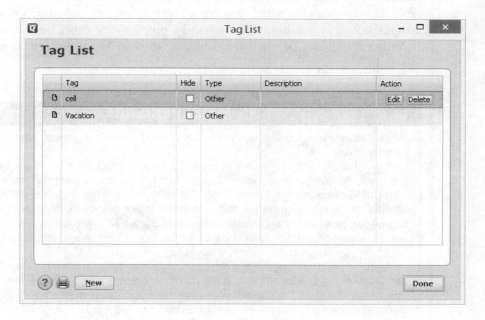

Creating a New Tag

Click the New button in the Tag List window. The New Tag dialog, shown next, appears. Use it to enter information about the tag.

Only one piece of information is necessary: the tag name. You may want to make it short so it's easy to remember and enter. The description can be used to provide additional information on the tag's use. The copy number enables you to associate tags with different but similar activities. For example, if you have two separate businesses for which you report activity on two Schedule Cs, you can assign Copy 1 to one business's tags and Copy 2 to the other business's tags.

When you click OK, the tag is added to the list. You can create as many tags as you like.

IN MY EXPERIENCE

While not everyone uses tags, here are a couple of ways in which tags can prove very useful.

If you have children, you might create a separate tag for each child. Then, when you've got expenses for a specific family member, record the transaction with the appropriate tag name. (If you've got income related to that child, that's terrific; be sure to include the tag name with those transactions, too.) Then, when that partially grown bundle of joy asks for $457.49 to buy a new computerized tablet, you can show him a report of how much he's cost you so far when you suggest he save his allowance instead.

Another creative use of tags relates to tracking dues or membership fees for small groups in Quicken. Make each member's name a tag. Then, when you enter their dues for the current year—for example, using the category 2015 Dues—you can add each member's name in the Tag field.

Since nearly all reports include the ability to customize and include tags, you can create some very useful information, whether it be for your family or that group for which you are acting as treasurer.

Working with the Tag List Window

You can use buttons that appear beside a selected tag in the Tag List window, as shown earlier, to work with the tag list or a selected tag:

- **Edit** enables you to modify the currently selected tag name or other information.
- **Delete** enables you to delete the currently selected tag. When you delete a tag, the tag name is removed from all transactions in which it appeared, but the transaction remains properly categorized.

You can easily toggle the Tag display off and on in your register.

1. Open the account register. Click the small "gear" icon found at the top of the scroll bar below the Action gear icon. You can also click the Action gear icon | Register Columns to open the same list.
2. From the drop-down list, check or clear the Tag check box.

When you are finished working with Quicken, close the program by clicking the red X on the title bar or choose File | Exit.

Remember always to back up your Quicken data file. See how to do it in Appendix A.

Getting Up and Running with Quicken Mobile

Chapter 2

In This Chapter:

- *Appreciating the "cloud"*
- *About your new mobile companion*
- *Understanding your Quicken Cloud Account*
- *Getting started from your desktop*
- *Setting Alerts*
- *Showing your budget*
- *Getting started on your mobile device*
- *Working with the Quicken Mobile app Overview page*

In today's hectic world, you are not always at your desktop computer when you need financial information. With the Quicken Mobile app you can check your credit card balance using your iPad on the way to work or glance at your smart phone to see if a check has cleared while you're at the gym. This chapter explains how to get started with the new Mobile app and discusses its features.

Understand Mobile Applications

A mobile application (or app) is a small program especially designed to run on smart phones, tablet computers, or other mobile devices. If you have ever downloaded a game like Angry Birds onto your cell phone, your favorite tune to your MP3 player, an e-book from the library to your e-book reader, or a map to your tablet computer the last time you took a trip, you have used a mobile app. Many apps, like the Quicken Mobile app, are free and others are available for a small price. Of the price for the apps sold to the user, a percentage of the cost goes to the distributor (such as iTunes) and the rest goes to the person or company that created the app.

Appreciating the "Cloud"

The "cloud" seems to appear everywhere in our world today: in advertisements, news programs, even schools. Just what is the "cloud" and how is it used? The term, whose original use is obscure, refers to storing programs and data at a location other than the owners' (or users') physical location and allowing users to access that information via the Internet.

If you have ever viewed a YouTube video, have a G-mail account, or used a website to share family photos, you've accessed the "cloud." The reality is that much of what we do each day on the Internet is done on the cloud. There is even an e-book edition of this book downloadable from the cloud!

Meet Quicken's Mobile App

Quicken 2014's Mobile app is designed for Quicken users who want the ability to access their information from anywhere with an Internet connection. Are you required to use the Mobile app? No—Quicken's desktop works for many Quicken users. However, by installing and using the free Quicken Mobile app on your Android or Apple device, you can keep up with any of your spending accounts—checking, savings, and credit cards—no matter where you may be.

About Your New Mobile Companion

Quicken's Mobile app is available only for those who have purchased Quicken 2014 and installed the program on their laptop or desktop computer. It is useful as an add-on your program, not as a stand-alone product. Only after you have set up your accounts and created your Quicken Cloud ID as discussed in Chapter 1, can you start using Quicken's Mobile app.

Some Quicken users never use this tool. Others find it invaluable. It is up to you to decide. So what are the requirements for using Quicken's Mobile app?

- You must have either an Apple (iOS) or Android mobile device such as a tablet, smart phone, or e-reader that has the ability to connect to the Internet.

- You must have set up your accounts (and budget if you want to use that feature) on your desktop computer.
- You must create a Quicken Cloud ID as discussed in the section "Understanding Your Quicken Cloud ID" later in this chapter. You'll notice throughout Quicken that the terms Quicken Cloud ID and Intuit ID are used interchangeably. The Intuit ID you created when first installing (or first setting up online access) is your Quicken Cloud ID, also known as your Intuit ID. Throughout the rest of this chapter, we are using Quicken Cloud ID to describe this identifier.

The illustrations throughout this chapter are from an Android smart phone and an Android tablet. On your device, the screens may look a bit different.

Beginning with Quicken's Mobile App

If you are excited about the ability to see your financial information from any location with an Internet connection, it's time to get started. When you first installed Quicken on your computer, you created your Quicken Cloud ID. At the time, you may have chosen to not create a cloud account, as using the cloud is strictly optional. However, if you choose to access your information from the cloud, this section explains both the advantages of using the Quicken Mobile app and how to set it up from your desktop.

Understanding Your Quicken Cloud ID

Quicken uses your Quicken Cloud ID to enable access of your financial information from anywhere using either your smart phone or a tablet. Having that capability can make your financial life easier and eliminate the "oh my gosh" feeling that you might not have instructed Quicken to send the insurance payment. This ID is used by Quicken to send both e-mail and text alerts regarding the accounts you choose to access on your mobile device. It is very useful to know that your salary check was, indeed, deposited yesterday or that a new charge was placed on your credit card.

The ability to monitor your credit card accounts may be one of the most useful features of the Mobile app. The moment you see a charge that you have not made, you can call your financial institution to report the error.

Getting Started from Your Desktop

If you have not yet done so when installing Quicken, you start the process by creating a Quicken Cloud ID directly from your Quicken desktop program.

1. Click the Mobile & Alerts tab and click Create Your Quicken Cloud ID to see this dialog. (Again, Quicken uses both the Quicken Cloud ID and Intuit ID interchangeably.)

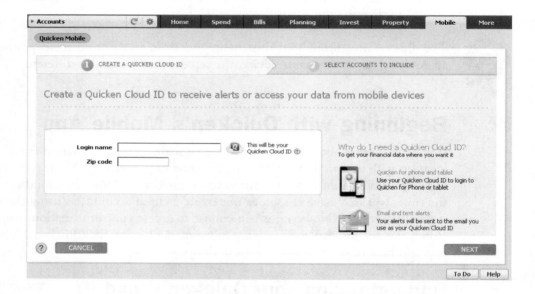

2. Enter the log-in name you chose when installing Quicken and enter your ZIP code in the Zip Code field. Quicken uses this to help should you ever forget your Quicken Cloud ID password.
3. From the Create A Quicken Cloud ID dialog, click the Help (question mark) icon for additional information about your Quicken Cloud ID or choose the Cancel button to stop the process.
4. Click Next to open the Select Accounts To Sync dialog.
5. From the Select Accounts You Want to Access From Mobile Devices dialog, seen next, you'll see a list of accounts that are available.
6. Click the check box for each account you want to synchronize with your mobile device. You can choose checking, savings, or credit card accounts.
7. Enter the online banking password for that account.
8. Click Done to complete the process.

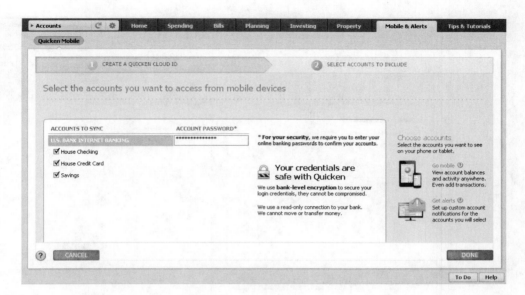

 Some Quicken Mobile users have reported that all of the accounts were checked when they accessed the screen shown in the above illustration and they had to uncheck the accounts they did not want to sync.

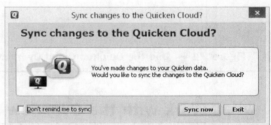

When the information has been synchronized, a message appears that your sync is complete. The Overview screen, discussed next, appears.

Figure 2-1 • Use the Quicken Cloud Overview screen to set up your mobile settings.

Work with the Overview Screen

Figure 2-1 shows the Quicken Cloud Overview screen. After you have set up your Cloud connection, this screen appears when you click the Mobile & Alerts tab.

Edit Your Profile   When you click Edit Profile at the upper left of the Overview screen, the Quicken Preferences dialog appears at the Intuit ID, Mobile & Alerts section as seen next. Your current Intuit ID Profile appears at the top of the dialog. With the options in the Settings section, you can change the accounts you want to sync as well as your Alert settings. See "Setting Alerts" later in this chapter for more information about Alerts.

In the Troubleshooting section you can reset or delete your Cloud Data and unlink either your Cloud Data or Quicken Cloud ID with your online accounts.

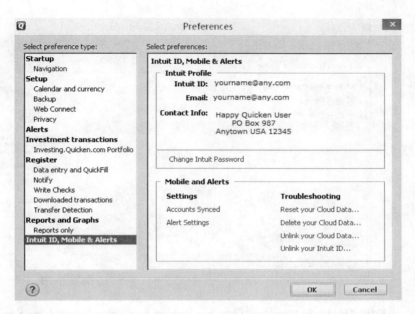

Sync Now   Use the Sync Now link at the upper right of the Overview screen to sync your accounts with the Quicken Cloud. When the operation has completed, the following screen appears.

Edit Account Settings   Click Edit Account Settings in the Accounts Enabled For Mobile and Alerts section to add or delete accounts you want to access via your mobile device. The Edit Account Settings dialog, shown next, appears. After you are done making changes, click the Update Accounts button to let Quicken know of the changes. Otherwise, click the Cancel button to close.

Edit Alerts Settings Use this link to open the Edit Alerts Settings dialog as discussed in the "Settings Alerts" section, next in this chapter.

Setting Alerts

One of the great reasons to use Quicken's Mobile app is its ability to tell you about various financial happenings, even when you are not at home in front of your desktop computer. To let Quicken know the information you would like to see, from anywhere in Quicken, click the Mobile & Alerts tab. At the Overview screen that appears, select the Edit Alerts Settings link which will open the Edit Alerts Settings dialog, as seen here.

Each section allows you to set different types of alerts.

How Often Do You Want Alerts?

The first section of the Edit Alerts Settings dialog lets you tell Quicken how often you want summary e-mail information sent to you. The drop-down list gives you the option of receiving e-mails Monthly, Weekly, or Never, with Weekly being the default.

Email & Text Alerts

In this section you can add a secondary e-mail address for Quicken to use for alerts. Your Quicken Cloud ID e-mail address is the primary e-mail by default.

What Type of Alerts Do You Want to Receive?

The bottom half of the Edit Alerts Settings dialog is how you tell Quicken both the information you want to see and how you want it delivered. You can choose to have each item delivered via a text message or by e-mail or both. Click the check box to the left of each alert type for the method of delivery and choose from these alert types:

- **Credit Available**   This option warns you if you are getting near your credit limit on the credit card accounts you have enabled for mobile access. The drop-down list to the right of the Credit Available option lets you choose between $500, $1000, $2000, and $5000.
- **Bank Fees**   If any of the banks you have enabled for mobile access charges a fee above the amount you specify, choosing this option will alert you to that fact. The drop-down list offers four choices: $1, $5, $10, and $50.
- **Unusual Spending**   This alert warns you of above-average spending in any category. The drop-down list lets you choose how much over the average amount requires you to be notified. The options are $200, $500, $1000, and $2000.
- **Large Deposits**   Expecting those lottery winnings any day? This option lets you know when a deposit over the amount you designate is posted to your account. You can choose from $500, $1000, $2000, or $5000.
- **Large Purchases**   By choosing this option you are advised of any purchases that are over your designated amount that appear on any of your accounts. You can choose to be told about purchases that are over by $500, $1000, $2000, or $5000.
- **Low Balance**   This selection alerts you to low balances in any of your accounts. You can choose to be warned of any balances below $200, $500, $1000, or $2000.

- **Overbudget**   Selecting this check box asks Quicken to warn you of any category in which the amount has gone over what you budgeted.
- **Interest Rate**   This selection lets you know about any interest rate changes made on any of your spending accounts.
- **Total Credit Available**   Selecting this option sends a warning if you have used so much credit that your credit score might be affected.

After you have made all of your choices, click OK to continue. You will see that your alert settings are being updated. When that message disappears, you are back at the Mobile & Alerts tab screen.

Enable Text Alerts Button

You can tell Quicken to send both e-mail and text alerts using your Quicken Cloud ID. To set these alerts, click the Edit Alerts Settings to open the Enable Text Alerts dialog as seen in the following illustration. Enter your mobile number and read the important information about possible charges when using this feature. Click OK to close the dialog.

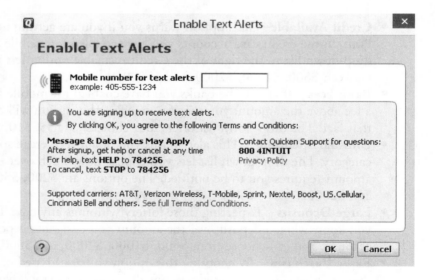

When you have completed your Alerts settings, click OK to close the dialog and return to the Overview screen.

Showing Your Budget

When you first set up your accounts for mobile access, you may not yet have entered a budget. If not, you can create one by clicking the Make A Budget link in your Mobile & Alerts Overview screen. For more information about creating budgets, see Chapter 12. If you have set up a budget in Quicken, you can transfer your budget information to your mobile device. To do so, from anywhere in Quicken, choose the Mobile & Alerts tab.

- In the Budget To Show On Phone Or Tablet field, select the budget that shows, or click the Change link, as seen here, to open the Edit Budget Settings dialog.

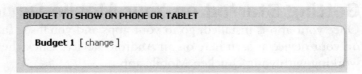

- If you have more than one budget or do not want to sync your budget data, click the Change link to choose the budget to upload to your mobile device. The Edit Budget Settings dialog appears as seen here.

- If you want to use another budget, choose the drop-down arrow to show the available budgets and select the one you want to use.
- If you do not want to see your budget information on your mobile device, click Don't Sync Budget Data.
- When you have made your selection, click OK to close the dialog. You see the Edit Budget Settings synchronizing to the cloud to be available on your mobile device.

Using Your Mobile Device

After you have completed your settings on your desktop, you are ready to begin using the information on your mobile device. The first step is to obtain the free Quicken Mobile app and install it on your mobile device. You can obtain the app from the sources shown below or visit the Quicken.com website for more details.

- The App Store
- iTunes
- Google Play
- Amazon Appstore

Getting Started on Your Mobile Device

Once your app is installed, go to your apps and you'll see Intuit Quicken 2014 on your device as seen here on an Android device. Click the app to begin working with your Quicken Mobile app.

 You may find the Quicken Mobile app in one of the app stores and install it on your mobile device. After you have installed the app and opened it, you will be prompted to purchase Quicken 2014 as you cannot use the app without Quicken 2014 installed on a Windows computer.

 As mobile operating systems differ, you may find that some of the illustrations shown in this chapter are different or not available on your mobile device.

To ensure your accounts are available on your mobile device, set up your mobile accounts using your desktop Quicken program as described in "Choose Your Quicken Mobile Accounts" earlier in this chapter. Once you've selected the Quicken 2014 app on your device, you'll see the Let's Get Started screen, shown here.

Sign In with Your Cloud ID

When you click Sign In to enter your Quicken Cloud ID, the sign-in dialog appears as seen next. Enter the e-mail address you designated when creating your Quicken Cloud ID and use the ID password. You'll notice throughout Quicken that the Quicken Cloud ID and Intuit ID are used interchangeably. The Quicken Cloud ID you created when first installing (or first setting up online access) is your Quicken Cloud ID, also known as your Intuit ID.

If you see a message that your sign-in failed and you are sure you entered the correct e-mail address, try re-entering your password. Depending on your mobile device, it is very easy to type incorrectly.

Working with the Quicken Mobile Overview Page

After you have correctly entered your Quicken Cloud ID, the home or Overview page of the Quicken Mobile app appears as seen next on a smart phone. Each section enables you to see more information as discussed next.

Since each device and operating system differs, what you see on your device may look more like this example on an Android tablet.

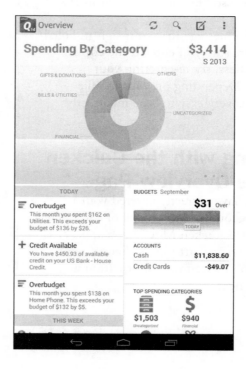

Recognize the Quicken Mobile App Tools

When your Overview page opens, you see a screen similar to the one shown above. As each mobile device varies, so may your display vary as well. If you are using a tablet, small icons appear at the top of your screen, as seen here.

If you use the Mobile app on a smart phone, you may have to click an action button to use the tools as seen here at right.

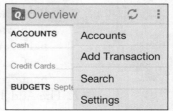

- **Search**   The small magnifying glass opens a Search dialog as seen next. At the bottom of this screen is a keyboard (not shown). With this dialog you can type the name of a payee, a category, or, if you use them, a tag name. Learn more about tags in Chapter 1.

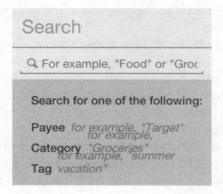

Depending on your device, you may only see the Search field once you have opened an account.

You may note the device name is in the upper-left corner of the screen on the iPad. The iPhone has signal bars and the carrier in the upper-left corner of the screen.

- **Transaction**   The Transaction tool opens the Add Transaction dialog, shown here. To work with this dialog:

1. Press the Choose A Payee field to open the Choose Payee dialog. You may
   - Choose a payee from the list if it is available. On some devices you may not see any payees until you start typing the first letter of a payee name.
     –Or–
   - Press the Enter Payee Name field to open a keyboard with which you can type a new payee name. After you have typed the name, you will see Create "nnnn" (with *nnnn* being the payee name you just typed). Press Create "nnnn" to save the payee name.
2. The Add Transaction dialog appears again with the name of your newly created payee in the Payee field.
3. Press the Expense field to select the account from which this transaction is being paid if the appropriate account name is different from the name in the field.
4. The Transaction Type dialog appears. From this dialog you can select
   - Whether this transaction is an income or an expense item.
   - Whether the transaction is cash, credit card, or a check.
   - The account for this transaction. If the appropriate account for this transaction does not show, click the right-facing arrow to open the Choose Account list.
   - Press the appropriate account, and you are returned to the Transaction Type dialog. Enter a check number if necessary and press Done. Click Back to return to the Add Transaction dialog.
5. Enter the amount of the transaction from the calculator keyboard. Click Next.
6. The Add Transaction dialog shows the amount, account, payee, date, and category of the transaction. Click Done. You see a message indicating the transaction is being entered into your account. After the message completes, you are returned to the Overview page. (Depending on your mobile device, you may find that, depending on the screen you are using when you click the Transaction icon, you may not be returned to the Overview page.)

- The last tool opens the Settings dialog as seen here.
- **Options**   Here is where you can give Quicken's Mobile app instructions on when to Auto-Refresh, use Widgets, or, depending on your operating system, display notifications for new alerts.
- **Accounts**   This dialog displays the accounts with which you have selected to work. Each account shows the name of the financial institution, the account type and name, and the balance that was current as of your last download. You may also see the last update date and time.
- **Security**   If you share your device with someone else, you can protect your financial information by using the Quicken Passcode feature. Click the link to Passcode dialog. Use the keyboard to enter a four-digit passcode. Re-enter the code and after you have done so, you are returned to the Settings dialog.

IN MY EXPERIENCE

Why would someone use a passcode? By creating a passcode, your financial data will only be available when that passcode is entered.

You can remove or reset the passcode from the Settings dialog by opening the Passcode dialog and entering your passcode. From the dialog that appears, press Turn Passcode Off to delete the passcode. After you press that option you are returned to the Settings dialog.

To change your passcode, choose Change Passcode. After you have made that choice, the Enter A Passcode dialog appears. Enter a new passcode and then enter it again. In an iPad, you are then returned to the Settings dialog. If you have another device, you may be returned to the Passcode Lock screen and be required to click Settings to get back to the Settings screen.

- **Logout**   Click here to log out of your Quicken Mobile app. Get into the habit of signing out each time you use Quicken Mobile as the process removes your financial information from the device.
- **About Quicken**   This section tells you what version of the Quicken Mobile app you are using and other information about the program.
- **Help**   This option opens the Help And Legal dialog.

To return to the Overview, click the small Quicken icon at the upper left of your screen.

The Spending By Category Snapshot

As you saw earlier, if you are using a tablet, the top of your Overview page shows a colorful chart showing the categorized and uncategorized expenses for the current month. At the upper-right corner of the screen is the total amount you have spent for the current month. On other devices, such as a smart phone, you may see a bar chart.

Press any of the category sections to open a larger screen from which you can look at the totals for that category and any others, as seen here. From this screen you can

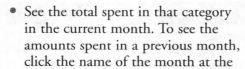
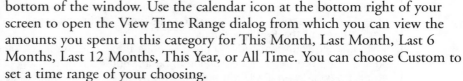

- See the total spent in that category in the current month. To see the amounts spent in a previous month, click the name of the month at the bottom of the window. Use the calendar icon at the bottom right of your screen to open the View Time Range dialog from which you can view the amounts you spent in this category for This Month, Last Month, Last 6 Months, Last 12 Months, This Year, or All Time. You can choose Custom to set a time range of your choosing.
- Press the left-facing arrow to move the circle to the next category in the circle to the left of the category you originally selected.
- Press the right-facing arrow to move the circle to display the category on the right of the one you originally selected.
- Press the Transactions link to see what transactions are included in this total.
- Press the Details link to see additional information about the expenditures.
- Press the left-facing arrow to the left of the dialog to return to the Overview page.

The illustration shown above may appear substantially different in other mobile devices.

More Spending Reports

If you slide the Spending By Category snapshot, seen on tablets, you will see two more snapshots.

Spending Over Time   This snapshot displays your total spending for the last six months as a columnar graph, as seen next. Click any column to enlarge the graph. When you select a month, the total spending for the month (or month to date if you are working with the current month) displays at the bottom of the graph.

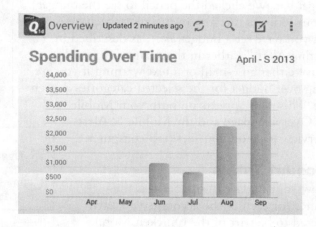

Not all mobile devices contain the Spending Over Time graph.

Press Transactions to see each transaction for the month. Press See Details to open a Spending By Category snapshot.

Net Income Over Time   When using your tablet, slide once again to see the Net Income Over Time snapshot. The information again shows in columnar graph form. Select any month to see both the income and expenses for that month.

Your smart phone may not have a Net Income snapshot.

There are three small circles at the bottom right of the Spending By Category snapshot. Press each circle to cycle through the main Spending By Category, Spending Over Time, and Net Income Over Time snapshots.

Your Budget in Quicken Mobile

If you have chosen to include budget information, that data displays on your Overview page. Click the section to open the Budget window. The budget categories you have chosen to include show how much you have spent in addition to how much you have left for each category, as well as the total month. On some smart phones, you may see a small gray circle with a pencil at the right end of each budget bar. We clicked the pencil to see the budget for our Utilities category over time, as seen here.

If you have set a budget alert, as described in "Setting Alerts" earlier in this chapter, you will receive either an e-mail or a text warning if you are going over budget for the selected categories as seen here. This alert appears on both your Mobile app Overview page and the Mobile & Alerts Overview page on your desktop computer.

Account Totals

Below your budget information is the balance for each of the accounts you have selected to be part of the Quicken Mobile app. Click any account name to see the recent transactions for that account. Depending on your device, you may have two clicks to accomplish this task. The first click takes you from the Overview Accounts section to Accounts. Clicking any account on the list takes you to a list of the transactions for that account. Click any transaction to open the Transaction Detail window.

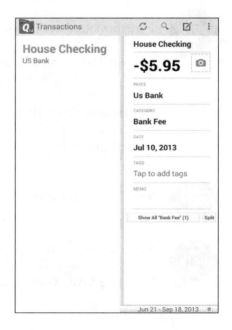

Transaction Detail Window

When you choose a specific transaction, the Transaction Detail window allows you to make changes, view information, and split the categories for the transaction, as seen in the illustration at right.

Several Quicken Mobile users use their own personal "shorthand" for memos. Some smart phones try to correct the "misspellings," so this feature is not as useful for them.

See All Similar Transactions   At the bottom of the Transaction Detail window, press the Show All "*nnnn*" (n) link to see all of the transactions for this category. The small number in the parentheses is the total number of transactions. If you are using another device, you may not see the Show All "*nnnn*" functionality.

Split a Downloaded Transaction   In the Transaction Detail window, click the Split button to open the Split dialog. On an iPhone the Split button is at the top right of the transaction details screen.

- To add a new category, press Add or the white cross within the green circle. A new category line appears along with a calculator. Press the right-facing arrow in the category field to choose from the list of categories.
- Press the amount field for that category and enter the numbers from the calculator. You do not need to enter the decimal point.
- Repeat the process for each new category. As you enter new amounts, the original amount adjusts to reflect your entries. If you enter a number that would make the total less than zero, you will see a warning that the amount you are entering is too large.
- Press the white minus sign inside the red circle by any category and a small Delete message appears in the amount field. Press the message to delete that category.
- Press Save when you have completed your changes, or Cancel if you decide you don't want to split the transaction.

After you have reviewed your transaction, press the white left-facing arrow to return to the previous screen. Repeat the process until you are back at the Overview page.

In some mobile devices, you may have to click the <Your Account Name> button to return to the transaction listing the account.

Banking

This part of the book explains how to use Quicken Personal Finance Software to keep track of your bank and credit card accounts. It starts by explaining the basics of manually recording bank and credit card transactions, and then tells how you can take advantage of online transaction entry and payment processing features such as Transaction Download and Online Bill Pay. It provides details about how you can tap into the power of Quicken to automate many entry tasks, thus saving you time. It also explains how to reconcile accounts and how to use Quicken's reporting features to learn more about what you have and how you're doing financially. This part has three chapters:

Chapter 3:   Recording Bank and Credit Card Transactions

Chapter 4:   Using Online Banking Features

Chapter 5:   Reconciling Your Accounts and Examining Your Banking Activity

Part Two

Recording Bank and Credit Card Transactions

In This Chapter:

- *Reviewing account and transaction types*
- *Working with bank accounts*
- *Using account registers*
- *Understanding splits*
- *Tracking credit cards with Quicken*
- *Writing checks*
- *Printing Quicken checks*
- *Transferring money*
- *Searching for transactions*
- *Adding notes, flags, and alerts*
- *Attaching checks, receipts, or other images*

The heart of Quicken is its ability to manage your bank accounts. This is probably Quicken's most used feature. You enter or download the transactions, and Quicken Personal Finance Software keeps track of the source of your money, where you spent it, and your account balances. Quicken will even print your checks.

In much the same way, Quicken helps you track your credit card accounts. You may choose to enter transactions as you make them, download your transactions daily, or enter an entire month's charges and payments when you receive your credit card statement.

Quicken keeps track of balances and offers you an easy way to monitor what you used your credit card to buy. Equally important today, Quicken shows you how much your credit cards cost you in terms of finance charges and other fees.

Getting Started

Quicken groups its account types into four general categories:

- **Spending & Saving** accounts, which include checking, savings, credit card, and cash accounts
- **Investing & Retirement** accounts, which include brokerage, IRA or Keogh Plan, 401(k) or 403(b), and 529 Plan accounts
- **Property & Asset** accounts, which can include your house, vehicles, and other assets
- **Loans & Debt** accounts, which include loans and other non–credit card liability accounts

This chapter focuses on what Quicken calls the "Spending & Savings" accounts, such as those you have at banks, credit unions, or similar financial institutions. Before you can use Quicken to track bank and credit card transactions, you should prepare by creating the necessary accounts and learning how recording transactions works. This section provides an overview of the spending account types, along with examples of transactions you might make. This chapter also reviews how to create these accounts.

Reviewing Account and Transaction Types

Many of the transactions you track with Quicken will involve one or more of its bank, credit card, and cash accounts. Here's a closer look at each account type, along with some transaction examples. As you read about these accounts, imagine how they might apply to your financial situation.

Bank Accounts

Quicken offers two types of accounts that you can use to track the money you have in a bank:

- Checking accounts are usually the first type of account you create in Quicken.
- Savings accounts are for your savings. These accounts normally don't have as much activity as checking accounts. You can use a Quicken savings account to track the balance in a certificate of deposit (CD), vacation savings plan, or similar savings account.

Some financial institutions consider CDs to be investment accounts, so you may not be able to download interest as you would with a regular savings account.

Both of these account types have the following types of transactions:

- **Payments**   Payments are funds going out of your account.
- **Deposits**   Deposits are funds put into your account.
- **Transfers**   A transfer is a movement of funds from one account to another.

Credit Card Accounts

Credit card accounts track money you owe, not money you own. Some credit cards, such as MasterCard, Visa, American Express, and Discover, can be used in many locations. Other credit cards, such as Macy's or Shell, can be used only in certain stores. But they all have one thing in common: if there's a balance, it's usually because you owe the credit card company money.

Credit card account transactions can also be broken down into three categories:

- **Charge**   Charges result when you use your credit card to buy something or the credit card company charges a fee for services.
- **Credit**   The opposite of a charge is a *credit*. Think of it as a negative charge; don't confuse it with a payment. An example is when you return an item to a store where you bought it and receive credit on your Visa card.
- **Payments**   Payments are amounts you send to a credit card company to reduce your balance, such as paying the balance on your American Express card or $150 of the $227 balance on your Visa card, as the rest of the balance is not yet due.

Cash Accounts

From within Quicken, you can also use a cash account to track your cash expenditures. For example, you might create an account called My Wallet or Spending Money and use it to keep track of the cash you have on hand. Cash accounts are like bank accounts, but there's no bank. The money is in your wallet, your pocket, or the Mason jar on your dresser.

Cash accounts have two types of transactions:

- **Receive**   When you receive cash, you increase the amount of cash you have on hand such as receiving a $20 bill in a birthday card.
- **Spend**   When you spend cash, you reduce your cash balance.

Working with Bank Accounts

In Chapter 1, you learned how to add new accounts. Here are a few additional things to keep in mind when creating Quicken accounts:

- Ensure that each account has a name that clearly identifies it. For example, if you have two checking accounts, don't name them "Checking 1" and "Checking 2." Instead, include the bank name (such as "USA Bank Checking") or account purpose (such as "Joint Checking") in the account name. This prevents you from accidentally entering a transaction in the wrong account register. Remember, the name of the account register displays on the title bar of the Quicken window and at the top of each register, as shown next. In addition, at any time, you can change an account's name in the General tab of the Account Details dialog.

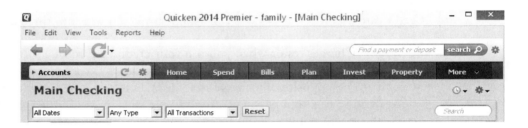

- If you create an account for which you manually enter transactions and include the balance date and amount from a bank statement, be careful not to enter transactions that already have been cleared on previous statements.
- Entering your credit limit for a credit card account enables Quicken to alert you when you get close to (or exceed) your limit. If a credit card account doesn't have a credit limit—for example, a store charge card—you may want to enter your own personal spending limit. This makes it possible to take advantage of Quicken's alerts feature to prevent overspending in that account.
- Using a cash account to track every penny you spend, from the cup of coffee you buy at work in the morning to the half-gallon of milk you pick up on your way home that evening, isn't for everyone. You may prefer to track only items that might be income tax related, such as donations or large purchases, and record the rest as miscellaneous expenses.

Adding Other Account Information

As you work with your accounts, there may be other information you want to include, such as interest rate changes on a money market account. To enter the new information:

1. From the Account Bar, right-click the name of the account you want to edit. From the context menu, select Edit/Delete Account to open the Account Details dialog.

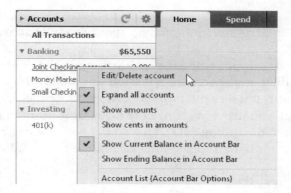

2. Enter or change the account information on the left side of the General tab, as seen here. The dialog has different fields depending on the type of account. All account types allow you to change their account name and description. In addition checking and savings accounts let you change the following:

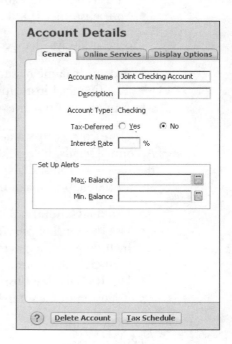

- Whether the account is tax deferred
- Interest rate
- Maximum and minimum balances for which you can be alerted

In credit card accounts, you can change the following:

- Interest rate
- Credit limit

Investing accounts let you change the following:

- Whether the account is tax deferred
- An option to show the cash in some types of investment accounts in a checking account

 Chapter 6 has more information about investing accounts.

For all account types, the information on the right side of the dialog is similar, depending on the account type. You can modify the information *only* if the account is not set up for online services. Once the account is set up for online services, you may not change the financial institution name, account and routing numbers, or customer ID. (However, if you deactivate an account you have enabled for online access, you can edit the fields.) You see the following:

- The financial institution
- The account and bank routing numbers
- Your customer ID, if applicable to this type of account

You can always change:

- A contact name or the phone number at the financial institution
- The financial institution's web page, including the banking activity pages
- Any other comments you have about the account

Before you set up an account for online services, there are two tabs in the Account Details dialog. After that, there are three. From all three, you can access the Delete Account dialog and change the Tax Schedule information. Use the appropriate tab to make these changes:

- Use the **General** tab to make any changes.
- Use the **Online Services** tab to activate or deactivate online services, including online payment services, if they are available through your financial institution.
- Use the **Display Options** tab to tell Quicken how to display this account, as discussed in Chapter 1.

When you have made all of your changes, click OK to close the Account Details dialog.

Quicken's Registers

To make the most of Quicken, you must enter transactions for the accounts you want to track. You can do this manually, as discussed in this chapter, or, if the account is enabled for online account services, you can track your account activity automatically via download, as discussed in Chapter 4. Either way, you'll need to know how to work with register transactions for your accounts.

You can enter transactions in several ways, based on the type of transaction:

- Use registers to record virtually any type of transaction, including manual checks, bank account payments and deposits, credit card charges and payments, and cash receipts and spending.
- Use the Write Checks window to record checks to be printed by Quicken.
- Enter transfers to transfer money from one account to another. You can also enter transactions via transaction reminder or scheduled transaction.

Using Account Registers

Quicken's account registers offer a standard way to enter all kinds of transactions. As the name suggests, these *electronic account registers* are similar to the paper checking account registers that come with your checks. To open an account's register, from the Account Bar, click the name of the account you want to open. The register opens to the right of the Account Bar, as seen in Figure 3-1.

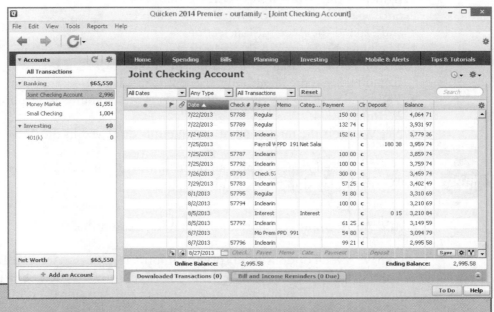

Figure 3-1 • Use the account register to work with your bank accounts.

The Account Bar

The Account Bar displays a list of the accounts
you've chosen to display, including the total balance
if you choose to display it. As seen at right, the
Account Bar displays your accounts in several
sections: Banking, Investing, and Property & Debt.
You can choose to show all accounts in each
section, such as Banking and Property & Debt as
we've done here. Or, you can choose to collapse the
section and show only the total as we've done in
the Investing and Savings Goals sections. In
general, you can designate the section in which you
want your account to appear, or you can choose to
show all accounts in each section.

- The small downward arrow to the left of the
  word Accounts allows you to minimize the
  Account Bar to save room when working with
  other Quicken processes. When you click this
  arrow to minimize the Account Bar, it turns
  into an arrow pointing to the right. Click that
  right-pointing arrow to open the Account Bar
  once again. In the same way, you can collapse
  and expand the Account Bar sections.
- The blue curly arrow to the right of the word
  Accounts is a shortcut for updating your online
  accounts. See more about online accounts in Chapter 4.
- The small gear icon at the far right of the word Accounts is a shortcut to the
  Account List.
- **Net Worth** is the total of all of the amounts displayed in the Account Bar.

If you have chosen to not display amounts in the Account Bar, you will not see
Net Worth displayed in the Account Bar.

- **Add An Account** is a shortcut to the Add Account dialog.

You have several options for displaying information in the Account Bar. While
most of the display options can be set in the Account List as described in
Chapter 1, you can also open a context menu in the Account Bar with a right-
click. The following menu options are available.

- If you right-click a specific account, the context menu includes **Edit/Delete Account**. This link opens the Account Details dialog for the account you selected.
- **Expand All Accounts** tells Quicken to display all of the individual accounts in each separate section of the Account Bar.
- **Show Amounts** tells Quicken to display the balance of each account. If you choose not to display the balance amount, you do not see the Net Worth total in the Account Bar.
- **Show Cents In Amounts** tells Quicken to include the cents rather than just the dollar amount of each account's balance.
- **Show Current/Ending Balance In Account Bar** tells Quicken whether to display the balance as of today or include transactions you've entered for future dates in the balance.
- **Show Savings Goals Transactions** appears only if you have established savings goals. Learn more about Savings Goals in Chapter 12.
- **Account List (Account Bar Options)** opens the Account List when chosen from this context menu.

Overview of the Account Register

Before we discuss entry techniques, let's take a closer look at the account register window.

Range Selection Options   At the top of most account registers are options to customize the information displayed in your register. Drop-down lists enable you to filter the transactions that appear in the current register:

- The Dates drop-down list lets you filter the register to include all dates, specific time periods, or create a customized date range to display.
- The next drop-down list in bank account registers gives you the ability to filter for Any Type (meaning the type of transaction), Payment, or Deposit. In credit card account registers, your choices are Any Type, Charge, or Payment. A cash account shows Any Type, Spend, or Receive.
- The next drop-down list allows you to filter the register by several criteria: Uncategorized, Unreconciled, Cleared, Uncleared, Flagged, and the default All Transactions.
- Reset sets the transactions register back to the default settings of All Dates, Any Type, and All Transactions.
- The Search field allows you to search for transactions within this register.
- Reminders menu lets you set reminders to appear in your register. See "Reminders Menu" later in this chapter.

See "Gear Icon Actions Menu" later in this chapter for information about the Actions button (icon).

Downloaded Transactions   At the bottom of the account register are two tabs of information, Downloaded Transactions and Bill And Income Reminders, as seen in Figure 3-1. If these tabs are not visible, you may have told Quicken to automatically add downloaded transactions to the banking registers. While this is covered in Chapter 4, you can quickly check your settings.

1. From the menu bar, click Edit | Preferences | Register | Downloaded Transactions | Downloaded Transactions Preferences | After Downloading Transactions.
2. Clear the Automatically Add To Banking Registers check box. Even if you clear the file preference, you may still have an individual account register preference set for the particular account register. Check the Online Services tab of the Account Details dialog to verify your settings.
3. If you do not want your investment accounts transactions added automatically to your investment account register, clear the Automatically Add To Investment Transactions Lists check box. See Chapter 7 for more information about downloaded investment transactions.
4. Click OK to save your settings and close the Preferences dialog.

Download Transactions (or Downloaded Transactions if there are transactions that have been downloaded and need to be reviewed) displays either a link to set up downloading for each account or a list of transactions that have already been downloaded but not yet accepted into the account, respectively. Learn how to set up and work with the Transaction Download and Online Payment features in Chapter 4.

Bill and Income Reminders   The Bill And Income Reminders tab displays a list of upcoming, due, and overdue scheduled transactions. See Chapter 4 for more information about scheduled transactions.

You can show or hide this information in the bottom half of the register window by clicking the small arrow button on the right end of the bar on which the tabs appear.

Reminders Menu

Use the choices on this menu to tell Quicken when (or if) to display Bill & Income Reminders that you have set earlier. These scheduled reminders display in the register, as seen below. You have a choice of how far ahead the reminders should appear or to not show them at all, as seen on the menu at right.

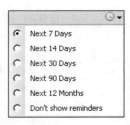

	Next 7 Days
	Next 14 Days
	Next 30 Days
	Next 90 Days
	Next 12 Months
	Don't show reminders

Checking

All Dates	Any Type	All Transactions	Reset				Search

Date ▲	Check #	Payee		Payment	Clr	Deposit	Balance
		Category	Memo				
9/10/2013		Gas		85 00			9,814 40
		Auto & Transport:Fuel					
9/11/2013		Big Electric		81 22			9,733 18
		Utilities:Gas & Electric					
9/15/2013	Sched	2011 Ford Fusion Loan		356 46			9,376 72
		--Split--					
9/16/2013		Retail Firm				1,160 19	10,536 91
9/20/2013	Sched	Loan 3		258 64			10,278 27
		[Loan 3]					
9/22/2013		Big Electric		81 22			10,197 05
		Utilities:Gas & Electric					
9/27/2013	Sched	Rental House Loan		1,649 10			8,547 95
		[Rental House Loan]	N/A				

	Current Balance:	9,733.18	Ending Balance:	9,055.05

IN MY EXPERIENCE

For many Quicken users, the ability to show scheduled payments (or deposits) in account registers is very useful. Note that there is no check number, but the indication "Sched" that displays in the check number column. See if this new feature works for you! You'll never forget that annual insurance payment or property tax payment when you use this feature.

You can choose to change this Quicken 2014 feature by changing how far ahead you want the reminders to display or by simply choosing **Don't Show Reminders** on the Reminders menu.

Gear Icon Actions Menu

This register window's Account Actions menu (gear icon), as seen here, includes a number of options you can use while in the register. There are three sections: Transactions, Reporting, and Register Views And Preferences. Note that many of sections include keyboard shortcut commands. Learn more about keyboard shortcuts in Appendix A.

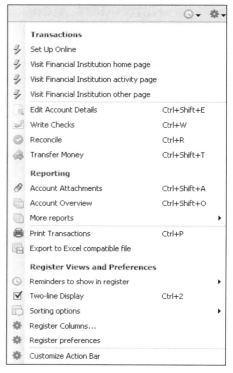

Transactions Section   In the Transactions section you can

1. Click Set Up Online to activate Online Services for the current account. If you have included the financial institution's home page, or an activity or other page in the Account Details dialog, you will note additional options that are links to those websites.

2. Click Update Now (not shown) to open the One Step Update Settings dialog for accounts that have online services. Enter the password given by your financial institution, and click Update Now.

If the account is set up for Web Connect, when you click Update Now, your Internet connection will open your browser at the login page for that financial institution's website.

3. Click Edit Account Details to open the Account Details dialog as described in Chapter 1.

4. Click Write Checks to open the Write Checks dialog. See "Writing Checks" later in this chapter. If this is a cash or credit card account, that option is not available.

5. Click Reconcile to open the Reconcile Details dialog. See Chapter 5 for complete instructions on reconciling your accounts. Depending on the account type and online status of the account, you may see an Update Balance dialog or you may be prompted to download transactions before

reconciling. If the account is a checking or credit card account not enabled for online access, you will go directly to the Reconcile Details screen.

Reporting Section   The Reporting section allows you to

1. Click Account Attachments to open the Account Attachments dialog. See more information in the section "Working with Attachments" later in this chapter.
2. Click Account Overview to display a graphical recap of the selected account as well as the account's current status.
3. Click More Reports to see the information about this account in various report formats. Read more about creating reports in Chapter 5.
4. Click Print Transactions to open the Print dialog where you can print the register for this account. See Chapter 5 for more information about printing reports and graphs.
5. Click Export To Excel Compatible File to export this file in a tab-delimited text format. See more information about exporting files in Chapter 5.

Since the export utility prints your transactions to a text file, if your account has many years of transactions, the process may take a few minutes to complete.

Register Views and Preferences   The Register Views And Preferences section lets you set how this register displays.

1. Click Reminders To Show In Register to open the Reminders menu as discussed earlier in this chapter.
2. Click Two-line Display to show your register information on two lines, as seen in Figure 3-1. If you clear that check box, you'll see the payee, the category, and the amount on just one line. One-line display is the default for Quicken 2014, as shown next.

8/2/2013	57794	Inclearing Chk			100 00	c		3,210 69
8/5/2013		Interest Deposit		Interest Inc		c	0 15	3,210 84
8/5/2013	57797	Inclearing Chk			61 25	c		3,149 59

3. Click Sorting Options to tell Quicken how to organize your transactions in this register menu. See "Sorting Transactions" later in this chapter for more information.
4. Click Register Columns to open the Register Columns list. You can also click the small gear icon at the top of the register's vertical scroll bar to see

this list. Learn more about this topic later in this chapter in the "Using Register Columns" section.

5. Click Register Preferences to open the Preferences dialog at the Register section. See Appendix B for more information on Quicken Preferences.

6. Click Customize Action Bar to open the Customize Action Bar dialog, as seen next. From here you can add toolbar buttons that will show to the left of your Account Actions (gear) icon at the top of your account register. As seen in our Customize Action Bar illustration, the Reminder menu, the Reconcile shortcut, and the Write Checks icons appear on our Action Bar.

Basic Entry Techniques

To enter a transaction into a register, first, open the register by clicking the account in the Account Bar. Begin by clicking in the first empty line at the end of the account register window (refer to Figure 3-1). This activates a new, blank transaction. (You will see grayed-out indications of what is to be entered in each field, as seen next.) You can then enter transaction information into each field and press ENTER to complete the transaction.

Although the entry process is pretty straightforward, here are a few things to keep in mind when entering transactions.

Advancing from Field to Field

To move from one text box, or field, to another when entering transactions, you can either click in the next field's text box or press the TAB key. Pressing TAB is usually quicker.

Many users feel more comfortable using the ENTER key to move between fields. To set this option, go to Edit | Preferences | Register | Data Entry And QuickFill | Data Entry. Click the Use Enter Key To Move Between Fields check box.

Using Icons   Icons appear when certain fields are active:

- When the Date field is active, a calendar icon appears. You can click it to display a calendar, and then click calendar buttons to view and enter a date.
- When either the Payment or Deposit Amount field is active, a calculator icon appears. You can click it to use a calculator and enter calculated results.
- When the Payee or Category field is active, a Report button appears. Click the Report button to display a pop-up report of transactions in that category or for that payee, like the one shown here. Click the X to close the report.

If you do not see the calendar, calculator, or report icons, you can turn them on by going to Edit | Preferences | Register | Data Entry And QuickFill and ensuring that the Show Buttons On QuickFill Fields check box is selected.

Menu buttons, which look like triangles pointing down to a horizontal line, display drop-down lists of items applicable to the active field. You can enter an item by choosing it from the list's options or by simply typing the information.

Using the Number Field   The Check # (or Reference # in non-banking accounts) field is where you enter a transaction number or type. You can enter any number you like, or use the drop-down list (shown here) to display a list of standard entries; click an option to enter it for the transaction. You can also press the + or − key on the keyboard to increase or decrease the check number, respectively, while the field is active.

Savings and Credit Card accounts have a default one-line display with no reference field. Turn on the Reference # field by clicking the Register Columns gear icon at the top of your register (above the vertical scroll bar). Click the Reference # check box and then click Done to close the list.

- **Next Check Num** automatically increments the most recently entered check number and enters the resulting number in the Check Number field.
- **ATM** is for ATM transactions. You may also want to use it for debit or check card transactions.
- **Deposit** is for deposits.
- **Print Check** is for transactions for which you want Quicken to print a check. Quicken automatically enters the check number when the check is printed.
- **Send Online Payment** is for accounts for which you have enabled Online Bill Pay.
- **Online Transfer** is for accounts you have activated to transfer funds from one online account to another online account.
- **Transfer** is for a transfer of funds from one account to another.
- **EFT**, which stands for electronic funds transfer, is for direct deposits and similar transactions.
- **Edit List** opens a dialog with which you can create your own item names. If you have periodic items, such as insurance payments, withdrawn from your account, you might create an item named INS.

The Payee Drop-Down List and QuickFill   When you begin to enter information in the Payee field, a drop-down list of existing payees or payers appears. As you type, Quicken narrows down the list to display only those names that match what you have typed. You can enter an existing name from the list by selecting it. Quicken will fill in details from the most recent transaction for that name for you. This is Quicken's QuickFill feature, which you will learn more about in Chapter 4.

Automatic Categorization   After entering a payee for the first time, Quicken may fill in the category for you. This is Quicken's automatic categorization feature, which enters categories based on thousands of payee names programmed into it. You'll find that in most cases, Quicken assigns an appropriate category. But you can change the category if you like and, from that point on, Quicken's QuickFill feature uses your newly assigned category for future transactions to that payee. Chapter 4 provides more information about QuickFill.

Using the Category Drop-Down List   The Category drop-down list organizes category and transfer accounts in the Category List window, as discussed in Chapter 1. This drop-down list may appear automatically when you begin to enter a category in the Category field of the transaction area. If it does not, you can click the menu button on the right side of the field to display it. You can narrow down the display of categories by clicking a heading on the left side of the drop-down list. Then click the category name to enter it into the field.

Entering New Categories   If you type in a category that does not exist in the Category List and press ENTER, Quicken displays a message asking if you want to create a new category with that name. (You may also see the prompt if you use the TAB key.) Click Yes to open the Set Up Category dialog to create a new category, or click No to return to the register and enter a different category.

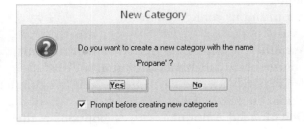

If you turn off the Prompt Before Creating New Categories check box, Quicken automatically displays the Set Up Category dialog every time you enter a category that does not exist in the Category List. See more about categories in Chapter 1.

Entering Subcategories   When you choose a subcategory from the Category field's drop-down list, Quicken automatically enters the subcategory's parent category name, followed by a colon (:) and the subcategory name. To type a subcategory, use the first letter or two of the category, the colon, and then the first letter or two of the subcategory. QuickFill will match the category:subcategory.

Entering Multiple Categories   To enter more than one category for a transaction, click the Split button (a small, two-headed arrow pointing upward, as shown here) on the right side of the transaction entry area. See how to enter transactions with splits a little later in this chapter, in the section titled "Understanding Splits."

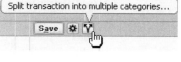

Using Register Columns   Use the small gear icon at the top of the vertical scroll bar to tell Quicken which columns to display in your register and which ones to hide. (You can either click the Register Columns gear icon at the top of the vertical scroll bar or choose Register Columns from the gear icon Actions menu to open the list, as shown right.) Each item toggles the selected column in your register off and on. While many of the items seem self-explanatory, there are several that might cause some confusion, so we explain the options here. You may see a slightly different list, depending on your register, its online services activation, and its configuration.

- **Amount**   Selecting this option adds an amount column before the balance column. It displays deposits in black and payments in red. This column is not editable.
- **Downloaded Amount**   This "suboption" of the Amount column displays the amount that was actually downloaded for this transaction. It is a

great way to see if the bank cleared a check (or deposit) for the same amount that you entered into Quicken!

- **Balance**   This column shows the balance in the account after each transaction.
- **Action Buttons**   When this is selected, the Save/More Actions/Split Transaction Into Multiple Categories buttons display in the selected transaction. See "Using Transaction Buttons" later in this chapter for more information.
- **Attachments, Flags, Status, Tax-Line Item, and Tax-Related**   If any of these items are selected, the appropriate button (Sort By Attachment, Sort By Status, and/or Sort By Tax-Related) appears at the top of the Date column. See "Sorting Transactions" later in this chapter for more information. The small flag and attachment icons also appear before or underneath the date when entering a new transaction.
- **Date**   This column cannot be omitted.
- **Downloaded** *xxxxx*   These items are covered in Chapter 4.

After you have made your selections, click Done to close the Register Columns list.

If you don't like the way your register columns appear, open the Register Columns list and click the small gear icon at the bottom-left corner. From there you can choose to make all of your similar registers' displays the same one-line or two-line registers as your current register or reset the columns to their default settings.

Using Tags   As discussed in Chapter 1, a tag is an optional identifier for specifying what a transaction applies to. Quicken displays a Tag field in the register. To include a tag in a transaction, simply enter the tag in that field. Quicken may display a drop-down list of valid tags from which you can choose. If you type a tag name that is not on the Tag List, Quicken displays the Set Up Tag window so you can create the tag on the fly. Review how to create tags in Chapter 1. You can use the Register Columns menu to turn off the Tag field display.

Entering Memos   You can enter a brief memo (up to 64 characters) about the transaction in the Memo field to the right of the Category (or Tag) field. This memo can help you recall why you made the transaction.

Using Transaction Buttons   If you have set the option to display the Action Buttons, three buttons appear in the second line of a two-line display register and inline with the active transaction in a one-line display register as shown here. You can use these buttons to work with the transaction, as follows.

- **Save** enters the transaction into the account register. If Quicken's sound option is turned on, you should hear a cash register cha-ching sound when you click it. (You can turn Quicken sounds on or off in the Preferences dialog, which is covered in Appendix B.)
- **More Actions**, a small black gear icon, displays a menu you can use to edit this transaction. See some of the More Action menu commands later in this chapter, in the section titled "Changing Transactions."
- **Split Transaction Into Multiple Categories**, a small two-headed arrow pointing upward, opens the Split Transaction window. The next section explains how to enter a transaction with splits.

Understanding Splits

A split is a transaction with more than one category. For example, suppose you pay one utility bill for two categories of utilities—electricity and water. If you want to track each of these two expenses separately, you can use a split to record each category's portion of the payment you make. This enables you to keep good records without writing multiple checks to the same payee.

To record a transaction with a split, click the Split icon in the account register or the Split button in the Write Checks window when entering the transaction. The Split Transaction window, which is shown on the following page, appears. Click in the first blank line and select a category. If desired, enter a memo for the category in the Memo field. Then enter the amount for that category in the Amount field. Repeat this process for each category you want to include in the transaction. The illustration shows what the Split Transaction window might look like with three categories entered.

If you entered a transaction amount before clicking the Split button, you can monitor the Remainder and Transaction Total values in the Split Transaction window to make sure you've accounted for the entire transaction amount. If you entered an incorrect amount, you can click the Adjust button to adjust the transaction amount to match the split total. You may also allocate how the split distributes a remainder amount.

If you need more lines to record all of the split amounts, click Add Lines. To clear all of your entries and start over, click Clear All.

When you're finished entering transaction categories, click OK or press ENTER. If you left the transaction amount empty before clicking the Split button,

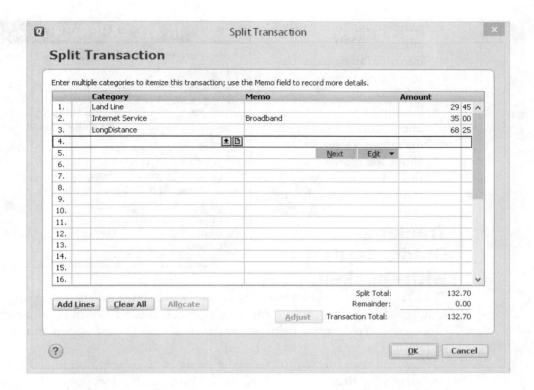

a dialog appears, asking if you want to record the transaction as a payment or deposit. Select the appropriate option and click OK.

If the split is in a credit card account, the dialog will be "Charge Or Payment."

As shown here, the word "Split" appears in the Category field for the transaction in the account register window.

Three buttons appear beside the Category field when you activate a transaction with a split:

Payee		Payment
Category	Memo	
Our Phone Company		132 70
--Split-- ✓✗🗋	Memo	

- The green check mark displays the Split Transaction window so you can review and edit the transaction.
- The red X opens a message that allows you to clear all lines from the split. Use this option with care—it removes all category information from the

transaction. You can then add new category information or redo the previous category information.

- Clicking the Report icon opens a mini-report pop-up showing a report about the categories in this transaction for a time period you can set.

IN MY EXPERIENCE

As you are entering categories in a split transaction, you may notice that the Allocate button at the bottom of the Split Transaction dialog is activated. If you have entered several amounts and have just one remaining amount, you have two options for that remainder.

1. Click Allocate to open the Allocate Empty Split Line dialog.
2. Choose Distribute Proportionally Between All Other Split Lines to apportion the remaining amount in the same ratio as the other lines.
3. Choose Distribute Evenly: *$nn.nn* To All Other Split Lines.

Tracking Credit Cards with Quicken

Tracking bank account transactions and balances is just one part of using Quicken. It's also a great tool for tracking credit cards. Knowing how much you owe on your credit cards helps you maintain a clear picture of your financial situation.

How you use Quicken to track your credit cards depends on how accurate you want your financial records to be and how much effort you're willing to spend to keep Quicken up-to-date.

Credit Card Tracking Techniques

You can use either of two techniques for paying credit card bills and monitoring credit card balances with Quicken:

- Use your checking account register or the Write Checks window to record amounts paid to each credit card company for your credit card bill. Although this does track the amounts you pay, it doesn't track how much you owe.
- Use a credit card account register to record credit card expenditures and payments. This takes a bit more effort on your part, but it tracks how much you owe and categorizes what you bought. And, if you utilize Quicken's Transaction Download feature for your credit card accounts, as discussed in Chapter 4, it won't take much time or effort to get the job done.

Many Quicken users feel it is well worth the effort to track their credit card expenditures and balances in individual credit card accounts.

Recording Strategies

You can also use two strategies for recording transactions in credit card accounts. Choosing the strategy that's right for you makes the job easier to handle.

Enter as You Spend   One strategy is to enter transactions as you spend. To do this, you must collect your credit card receipts—which might be something you already do. Don't forget to jot down the totals for any telephone and online shopping you do. Then, every day or every few days, sit down with Quicken and enter the transactions.

While this strategy requires you to stay on top of things, it offers two main benefits:

- Your Quicken credit card registers always indicate what you owe to credit card companies. This prevents unpleasant surprises at month-end or at the checkout counter when you're told you've reached your card's limit. It also enables you to use the alerts feature to track credit card balances. Learn more about those features in Chapter 5.
- At month-end, you won't have to spend a lot of time entering big batches of transactions. All (or at least most) of them should already be entered.

Many just don't like holding on to all those pieces of paper. (Of course, once you have signed up for Transaction Download, all of the information can be downloaded from your card company and entered automatically.) This method has an added bonus, as it allows you to spot any fraudulent charges earlier than waiting for a paper statement.

Enter When You Pay   The other strategy, which you may find better for you, is to enter transactions when you get your monthly statement. With this strategy, when you open your credit card statement, you'll spend some time sitting in front of your computer with Quicken to enter each transaction. If there aren't many, this isn't a big deal. However, it can take some time if you have a large number of transactions to enter.

Of course, the main benefit of this strategy is that you don't have to collect credit card receipts and spend time throughout the month entering your transactions. However, you still have to enter them!

Entering Credit Card Transactions

Entering credit card transactions isn't very different from entering checking account or savings account transactions, as seen in Figure 3-2.

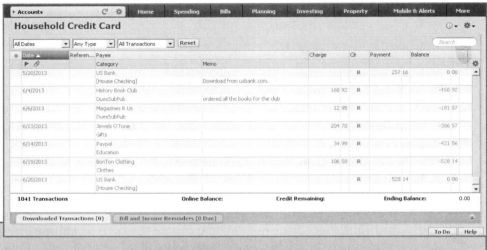

Figure 3-2 • Your credit card register looks much like your checking and savings registers.

Entering Individual Charges   Open the account register for the credit card account. Then enter the charge transaction, using the name of the merchant that accepted the charge as the payee name. Press TAB to move between the fields.

If you want to record a reference number for a credit card transaction, choose the Register Columns icon at the top-right area of the register and click in the Reference # check box at the bottom of the list. This column then appears to the immediate right of the Date column. Don't forget to click Done to save your column display changes.

Entering Credits   Enter the transaction just as if it were a charge, but put the amount of the credit in the Payment box. This subtracts it from your account balance.

Entering Finance Charges   In the credit card account register, enter the name of the credit card company as the payee and the amount of the finance charge as a charge. You can use the Interest Exp category for the transaction.

Entering Payments   In the account register for your checking account or in the Write Checks window, enter a payment transaction with the credit card company name in the Payee box. Enter the credit card account name in the Category text box; you should find it as a transfer account in the Category drop-down list that appears when you activate the field. The credit card account register transaction should look like the one shown here.

●	Date ▲	Reference #	Payee		Charge	Clr	Payment	Balance
	▶ 🖉		Category	Memo				
	6/20/2013		US Bank				528 14	0 00
			[House Checking]					

Recording Credit Card Rebates   Some credit card companies offer rebates for purchases. How you record a rebate depends on how the rebate is received:

- To record a rebate received as a check, deposit the check as usual and enter the amount of the rebate as a deposit in that account.
- To record a rebate received as a reduction in the credit card account balance, enter the amount of the rebate in the credit card account as a payment. (Just remember that a rebate is not a payment that counts toward your monthly obligation to the credit card company.)

What you use as a category for this transaction is completely up to you. You may want to use the Interest Exp(ense) category, thus recording the rebate as a reduction in your interest expense. Or, perhaps, if the rebate applies to a certain purchase only, use the category you originally used for that purchase. For example, if you have a credit card that gives you a 5 percent rebate on fuel purchases, you might record the rebate using the Fuel category you created to track fuel expenses. If you have many credit cards that offer rebates, you may want to create a rebate income account or rewards account and use that as the category for all rebate transactions. These are just suggestions. There is no right or wrong way to do it.

Entering Cash Transactions

Although Quicken enables you to keep track of cash transactions by creating a "cash" account, not everyone does this. The reason: Most people make many small cash transactions every day. Is it worth tracking every penny you spend? That's something you need to decide.

Many people track only expenditures that are large or tax-deductible—for example, the $20 you gave to the local Lions Club. You may want to do the same. If so, you still need to set up a cash account, but you don't need to record every transaction.

Cash Receipts   Cash receipts may come from using your ATM card, cashing a check, or getting cash from some other source. If the cash comes from one of your other accounts through an ATM or check transaction, when you record that transaction, use your cash account as the transfer in the Category field. That increases your cash balance.

Important Cash Expenditures   In your cash account, record large, tax-deductible, or other important cash expenditures like any other transaction. Be sure to assign the correct category.

Other Cash Expenditures   Throughout the week, you may spend $1 for a newspaper, $3 for a soft drink, and about $12 for lunch at your favorite coffee shop. Recording transactions like these can be tedious, so don't bother if you don't want to. Instead, at the end of the week, compare your cash on hand to the balance in your cash account register. Then, enter a transaction to record the difference as an expenditure. You can use the Misc category and enter anything you like in the Payee field.

Writing Checks

Quicken's Write Checks window uses a basic check-like interface to record checks. You enter the same information that you would write on an actual check. You then tell Quicken to print the check based on the information you entered. (See how to print checks later in this chapter, in the section titled "Printing Checks.")

To open the Write Checks window, from your account register, click the Actions gear icon | Write Checks or press CTRL-W. The Write Checks window, shown in Figure 3-3, appears. The name of the account from which you are writing this check appears in the drop-down list near the top of the window. If you need to choose another account, click the down arrow. Enter the necessary information for a check, and record the transaction.

Overview of the Write Checks Window

The top of the Write Checks dialog looks much like the checks you write by hand, including a space for a memo. If you have enabled Online Bill Pay for the selected account, the Use Online Bill Pay check box will appear to the right of the account name, as seen in Figure 3-3. Other options are discussed here:

- **Edit Address**   If the address that appears in the Bill Pay Address field is incorrect, click Edit Address to open the Edit Address Book Record dialog. The Address Book is discussed at length in Chapter 4.
- **Category**   Use the Category field to enter the category for this check. Click the Split icon should you need to use more than one category.

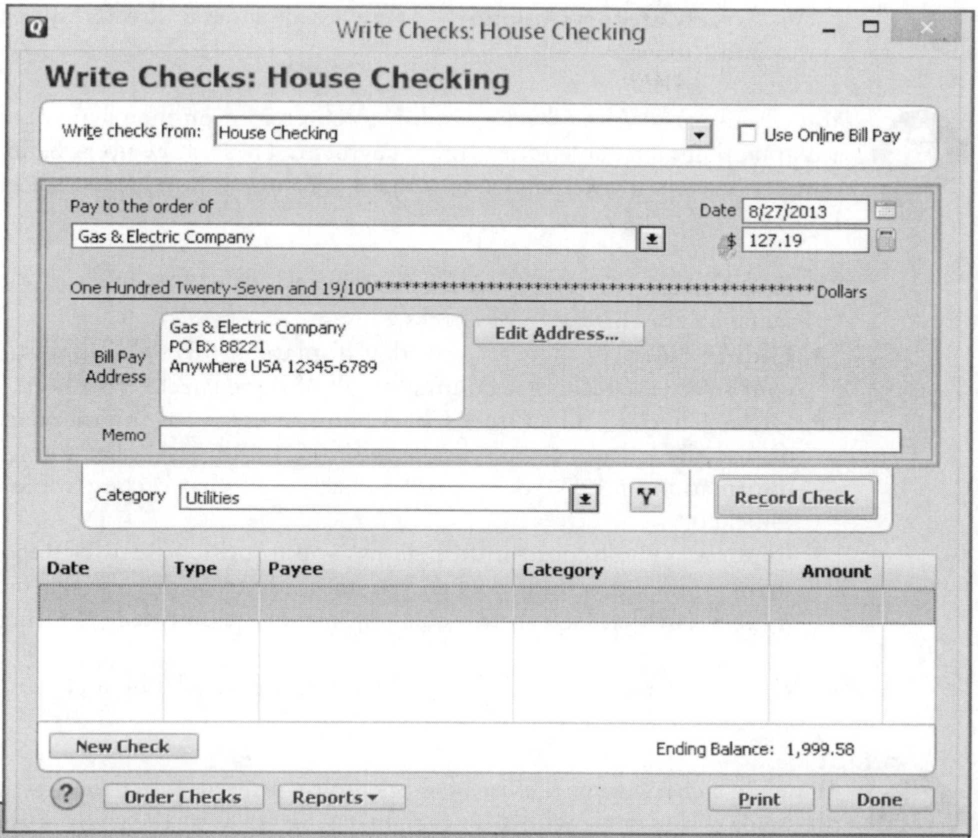

Figure 3-3 • The Write Checks window makes printing checks from Quicken easy.

- **Split**   Use the Split Transactions icon to split the categories as you do in your check register.
- **Record Check**   The Record Check button records your check in the appropriate check register. You do not have to enter it twice!
- **Check Data**   Quicken uses the space below Category, Split, and Record Check to show a list of the checks that are ready to print. This makes it easy to enter a number of checks and print them all at once. The information displayed is
  - **Date**   This is the date you entered in the Date field in your check body.
  - **Type**   Normally, Print will appear in this field as the check is to be printed using Quicken.

- **Payee/Category/Amount** These are all entered directly from the check body above.

You can use the Write Checks window to enter your online payments for accounts that are enabled for Online Payment. These show up as Send transactions when entered. See Chapter 4 for more information on Online Payment.

- **New Check** Select the New Check button to add the next check in sequence for this batch of checks.
- **Ending Balance** The amount that displays in this field is the balance in your selected checking account after all of these checks have been printed.
- **Order Checks** The Order Checks button uses your Internet connection to display the Checks & Supplies page of the Intuit Market window, with information on how you can order check stock that is compatible with Quicken.
- **Reports** The Reports button allows you to print a Register Report.
- **Print** Click this button when you are ready to print your checks. Learn more about that later in this chapter, in the section titled "Printing Checks."

When you have made all of your choices and entered all the checks for this work session, click Done to close the dialog.

To delete a check from the list of checks to be printed, select the check and click the small, white circle with a blue, right-facing arrow at the right of the check information. Click this arrow and select Delete. A message appears asking if it is okay to delete the current transaction. Choose OK or Cancel. You can use this same menu to Void or Memorize a check.

Entering Transactions in the Write Checks Window

The Write Checks window (refer to Figure 3-3) is like a cross between a paper check and Quicken's account register window. You fill in the check form just as you would fill in the blanks on a paper check. Quicken's QuickFill feature makes data entry quick and easy by recalling entry information from similar transactions to the same payee, and its automatic categorization feature can automatically "guess" the category for many new transactions. You must enter a valid Quicken category in the Category field, just as you would when entering a transaction in the account register. Clicking the Record Check button completes the transaction and adds it to the checks to print list as well as the account register.

Consult the section "Using Account Registers," earlier, for details about the information that should be entered into most fields. Here are a few additional things to consider when entering transactions in the Write Checks window.

Addresses on Checks   If you enter an address on the check, you can mail the check using a window envelope. The address is automatically added to the Quicken Address Book. You can click the Address button in the Write Checks window to display the Edit Address Book Record dialog, which you can use to modify an address in the Address Book.

Check Memos   Be careful when using the memo field if you are using window envelopes. Some envelopes display part of the memo field. If you have included account numbers or other personal information in the memo, that information may be visible to others.

Printing Checks

Quicken's ability to print checks enables you to create accurate, legible, professional-looking checks without picking up a pen (or a typewriter). In this section, you'll learn how to print the checks you enter in the Write Checks window, discussed earlier.

Before you can print checks from Quicken, you must obtain compatible check stock. Quicken supports checks in a number of different styles:

- Standard checks print just checks. There's no voucher or stub.
- Voucher checks pair each check with a similarly sized voucher form. When you print a voucher check, the transaction category information, including splits and tags, can be printed on the voucher portion.
- Wallet checks pair each check with a stub. When you print a wallet check, the transaction information is printed on the stub.

Wallet checks are being phased out and have been replaced by Check 21 Compatible Wallet checks.

- Wallet checks (Check 21 Image Compatible).

In addition to these styles, you can get the checks in two different formats for your printer:

- Page-oriented checks are for laser and inkjet printers.
- Continuous checks are for pin-feed printers.

A catalog and order form for checks may have been included with your copy of Quicken. If so, you can use it to order checks. If you have an Internet connection, you can order checks online from within Quicken by clicking the Order Checks button in the Write Checks window (see Figure 3-3), or by clicking the Order [check type] checks link below the check style field in the Select Checks To Print dialog.

Quicken must also be set up to print the kind of checks you purchased. You do this once, and Quicken remembers the settings.

Choose File | Printer Setup | For Printing Checks to display the Check Printer Setup dialog, shown next. Use the drop-down lists and option buttons to specify settings for your printer and check stock. The following are a few things to keep in mind when making settings in this dialog.

Partial Page Printing Options

If you select the Page-Oriented option and either Standard or Wallet checks in the Check Printer Setup dialog, you can also set options for Partial Page Printing Style. This enables you to set up the printer for situations when you're not printing an entire page of checks.

- **Edge** is for inserting the page against one side of the feeder. The left or right edge of the checks enters the feeder first.
- **Centered** is for centering the page in the feeder. The left or right edge of the checks enters the feeder first.
- **Portrait** is also for centering the page in the feeder, but in this case, the top edge of each check enters the feeder first.

If your printer supports multiple feed trays, you can also set the source tray for partial and full pages by choosing options from the Partial Page Printing and Full Page Printing drop-down lists.

Continuous Printing Options

If you select the Continuous option and either Standard or Wallet checks in the Check Printer Setup dialog, the dialog changes to offer two Continuous options:

- **Bypass The Driver**   Check this check box for a continuous printer that skips checks or prints nothing.
- **Use Low Starting Position**   This should be turned on for a continuous printer that cuts the date or logo off your checks.

Checking the Settings for Page-Oriented Checks

If you're using page-oriented checks, you can check your settings by printing a sample page on plain paper. Here's how:

1. Click the Alignment button in the Check Printer Setup dialog.
2. In the Align Checks dialog, choose the Full Page, Two Checks, or One Check button. The Fine Alignment dialog appears.
3. Click Print Sample.
4. When the sample emerges from your printer, hold it up to the light with a sheet of check stock behind it. The sample should line up with the check.
5. If the sample does not line up properly with the check stock, set Vertical and/or Horizontal adjustment values in the Fine Alignment dialog. Then repeat steps 2 through 4 until the alignment is correct.
6. Click OK in each dialog to accept your settings and close it.

Printing Quicken Checks

Once setup is complete, you're ready to print checks.

Open the account register for which you want to print checks. Then insert the check stock in your printer and choose File | Print Checks, or click the Print button in the Write Checks window. The Select Checks To Print dialog appears. Enter the number of the first check to be printed in the First Check Number box. Then set other options as desired. If you select the Selected Checks option, you can click the Choose button to display a list of checks and mark off the ones you want to print. Click Done in that window to return to the Select Checks To Print dialog.

When you click Print First Check or OK, Quicken sends the print job to your printer. It then displays a dialog asking if the checks printed correctly. You have the following two options:

- If all checks printed fine, just click OK.
- If a problem occurred while printing the checks, enter the number of the first check that was misprinted, and then click OK. You can then go back to the Select Checks To Print dialog and try again. Click OK or Cancel to close the Select Checks To Print dialog.

Transferring Money

You can easily record the transfer of funds from one account to another. You might find this feature especially useful for recording telephone or ATM transfers.

Recording a Transfer in the Account Register Window

You can record a transfer in the account register window of either the source or destination account. When you choose Transfer (TXFR) from the Check # drop-down list, the Category drop-down list displays only transfer accounts. Choose the other transfer account from the list and complete the transaction. (If you don't see a Check # column in your account register, you can display it by clicking the Register Columns gear icon at the upper-right corner of your account register and marking the Register Columns check box in the list. Click Done to close the Register Columns list.)

You can also click the Account Actions (gear) Transfer Money icon to open the Transfer Money Within Quicken dialog, or simply enter the transfers directly into an account register.

Working with Existing Transactions

So far, this chapter has concentrated on entering transactions. What do you do when you need to modify a transaction you already recorded? That's what this section is all about.

Searching for Transactions

Each type of register (checking, savings, and credit card) has a specific Search field with which you can search the register for specific payees, categories, and even amounts. Simply type the item into the Search field and all transactions that match what you typed will appear in the register, as seen in Figure 3-4. When you have finished reviewing the information, click the red X in the Search field to return to the register with its normal display.

As you type into the Search field, it filters the register to show transactions that match the text you type in the field. You can use this to make a quick register report or find a set of transactions quickly, which is a great feature.

The search is register-specific, meaning that it is only for the register in which you are working. Should you want more detailed information, use the Quicken Find command as discussed next.

The Search field is available in asset registers as well as spending registers. Investment Transaction Lists use the Find command.

Using the Find Command

The Quicken Find dialog includes several drop-down lists to help you locate and work with transactions. To use the Find command, from the Quicken menu,

Checking									
All Dates ▼	Any Type ▼	All Transactions ▼	Reset					Search	
Date ▲	Check #	Payee			Payment	Clr	Deposit		Balance
▶ 🖉		Category	Memo						⚙
8/16/2013	DEP	Retail Firm					1,160 19		-76 59
		--Split--							
8/24/2013	DEP						12,000 00		11,923 41
		[Money Market]							
8/24/2013	Sched	Bank			187 64				11,735 77
		--Split--							
8/27/2013	Sched	Rental House Loan			1,649 10				10,086 67
		--Split--	N/A						
9/1/2013	Sched	TownBank			246 24				9,840 43
		--Split--							
9/1/2013		Big Electric			81 22				9,759 21
		Utilities:Gas & Electric							
9/1/2013	DEP	Retail Firm					1,160 19		10,919 40
		--Split--							

Current Balance: 9,733.18   Ending Balance: 9,055.05

Download Transactions | Bill and Income Reminders (0 Due)

To Do | Help

Figure 3-4 • Use the Search field in a register to find specific transactions.

click Edit | Find or press CTRL-F. (In an Investment Transaction List, use the Find icon found at the right side of the list, shown here.)

The Quicken Find dialog appears:

Start by choosing an option from the Find drop-down list, which includes all register fields for a transaction. Then choose the matching option from the next field to indicate how the search criteria should be matched (this field is not labeled, but the first choice on the list is "Contains"). Enter the search criteria in the next field. To search backward (relative to the currently selected transaction), turn on the Search Backwards check box.

After setting up the search, if you click the Find button, Quicken selects the first match found in the account register and takes you to that transaction. If you click the Find All button, Quicken displays the Search Results window, which lists all the matches it found. You can double-click a match to view it in the account register window.

Be specific when typing in a name. For example, "IntuitQuicken" will return nothing if you have entered the name of the payee as "Intuit-Quicken."

Using the Edit Transaction Command

To edit transactions, first find them. Then, in the Search Results window, select the transaction(s) by clicking the check box(es) in the Select column. Then click the Edit Transaction(s) button at the bottom right of the Search Results window. The Find And Replace dialog appears with the items you selected as seen in Figure 3-5.

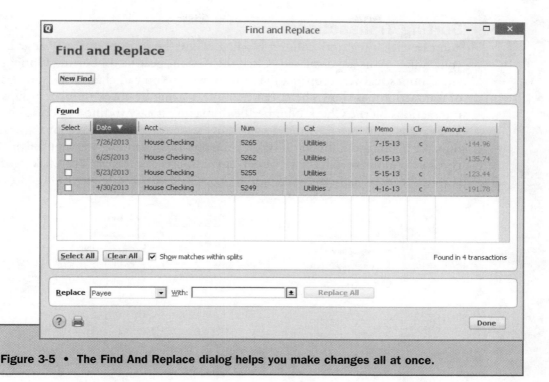

Figure 3-5 • The Find And Replace dialog helps you make changes all at once.

The items you selected in the Find And Replace dialog appear in the Found section of the dialog. You can click the New Find button to make the top part of the dialog look and work much like the Quicken Find dialog. You can turn on the Show Matches Within Splits check box at the bottom of the dialog if you want Quicken to find all matches, including those that appear in splits. Once you set up the search and click the Find button, a list of matches appears in the Found section of the dialog. Click beside each found item you want to change to place a check mark there. Then set options in the Replace and With fields. Click Replace All to replace all selected items with the replacement option you specified. Click Done to close the Find And Replace dialog.

You can also access the Find And Replace dialog by pressing CTRL-H or choosing Edit | Find/Replace.

Remember to create a backup before you make any mass changes in your data.

Sorting Transactions

You can click a register's column heading or use the sort options to change how your transactions are displayed. Click the Actions gear icon | Sorting Options in an account's register to open a menu from which you can change the sort order of transactions, as shown here. For example, sorting by check number groups the transactions by the Check Number field, making it easy to find a specific check. You can quickly move up and down your register to a specific date or transaction number by dragging the scroll box on the scroll bar. However, except for the last two sort options pertaining to Order Entered, it is easier to sort by clicking the account register's column headings.

You can even sort by the flags. See "Adding Notes, Flags, and Alerts" later in this chapter.

Changing Transactions

Quicken enables you to change a transaction at any time—even after it has been cleared. This is especially useful when you find that a check has been categorized as groceries when it should have been categorized as a charitable donation.

Making Simple Changes If all you want to do is change one of the fields in the transaction—such as the category, date, or number—simply find the transaction in the appropriate account register, make changes as desired, and click the Save button to record them.

Using the More Actions Menu   When you need to make additional changes, use the More Actions menu. The More Actions menu appears when you click the small gear icon between the Save and Split icons. These icons are available when you have selected a specific transaction (or multiple transactions) in your register.

> ### IN MY EXPERIENCE
>
> Several Quicken users have mentioned how easy it is to inadvertently sort by a column heading in a register. If your data suddenly looks odd, your balances seem to calculate incorrectly, or you seem to have lost transactions, first check your sort order. Often, simply clicking the Date column header will resolve the issue.

The More Actions menu, as shown below, offers a number of options for working with your transactions. Each is explained here:

Many of these actions can be also be accessed by right-clicking and choosing from the resulting context menu.

Save	
Restore transaction	Esc
Split...	Ctrl+S
Notes and flags...	
Attachments...	
Tax Line Item Assignments	
Copy transaction(s)	
Cut transaction(s)	
Paste transaction(s)	
Edit transaction(s)	
New	Ctrl+N
Delete	Ctrl+D
Undo delete	
Insert transaction	Ctrl+I
Move transaction(s)	
Undo Accept All Transactions	
Memorize payee...	Ctrl+M
Schedule bill or deposit	
Void transaction(s)	Ctrl+V
Reconcile	▶
Find...	Ctrl+F
Find Next	Ctrl+Shift+F
Go to matching transfer	Ctrl+X
Go to specific date...	Ctrl+G
Cancel Payment	
Payment Inquiry	
Properties	

- **Save** enters the transaction in the register. Choosing this command is the same as clicking the Save button or pressing ENTER.
- **Restore Transaction** enables you to change a transaction back to the way it was before you started changing it. This option is available only if you have made changes to the selected transaction.
- **Split** opens the Split window for the transaction. Choosing this command is the same as clicking the Split button. You learned how to use the Split feature earlier in this chapter, in the section titled "Understanding Splits."

You can also press CTRL-S on your keyboard to open the Split window.

- **Notes And Flags** displays the Transaction Notes And Flags dialog (which is shown later in this chapter, in the section titled

"Adding Notes, Flags, and Alerts") so you can add transaction notes, flag the transaction in a specific color, or create an alert for follow-up.

> ## IN MY EXPERIENCE
>
> Cutting, copying, and pasting are basic computer processes that many programs use. Often, it is quicker to copy a transaction and simply paste it into the new register. While that does require you to return to the first register to delete the transaction from its original location, using copy protects against loss of the transaction. If you have children, pets, or power issues that might impact your computer during a cut-and-paste process, you might want to consider using copy instead of cut when moving information. Or, you can use the Move Transaction option to move the transaction back to its original register.

- **Attachments** displays the Transaction Attachments dialog (shown later in this chapter, in the section titled "Attaching Checks, Receipts, or Other Images") so you can attach scanned copies of paper information to the transaction.
- **Tax Line Item Assignments** displays the dialog with which you can assign a Tax Line Item to the transaction's category as discussed in Chapter 13.
- **Copy Transaction(s)** copies the selected transaction without removing it from the account register.
- **Cut Transaction(s)** selects the selected transaction and removes it from the account register so that it can be put in another register.
- **Paste Transaction(s)** pastes the last-copied transaction into the current account register. This option is available only after a transaction has been cut or copied. You might want to cut a transaction to paste it into another register if you realize that you entered it in the wrong register.

Copy/Cut/Paste can all be used with multiple transactions. You just need to select the transactions first before selecting the command.

- **Edit Transaction(s)** displays the Find And Replace dialog (shown earlier in this chapter, in the section titled "Searching for Transactions") so you can use the Replace feature to modify the selected transaction(s).
- **New** enables you to create a new transaction for the account. This does not affect the currently selected transaction.
- **Delete** deletes the selected transaction. Remember that deleting a transaction removes the transaction from the Quicken data file, thus changing the account balance and category activity.
- **Undo Delete** restores the transaction you just deleted. You must use this command immediately after deleting a transaction to restore it.

- **Insert Transaction** enables you to insert a transaction before the selected transaction in the account register. This does not affect the currently selected transaction.
- **Move Transaction(s)** displays the Move Transactions(s) dialog, which you can use to move a transaction from the current account register to a different account register. Simply choose an account name from the drop-down list and click OK to complete the move. This is sometimes a better option than the cut-and-paste option.
- **Undo Accept All Transactions** restores accepted transactions to unaccepted status when you have accepted all transactions. This command is available only if the last thing you did was accept the transactions. Learn more about accepting transactions in Chapter 4.
- **Memorize Payee** tells Quicken to add the selected transaction to its list of memorized payees.
- **Schedule Bill Or Deposit** enables you to schedule the transaction for a future date or to set up the transaction as a recurring transaction. Learn more about scheduling transactions in Chapter 4.
- **Void Transaction(s)** marks the selected transaction as void. This reverses the effect of the transaction on the account balance and category activity without actually deleting the transaction. You can void a single or multiple transactions.
- **Reconcile** enables you to indicate whether the transaction should be marked as Uncleared, Cleared, or Reconciled. Learn how to reconcile accounts in Chapter 5.
- **Revert To Downloaded Payee Name** (not shown) enables you to revert to the transaction payee downloaded from your financial institution's server. This option only appears if the transaction has been downloaded and its payee name has changed.
- **Find** displays the Find dialog, which is discussed earlier in this chapter, in the section titled "Searching for Transactions."
- **Find Next** searches for transactions matching the previously entered Find criteria.
- **Go To Matching Transfer** displays the selected transaction in the account register for the other part of a transfer. For example, if the selected transaction involves the checking and savings accounts and you are viewing it in the checking account register, choosing the Go To Transfer command displays the same transaction in the savings account register. This command is available only if the selected transaction includes a transfer.
- **Go To Specific Date** enables you to move to a different date within the register. This does not affect the currently selected transaction.

- **Use Calculator** (not shown) opens the Quicken Calculator. This option is available when your cursor is in a field other than the category or payee fields when you select More Actions.
- **Cancel Payment** sends a cancel payment instruction to your bank to stop an online payment. This option is available only for online payments that have not yet been made.
- **Payment Inquiry** shows the status of an online payment and offers a link to create an e-mail to your financial institution.
- **Properties** displays the date this transaction was posted by your financial institution.
- **View As A Check** (not shown) displays the selected transaction as a check in the Write Checks dialog if the transaction is marked to print. You can then easily print the transaction or make any other changes.

The following items appear, as shown next, if your cursor is in the Category field when you select More Actions.

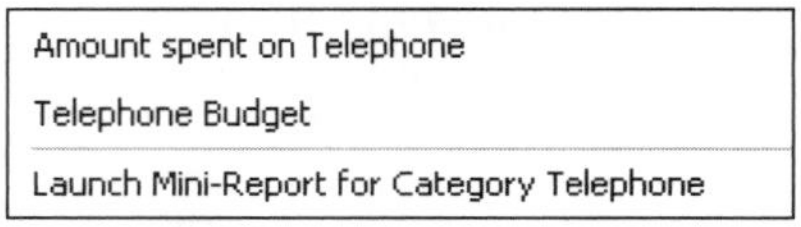

- **Amount Spent On <category>** will display a Category Report for this category if your cursor is in the category field in the selected transaction.

| Amount spent on Telephone |
| Telephone Budget |
| Launch Mini-Report for Category Telephone |

- *nnnnnn* **Budget** displays budget information about the selected category, if your cursor is in the category field. This action works only with a single category you have included in a Quicken budget.
- **Launch Mini-Report** displays a small report window of the current category's transactions. The option that appears depends on the field that is selected when you display the menu.

The following items appear, as shown at right, if your cursor is in the Payee field when you select More Actions.

| Payments made to Pickles Deli |
| Launch Mini-Report for Payee Pickles Deli |

- **Payments Made To <payee>** will display a Payee Report for this payee if your cursor is in the Payee field in the selected transaction.
- **Launch Mini-Report For Payee <payee>** displays a small report window of the current payee's transactions.

Selecting More Than One Transaction   You may need to work with more than one transaction at a time. To do this, you need to select multiple transactions. Here's how:

- To select several individual transactions in an account register, hold down CTRL and click each transaction you want to include. The transactions change color to indicate they are selected.
- To select a range of transactions, click to select the first transaction in the range. Then hold down SHIFT and click the last transaction in the range. All transactions between the first and the last transaction change color to indicate they have been selected.

It may be helpful to sort the register first to get the transactions you wish to select grouped together. You can also filter using the drop-down boxes at the upper left of the register, or use the Search field to enter a payee, category, or name on which to filter.

Quicken's Other Account Features

If you have ever spent several hours (or even days) looking for an invoice that contained a guarantee, Quicken's attachment feature is for you. You can add notes, flags, reminders, and image files to any transaction in your account. This makes it possible to store all kinds of digital information in your Quicken data file, including cancelled checks, receipts, or photographs.

If there's such a thing as a "Paperwork Reduction Act," then why do we seem to keep accumulating more and more paper? Bank statements, canceled checks, receipts…it seems endless. Then, somehow, the moment we throw away an important property tax-related document, the next day we get a letter from the county, asking to see it.

This is when Quicken's electronic image attachment feature can help. If you have a scanner, you can digitize important papers and attach their image files to the transactions or accounts they relate to. Then, when you need to consult the document, you can quickly and easily find it in Quicken and view it on-screen. You can even print a copy with the click of a button! Sure beats dealing with file boxes.

Adding Notes, Flags, and Alerts

You can add a note, color-coded flag, or follow-up alert—or all three—to any Quicken transaction. First, select the transaction to which you want to add the item. Click the More Actions button, and from the menu, click Notes And Flags to open the Transaction Notes And Flags dialog seen here. You can also use the small flag or paper clip icons beneath or to the left of the date on a register line.

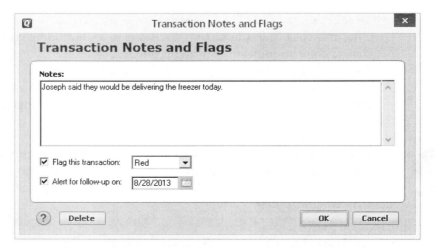

- To add a note, type the text of the note into the Notes box. This adds a flag icon to the transaction beneath the date. Pointing to the icon displays the note in a screen tip box.
- To flag the transaction, click the Flag This Transaction check box. Then choose a color from the drop-down list. This colors the flag icon placed above.
- To create a follow-up alert, turn on the Alert For Follow-Up On check box and enter a date in the box beside it. (You can add a follow-up alert only if the transaction is already flagged.) This adds an alert to the Alerts Center window, which is discussed in Chapter 4.

Click OK to save your settings.

Attaching Checks, Receipts, or Other Images

Quicken enables you to attach image files from a file on disk, a scanner, or the clipboard to transactions or accounts. You can use this feature to file digital copies of important documents with the transactions or accounts to which they relate.

Attaching Images to Transactions

You attach an image to a transaction in the account register window. Begin by selecting the transaction you want to attach the item to. Then click the More Actions button and select Attachments.

The Transaction Attachments dialog appears (shown right). Click the Add downward arrow to open the drop-down list. Choose the location of the attachment you want to add:

- **Add File** displays the Select Attachment File dialog, with which you can locate, select, and open a file on disk. The file must be in a format readable by your browser, such as JPG, GIF, TXT, HTML, PDF, or PNG. When you select the file, it appears in the Transaction Attachments dialog, as seen next.
- **Add From Scanner** displays the Select Source dialog, which you can use to select your scanner. It then displays your scanner's standard scanning interface, which you can use to scan an image. When the scan is complete, the image appears in the Transaction Attachments dialog.
- **Add From Clipboard** pastes the contents of the clipboard into the Transaction Attachments dialog.

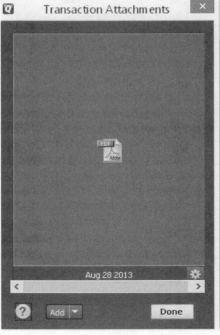

Quicken allows you to add as many attachments as you like to a transaction. To add other attachments, just repeat the process. When you're finished, click Done to close the Transaction Attachments dialog. An Attachment icon appears beneath the transaction date to indicate that items are attached.

Working with Attachments

Once a file is attached to a transaction, you can view, export, delete, or print it at any time.

- To work with a transaction attachment, click the More Actions icon for the transaction and select Attachments. The Transaction Attachments dialog opens. The question mark Help link displays the Quicken Personal Finances Help window, with links to topics about attaching digital images to transactions and accounts. Click a link to view the help information. Click the gear icon shown beneath each image or icon to open the menu shown at right.

You can use buttons in the Transaction Attachments dialog to work with attachments:

- **View/Open** opens the attachment with the .pdf reader included with Quicken.
- **Export** saves the attachment as a file on a disk.
- **Upload to Cloud** saves the attachment in your Quicken Cloud file.
- **Delete** removes the attachment.

The menu items you see will depend on the type of attachment you have created.

Click Done to close the Transaction Attachments dialog.

Using Online Banking Features

Chapter 4

In This Chapter:

- *Understanding Transaction Download*
- *Introducing Online Payment and Quicken Bill Pay*
- *Setting up Online Account Services*
- *Checking Online Account Service Status*
- *Using the Online Center window*
- *Downloading transactions*
- *Making online payments*
- *Being reminded*
- *Creating reminders from downloaded transactions*
- *Working with the Bills tab*
- *Managing reminders*
- *Using QuickFill and memorized payees*
- *Using the financial Calendar*
- *Minding your bills*
- *Using the Paycheck Setup Wizard*
- *Creating the Address Book*
- *Viewing available alerts groups*

Life can be hectic sometimes, too hectic to keep track of your bank accounts, pay bills before they're overdue, and buy stamps to mail those bills. Quicken Personal Finance Software's Online Account Services enable you to do most (if not all) of your banking from the comfort of your own home so banking can be a lot less of a chore. You can use these features separately or together:

- **Transaction Download** enables you to download bank and credit card account activity, and transfer money online between accounts.
- **Online Payment** enables you to pay bills online without manually writing or mailing a check. (Quicken Bill Pay offers the features of Online Payment, even if your bank does not support it.)

This section explains how these features work and how you can use them to save time while keeping track of your finances. The instructions assume that you have already configured Quicken for an Internet connection. If you have not done so, do it now.

Just a reminder: Quicken does not handle the characters &, <, or > as part of a password. In addition, each financial institution designates both the password length and its allowable (and disallowable) characters.

Online Account Services

Here's a closer look at Quicken's Online Account Services, including what the services are, how they work, and how you can expect to benefit from them.

Understanding Transaction Download

Quicken's Transaction Download feature can perform several tasks, depending on your financial institution. Generally speaking, financial institutions support Transaction Download three ways. You can quickly determine which method is used for a specific account. Press CTRL-A to open your Account List. (You can do this from any screen within Quicken.) The type of connection for each account shows in the Transaction Download column of the list. If you do not see the Transaction Download column in your Account List, click the Options button at the bottom left of the Account List and choose Show Transaction Download Status. See Table 4-1 for the download features that are available for each download method.

If you have more than one account that uses Web Connect, consider downloading one account at a time the first time you download, if your financial institution allows it. This way you won't inadvertently import the wrong account's information into your register.

	Connection Type		
Item	**Direct Connect**	**Express Web Connect**	**Web Connect**
Bill Pay	Available from within Quicken	Not available from within Quicken. Consider Quicken Bill Pay services.	Not available from within Quicken. Consider Quicken Bill Pay services.
Data	Two-way connection with your financial institution. Data is stored on the financial institution's server. All passwords are stored on the financial institution's server.	One-way connection for download and updating account balances. Data and passwords are stored on Intuit's aggregation servers.	One-way connection for download and updating account balances. All imported information is encrypted and stored on your computer.
Features	Download transactions; update account balances; pay bills, transfer money between accounts. You can transfer funds between accounts and send e-mail to your financial institution.	Download transactions and update account balances in Quicken.	Download transactions and update account balances in Quicken.
Fees	Check with your bank as many institutions charge a fee for this type of connection. Your financial institution pays a fee to Intuit for this support.	Normally, there are no fees charged by your financial institution. Your financial institution pays a fee to Intuit for this support.	Normally, there are no fees charged by your financial institution. Your financial institution pays a fee to Intuit for this support.
Setup	Contact your financial institution.	Use the financial institution's website's login when you create the account in Quicken.	Create a login on the financial institution's website to be used each time you want to download your data.
Use	No need to leave Quicken to use all of the banking features.	Just update your account and all transactions and balances are downloaded into Quicken.	Log on to your financial institution's website, using their login information. Locate a link called "Download" or "History" and follow the directions on that website.

Table 4-1 • Connection Options for Downloaded Transactions

One important feature of Web Connect is you may be able to download a greater range of transactions by date than you can with Direct Connect and Express Web Connect. This is especially useful when you first set up your accounts so you can get the longest transaction history possible.

Introducing Online Payment and Quicken Bill Pay

Online Payment enables you to send a check to anyone without physically writing, printing, or mailing a check. You enter and store information about the payee within Quicken. You then create a transaction for the payee that includes the payment date and amount. You can enter the transaction weeks or months in advance if desired—the financial institution sends payment on the date you specify.

Explaining the Process

Suppose you use Quicken to send online payment instructions to pay your monthly bill at Jim's Hardware Store. You've already set up Jim's Hardware as a payee by entering the name, address, and phone number of his store, as well as your account number there. Quicken sends your payment instructions to your bank, which stores it in its computer with a bunch of other online payment instructions. When the payment date nears, the bank's computer looks through its big database of payees that it can pay by wire transfer. It sees phone companies, credit card companies, and other banks. However, because Jim's store is small, it's probably not one of the wire transfer payees. So the bank's computer prepares a check using all the information you provided. It mails the check along with thousands of others due to be paid that day.

The date the money is actually withdrawn from your account to cover the payment varies depending on your bank. There are four possibilities: one to four days before the payment is processed for delivery, the day the payment is processed for delivery, the day the payment is delivered, or the day the paper check or electronic funds transfer clears your bank.

Check with your bank to find out when funds are withdrawn from your account for online payments. You can also search the Quicken Live Community to see the experiences other Quicken users have had with that financial institution. To access the Quicken Live Community, from the Quicken Toolbar, click Help | Quicken Live Community. While the name is now the Quicken Community, the link still says "Quicken Live Community," although the forum is not "live."

Online Service Costs

The cost of Quicken's Online Account Services varies from bank to bank. Check with your bank to determine the exact fees.

Setting Up Online Account Services

To use the Online Account Services supported by Quicken, you must configure the appropriate Quicken accounts. This requires that you enter information about your financial institution and the account with which you want to use these features. To apply for online account services, normally all it takes is a phone call, although some banks and credit card companies allow you to apply online. The setup information usually consists of the following:

- **PIN (Personal Identification Number)**   You'll enter this code into Quicken when you access your account online. This is a security feature, so don't write down your PIN on a sticky note and attach it to your computer monitor. Many financial institutions send this information separately for additional security.
- **Customer ID Number**   This is often your Social Security number or taxpayer identification number.
- **Bank Routing Number**   Although your bank might send routing number information, Quicken won't need it. It knows what financial institution you're using based on the information you provide when you create the account. That's why it's so important to choose the correct financial institution when you create each account. You may see the routing information received by Quicken in the Routing Number field in the General tab of the Account Details dialog.
- **Account Number for Each Online Access–Enabled Account**   This tells your financial institution which account you want to work with. Quicken may not need this information. Depending on your financial institution, the account number may appear in the Account Number field of the General tab of the Account Details dialog.

Getting Started with Online Account Services

With customer ID and PIN in hand, you're ready to set up your account (or accounts) for Online Account Services. You can verify this by following the instructions in the "Checking Online Account Service Status" section, later in this chapter.

Some companies, such as department stores, that offer online access on their web pages, may not have the capability of downloading your transactions into Quicken.

Setting Up for Direct Connect, Express Web Connect, and Quicken Bill Pay

If you entered your accounts manually when you first used Quicken, from the Account Bar, click the account you want to set up to open its register. Click the

Account Actions gear icon (shown at right). From the menu, select Set Up Online as shown below. (If the account is already set up for online access, the Actions menu shows Update Now instead of Set Up Online.)

 The Account Actions gear icon is at the top right of your account registers. If you have customized an account to show account toolbar icons, there may be additional icons showing. The Actions icon is furthest to the right. You can always use the keyboard shortcut CTRL-SHIFT-N to open the Actions menu.

Follow the directions in Chapter 1 to set up this account with online services.

 When logging in to your financial institution, you may have to place the cursor each time so that it is in the password/security question field if there are multiple security questions.

Checking Online Account Service Status

You can confirm that an account has been set up for Online Account Services and determine what kind of connection it uses. Right-click the account from the Account Bar and choose Edit/Delete Account. Then, click the Online Services tab to display the type of connection, as shown next.

- **Deactivate**   Use this button if you want to stop online connection for the account. However, you must still contact the bank to deactivate the connection on their side. To deactivate (or disable) an account from online services:
  - Click Deactivate. (If you currently have unaccepted transactions, you must either accept the transactions or delete them before you can deactivate online services.) A message appears asking if you would like to deactivate the service. Click Yes to complete the deactivation.
  - A connection message box briefly appears while the service is deactivated. Depending on the type of connection your financial institution offers, you may see a Remove Connection button. If so, click it.
  - Click OK to close the Account Details window and complete the deactivation.

If your financial institution has changed or if you have problems deactivating an old (or closed) account, try disconnecting your Internet connection before you deactivate.

- **Reset Account**, can be used when a download problem has occurred. None of your data is deleted from Quicken; the account is reset to, hopefully, solve the issue. Click this button, enter your bank password, and the account's online access is reset. You are prompted to choose the account with which downloaded transaction are connected. Make your choice and click OK.

- **Automatic Entry Is: On/Off**   This link opens the Automatic Transaction Entry dialog, shown next. From this dialog, you tell Quicken how to handle downloaded transactions for this specific account.

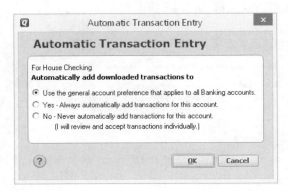

Some banks use different passwords for Direct Connect services than for Web Connect or Express Web Connect.

By default, when you first create your accounts in your Quicken file, your downloaded transactions are entered into your register. If you want all downloaded transactions to be loaded into your register automatically, click Edit | Preferences | Downloaded Transactions | Downloaded Transaction Preferences | After Downloading Transactions, and select the Automatically Add To Banking Registers check box. Many Quicken users avoid automatically adding downloaded transactions to the account register. If the matching does not work correctly, it's very difficult to determine what went wrong.

The Online Center

While you can access online services from several of the various tabs, you can also use the Online Center to work with Quicken's online features. This window gives you access to all the lists and commands you need to download transactions, and, if you have Direct Connect, to create payments, transfer money, and exchange e-mail with your financial institution.

Using the Online Center Window

To open the Online Center window, choose Tools | Online Center. This illustration shows the available tabs with one financial institution selected.

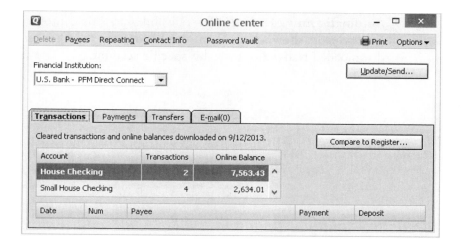

A number of buttons and menus enable you to work with the window's contents:

- **Delete** removes a selected item. This button is not available in all tabs of the Online Center window.
- **Payees** (if you have set up online payments) displays the Online Payee List window, which is discussed later in this chapter in the section titled "Entering Online Payee Information."
- **Repeating** (if you have set up online payments) displays the Repeating Online tab of the Bill And Income Reminders list window. Learn more about using this feature later in this chapter, in the section titled "Scheduling Repeating Online Payments."
- **Contact Info** displays the Contact Information dialog for the currently selected financial institution, if it is offered. You can use the information in the dialog to contact the bank or credit card company by phone, website, or e-mail. Not all financial institutions have these options.
- **Password Vault** gives you access to Quicken's Password Vault feature, which is discussed later in this chapter. (This option may appear only if you have online banking features enabled for accounts at more than one financial institution.)
- **Print** prints the transactions that appear in the Payments tab window. It will also print any e-mails you have in the E-mail tab. You may be able to print downloaded transactions that have not yet been accepted.
- **Options** displays a menu of commands for working with the current account or window.

Downloading Transactions

One of the main features of Online Account Services is the ability to download transactions from your financial institution into Quicken. There are several ways to start downloading your transactions after you have set up your online accounts:

- Use the Update/Send button of the Online Center window.
- Click the blue right-curling arrow at the top of the Account Bar.
- Click the One Step Update arrow on the Quicken Toolbar, as seen here.
- From an account's register, click the Account Actions gear icon at the top right of the register and choose Update Now from the menu that appears.
- From the Quicken menu, choose Tools | One Step Update.

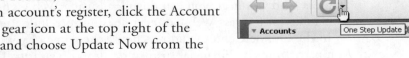

Connecting to the Financial Institution with Direct Connect or Express Web Connect

If your financial institution supports Direct Connect or Express Web Connect, you can download all transactions from within Quicken.

Using the Online Center window, choose the name of your bank or credit card company from the Financial Institution drop-down list. Click the Update/Send button. The One Step Update Settings dialog for that institution appears. Click to toggle the check marks beside any instructions that appear, enter your password, and click Update Now.

Quicken may display a dialog offering to save your passwords. If you click Yes, follow the instructions to set up the Password Vault feature. You may then need to reinitiate the download procedure. Depending on whether you have added the Intuit ID to your Password Vault or not, you may be prompted to enter your Intuit ID before the One Step Update Settings dialog appears.

Wait while Quicken connects to your bank. A status dialog may appear while Quicken collects your data. When Quicken has finished exchanging information, the status dialog disappears and the One Step Update Summary window takes its place. Continue following the instructions later in the chapter, in the section titled "Comparing Downloaded Transactions to Register Transactions." Depending on your preference settings, you may only see the One Step Update Summary window if there is an error in the online session.

If you have chosen One Step Update by using the blue right-curling arrow, you see a list of all of your accounts that have been activated for online services. You may choose to download transactions from one or all of them by entering your password(s).

Downloading a Web Connect File

If your financial institution supports Web Connect but not Express Web Connect, you'll log in to your financial institution's website and manually download the statement information, just as you did when you first set up the account for Online Account Services. Even if your financial institution supports Express Web Connect, you can download using Web Connect if you wish. The availability of Express Web Connect does not preclude use of Web Connect.

In the Online Center window, choose the name of your bank or credit card company from the Financial Institution drop-down list. If necessary, click the Update/Send button. Quicken connects to the Internet and displays your

IN MY EXPERIENCE

Many Quicken users set up accounts in Quicken and decide later to activate online services for these accounts. The first time you download transactions into a Quicken file for which accounts have been set up, you are prompted to either add the downloaded transactions into a new account or link to an existing account.

   If your link is to an incorrect account, the transactions download into that incorrect account. If you have not accepted the transactions, simply delete the downloaded transactions. Then, download the information into the correct account. If you have accepted the transactions and they are in the register of the wrong account, you can move them into the correct account. However, if you have linked the accounts, you may have to deactivate the accounts to break the connection.

 It's not so easy to delete transactions from the Downloaded Transactions tab. You must delete the downloaded transactions one at a time. If you have many transactions in the Downloaded Transactions tab, it may be easier to accept them all, sort your account by date/order entered, and then select all the downloaded transactions and either delete or move them to the correct account.

   If you have several months' (or years') worth of downloaded transactions, one way to solve this issue is by deactivating online services for both accounts, moving any transactions that are in the wrong account into the correct account, and then reactivating the online service for both accounts. See "Moving Transactions" later in this chapter. However, as always, before making any changes, back up your Quicken data, "just in case."

financial institution's login page. Log in, navigate to the page where you can download statements, and download the statement or transactions you want.

   If necessary, switch back to Quicken. It should automatically import the transactions you downloaded into the correct account. If you have chosen to accept your downloaded transactions automatically, you will see a small blue ball icon at the left of each of the downloaded transactions in your account register. Transactions that have been matched to scheduled transactions have a calendar icon in the same location.

 If Express Web Connect or Direct Connect is available for an account, you may see a dialog offering to upgrade your connection. You may see a prompt to handle your Web Connect transactions now or save the transactions for later processing. To set this, go to Edit | Preferences | Downloaded Transactions and make your selection.

Click the Close button in the One Step Update Summary window to dismiss it. Then, click that account's name in the Account Bar to open the register for that account.

Unless you have chosen to turn on the Automatically Add To Banking Register preference, your downloaded transactions will appear in the Downloaded Transactions tab at the bottom of the register window. From there, you can use the directions in the next section "Comparing Downloaded Transactions to Register Transactions."

Keep in mind that the first time you connect via Direct Connect, the bank normally sends all transactions from the past 60 or more days. (Some banks send a full year of transactions!) After that, only new transactions (items that have not been downloaded) will be downloaded. For Web Connect downloads, you can often specify the transaction period when you set up the download.

IN MY EXPERIENCE

If you have trouble downloading your transactions from a specific financial institution using One Step Update, use the Update Now command from the Account Actions gear icon menu in your account's register. If that doesn't solve the problem, try going online to your bank's site and downloading the transactions manually. Some of my clients experienced issues when there were no transactions to download, and downloading manually solved the problem.

If the account is set up for Direct Connect or Express Web Connect, being able to successfully download from the financial institution's website does not necessarily eliminate that institution as the cause of the issue. Often Direct Connect and Express Web Connect use entirely different servers. Because the servers are different, it may be that the problem is with one of the server computers.

Consider using the Quicken Live Community forums using the name of your financial institution as the search term. If the financial institution is having problems, it's very possible another Quicken user has already posted a question. To access the Quicken Live Community, from the Quicken Toolbar, click Help | Quicken Live Community.

Comparing Downloaded Transactions to Register Transactions

If you have opted to accept downloaded transactions manually, you will compare the downloaded transactions to the transactions already entered in your account register. This process enables you to review or identify transactions that may have been entered incorrectly, by either you or the bank.

If you do not see the Downloaded Transactions tab at the bottom of your register you may have told Quicken to automatically add downloaded transactions to the banking registers. To allow the tab to display, click Edit | Preferences | Downloaded Transactions | Downloaded Transaction Preferences | After Downloading Transactions, and clear the Automatically Add To Banking Registers check box.

The bottom half of the account register window is the Downloaded Transactions tab (refer to Figure 4-1). It shows three ways to identify downloaded transactions:

- **Match** identifies transactions that match those in the register. This will happen if the transaction has already been entered in the Quicken register and matches the information in the downloaded transactions.

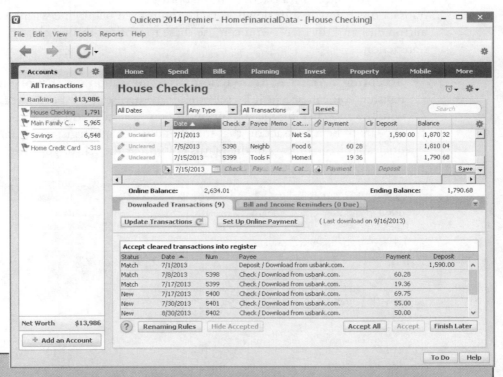

Figure 4-1 • **You can review each downloaded transaction before it is entered into your register.**

- **New** identifies transactions that are not in the register, or that are in the register but are different from the downloaded transactions. Maybe you transposed a number or the date is different. You need to manually match these transactions so you do not get duplicates.

Be sure to check each New transaction carefully to ensure that you were the one who actually initiated the transaction and that the transaction is to the payee and in the amount you created. If you suspect any type of fraud, call your bank immediately.

- **Accepted** identifies matched transactions that you have accepted. When a downloaded transaction has been accepted, a small "c" appears in the Clr column of the account register to indicate that the item has cleared the bank but has not yet been reconciled.

When you select a transaction in the bottom half of the register window, the transactions below it shift down to make room for a blank line with an Accept button and an Edit menu. You can use these to work with the selected transaction.

- **Accepting a Matched Transaction** If a transaction matches one in the register, you can accept it by selecting it in the list at the bottom of the window and clicking the Accept button, as seen next. If Quicken sees what appears to be a transaction that matches one in your register, a small, uncleared icon appears in the Status column at the left of your register, as

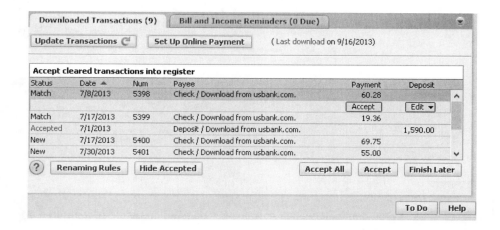

seen here. Click the icon to match the register entry to a downloaded transaction. Even if there is not an apparent match, any time you see the

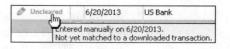

uncleared icon, you can click it to get the Match To A Downloaded Transaction context menu item and, by clicking that menu item, get to the Manual Match window.

- **Entering and Accepting a New Transaction** To enter and accept a new transaction, select the transaction in the bottom half of the window. If the information on the transaction is complete and correct, click Accept. If you have entered the part of the transaction in the register (the top half of the window), fill in any missing details, including the payee, category, and memo. Then click Save in the top half of the window or Accept in the bottom half. Quicken marks it as Accepted and a small "c" appears in the Clr column of the register.
- **Unmatching a Matched Transaction** If a matched transaction really shouldn't be matched, select it in the bottom half of the window and choose Unmatch from the Edit pop-up menu as seen here.
  - **Unmatch** tells Quicken that it got the match wrong, but this command lets Quicken attempt to match it to another transaction. As a result, it may come up with another match. It's your job to determine whether the new match is correct. If it can't find a match, the status changes to New.

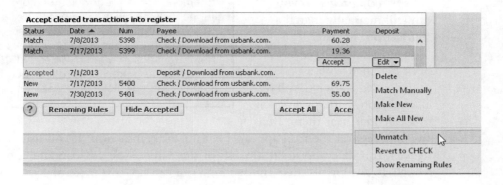

- **Make New** tells Quicken that the transaction shouldn't match any existing transaction. The status changes to New, and Quicken can then treat it as a new transaction.
- **Make All New** tells Quicken to make all of the downloaded but not yet accepted transactions new so you can manually match them or enter them as a new transaction.

- **Manually Matching a Transaction** If a downloaded transaction identified as New should match one in the register, or if a single transaction corresponds to multiple transactions in your account register, you can manually match them up. In the bottom half of the window, select the transaction that you want to match manually, and click the Edit button. Click Match Manually to open the Manually Match Transactions dialog. Turn on the check box(es) for the transaction(s) you want to include in the match. When you click Accept, Quicken marks the transaction in the Clr column with a small "c".

If the transaction included multiple register transactions, the entry Quicken creates includes each of the register transactions on a separate split line. You can click the Split button for the transaction to edit it as desired. See Chapter 3 to review working with split transactions.

If you see a transaction that displays as "New" but you're sure you've entered it, check for small discrepancies, perhaps in the amount. You can force a manual match, or simply correct the item you've entered into your register and the item status will change to Match.

If you choose to have Quicken add your downloaded transactions into your banking register, you can still manually match a transaction. Register transactions that have not been matched with a downloaded transaction have a small icon, perhaps a pencil or a calendar near them. In a

IN MY EXPERIENCE

If you reconcile your accounts using a paper statement and don't download before you do the reconciliation, you may encounter a transaction that indicates it has been reconciled in your register but appears as a "New" transaction when downloaded. Use the Match Manually procedure to connect the two, or delete the downloaded transaction.

two-line register the icon appears beneath the transaction. If you use a one-line register, this icon appears to the left of the date. Click the icon and choose Match To A Downloaded Transaction. You can use this matching method whether you auto-enter your downloaded transactions or manually review/accept your downloaded transactions.

Deleting a New Transaction To delete any transaction, select it in the bottom half of the account register window, click Edit, and choose Delete from the Edit pop-up menu. A confirmation dialog appears; click Yes to remove the transaction from the list.

Sometimes the matching issue can be resolved, especially when reconciling an account, by choosing to display the Downloaded Posting Date column in your register. Display this column (field) in your register by choosing the Account Actions gear icon | Register Columns | Downloaded Posting Date. Since reconciliations are date-driven, the posting date may be after the cutoff date of the reconciliation. Click Done to close the Register Columns list and return to the register.

Moving Transactions   If you have several accounts at the same bank and inadvertently accept transactions into the incorrect account, you can move either a single or multiple transactions. You can use this procedure to move transactions between accounts at different banks or to move transactions between accounts that are not online accounts.

1. To move a single transaction, right-click the transaction in the account register. Choose Move Transaction(s) from the context menu.
2. The Move Transaction(s) dialog box appears. Choose the account into which you want to move the transaction from the drop-down list.

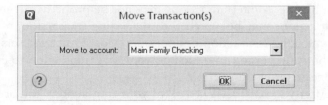

3. Click OK and you are returned to the original register.

To move multiple transactions as a group in your register:

1. Click the first transaction in the register to highlight it.
2. Hold down your SHIFT key and, while still holding it, click the last transaction in the group. All of the transactions will be selected. Release the SHIFT key.
3. Right-click in the highlighted area, and from the context menu, choose Move Transaction(s).
4. The Move Transaction(s) dialog box appears. Choose the account from the drop-down list into which you want to move the transactions.
5. Click OK to return to your original register.

To select multiple transactions that are scattered throughout your register:

1. Click the first transaction in the register to highlight it.
2. Hold down your CTRL key and, while still holding it, click each transaction you want to move. All of the selected transactions will be highlighted. Release the CTRL key.
3. Right-click in the highlighted area, and from the context menu, choose Move Transaction(s).
4. The Move Transaction(s) dialog box appears. Choose the account from the drop-down list into which you want to move the transactions.
5. Click OK. You are returned to the original account register.

 You may be able to get all the transactions together in a contiguous group by sorting or filtering the account register.

In each case, the transactions are moved to the account you designated.

Accepting All Downloaded Transactions   The Accept All button accepts all transactions into your account register. If you select this without reviewing them one by one, some transactions may not be properly categorized. Also, some transactions may be matched to the wrong transaction, making it appear as if the downloaded transaction disappeared. Most Quicken users don't use Accept All without first examining each downloaded transaction to ensure it matched to the proper register transaction.

After you have reviewed all of your transactions and accepted, matched, or deleted the transactions, click Done to close the Downloaded Transactions tab. Choose Finish Later if you cannot complete the task at one sitting.

Renaming Downloaded Payees

One of the potentially annoying things about entering transactions by accepting downloaded activity information is the way your bank identifies payees. For example, one bank identifies the payee as "Safeway 23456" instead of plain old "Safeway". Fortunately, Quicken's Renaming Rules feature can automatically rename bank-assigned payee names with names you prefer. You can also create and apply your own renaming rules. You do this with the Renaming Rules dialog, which allows you to control how Quicken deals with the differences between the payee names in your records and those of the bank's.

To open this dialog, click the Renaming Rules button at the bottom of the Downloaded Transactions tab of the register window, or choose Tools |

Renaming Rules. You can also select a payee in your register, click the small downward arrow at the right of the Payee field, and click the Renaming Rules button.

The Renaming Rules dialog lists all the renaming rules you have already created. Click the Add A Rule link, or the white cross within the green circle icon, to add a new rule. Click the Do Not Rename Rules tab to add a payee to the Do Not Rename list. (You can add a rule from that tab as well; just click the Add A Rule link.)

If you want to delete a rule, simply select the rule, and click the icon with the small white line within the red circle. A confirmation message appears. Click OK in the confirmation dialog to remove the rule.

To modify a rule, select the payee to display three icons: a pencil, a green circle with a white plus sign, and a red circle with a white line. Click the pencil icon to open the Edit Payee Name dialog. Use this dialog to modify settings for the selected payee.

After you have made all of your changes, click Done to return to the register.

However, be careful when renaming generally named downloaded transactions. In the following example, we've written a check to Car Repair By Royce in the amount of $202.26. Our US Bank account downloads transactions as "CHECK Download from usbank.com". If we use the Add A Renaming Rule dialog, all downloaded checks will be renamed as Car Repair By Royce!

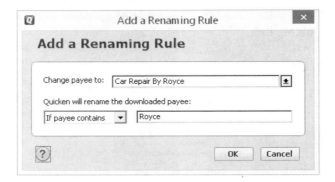

When you are in the Renaming Rules dialog and select the Add A Renaming Rule link, it opens the Add A Renaming Rule dialog. Enter the name you want to see as the payee name in the Change Payee To box. Then, from the drop-down list, choose If Quicken Name Is or If Payee Contains and then enter the word (or words) that most likely will appear in the downloaded transaction. When you click OK in the dialog, you are returned to the Renaming Rules dialog and see the new renaming rule added to the list.

Making Online Payments

Paying your bills from within Quicken can save you both time and effort. If your bank supports Online Bill Pay, this may be the best choice for you. This section explains how to set up online payees, enter payment information for one-time and repeating payments, and work with payment instructions.

> **IN MY EXPERIENCE**
>
> One of the reasons to download your transactions is to eliminate the need to enter all of your checks into your register. However, some banks do not include check numbers or payees in their downloaded transactions. For these accounts, you might consider entering your checks so that you only need to match them to the downloaded item. Otherwise, if you have many transactions, it can take a bit of time to enter the information for each downloaded item. You can cut down on your data entry time by using scheduled reminders and memorized payees.

Entering Online Payee Information

To send payments from your account, your bank must know who each payee is and where they are located. To ensure that your account with the payee is credited properly, you must also provide account information. You do this by setting up online payees in the Online Center.

- From the Tools menu, click Online Center to open the Online Center dialog. Select Payees to open the Online Payee List. You can also choose Online Payee List from the Tools menu to open the list.
- The Financial Institution drop-down list shows the institutions for which you have enabled Online Bill Pay. If there is more than one, choose the institution that has the account from which you will be paying this payee. The payees you have added for the displayed institution, showing the payee name, the lead-time for this payee, and the account number. Some financial institutions do not provide the lead-time for online bill payments. There are several buttons at the bottom of the list, as discussed later.

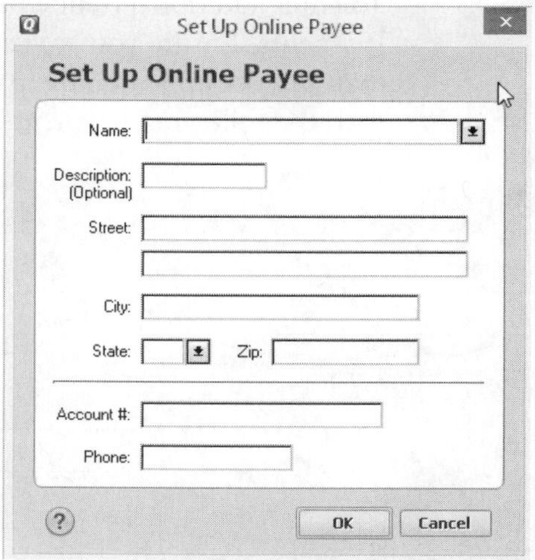

NOTE If you have not yet set up Online Bill Pay, the Payees menu item may be disabled. This is also true of the Online Payee List option in the Tools menu.

- New opens the Set Up Online Payee dialog, shown here.
  - Enter the name of the online payee in the Name field and any description that might be needed

in the optional Description field. Verify (or enter, if this is a new payee) the mailing address, account number, and phone number. If you skip over one of these required fields, Quicken will prompt you for the information.

- Click OK when you have completed entering the information. The Confirm Online Payee Information message appears displaying the information you just entered. Check the information in this box carefully. When you're satisfied that the information is correct, click Accept. The new payee is added to the Online Payee List. If the information is not correct, click Cancel and you are returned to the Online Payee dialog.

- **Help** (the small question mark in the yellow circle) opens the paying bills online section of Quicken Help.
- **Print** (the printer icon) prints a list of online payees.
- **Edit** enables you to modify the information for the selected online payee. However, note that you cannot change the account number without deleting the payee and setting up a new payee.
- **Use** switches you back to the Payments tab of the Online Center window and inserts the selected payee into the payment form.
- **Report** displays a report of all payments made to the selected online payee.
- **Delete** removes the selected online payee. Deleting a payee simply deletes the payee's information from the Online Payee List window. It does not change any transactions for a payee. You cannot delete a payee for which unsent payment instructions exist.
- **Done** closes the Online Payee List.

Entering Payment Instructions

To enter additional online payment instructions, click Tools | Online Center | Payments. Ensure you are using the correct financial institution if you have more than one set up for online payments. Fill in the fields in the middle of the window with the following payment information:

- **Processing Date** is the date the bank should begin processing the payment. For some banks, this date is fixed based on the Delivery Date field and can't be changed.
- **Delivery Date** is the date you want the payee to receive payment. This should be before the date the bank will either create and mail the check or make the electronic funds transfer. The check may be received before the delivery date, depending on the mail (if the check is mailed). The date you enter, however, must be at least the same number of business days in advance as the lead time for the payee—often four business days. For some banks, the delivery date cannot be changed; instead, specify a processing date that allows enough time for the payment to be made on a timely basis.
- **Payee** is the online payee to receive payment. Quicken's QuickFill feature fills in the payee's name as you type it. If desired, you can choose it from the drop-down list of online payees. If you enter a payee that is not in the Online Payee List window, Quicken displays the Set Up Online Payee dialog so you can add the new payee's information. This enables you to create online payees as you enter payment instructions.
- **$** is the amount of the payment.

 If you have set your Quicken Preferences to use the ENTER key when moving between fields, this process ignores your Preference setting and uses ENTER to enter the online payment.

- **Category** is the category for the transaction. You can enter a category, choose one from the drop-down list, or click the Split button to enter multiple categories.
- **Memo**, which is optional, is for entering a note about the transaction.

When you've finished entering information for the transaction, click ENTER. Depending on your financial institution, a message box may appear reminding you that you need to allow enough time for the payment to be processed by your financial institution. Click OK to continue or Cancel to return to the payment. Click the Don't Show This Message Again check box to keep the message from appearing for future transactions.

The transaction appears in the list in the bottom half of the window with the words "Payment request ready to send" in the Status column beside it. You can repeat this process for as many payments as you want to make.

 You can also enter an online payment instruction directly into the appropriate account register and choose Send Online Payment in the Check # column.

Sending Payment Instructions

Once your payment instructions have been completed, you must connect to your bank to send the instructions. In the Online Center window, click the Update/Send button. Quicken displays the One Step Update Settings dialog, which lists all of the payment instructions, including any repeating payment instructions. Enter your password and click the Update Now button.

Quicken connects to your bank's server and sends your payment (or payment cancellation) instructions. When the process is complete, you see the One Step Update Summary window. Click Close. In the Payments tab of the Online Center window, the words "Scheduled for delivery on" followed by the payment date appear in the Status column beside the payment instructions that have been sent to your bank.

Canceling a Payment

Occasionally, you may change your mind about making a payment. Perhaps you find your spouse already sent a check or that you set up the payment for the wrong amount. For whatever reason, you can cancel an online payment that you have sent to your bank, as long as there's enough time to cancel it.

When you send a payment instruction to your bank, it waits in the bank's computer. When the processing date (determined by the number of days in the payee's lead-time and the payment date) arrives, the bank makes the payment. Before the processing date, however, the payment instructions can be canceled. If you send a cancel payment instruction to the bank before the processing date, the bank removes the instruction from its computer without sending payment to the payee. Quicken won't let you cancel a payment if the processing date has already passed. If you wait too long, the only way to cancel the payment is to call the bank directly and stop the check.

Keep in mind that canceling a payment instruction isn't the same as stopping a check. If you send the cancel payment instruction in time, the bank should not charge a fee for stopping the payment. In the Online Center window, click the Payments tab, select the payment that you want to cancel, and click the Cancel Payment button. Click Yes in the confirmation dialog that appears. Use the Update/Send button to send the cancel payment instruction.

Transferring Money Between Accounts

Quicken makes it easy to record your transfers between accounts. If you have more than one account enabled for Online Bill Pay via Direct Connect at the same financial institution, you can even transfer money from one account to the other directly from within Quicken.

To record a transfer of funds that you make with a phone call or on the financial institution's website:

1. From the Account Bar, select the account from which you want to transfer the funds.
2. Click the Account Actions gear icon | Transfer Money or press CTRL-SHIFT-T to open the Transfer Money Within Quicken dialog appears.

3. Enter the transfer information—source account, destination account, and amount—in the fields in the middle of the window.
4. Click OK. The information is added to the list of transfers at the bottom of the window. The transaction will appear in both check registers.
5. Be sure to call the bank or go to the website to actually give them the instructions to transfer funds.

To create an online transfer, both accounts must be activated with Direct Connect and be at the same bank under the same customer identification number. Some financial institutions allow you to pay a credit card that is associated with the same identification number in this manner as well.

To create the online transfer:

1. In a new transaction line, click the Date field and enter today's date. You may not schedule an online transfer in the future. Financial institutions process transfer instructions on the same day the request is received.

2. In the Check # field, click the downward arrow, and select Online Transfer from the list. It will appear in your Check # field as OXfr.
3. Enter a description, if you choose, in what is normally the Payee field.
4. In the Payment column, enter the amount of the transfer. Press TAB to move to the Category field. Choose the account to which you want to transfer the money from the drop-down list that appears.
5. Click Save to enter the transaction.

Use the One Step Update dialog to send the instructions to your financial institution. You may also use the Online Center to send an online transfer.

1. Click Tools | Online Center.
2. Select the appropriate financial institution from the drop-down list.
3. Click the Transfers tab.
4. In the Transfer Money From field, choose the account from which you want to transfer the funds from the drop-down list.
5. In the To field, choose the account where the money is going from the drop-down list. Enter the amount in the Amount field.
6. Press ENTER.
7. Click Update/Send to send the instructions to the bank.

Whether you use the Online Center method or the account register method, you must send the transfer instructions to the bank in order for the transaction to take place.

Transfer Detection

A Quicken feature scans your transactions as they are being downloaded to detect transfers between your accounts. When Quicken finds what looks like a matched pair of transfer transactions, it can automatically create the transfer in Quicken for you or ask you for confirmation first. To select this feature, from the Quicken menu bar, click Edit | Preferences | Transfer Detection. Be cautious with this preference—it may detect matches that are not truly transfers. Select the option for Quicken to ask for confirmation first.

Exchanging E-mail with Your Financial Institution

You can use the E-mail tab of the Online Center window to exchange e-mail messages with financial institutions for which you have enabled Online Account Services via Direct Connect. Keep in mind that not all financial institutions support this feature. Also, remember that this communication is between you and your financial institution, not Intuit (the makers of Quicken). It is intended primarily for exchanging information about your account, not technical support for using Quicken.

- **Creating an E-mail Message** In the E-mail tab of the Online Center window, click Create. If a Create dialog appears, use it to set general options for your e-mail message. If your message is about an online payment, choose the account from the Account drop-down list, and select the payment from the Payments list. Even if there is only one payment in the list, you must select it or the OK button remains disabled. When you click OK, a Message window appears. Use it to compose your e-mail message. Click OK again to save the message. The message appears in the bottom half of the E-mail tab of the Online Center window, ready to be sent to your financial institution.

 If you elected to e-mail your financial institution regarding a payment, the window is titled Payment E-mail.

- **Exchanging E-mail Messages** In the Online Center window, click the Update/Send button. Quicken displays the Online Update window, which includes any e-mail messages you may have created that need to be sent. Enter your password and click the Update Now button. Then wait while Quicken establishes an Internet connection with your bank and exchanges e-mail.
- **Reading an E-mail Message** When your bank sends you an e-mail message, it appears in the E-mail tab of the Online Center window. To read the message, select it and click Read. The message appears in a message window. If desired, you can click the Print button to print the message for future reference. You can also click Delete to delete the e-mail once you no longer need it.

Bills and Income Reminders

A favorite Quicken feature is the ability to tell Quicken about the bills, deposits, and other transactions that need to be made in the future, especially the ones that happen on a regular basis. This feature, when fully utilized, doesn't just prevent you from forgetting to pay bills; it can completely automate the transaction entry process. Starting from the time you first create your Quicken file, you can create reminders to help you stay on top of your monthly bills. This part of the chapter discusses bill and income reminders, including how to set up and use them.

Being Reminded

Reminders aren't only for payments. You could create a reminder for incoming funds, such as an expected bonus or a monthly child-support check you receive. You can even schedule your paycheck—but it's better to use Quicken's Paycheck Setup feature, which is discussed later in this chapter, to do that.

Quicken's Reminders feature is one of the best timesaving features Quicken offers. By taking full advantage of this feature, you can minimize the time you spend entering transactions into Quicken. Generally speaking, you can be "reminded" about two types of transactions:

- One-time transactions are future transactions that you expect to record only once. For example, suppose you are arranging to purchase some furniture. You have already paid a deposit for the furniture and you know that the balance will be due at month-end, when the furniture is delivered. You can schedule that month-end payment in advance.
- Recurring transactions are transactions that occur periodically on a regular basis. Many of your monthly bills are good examples: rent or mortgage payments, car payments, utility bills—unfortunately, there are too many to list!

 Throughout this chapter and this book, bill reminders, scheduled transactions, and scheduled reminders all are used and mean the same process, saving information about a payee or a transaction so that you can pay or enter the information at a future time.

Remember that creating a reminder is not the same as recording a transaction, even if you opt to show the reminder in your account register. You must print a check or send an online payment instruction to record the transaction. Creating the reminder is only part of the job.

Creating Reminders from Downloaded Transactions

You can create a scheduled transaction in Quicken in several ways. When you first install Quicken, in the Home tab's Main View, click the Get Started button in the Stay On Top Of Monthly Bills snapshot. If you have downloaded your bank account transactions, you may already see outgoing transactions that appear to be recurring transactions. The Review Bills dialog lists these transactions, as seen next. (If you do not see the Get Started button in the Stay On Top Of Monthly Bills snapshot, skip ahead to "Work in the Home Tab's Main View," later in this chapter.)

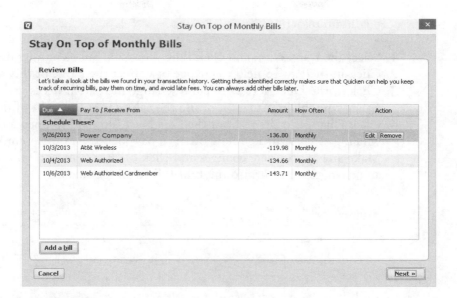

 If you have not downloaded your transactions, nor created a bank account, you may see three different Get Started buttons. However, until you create your first bank account, the only available Get Started button will be in the See Where Your Money Goes snapshot.

You may remove the transactions or edit them, as shown next. If you do not want to enter a transaction as a recurring transaction into Quicken, select that transaction and click Remove in the Action column.

To edit a transaction:

1. Select the transaction and click Edit. The Edit Bill Reminder dialog appears.
2. Click in the Pay To field to change or correct the payee of this transaction.
3. Click in the Due Next On field to change the date if necessary. You may either type the information or use the calendar at the right of the field.
4. Click Change to the right of the Due Next On field to open a dialog in which you tell Quicken how often to pay (or receive) this item, as seen next. Make any appropriate changes and click OK (or Cancel if you've not made any changes) to return to the Edit Bill Reminder dialog.

 If you have a bill that is due on the second Tuesday of each month, to schedule this bill, select Monthly. Leave the second field at Every 1 Month and set the third field at 2. In the final field, select Tuesday. Until you select 1 through 4 in the third field, the last field will only contain Day.

5. Click the Amount Due field to change the amount, if necessary. You may either type the new amount or use the small calculator to the right of the field.
6. Click Change to the right of Amount Due to open the variable payment dialog, seen here, to tell Quicken how to estimate payments that differ from month to month. Make any appropriate changes and click OK (or Cancel if you've not made any changes) to return to the Edit Bill Reminder dialog.

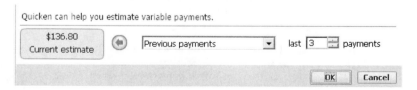

7. If necessary, open the drop-down list in the From Account field to change the account from which this payment is to be made or to which the deposit is to be deposited.

8. Click anywhere within the Details section to add a category, tag, or memo, as seen here. Click OK (or Cancel) to close the dialog and return to the Edit Bill Reminder dialog.

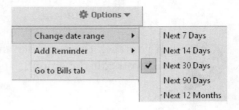

Power Company

Category: Bills & Utilities:Utilities   Tag:

Memo: Download from usbank.com.

OK   Cancel

You may also see the split button to the right of the Category field, a small two-headed arrow.

9. The Optional Settings section is covered in the section "Setting Up Reminders in the Bills Tab" later in this chapter.
10. After you have completed changing or entering the information, click Done/Next. If you have additional recurring items, the Stay On Top Of Monthly Bills | Review Bills dialog asks that you follow the same process for each item on the list.
11. If you have recurring income items, follow Steps 1 through 9 for each income item. When you have completed the income items, click Done. You are returned to the Home tab's Main View in the Stay On Top Of Monthly Bills snapshot. Note that the Bill And Income Reminders section now includes the recurring items.

Work in the Home Tab's Main View

After you have set up recurring bills from downloaded transactions, you can continue to work in the Stay On Top Of Monthly Bills section in the Home Tab's Main view. Click the Options menu, from which you can do the following:

- Choose to display the reminders for the next 7, 14, 30, or 90 days, or 12 months, as seen at right.
- Open the Add Reminder dialog to add a new Bill, Income, or Transfer reminder. Each option opens the appropriate reminder dialog for that specific task.

⚙ Options ▾

Change date range   ▶   Next 7 Days
Add Reminder   ▶   Next 14 Days
Go to Bills tab   ✓ Next 30 Days
                              Next 90 Days
                              Next 12 Months

- Go to the Bills tab, from which you can work with reminders, see what bills and income are due in the near future, and see your projected balances for the next 12 months or even longer, if you choose. See the upcoming section "Setting Up Reminders in the Bills Tab" in this chapter.

Each reminder displayed on the Stay On Top Of Monthly Bills list is a link. Click the small, right-facing arrow to the right of the amount to see a menu, shown here, from which you can do the following:

Due ▲		
Power Company	9/26/2013	-136.80
At&t Wireless	10/3/2013	-119.98
Web Authorized	10/4/2013	-134.66
Web Authorized Cardmember	10/6/2013	-143.71

- Enter into Register
- Skip this one
- Edit ▶

- Enter the reminder into the appropriate register, which opens the Enter Into Register dialog. With this dialog, you can enter the transaction into the register immediately rather than waiting for the date you set earlier. The transaction will reflect the date you specify, showing in the register with that date in the future.
- Skip this one entry.
- Click Edit to open a submenu from which you can
  - Edit Only This Instance of the reminder, which opens the Edit Reminder dialog.
  - Edit This And All Future Reminders, which opens the Edit Bill Reminder dialog. If the reminder is an income or transfer reminder, the Edit Income Reminder or Edit Transfer Reminder dialog opens.
  - Delete This And All Future Reminders, which opens a message that you are about to delete a scheduled bill or deposit. You must click OK to delete the reminder or click Cancel to close the message without deleting the reminder.

If you click the reminder amount, the Edit Reminder dialog appears. This dialog lets you edit the amount and due date for the next instance only.

See What's Left

The What's Left section at the right of the Stay On Top Of Monthly Bills section shows how much is available for the date range you selected in the

Options menu. If any of your accounts are close to being overdrawn, you will see "Risk of Overdraft" displayed at the bottom of the What's Left section. Click the link to display the Projected Balances dialog. In this case, the Projected Balances shows only the overdrawn accounts.

If your accounts are all positive (not overdrawn), you will see a See Projected Balances link instead of the Risk Of Overdraft link. Click See Projected Balances to display the balances in each of your spending accounts. This is the same information you see in the Bills tab's Projected Balances view. Click Close to dismiss the Projected Balances dialog.

Setting Up Reminders in the Bills Tab

The Bills tab is the place to work with your reminders. If you did not download any recurring transactions when you created your first bank account, when you first click the Bills tab, you will see a Get Started button.

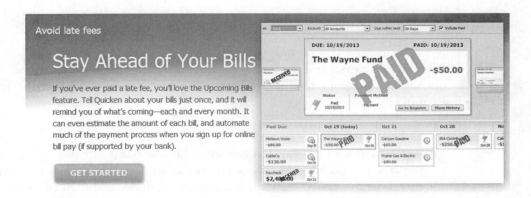

To begin, click the Get Started button. The Stay On Top Of Monthly Bills Review Bills dialog appears as you saw in "Creating Reminders From Downloaded Transactions" earlier in this chapter. Click the words "Set Up" in the sentence "Set Up A Scheduled Bill Or Deposit" to open the Add Reminder dialog, shown next.

To go directly to the Add Bill Reminder dialog, click the Add A Bill button at the bottom left of the Stay On Top Of Monthly Bills dialog.

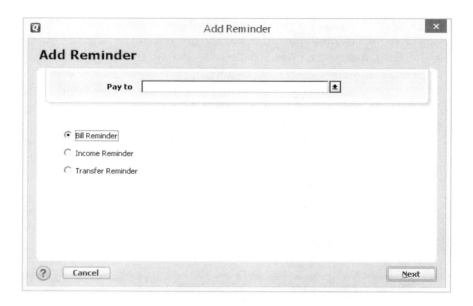

 When you are first working with your Quicken file, you only see the choice to open bill and income reminders. As you add more accounts, you see the Transfer Reminder option.

1. Enter a name in the Pay To or From field. The name of this field depends on the type of reminder you choose from the list. While it does not appear in this order, it's easier to choose the type of reminder and then enter the name.
   a. If this is a bill reminder and you have entered payees before, click the drop-down arrow to choose from a list of existing payees. If you are setting up a bill reminder in a new Quicken file, you will probably not yet have any payees on your list.
   b. If you are creating an income reminder, type the name of the income source in the From field. This field also has a drop-down list from which you can choose if you have entered other income sources.
   c. Click Next to continue.
2. The Add Bill Reminder dialog appears, as seen in the next illustration, with the Pay To field prefilled with the information you entered in Step 1.
3. Enter a date in the Due Next On date field. You can also choose a date from the Calendar to the right of the field.
4. Click Change to set how often you need to be reminded about the bill. The Change dialog appears, from which you can change

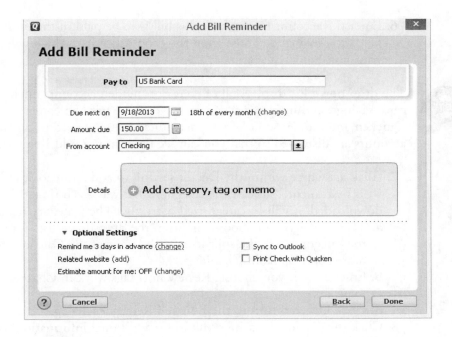

a. The start date.

b. How often the item is deducted from your account. Choose an option from the drop-down list. Your options are Weekly, Bi-Weekly, Monthly, Twice A Month, Quarterly, Yearly, Twice A Year, Only Once, and To Pay Estimated Tax (which follows the IRS estimated tax payment schedule). Then set options in the area to the right of the How Often field; the options change based on the frequency you select.

c. Click the End Date field's drop-down arrow to display the End Date options. These specify when the recurring transaction should end.

- **No End Date**, the default option, keeps the transaction scheduled until you delete it or set another option in this dialog.
- **End On** enables you to set a specific date for the last transaction.
- **End After** or **End Date** enables you to specify the number of transactions before they automatically end or the date on which the payments end. What you see will depend on what you enter in the How Often field.
- If all of the information on the Change dialog is correct, click OK to close the dialog and return to the Add Bill Reminder dialog.

5. Enter an amount in the Amount Due field, or use the Calculator to the right of the Amount Due field. You cannot leave this field blank, but you can change the amount when it is time to enter the bill in the register.

6. Enter the account from which this bill is to be paid in the From Account field. You may also choose from the drop-down list, which will display all of your non-hidden accounts.

The drop-down list displays all of your non-hidden accounts, including credit card, savings, and investing accounts. If you have used an earlier version of Quicken and hidden some of your accounts, you may need to update how those accounts are displayed so that you can see them in the Add Reminder dialog.

7. Click anywhere within the Details section to add a category, tag, or memo. (It is best to enter at least the category; that way, each time this transaction is downloaded, it will be categorized correctly.) The Category dialog appears:

a. Type a category or choose one from the drop-down list. You can even split the category—see the split icon to the right of the Category field? (Learn more about splits in Chapter 3.)

b. Enter a tag if you choose. Review how tags work in Chapter 1.

c. Type a memo.

d. Click OK to return to the Edit Bill Reminder dialog.

8. Click the Optional Settings link to set additional information for this bill. Click the Change link by the Remind Me 3 Days In Advance option to be reminded according to a different time schedule. From this dialog:

a. Use the up or down arrows to increase or decrease the number of days before the bill is due to be reminded. You can also type in the number of days.

b. Tell Quicken to enter the bill for you automatically and specify the number of days before the bill is due that you want the bill to be entered.

c. Tell Quicken to count only business days when calculating the reminder days.

d. Click OK when you've made your changes to return to the Add Bill Reminder dialog.

9. Click the Add link next to the Related Website option to add the payee's website. Click OK after you have typed the website address to return to the Add Bill Reminder dialog. You can also copy the web address directly from the appropriate website and paste it in the field. This will ensure you don't make a typo when you enter the web address.

10. Click the Change link next to the Estimate Amount For Me option to open the Estimate dialog.

a. The Fixed Amount option displays a text box you can use to enter a dollar amount that the transaction will always use. You can change the amount when the transaction is entered, if necessary.

b. Click the drop-down list to choose Previous Payments. This option tells Quicken to create an estimate based the payments you have made previously on which to base the estimate.

c. The other option on the drop-down list is Time Of Year. This is used when you make recurring payments at a specific time of year, such as real estate or other taxes.

 If your Quicken file does not have enough data to estimate either Previous Payments or Time Of Year information, you will see a pop-up message telling you this.

d. If you have set any estimates in the Estimate dialog, click OK. Otherwise, click Cancel to close the dialog and return to the Add Reminder dialog.

11. If you use Microsoft Outlook, select the Sync To Outlook check box to synchronize your due date reminder with the Outlook calendar.

12. Select the Print Check With Quicken check box to tell Quicken to print the check for this bill when it is due. Print Check With Quicken records the transaction as a payment using a check to be printed. Entering the transaction, of course, decreases the balance in a banking account. The Check Number field in the account register is set to PRINT, which signals Quicken to include the transaction with other checks to be printed.

13. Click Done to close the Add Bill Reminder dialog.

Working with the Bills Tab

You can view your reminders in your account registers if you have elected to display Reminders in the account registers, or

- From the Bills tab, by clicking the Manage Reminders button.
- From the Quicken menu bar when you click Tools| Manage Bill & Income Reminders.
- From the default Main View of the Home tab, in the Stay On Top Of Monthly Bills section, as discussed in the section "Work in the Home Tab's Main View," earlier in this chapter.

Use the Bills tab, shown in Figure 4-2, to view upcoming bills and other scheduled transactions in a number of different ways:

- Add Reminder enables you to add a bill, income, or transfer reminder as discussed earlier in this chapter.
- Manage Reminders displays the Bill And Income Reminders window.

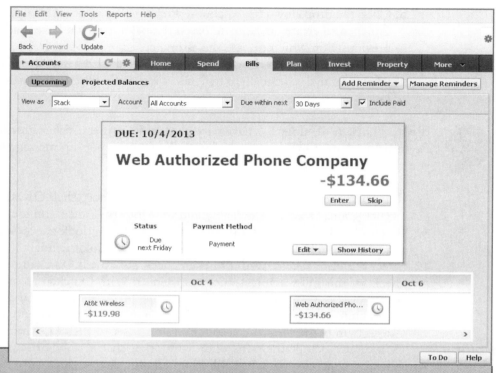

Figure 4-2 • The Stack view in the Upcoming view of Quicken's Bills tab is useful for seeing payments you must make soon.

Upcoming Button

The Upcoming button's view, as seen in Stack view in Figure 4-2, shows each upcoming scheduled transaction with a note-like interface. Click one of the transactions, and its details appear in the middle of the window. Use the horizontal scroll bar at the bottom of the window to display upcoming transactions. You can use a transaction's buttons to enter, skip, or edit the transaction. Clicking a Show History button displays a payment history for that payee.

You may change the way the information shows by clicking the View As drop-down list, as shown here.

- **Stack** displays each item in a "stack" as if they were papers on top of each other. You can use the Due Within Next drop-down list to choose the date range. Your options are 7, 14, and 30 days. You can choose to not include items that have been paid by clearing the Include Paid check box, located to the right of the Due Within Next field.

- **List** displays information about the status, due date, pay to or receive from information, and amount of each transaction. From this view you can enter, edit, or skip the transaction. The Due Within Next and Include Paid options are the same as in the Stack view.

- **Calendar** shows all transactions in a calendar view that includes transactions and their amounts, as well as the ending total banking account balance. You can use the arrows by the current month area to scroll through months.

The Calendar view does not show cash or bills paid from any Brokerage accounts, nor can you indicate which accounts to include on the Bills tab's Calendar view, even if you have designated those accounts in the full Calendar view. See "Using the Financial Calendar" later in this chapter.

- **Monthly List** shows all scheduled transaction reminders for the current month. You can choose another month by using the arrows to the left and right of the current month.

- The **Account** drop-down list allows you to select the accounts to show in each view.

- Select the date range for which you want the reminders displayed in the **Due Within Next** drop-down list. You may choose to see what is due for the next 7, next 14, or next 30 days. This drop-down list appears only in the List and Stack views.

Projected Balances

This button's view, seen next, shows projected balances and your upcoming transactions in a list view, as shown in the next illustration. While the default is to display all spending accounts, you can select a single account to view from the Select Accounts drop-down list or choose Multiple Accounts to open the Projected Balance selection dialog. This dialog allows you to choose two or more spending or credit card accounts to display. Click the Show (Hidden Accounts) check box to include them in the cash flow view. Click Tools | Manage Hidden Accounts if you don't see the accounts you expect to see here.

Click Select All to choose all displayed accounts or Clear All to start over with your selection. Click OK to close the dialog.

You may choose a date range to display by clicking the Time Range drop-down list. You may choose the next 7, 14, 30, or 90 days; the next 12 months; or create a customized date range.

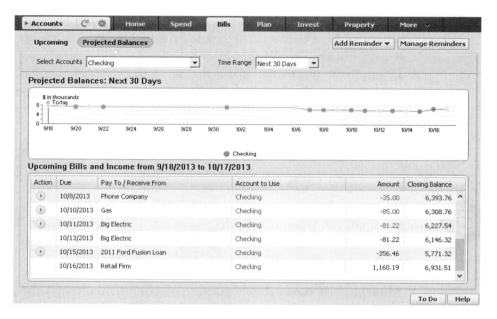

The Projected Balances snapshot of the graph includes all of the accounts you have selected for the date range you select. A legend showing the account or accounts represented in the line graph appears at the bottom of the section. For example, in the illustration above, only one account was chosen.

In the Upcoming Bills And Income From *nn/nn/nnnn* to *nn/nn/nnnn* section, you can work with your transaction reminders as follows:

- Click the right-pointing arrow in the circle icon in the Action column to enter, skip, or edit the selected transaction.
- Click the account name in the Account To Use column to be taken to that account's register.
- Click the transaction's amount in the Amount column to open the Edit Reminder dialog.

Working with Reminders

Scheduling a transaction was the hard part. (Not very hard, though, was it?) Entering, editing, and skipping a scheduled transaction is easy. Here's one way that some say is the quickest and easiest, to work with reminders.

Click the Bills tab, and then click the Upcoming button to display the view you prefer, and select a reminder. The options described here may be on the selected item's transaction list, as in the List or Monthly List views, the Calendar date in the Calendar view, or the reminder itself in the Stack view.

- **Enter**   In all views except the Calendar view, if the transaction has not already been entered, the Enter button displays the Enter Transaction dialog. Use this dialog to finalize settings for a transaction. When you click Enter Transaction, the transaction is entered into the account register. The dialog will be labeled Enter X Transaction, where X is Expense or Income.
- **Skip**   In all views except the Calendar view, the Skip button skips the transaction if it has not already been entered into the account register. The transaction moves down in the list, and its due date changes to the next due date.
- **Edit**   In all views except the Calendar view, the Edit button displays the Edit Transaction Reminder dialog when the transaction has not yet been entered into the account register. This dialog looks and works very much like the Add Income Reminder dialog shown earlier. Use this dialog to modify settings for the transaction's future entries. If the transaction is an instance of a recurring transaction, the Edit button appears as a menu with the following two options:
  - **Only This Instance** displays the Edit Reminder dialog that enables you to change the date and amount of the transaction.
  - **This And All Future Reminders** displays the Edit Transaction Reminder dialog, as discussed earlier. The dialog will be labeled Edit *X* Reminder, where *X* is Income or Expense.

While the Calendar view does not feature an Edit button, you can double-click each day's transactions to open a dialog with which you can choose to enter, edit, or skip the transactions.

Managing Reminders

In the Bills tab, click Manage Reminders or press CTRL-J to open the Bill And Income Reminders window, which displays both current and future transactions. If you have previously scheduled transactions or repeating online transactions, the Bill And Income Reminders window has four tabs, as shown next. Until you have created either one or both, there are only two tabs visible.

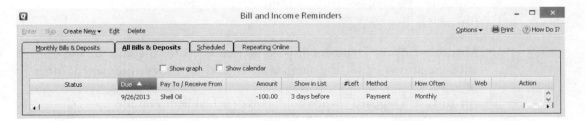

Bills and Income Reminder Button Options

You can use button options in both the Monthly Bills & Deposits and the All Bills & Deposits tabs to enter, skip, create, edit, or delete scheduled transactions. You must select a transaction to activate all but the Create New option.

- **Enter** opens the Enter [type of] Transaction dialog. Enter the appropriate information, and click Enter Transaction. If the reminder is for investment income, you may see a dialog titled Edit Income – Income (Div, Int, etc.).
- **Skip** enables you to skip the payment (or next payment) of that transaction.
- **Create New** enables you to create a new scheduled transaction. See "Setting Up Reminders in the Bills Tab" earlier in this chapter.
- **Edit** opens the Edit Bill (or Income) Reminder dialog in which you can modify each area of the reminder.
- **Delete** removes the scheduled transaction. It does not remove any transactions that have already been entered in a register.
- **Options** offers commands for changing the way the Bill And Income Reminders window is sorted. You can also change the sort order by clicking the Due, Pay To/Receive From, Payments, or Deposits column header. Depending on the tab in which you are working, you may also be able to sort by amount.
- **Print** prints a list of scheduled transactions.
- **How Do I?** displays the Quicken Personal Finances Help window with instructions for completing tasks with the Bill And Income Reminders window.
- **Action buttons** on individual transaction reminders can also be used. To access the action buttons, select a reminder and choose from the following:
  - **Enter** opens the Enter Transaction dialog discussed earlier in the chapter.
  - **Edit** opens a menu giving you the option to change only this reminder or this and all future reminders.
  - **Skip** tells Quicken to skip the reminder for this time only.

Bills and Income Reminders Tabs

There may be up to four tabs available in the Bill And Income Reminders window. Until you have scheduled some online payments, you will only see the first two tabs.

- **Monthly Bills & Deposits** displays all reminders for the month. You can click the arrows beside the name of the month to view reminders for other months.
- **All Bills & Deposits** displays all types of scheduled reminders.

- **Scheduled** displays the deposits and payments that you have scheduled for this month. Remember, until you have set up an account with Online Payment capabilities, you will not see the Scheduled tab.
- **Repeating Online** lists repeating payments you have scheduled for online payment.

Display Check Boxes

Two check boxes enable you to display additional information in the window:

- **Show Graph** displays a column chart showing cash flow for selected accounts for the month.
- **Show Calendar** displays one or two calendars that indicate scheduled transaction dates.

Schedule These?

You may see a Schedule These? list at the bottom of a Bill And Income Reminders window. When this is present, it displays transactions that Quicken "thinks" you might want to schedule for the future. It builds this list based on categories used in the transactions or transactions you have entered more than once.

- To schedule a transaction in the list, click the Yes button beside it. Quicken displays the Edit Bill (or Income) Reminder dialog so you can turn the transaction into a scheduled transaction.
- To remove a transaction from the list, click the No button beside it.

 You will not see the Yes/No buttons until you have selected a suggested reminder in the list.

Scheduling Repeating Online Payments

Some payments are exactly the same every month, such as your rent, a car loan, or your monthly cable television bill. You can set these payments up as repeating online payments.

The process begins when you schedule the online payment once, indicating the payee, amount, and frequency. Quicken sends the instructions to your bank. Thirty days before the payment is due, your bank creates a new post-dated payment based on your instructions and notifies you that it has created the payment. Quicken automatically enters the payment information in your account register with the appropriate payment date. The payment is delivered on the payment date. This happens regularly, at the interval you specify, until you tell it to stop. Because you don't have to do a thing to continue paying regularly, the more payments you make with this feature, the more time you save.

1. From the Bills tab, choose Add Reminders | Bill Reminder.
2. Enter the name of your payee in the Pay To field. Click Next.
3. In the Add Bill Reminder dialog, set the date, the amount, and the account from which you will be paying this bill. Be sure to choose an account in which you have activated Online Bill Pay!
4. Enter a category, tag, or memo if necessary.
5. Click the Use Online Bill Pay check box.
6. Click Optional Settings if necessary to display your options. Click the Make This A Repeating Online Payment check box. If you have made the payment a repeating online payment, you cannot ask Quicken to remind you to enter the payment or estimate the amount of the payment.
7. Click Done.

 If this is a new online payee, Quicken prompts you to enter address and account number information so that your payment can be processed by your bank.

There are two very important things to remember when using the Add A Reminder dialog to create a repeating online payment:

- Click the Use Online Bill Pay check box to tell Quicken that the payment will be made online.
- Click the Make This A Repeating Online Payment check box if you choose. This tells Quicken to send one instruction for multiple repeating payments.

When you click Done to save the payment instruction, it appears in the Repeating Online tab of the Bill And Income Reminders dialog. You can use the buttons at the top of the Bill And Income Reminders dialog to work with items listed in the Repeating Online list window. In each instance, if you have not clicked a transaction to select it, the appropriate button option is grayed out even if there is only one online transaction in the Repeating Online list.

- **Enter** records the selected repeating online payment in the register.
- **Skip** skips payment of the selected repeating online payment.
- **Create New** enables you to create a new scheduled transaction or paycheck.
- **Edit** displays the Edit Repeating Online dialog so you can modify the details of the repeating online payment.

If you right-click a repeating online transaction, you can select Enter, Skip, Edit, or Delete from the context menu.

- **Delete** removes the repeating online payment from the list, thus canceling future payments. You must click Delete in the confirmation dialog that appears to remove the transaction.
- **Options** offers commands for changing the sort order of payments in the list; however, you may have to click the header of the column by which you want to sort to make it sort properly.
- **Print** prints a list of repeating online payments.
- **How Do I?** displays the Quicken Personal Finances Help window with instructions for managing your spending and completing tasks with the Bill And Income Reminders list.

Stopping a Single Repeating Online Payment

In the Online Center window's Payments tab, select the payment you want to stop, and click the Cancel Payment button. Click Yes in the confirmation dialog that appears. Use the Update/Send button to send the cancel payment instruction. Note that the payment may not appear in the Online Center window unless you have reviewed and approved all downloaded payment transactions, as instructed earlier in this chapter.

Stopping All Future Payments for a Repeating Online Payment

Press CTRL-J to open the Bill And Income Reminders window. In the Repeating Online tab of the Bill And Income Reminders window, select the payment you want to stop, and click Delete. Click Delete in the confirmation dialog that appears. The transaction is removed from the list. Then use the Update/Send button in the Online Center window to send the cancel payment instruction.

Using QuickFill and Memorized Payees

As you enter transactions, Quicken is quietly working in the background, memorizing transaction information for each payee. It creates a database of memorized payees. It then uses the memorized payees for its QuickFill feature. QuickFill works in two ways:

- When you enter the first few characters of a payee name in the Write Checks or account register window, Quicken immediately fills in the rest of the name. When you advance to the next text box or field of the entry form,

Quicken fills in the rest of the transaction information based on the last transaction for that payee.

- You can select a memorized payee from the drop-down list in the Payee field of the Write Checks or account register window. Quicken then fills in the rest of the transaction information based on the last transaction for that payee.

QuickFill entries include amounts, categories, and memos. They can also include splits and tags. For example, you might pay the cable or satellite company for television service monthly. The bill is usually the same amount each month. The second time you create an entry with the company's name, Quicken fills in the rest of the transaction automatically. You can make adjustments to the amount or other information as desired and save the transaction. It may have taken a minute or so to enter the transaction the first time, but it'll take only seconds to enter it every time after that.

By default, the QuickFill feature is set up to work as discussed here. If it does not, check the QuickFill options to make sure they are set properly. To check these options:

1. Click Edit | Preferences | Register | Data Entry And QuickFill.
2. Ensure all of the check boxes are selected.
3. Click OK to close Quicken Preferences.

IN MY EXPERIENCE

If you use memorized transactions and the QuickFill feature is completing more information than you want it to, edit the transaction in the Memorized Payee List. For example, if you pay activity fees for each of your children to the local community center, you may want to use a different memo for each child's dues. After you have memorized the transaction, open the Memorized Payee List and clear out the Memo field or Tag fields. Then, click the Lock check box.

 You could also memorize the payee with a different memo for each child or create a tag for each one. Learn more about tags in Chapter 1.

To show the Lock column in the Memorized Payee List, click Options and click Show Locked Status Column In The List. Each time you enter the transaction, just change or enter the information that is different from the transaction that has been memorized.

Utilizing the Memorized Payee List

If desired, you can view a list of your memorized payees. Just choose Tools | Memorized Payee List or press CTRL-T. The list displays the last transaction you entered for each payee.

 Depending on the type or category for a payee, you may see more than just the last transaction in the Memorized Payee List.

 If a payee does not appear on the Memorized Payee List and you believe it should, check your Preferences. Click Edit | Preferences | Data Entry And QuickFill. Select the Remove Memorized Payees Not Used In Last nn Months check box or change the amount in the Months field.

Select a memorized payee to display the Edit and Delete action buttons. Edit displays the Edit Memorized Payee dialog for the currently selected transaction.

- The **Payee Name** field displays the payee name as it is currently entered. You may change the name or any of the other fields as required.
- You may also leave the **Category**, **Tag**, **Memo**, or **Amount** fields blank so that data can be changed each time you use this payee. If the amount paid to this payee changes each time, leave the amount blank.
- The **Never Auto-categorize This Payee During Quick Fill Or Downloads** tells Quicken you wish to enter the proper category for this payee.
- Click **Lock And Leave This Payee Unchanged When It Is Edited In A Register** to ensure the transaction stays blank in the Memorized Payee List.
- **Show This Payee In The Calendar Memorized Payee List**, which is selected by default, determines how this item is displayed in the Calendar. See "Using the Financial Calendar" later in this chapter.
- **Delete** displays a dialog asking you to confirm that you really do want to delete the selected item. If you delete the transaction, it is removed from the Memorized Payee List only, not from any register in the Quicken data file.
- The **Memorized Payee Report** icon is hard to see. It is located to the right of the Delete button. Click this icon to open a Payee Report about this payee.
- You can also print a report of transactions paid to this payee. Using the very faint report icon to the right of the Delete button in the Memorized Payee List, shown here, you can also print a report about this payee.

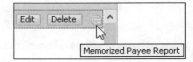

Use the ALT-A keyboard shortcut to save the transaction if the information is correct for the current entry. This shortcut works in an account register when entering a transaction.

You can also use the Memorized Payee List as follows:

1. Open the register from which the item will be paid, and click the next available line. Use the CTRL-T keyboard shortcut to open the Memorized Payee List.
2. Right-click the memorized payee transaction you want to use.
3. From the context menu that appears, click Use to paste the item into your register.
4. Click Save or use the ALT-A keyboard shortcut to save the transaction.

You may want to build a Memorized Payee List from all of your existing cash flow accounts. To do so:

1. From the menu bar, click Tools.
2. Hold down CTRL-SHIFT and click Memorized Payee List.
3. Your new Memorized Payee List displays.

Memorized Payee List Activities

You can use buttons at the bottom of the Memorized Payee window, as seen next, to change what displays in the list, add, merge, rename, or delete memorized payees on the Memorized Payee List:

- **New Payee** displays the Create Memorized Payee dialog, which is similar to the Edit Memorized Payee dialog. You use the Create Memorized Payee dialog to create brand-new transactions without actually entering them into any register of your Quicken data file. Just fill in the fields to enter transaction information, and click OK. The new transaction appears in the Memorized Payee List window.

- **Options** opens a menu that allows you to choose to display the "Lock" and the "Show On Calendar" columns in the Memorized Payee List. Click View Locked Items Only to display locked memorized payees only.
- **Merge/Rename** displays the Merge And Rename Payees dialog, which you can use to enter a new name for the selected payee. When you enter the new name, the Add A Renaming Rule dialog appears. Enter the new payee name, choose either If A Payee Contains or If Quicken Name Is from the drop-down list, and click OK.
- Use the **Delete** button to delete one or more payees from the list.
- The **Renaming Rules** button opens the Renaming Rules dialog, covered earlier in this chapter.
- The question mark icon opens the Quicken Personal Finances Help window with additional information for completing tasks with the Memorized Payee List window.
- The printer icon opens the Print dialog with which you can print the Memorized Payee List.
- Click **Done** to close the Memorized Payee List.

Use the CTRL-M keyboard shortcut after you have entered a transaction to memorize the payee and the category.

Using the Financial Calendar

Quicken's Calendar, shown in Figure 4-3, keeps track of all your transactions, past and future, by date. You may open the Calendar by choosing Tools | Calendar or by pressing CTRL-K.

Calendar Buttons

You can use buttons to work with the window's contents:

- **Go To Date** enables you to go to a specific calendar date. Click the Calendar icon to open a tiny calendar, and select the date you want. Or, enter the date in the Go To Date field and click the Go button.
- **Arrow buttons** on either side of the month's name enable you to move from one month to another.

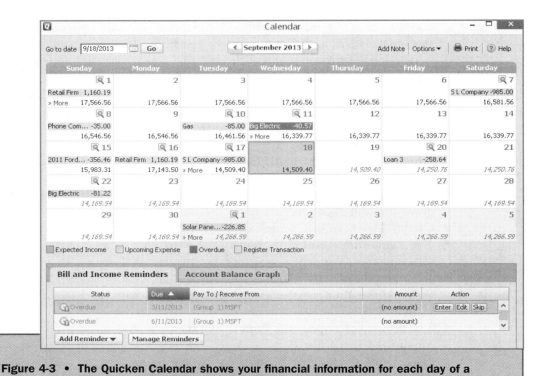

Figure 4-3 • **The Quicken Calendar shows your financial information for each day of a selected month.**

- **Add Note** enables you to enter a note for a selected date, as seen next. You can even change the color of your note. The Note icon then appears on the Calendar

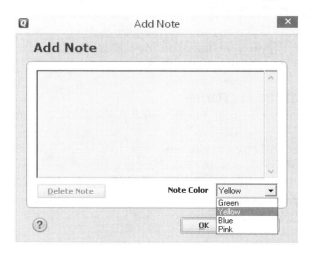

on that date. After you have selected the color of your note, check your monitor
settings. Depending on your monitor, the icon may be hard to see!

• **Options** offers commands for viewing and working with the contents of the
  Calendar window.

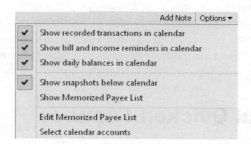

• **Print** opens the Print dialog from which you can print the Calendar.
• **Help** displays the Quicken Personal Finances Help window with
  information about using the Calendar.

The Transactions Window

When you double-click a calendar date (or single-click an already selected date),
the Transactions window, which lists all the transactions for that date, appears.
You can use the buttons in the Transactions window to work with transactions:

• **Enter** opens the Enter Expense Transaction dialog from which you can enter
  the selection into the register. If the transaction has already been entered into
  the account register, this button changes to Go To Register and opens that
  transaction in the register where it is entered.
• **Edit** enables you to modify the currently selected transaction. If this
  transaction has not been entered into the register, the Edit <type> Reminder
  dialog displays. If it has been entered into the register, the Edit Register
  Transaction dialog appears.
• **Delete** removes the selected transaction. This option is only available for
  transactions that have already been entered into the register.
• **Skip** lets you skip the transaction for this date. This option is only available
  for transactions that have not been entered.
• **Schedule** enables you to create a new scheduled transaction based on the
  selected transaction. This option is only available if the currently selected
  transaction is not a scheduled transaction.
• The **Help** icon opens Quicken Help at the section explaining how to work
  with the Calendar.

- **Add** enables you to enter a new transaction. From this menu you can add an expense or income transaction as well as a new reminder.
- **Close** closes the window.

The dollar amounts that appear in the bottom of each calendar date box show the total account balances for the accounts displayed in the window after taking all payments into consideration. (You can specify which accounts to include by choosing Select Calendar Accounts from the Options menu in the button bar.) This feature works, in effect, like a simplified forecasting tool.

Useful Quicken Features

In addition to the Bill and Income Reminders, Memorized Payees, and QuickFill, Quicken offers a number of other useful functions to help you with your financial recordkeeping.

Minding Your Bills

Quicken's optional Billminder feature, shown next, makes it possible for you to monitor upcoming bills and scheduled transactions without starting Quicken. This application displays a window that summarizes upcoming transactions. It also includes a convenient button to run Quicken, should you decide to take action on a listed item.

How you open Billminder depends on your operating system.

- **Windows 7 and earlier**   Choose Start | All Programs | Quicken 2014 | Billminder.
- **Windows 8**   Choose the Billminder tile located near your Quicken 2014 tile, shown at right.

To make the most of Billminder, you may want to configure it so it automatically starts each time you start your computer. To do this, click the Options button in the Billminder button bar to display Billminder Options as shown here. Select the Enable Billminder On Windows Startup check box. You can set other configuration options as desired to determine when Billminder should appear. Then click OK. Click Exit to close Billminder.

Billminder Options

☑ Enable Billminder on windows startup

☑ Only show Billminder if there are alerts or scheduled items due.

☑ Show scheduled bills and deposits

☑ Show checks to print

☑ Show online payments .

☑ Show investment reminders

☑ Show calendar notes

[OK]

[Cancel]

Using the Paycheck Setup Wizard

Quicken's Paycheck Setup Wizard feature offers yet another way to automate transactions. You use it to enter information about your regular payroll check and its deductions. Then, when payday comes along, Quicken automatically enters the payroll deposit information based on the Paycheck Setup transaction.

Quicken allows you to set up your recurring paycheck so that all the deductions can be fed into the appropriate categories. There are three ways to access the Paycheck Setup Wizard.

1. From the Planning tab, select Tax Center and from below the Taxable Income YTD section, click the Add Paycheck button.
2. From the Tools menu, click Manage Bill & Income Reminders | Create New | Income Reminder and choose the Paycheck Setup Wizard at the bottom of the dialog.

3. Some experienced Quicken users prefer to use the Classic menus instead of Standard menus as these menus offer easy access to the Paycheck Setup Wizard. Click View | Classic Menus | Bills | Add Reminder | Paycheck Reminder.

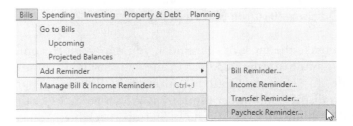

In all cases, the Paycheck Setup Wizard appears as shown in Figure 4-4. As you can see, you can choose to enter either the net amount of your paycheck or the gross amount which will help you track tax and other deductions. In the example outlined below, we have chosen to record the gross payroll. Quicken says that you will need your most recent paycheck and that you'll need to add any 401(k) accounts to Quicken before you begin.

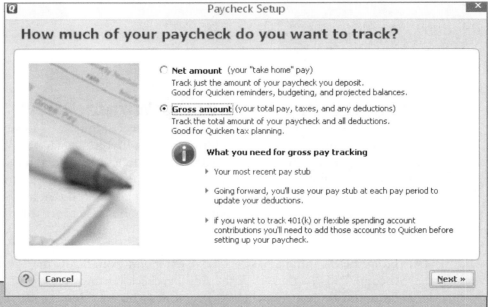

Figure 4-4 • Use the Paycheck Setup Wizard when creating your paycheck information in Quicken.

1. Once you have all the required information at hand and have entered any 401(k) or other accounts in Quicken, from the Paycheck Setup screen, click Next. If necessary, select Gross Amount, and then click Next.
2. Select the paycheck owner (you or your spouse), and type the name of the company from whom you earn the paycheck. Press TAB to move to the Memo field. Type any additional information in this optional field, for example, if you receive two checks, one for base pay and one for commissions. Click Next to open the Track Paycheck dialog, shown in Figure 4-5.
3. Click the Account field down arrow, and select the bank account into which this income is deposited. Press TAB, ENTER, or select the date, indicate

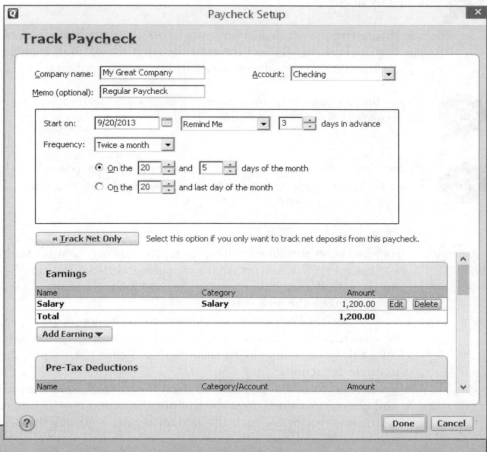

Figure 4-5 • **Enter your wages and deduction information to track your gross paycheck in Quicken.**

whether you want it automatically entered or just a reminder, and finally select the date you get paid. You can also change your mind and choose to track your net pay only by selecting the Track Net Only button.

4. Click Edit or Amount opposite Salary to open the Amount field. Enter the gross amount of income you receive. If you do not receive the same amount each time, enter an average.

5. If you have other components of your income, such as a regular bonus or commissions, click Add Earning, select the category of other earnings, enter the amount, and click OK.

If you select one of the pre-defined income items, you may not see the Category field.

6. If you have pre-tax deductions, such as 401(k) contributions, click Add Pre-Tax Deduction, select the category, select the account, enter both the contribution and employer-matching amounts, if applicable, and click OK.

Depending on your company's insurance plan, some health insurance premiums are deducted *after* taxes, not before.

By entering deduction information from your regular paycheck, Quicken can create tax reports, help you plan for taxes, and export information to TurboTax for year-end tax reporting.

7. Click in the amount field next to each of the tax items that are on your pay stub and enter the amount. If you want to make any changes to the name and category, click Edit, make the changes, and click OK. However, it is best to stay with the standard tax categories, as Quicken has already linked those categories with the proper tax-line items.

8. Click After-Tax Deduction, which can include health insurance and stock purchases, correct the name if needed, select the category you want to use to collect this deduction, enter the amount, and click OK. Repeat this for multiple deductions.

9. If you want to split your paycheck deposit over two or more accounts, click Add Deposit Account, select the additional account, type any memo information you want, enter the amount of your paycheck that will go into that account, and click OK.

10. When you have entered all of the paycheck information you want to track, click Done to close the Track Paycheck dialog.

11. Quicken asks if you want to enter year-to-date information. If you choose to enter that data, click OK, click in each of the Year To Date amount fields, type the requested information, and, when you've entered all the data you choose to include, click Enter to close the dialog box. Otherwise, click I Do Not Want To Enter This Information, and click OK.

Creating the Address Book

Quicken's Address Book feature stores the address information you enter when using the Write Checks window. You can also use this feature to modify or delete existing information or add new records. Keeping track of addresses with the Address Book makes it easy to insert addresses when writing checks and to look up contact information when you need to follow up on transactions.

Choose Tools | Address Book to display the Address Book window. This window lists all the records in the Address Book.

You can use buttons and menus to work with Address Book window contents as shown in the following illustration.

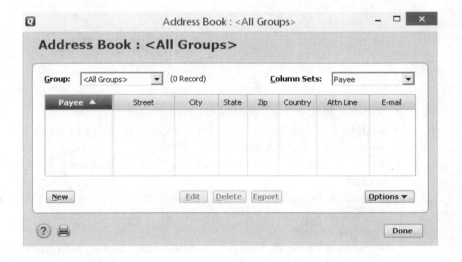

- The **Group** drop-down list lets you choose between All Groups and any other groups you have established within Quicken.
- The **Column Sets** drop-down list lets you view each of the various Address Book tabs in a columnar display. There are different columns in each column set. Each column set allows you to display different Address Book record data.

- **New** opens the Edit Address Book Record from which you can enter a new entry to the Address Book.

- **Edit** enables you to edit the selected record.
- **Delete** removes the Address Book record. It does not affect transactions that used the deleted Address Book record.
- **Options** opens a menu with which you can work with your Address Book entries:
  - **Switch Names And Organization** swaps the name you have entered as a contact into the Organization field in the Contact tab of the Address Book record.
  - **Switch Payee & Secondary Addresses** changes an address you have entered as the primary address to a secondary address.
  - **Format Address** opens a dialog with which you can format how the payee's address will appear on the checks you print.
  - **Assign To Groups** opens a dialog with which you can assign this payee to a group within Quicken.
  - **Select All/Select None** selects all or none of the payees in the Address Book.

- The **Help icon** displays the Help window with instructions for working with the Address Book.
- **Print** offers commands for printing Address Book record information.

 You cannot print envelopes from this section.

Adding or Modifying Address Book Records

To add a new Address Book record, click the New button in the Address Book window. The Edit Address Book Record dialog, shown earlier, appears. You also use the Edit Address Book Record dialog to edit an existing record. Simply select the record in the Address Book window, and click the Edit button in the button bar. You can also double-click the entry to open it if you choose.

The Edit Address Book Record dialog has five tabs for recording information. Click a tab to display its options, and then enter the information you want to store. Here's what you can enter in each of the five tabs:

- **Payee** is for the information that would normally appear in a Write Checks window, as well as some additional contact information. From this tab, you can also tell Quicken to include this payee in other lists.
- **Contact** is for the name, title, phone numbers, and website of a specific person.
- **Secondary** is for a secondary mailing address and e-mail address.
- **Personal** is for personal information, such as spouse and children's names, birthday and anniversary, an ID number if you need one, and still more phone numbers.
- **Miscellaneous** is for additional information, such as user-defined fields and notes. Click OK to save your entry.

Printing Entry Information

You can print the information in the list in three formats: list, labels, and envelopes.

Start by selecting a group from the Group drop-down list at the top of the Address Book window. From the group of records that displays, select a payee or several payees whose information you want to print. To change the format of a specific record, choose that record and click Options | Format Address to open the Format Print Check Address dialog. Set the options and click OK.

From the Address Book window, click the Print icon to open a drop-down list of printing options. These options are List, Labels, and Envelopes.

- **List**   Choose List to display a Print dialog just like the one that appears when printing Quicken reports. Use it to enter printing options, and then click OK to print the list.
- **Labels**   Choose Labels to display the Print Labels dialog. It includes a list of commonly used Avery label products; be sure to select the right one. Then select Contact To Print at the bottom of the Print Labels dialog. Click Print to open another Print Labels dialog from which you select the printer you want to use. Make sure you have label stock in the printer and choose the orientation of your labels, either Portrait or Landscape. Select Print Preview to see how your printed labels will look and click Print to print your labels.
- **Envelopes**   Choosing Envelopes displays the Print Envelope dialog. Use it to print #10 envelopes for Address Book records. To print your envelopes:
  1. Select the payees for which the envelopes are to be printed.
  2. Click the Print icon and select Envelopes.
  3. From the Print Envelope dialog, you may print either the contacts you have selected or select Print All Contacts to create envelopes for everyone in the group.
  4. Click Print Return Address if you want a return address printed on your envelopes. Select the return address.
  5. Click Print to open the Quicken Print Envelopes dialog. Your default printer appears in the Print To section.
  6. Select either a Horizontal or Vertical feed, depending on your printer's envelope printer. Set the Margin Offsets if necessary.
  7. If you want to use another printer, select Printer Setup and choose another printer.
  8. Click Font if you want to change the size of the printed information.
  9. Ensure you have envelopes in your printer's envelope feeder. When you have made your choices, click OK to print your envelopes.
  10. Click Done to close the Address Book window.

About Alerts

When you're juggling multiple bank, credit card, and investment accounts along with taxes, reminders, and several insurance policy renewal dates, Quicken's Alerts feature can really help you keep your sanity. After all, who can keep track of all those balances and keep them where they should be? Quicken can! Financial superhero!

The Alerts feature can also prevent embarrassment at a checkout counter by warning you when a credit card balance is getting dangerously close to its limit.

Likewise, it can remind you to pay your credit card bill so even if your balance is relatively low, you won't forget to make that monthly payment on time.

This section discusses the kinds of alerts Quicken offers and explains how to set them up.

Viewing Available Alerts Groups

Quicken offers four different groups of items for which you can set alerts. To enable them, open the Tools menu, choose Alerts Center, click the Setup tab, and then open the group with which you want to work. Here's an explanation of the alerts you can set in each group.

Banking Alerts

- **Account Min. Balances** enables you to set minimum balances for your checking and savings accounts. Quicken alerts you when the account balance falls below the reminder amount you specify.

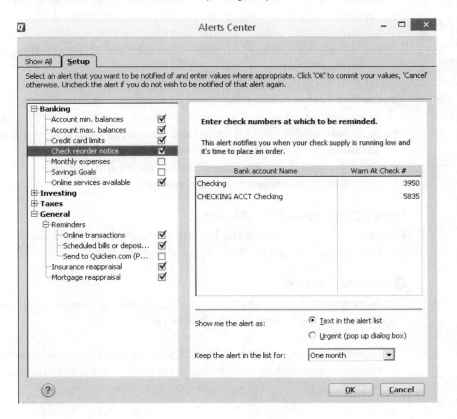

- **Account Max. Balances** enables you to set maximum balances for your checking and savings accounts. Quicken alerts you when the account balance climbs above the amount you specify.
- **Credit Card Limits** enables you to set limits for your credit card accounts. You can set a limit amount and a reminder amount. Quicken alerts you if the balance exceeds the reminder amount.
- **Check Reorder Notice** tells Quicken to alert you when you reach a certain check number. You can set this option for both checking and savings accounts.
- **Monthly Expenses** enables you to specify maximum monthly spending amounts for any Quicken expense category. If you exceed the limit you specified, Quicken alerts you to the fact.
- **Savings Goals** tells Quicken to alert you when you fall behind on a savings goal. This option works directly with Quicken's Savings Goals feature, which you learn about in Chapter 12.
- **Online Services Available** tells Quicken to alert you when one of your financial institutions supports Online Account Services.

In addition, Quicken offers three other General group reminder alerts that fall in the banking group:

- **Online Transactions** tells Quicken to remind you to download transactions from your financial institution if you haven't done so for 30 days or more.
- **Scheduled Bills Or Deposits Due Soon** tells Quicken to remind you in advance of any scheduled transactions that are due.
- **Send To Quicken.com** tells Quicken to remind you to export your portfolio to Quicken.com when holdings change.

Investing and Tax Alerts

Chapter 8 discusses setting the Investing group alerts while you can see Chapter 13 for a discussion on the three Taxes group alerts that are available for your use.

General Alerts

In addition to the three alerts discussed earlier in this section in "Banking Alerts," you can set alerts for the following:

- **Insurance Reappraisal** Use this alert to remind you of insurance policy renewal dates and to ensure that your current coverage amounts are up to date.

- **Mortgage Reappraisal**   This is a particularly useful alert if your mortgage has a variable interest rate, requires a balloon payment, or requires other, periodic attention.

Setting Up Alerts

You set up alerts from the Setup tab of the Alerts Center window. Click the name of one of the alerts to view and set it. To set an alert, select the name of the alert on the left side of the window. If necessary, click the checkbox to select it. Then click the value you want to change on the right side of the window and enter a new value. Not all alerts have values you can change; for example, the Online Services Available alert is a simple on or off setting made with the check mark.

You can tell Quicken how to notify you with the options in the bottom half of the Setup window.

- **Text In The Alert List** displays the alert as an item in an Alerts snapshot only, which you can see in the Alerts Center Show All tab and when you add alerts to another view.
- **Urgent (Pop Up Dialog Box)** displays the alert in a dialog when you first start Quicken each day.
- **Keep the Alert in the List For** lets you tell Quicken how long the alert should remain in the Alerts snapshot. The default setting is One Month, but you can use the drop-down list to choose One Day, One Week, One Month, One Quarter, or One Year.

When you're completely finished setting alerts, click OK to close the Alerts Center window. The alerts will work quietly in the background, watching your financial dealings. When it's time to go to work, they appear as you specified.

Working with Alerts

Once you've set up alerts, you can view, modify, or delete them as desired. Here's how.

- **Viewing Alerts**   View alerts in the Show All tab of the Alerts Center window. Click Tools | Alerts Center | Show All to display them.
- **Modifying Alerts**   Change the way an alert works at any time. Open the Tools menu, and choose Alerts Center | Setup. Then follow the instructions in the previous section titled "Setting Up Alerts" to change alert settings.
- **Deleting Alerts**   To delete an alert, display the Show All tab of the Alerts Center. Click the Delete button beside each alert you want to delete. A confirmation dialog appears. Click OK to delete the alert.

To prevent a deleted alert from appearing again, use the Setup tab of the Alerts Center window to clear the check box for the alert in the list on the left side of the window.

You can select multiple alerts and click one of the selected Delete buttons to delete all of the selected alerts. To select multiple alerts, click the first alert, then hold down SHIFT and click the last alert you want to delete. Click any of the Delete buttons within the highlighted selection.

Reconciling Your Accounts and Examining Your Banking Activity

Chapter 5

Once you have set up your banking and credit card accounts, it is important that you reconcile your Quicken information to that shown by your financial institution. Often, the task of reconciling or manually balancing your bank account each month is not your favorite chore. However, you may open your bank statement each month and, using the paper form and a hand calculator, total all the checks and deposits. There's a lot of adding when it comes to totaling the outstanding checks and deposits, and the longer you wait to do the job, the more adding you'll need to do. And for some reason, it hardly ever comes out right the first time you try. Maybe you've even failed so many times that you've given up.

In the first part of this chapter, you will learn why it is important to reconcile your bank statements and how you can do it, quickly and easily, with Quicken Personal Finance Software.

Reconciling Bank Accounts

Reconciling an account refers to the process of comparing transactions in your account register to transactions on the account statement sent to you by your bank. Transactions that match are simply checked off. You'll need to account for transactions that appear only in one place such as in your account register or the bank's account statement.

In this section, you'll review the basics of reconciling a bank account with Quicken: comparing transactions, making adjustments, and finishing up.

Starting a Reconciliation

You may reconcile your bank statement with the traditional paper statement sent by your bank or reconcile your account online. We'll begin with the paper statement with which you may already be familiar.

Open the account register for the account you want to reconcile. Click the Actions gear icon at the top far-right of the register, as seen here. Choose Reconcile. What happens next depends on whether the account is enabled for online access.

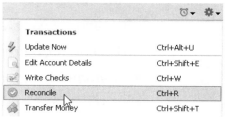

 Quicken does not supply a reconciliation form for cash accounts. However, you can update the balance, which marks the cash transactions with an "R" to indicate they have been reconciled.

Accounts Without Online Account Access

If the account is *not* enabled for online access, the Reconcile Details dialog, which is shown next, appears. It gathers basic statement information prior to reconciling the account. Enter information from your bank statement in the appropriate boxes. (Enter service charge and interest earned information only if you have not already entered it in the account register.) Then click OK to continue.

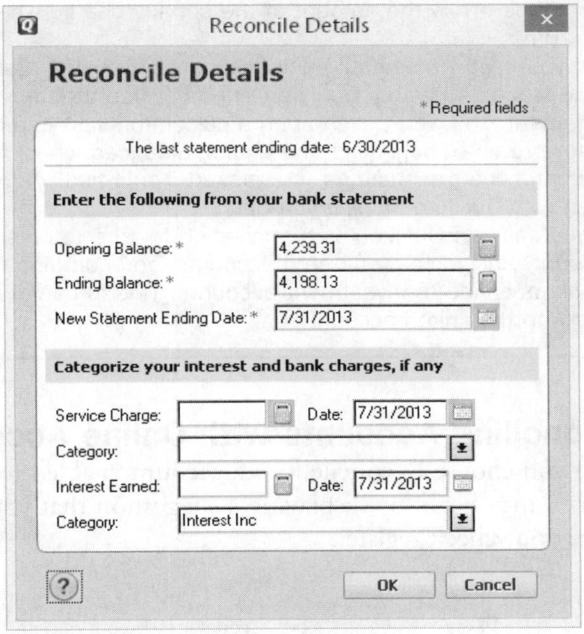

IN MY EXPERIENCE

While reconciling online may save you time, there are advantages to using your paper statement when reconciling your account:

- Paper statements make it easier to spot errors by your bank.
- Using a paper statement may help remind you of future payments you've authorized but not yet entered into your Quicken register, especially if you have not chosen to display your reminders.
- You may have forgotten to enter a debit card purchase or even a check. Using a paper statement will remind you to enter those transactions into your Quicken check register.

IN MY EXPERIENCE

Whether or not you are using an account with online access, be sure that the New Statement Ending Date that you enter in the Reconcile Details dialog is the same as the ending date shown on the paper statement. Several of my clients have inadvertently entered the date they are doing the reconciliation instead of the bank statement's ending date and have been unable to quickly complete the reconciliation process. Also, ensure the service charge and interest income dates are the dates shown on the bank statement. If your statement is dated the 29th of the month and you inadvertently enter the service charge as of the 30th, you will be off by the amount of the service charge when trying to reconcile as of the 29th.

If you keep track of all bank account activity with Quicken, reconciling your bank accounts is easy. You won't need to use the form on the back of the bank statement. You won't even need a calculator. Just use Quicken's reconciliation feature to enter beginning and ending balances, check off cleared transactions, and enter the transactions you missed. You'll find you're successful a lot more often with Quicken helping you out.

You can use Quicken's reconciliation feature to balance any Quicken banking account—including credit card accounts. You can also reconcile checking accounts linked to investment accounts. This is useful if you write checks or pay bills with the linked account.

Reconciling Accounts with Online Account Access

When you choose Reconcile for an account enabled for Online Account Access, Quicken may begin by displaying a suggestion that you download transactions to update your check register.

Downloading Transactions   If your account is not up to date, take the time to go online and update your account. Downloading is the only way you can be sure that all transactions recorded by the bank are included in your account register, unless you enter everything by hand. Choose Download Transactions For This Account, and click OK to download this account's latest transactions.

The One Step Update Settings dialog appears. Enter your password for this account, and click Update Now. After your update is complete and you have accepted the downloaded transactions, the One Step Update Summary dialog box displays. Click Close to close it and return to the account's register. If you have downloaded transactions, you will see a dialog stating you have unaccepted transactions. Quicken asks if you want to review them or continue reconciling without reviewing or accepting the transactions as shown here. If you have gone online with Quicken before and you store your passwords in the Password Vault, you may see the prompt to enter/create your Intuit ID here.

 Depending on your Preferences settings, you may not see the One Step Update Summary unless there are errors during your download. Also, unless you have told Quicken to automatically enter your downloaded transactions into your banking account register, you will have to accept and match your downloaded transactions. See Appendix B for additional information on setting your Preferences in Quicken.

Reconciling Without Downloading

If you have opted not to update your online account, click Reconcile Without Downloading to continue with the reconciliation, and click OK. Click Cancel if you want to stop the reconciliation process entirely. After you are up to date, or if you have chosen not to update at this time, Quicken displays the Reconcile <account name> dialog shown at right.

As you can see, this dialog offers two options for reconciling the account:

- **Use Paper Statement** helps you reconcile the information in your Quicken account register to your bank statement. It is a traditional account reconciliation, and it works just like the account reconciliation you perform for an account without Online Account Access. If you select this option, enter the bank statement ending date and ending balance in the appropriate boxes. The opening balance is the sum of all of the transactions in the register with "R" in the Clr column.
- **Use Online Balance** enables you to reconcile the account to the balance that was last downloaded for the account. When you select this option, you don't have to enter anything in the boxes. Selecting the Auto Reconcile Downloaded Transactions check box tells Quicken to reconcile the account to your financial institution's online balance automatically each time you download and accept transactions. With this Auto Reconcile feature enabled, you never have to reconcile the account again. However, you must trust the bank to make no mistakes.

After selecting your option in this dialog, click OK to continue.

 The fact that the "opening balance" is the sum of all of the register transactions that have been marked with an "R" or a "c" can cause Quicken users some aggravation. If there are any changed transactions in the register, you may have to re-reconcile in order to obtain the correct beginning balance.

Comparing Transactions to a Paper Statement

The next step in reconciling the account is to compare transactions that have cleared on the statement with transactions in your account register. For this, Quicken displays the Reconcile window, shown next, which displays all payments, checks, and deposits for the account you are reconciling.

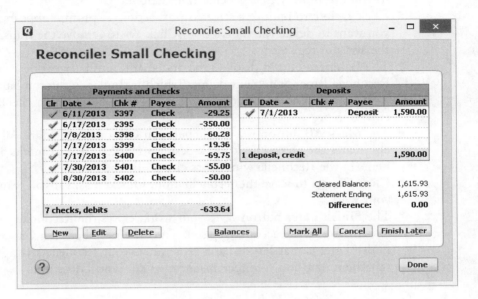

Understanding the Buttons

Quicken 2014 displays all of your button bar choices at the bottom of the Reconcile window, as seen in the above illustration. While by default the Reconcile window entries sort in ascending order with the most recent date at the bottom, you can sort the entries in either ascending or descending order by clicking the heading in each section. For example, to sort by check number, click Chk #. To reverse the order by which the column sorts, click the heading name a second time. Clicking any column heading re-sorts the columns in both the Deposits and the Payments and Checks sections. Use each button as follows.

- Click **New** to switch to the account register window for the account you are reconciling so you can enter a new transaction. To return to your reconciliation, click either the Reconcile:<name of account> button at the bottom-left corner of the check register or the Return To Reconcile button that displays at the top of your register to the left of the Search field.

The Return To Reconcile button works to return from both the New and Edit buttons.

- Select a transaction and click **Edit** to switch to the account register window so you can modify that selected transaction.
- Click **Delete** to remove a selected transaction. A prompt appears asking if you want to delete the transaction. Click Yes to remove the transaction from the account register.
- The **Balances** button displays the Statement Summary dialog or the Reconcile Paper Statement dialog (which is similar to the top half of the Reconcile Online Account dialog shown earlier) so you can check or change entries there.
- The **Mark All** button is a toggle between Clear All and Mark All that either eliminates the green check mark beside a marked item or marks all of the items in the Reconcile window as cleared by the bank.
- Click **Cancel** to leave the reconciliation. Quicken asks if you want to save your work.
- The **Finish Later** button saves your work, closes the Reconcile window, and returns you to the account register. The difference between Cancel and Finish Later is that Finish Later remembers your reconcile settings, such as statement date and reconcile balance, while Cancel does not.

To open the Quicken Help window when reconciling your accounts, click the question mark at the bottom-left corner of the Reconcile window. Click Done to close the Reconcile window.

Reconciling to a Bank Statement

While you're checking off transactions in Quicken and on your bank statement, look for differences between them. Here are some of the differences you might encounter:

- An item that appears on the bank statement but not in your account

---

IN MY EXPERIENCE

If you have set up Savings Goals (see Chapter 12), you may see "Contributions To Goals" or "Withdrawals From Goals" as items on your account register. These are only for your information and do not affect your bank account. To hide them while you are reconciling your account, click the Actions icon, and in the Register View And Preferences section, clear the Show Savings Goal Transactions In Register And Reports check box.

register is an item that you did not enter. You may have omitted the transaction for a number of reasons. Perhaps it was a bank adjustment that you didn't see. Or maybe you simply forgot to enter a check. To enter an omitted transaction, click the New button to switch to the register window. Enter the transaction in the register, click Enter, and click either the Reconcile:<account name> button at the bottom-left corner of the register or the Return To Reconcile button at the upper-right corner of your register to continue the reconciliation. Then click to place a check mark in the Clr column beside the item to mark it as cleared.

- An item that has a different date or amount in your register than that shown on the bank statement is usually due to an error, either yours or the bank's. If the error is yours, you can edit the transaction by double-clicking it in the Reconcile window. This displays the account register window with the transaction selected. Edit the transaction and click the Save button. Then click the Reconcile:<account name> button at the bottom-left corner of the register or the Return To Reconcile button at the upper-right corner of the register to continue the reconciliation.

- If the amount of an error is small, many people simply adjust their register to reflect what is shown by the bank, especially if the check has been written by hand. The check-reading machinery at the bank has sometimes mistaken the number 7 on my handwritten checks for a number 1, for example.

- Items that appear in your account register but not on the bank statement are items that have not yet cleared the bank. These are usually transactions prepared just before the bank's closing date, but they can be older. Do not

IN MY EXPERIENCE

A hidden field, Downloaded Posting Date, controls which transactions are presented in the Reconcile window for accounts with downloaded transactions. You can have this field display in your register by selecting the Actions icon | Register Columns. In the menu that appears, check Downloaded Posting Date, and a new column appears on your register next to the Date column. This is handy information if transactions you expect to appear in the current reconcile do not appear—the date the bank posted the transaction may be outside the date range of your reconciliation. Notice on the same menu there are other fields you can show in your register as well such as Downloaded Payee and Downloaded Memo. While these may not have any effect on your reconciliation, the fields may make categorizing these downloads easier. After you have made your choices, click Done to close the menu.

☐	Downloaded Amount
☐	Downloaded ID
☐	Downloaded Memo
☐	Downloaded Payee
☑	Downloaded Posting Date
☐	Downloaded Reference
☑	Action Buttons

✿▼   Done

check them off. Chances are you'll check them off the next time you reconcile. If, during a bank reconciliation, you discover any uncleared items that are older than two or three months, you should investigate why they have not cleared the bank. You may discover that a check (or worse yet, a deposit) was lost in transit.

Reconciling to an Online Balance

If you've recently downloaded and accepted transactions for the account, reconciling to an online balance shouldn't take much time. Items you've already reviewed and accepted will be checked off. Some more recent transactions may not be checked off because they haven't yet cleared your bank. Your job is to look for older transactions that appear in your Quicken account register that aren't checked off. These could represent stale payments that may have been lost in transit to the payee or errors (or duplications) you made when manually entering information into your Quicken account register. Follow up on all transactions more than 60 days old to see why they haven't been included with your downloaded transactions.

Identifying Reconciled Items

When you download your transactions during the month, Quicken marks the Clr column with a "c" because the transaction has been posted at the bank. This does not mean it has been formally reconciled. Once you have finished the reconciliation, whether reconciling to a paper statement or using the online balance as your accepted balance, Quicken will mark each of the transactions in the Clr column with a capital "R," meaning the transaction has been reconciled.

You can change a "c" to an "R" or clear the Clr column entirely. Click in the column to bring up the menu, as shown here. Be careful about changing a reconciled item unless you are making corrections. Quicken uses the Clr column in an account register to identify items that either have cleared the bank or have been reconciled:

If you want to change a transaction's cleared status, choose from the following:

- **Uncleared** indicates that the transaction has not yet been cleared by the bank.
- **Cleared** indicates that the bank has cleared the item, but the item has not yet been reconciled.
- **Reconciled** shows that the item has been reconciled. To make it even more obvious that a transaction either has cleared your financial institution or has

been reconciled, reconciled transactions appear in gray print rather than black.
- **Reconcile** CTRL-R begins the reconcile process as discussed earlier in this chapter.

You can toggle the gray color of reconciled transactions to black by clicking Edit | Preferences | Register | Register Appearance and unchecking Gray Reconciled Transactions. Gray Reconciled Transactions is the default.

Finishing Up

When you reconcile a bank account with Quicken, your goal is to make the difference between the cleared balance and the statement ending balance zero. You can monitor this progress at the bottom of the Reconcile window, as seen earlier.

When the Difference Is Zero

If you correctly checked off all bank statement items and the difference is zero, you've successfully reconciled the account and you can click the Done button.

If You Can't Get the Difference to Zero

Sometimes, try as you might, you just can't get the difference to zero. Here are a few last things to check before you give up:

- Make sure all the amounts you checked off in your account register are the same as the amounts on the bank statement. Keep in mind that if you made a transposition error—for example, 87.91 instead of 87.19—the difference between the two amounts will be evenly divisible by 9. In this case, 87.91 minus 87.19 is .72—a number evenly divisible by 9.
- Make sure you included any bank charges or earned interest.
- Make sure the ending date and balance you entered are the same as those on the bank statement.
- Check to see if any of the deposits were entered as checks or checks as deposits.
- Verify that none of the transactions were entered twice.
- Watch for penny differences. Occasionally the bank will see an 8 as a 3 or a 4 as a 1.
- Ensure that the opening balance shown in the Reconcile Details dialog matches your statement's opening balance. If there is a difference, you may have deleted or changed a previously reconciled transaction.

If you checked and rechecked all these things and still can't get the difference to zero, click Done. Quicken displays a message indicating the amount of the difference and offers to make an adjustment to your account register for the amount. Click Adjust to accept the adjustment. The amount of the adjustment will be recorded without a category. If you want to continue trying to find the difference, click Cancel to return to the Reconcile window.

IN MY EXPERIENCE

From time to time a deposit shows on the bank statement that does not seem to match anything in your register. It is possible you've deposited two or more checks together at the bank yet entered the deposits separately in your register. If you often have several checks to deposit at the same time, create a split deposit as explained in Chapter 3. This way, the total deposit will match the bank statement.

If any of the checks in a group is a "form," such as a payroll check, consider using two deposit slips so that each deposit shows separately on the bank statement. Some folks even use an Undeposited Checks account in Quicken where they enter the individual checks, then enter a transfer from the Undeposited Checks account to their checking account in the total amount of the group, because it is that total that will appear on your bank statement.

Be careful of old checks you have written that may suddenly clear. A good example of this is a check you wrote as a donation to a local charity. It may sit in someone's desk for several months before that person notices it and puts it into the bank. Each bank has their own policy on "stale-dated" checks, meaning that only checks within a certain period are honored. However, checks can slip through with dates as old as last year!

Other Reconciliation Tasks and Features

Quicken offers a number of other reconciliation features that you might find useful. Here's a quick look at them.

Reconciling Credit Card Accounts

You can reconcile a credit card account the same way you reconcile a bank account. If you try to enter all credit card transactions as you make them throughout the month, it's a good idea to use the reconciliation feature to compare your entries to the credit card statement, just to make sure you didn't miss any. If you simply enter all credit card transactions when you get your statement, reconciling to the statement really isn't necessary.

However, if you are going by what is on your credit card statement, you're counting on your financial institution to be correct. If you just enter in the transactions from your credit card statement, you may miss fraudulent charges or mistakes made by your financial institution.

When you access your credit card accounts online, you can quickly download or manually record your credit card transactions into your Quicken credit card account register. You can also use the Quicken Mobile app to enter your credit card charges as you make them!

Many Quicken users go online frequently to view both their bank account and credit card balances to ensure there are no fraudulent or unidentified charges.

Reconcile a Credit Card Without Online Access

Choose the account you want to reconcile from the Account Bar to open that account's register. Press CTRL-R to begin the reconciliation. When you reconcile an account for which you have not enabled Online Access, Quicken displays the Reconcile: Credit Card dialog as shown next.

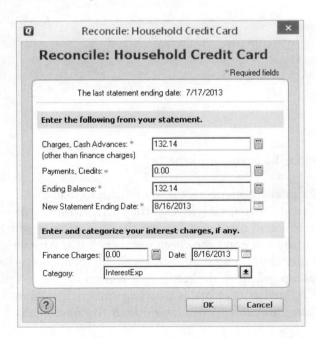

As you can see, Quicken asks for the total charges, including cash advances, you made during the billing period as well as any payments or credits that have been made on the account. You can find this information on your paper credit card statement. Enter the new statement ending date, any finance charges, and the date they were assessed. Note the red asterisks by the required fields. You must enter a number or date in these fields, even if the number is zero. Click OK to move to the Reconcile window, which looks and works almost exactly like the Reconcile window that was shown earlier.

As shown earlier, as you click each cleared transaction, a small green check mark appears. Click Mark All to clear every transaction shown in the Reconcile window. Click Done when the Difference field shows zero. A dialog appears asking if you want to make a payment on that credit card now, as shown next. If you choose to make a payment now, first select the account from which you want to make the payment from the Bank Account drop-down list.

Select the payment method:

- Printed Check opens the Write Checks dialog.
- Hand Written Check posts the check (without the check number) in the credit card register and opens the register from which that check was written so you can enter the check number of that handwritten check. Until you enter the check number and save the transaction, the check does not appear as a payment in the credit card register.
- Online Payment opens a message that online payments are not active for this account. Click OK to continue. If you have enabled an account for online

payments, this opens the Write Checks windows with the Use Online Bill Pay option checked and the payment fields populated.

If you do not want to be reminded to make a payment after each reconciliation, click Don't Show Me This Screen Again.

If you turn off this warning once and want to see it again, you will have to reset all of your warnings. Click Edit | Preferences | Alerts | Reset Quicken Warnings. Then click OK to close the Preferences dialog.

Click Yes if you have chosen one of the payment options and click No if you will be making the payment later.

You return to the account register, where you will see each reconciled transaction displays an "R" in the Clr column.

Reconcile a Credit Card with Online Access Enabled

Open the register for the credit card account you want to reconcile. Click the Actions icon | Reconcile. Quicken prompts you to either download any current transactions or proceed to the reconciliation process without downloading. See "Reconciling Accounts with Online Account Access" earlier in this chapter for more information. For this example, we are choosing to reconcile without downloading.

Click Reconcile Without Downloading, and click OK to proceed. The Reconcile Online Account window for the current account appears. Note this

window's similarity to the dialog for checking accounts. You may choose to reconcile to a paper statement, in which case you must enter a value (which can be zero) in each of the fields. If you accept the online balance method, note the Balance As Of date and recognize that the balance displayed is what the bank has cleared as of that date.

If you have chosen to reconcile the account to your online balance, click Auto Reconcile Downloaded Transactions to change the "c" in the Clr column of your register to an "R."

After you have completed the reconciliation, if there is a balance on the account, Quicken asks if you want to make a payment. If you choose to make a payment, select the bank account from the drop-down list and tell Quicken if you are going to print a check through Quicken or write the check or pay online. If your choice is to print or write a check, the Write Checks window displays. If you choose Online Payment, the Write Checks dialog also opens with an option to use Online Bill Pay if you have enabled that feature. If you choose not to make a payment at this time, click No.

When your credit card balance is zero, a message box appears stating that there is no payment required, as you have an outstanding balance of zero. Click OK to close the message box.

Adjusting Your Register

If you can't successfully get the credit card reconciliation to work, Quicken offers to make adjustments. If you simply cannot balance an account, use the Adjust Balance dialog to make your adjustments. Choose a date for the adjustment, and click Adjust to make the entry, which will show as a balance adjustment in your register as of the date you enter in this dialog.

Be careful about clicking any Don't Show Me This Screen Again check boxes. You only get one chance to do this, and at some point, you may want to see the dialog. To do so, you will need to reset the Quicken Warnings preference. Click Edit | Preferences | Alerts | Warnings | Reset Quicken Warnings.

Streamline Your Reconciliations

To make the reconciliation process even easier, you can place a reconciliation tool on the Quicken toolbar. To do so, from the Quicken menu bar, click View | Customize Toolbar. Scroll to Reconcile An Account, and click the Add button. This moves the Reconcile An Account button to the right side of the screen. You may move the Reconcile An Account button to another position with the Move Up or Move Down buttons in the Customize Toolbar dialog. Once you are satisfied with the location of the new button, click OK. The Reconcile An

Account button appears on your Quicken Toolbar, as seen at right.

Still quicker is adding a reconcile button to the top of your register. Click the Action icon (the small gear symbol at the top far-right of the register). From the menu, choose Customize Action Bar. In the list of Available Toolbar Buttons, choose Reconcile and click Add. A Reconcile icon appears pinned to the top of the register to the left of your Actions gear icon. Click Done to close the dialog. The reconcile icon is a small white check mark inside a green circle.

If you change back to using your paper statements after using online reconciliations, Quicken warns you the change may cause a problem.

Printing a Reconciliation Report

After you have completed an account reconciliation, Quicken displays a dialog that offers to create a reconciliation report, as seen next. If you click Yes, the Reconciliation Report Setup dialog appears. Give the report a title if you wish, set the date at which the balance is to be shown, and tell Quicken to show either all of the transactions as of the bank balance date or just a summary of all the transactions and each transaction that has not yet cleared the bank.

The reconciliation report is only available for bank accounts, not credit card reconciliations!

Click OK to open the Print dialog shown next. You may choose to print the report on paper or to the Quicken PDF printer, as seen in the illustration. Saving your report as a .pdf file allows you to electronically store the report in a location you choose on your hard drive. If your report is a long one, you can choose to print just one or two pages. In the Print Range section of the Print dialog, click Pages and enter the page number from which you wish to start in the From field and the page number with which you want to end in the To field.

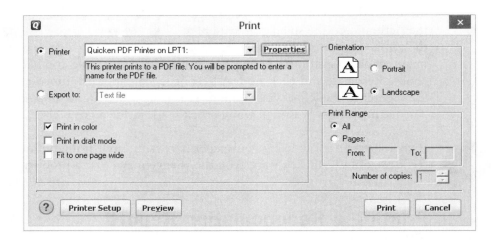

When you have finished making your choices, click Print to print the report.

You can print a current reconciliation report at any time. Open the register for which you want the report, and from the Reports menu, click Banking | Reconciliation to open the Reconciliation Report Setup dialog.

Since Quicken does not save copies of your reconciliations from previous months, if your reconciliation required an adjusting entry, it might be a good idea to document it by creating a report, either as a .pdf or a paper copy. You can then file the paper report with your bank statement and canceled checks, or store the .pdf with an electronic copy of your statement and pictures of your processed checks. To ensure you have a copy, either print a hard copy or save your report as a .pdf through the Quicken PDF Printer.

Undoing Reconciled Transactions

At times, you may have to clear previously reconciled transactions or even undo an entire reconciliation. Be aware, this is not recommended! However, computers are not always consistent, banks occasionally merge and their records get skewed, a user will sometimes make a mistake and so on. Before you make any changes to any reconciled transaction, do a backup of your data. See Appendix A for instructions on creating a backup.

To unclear a transaction you have inadvertently marked as reconciled:

1. Select the transaction and click in the Clr column.
2. Change the notation to Uncleared if it has not been downloaded or to Cleared if the transaction has cleared the bank.

If you need to clear several transactions in a row:

1. Click the first of the transactions, hold down your SHIFT key, and click the last transaction in the group.
2. Note that each selected transaction is highlighted. Right-click someplace within the highlighted area, and from the context menu that appears, click Reconcile and choose either Not Reconciled or Cleared.
   • Quicken opens a prompt asking if you want to mark the currently selected transactions. Choose Yes to mark the selected transactions and No to cancel the change.
   • Each transaction in the group now shows that it has not been cleared.

If the transactions you want to change are not in a row (listed one after the other), follow the procedure shown in Step 1, but hold down your CTRL key and click each transaction you want to change. These transactions are selected and you can continue.

A Closer Look at the Spending Tab

By now, you may agree that entering financial information into Quicken Personal Finance Software is a great way to organize it. However, sometimes organizing information isn't enough. Sometimes you need to see concise summaries of the information you entered in the form of balances, activity reports, and graphs.

Quicken provides the kind of information you're looking for in the form of snapshots, reports, and graphs. The next sections discuss Quicken's Spending tab by telling you about the snapshots of the information found there and how you can take advantage of its alerts. We also explain how you can create, modify, and save standard and custom reports and graphs for all Quicken tabs.

The Spending tab offers a place for examining the results of your work with your banking accounts. You will go on a guided tour of the Spending tab's reporting and graphing features so you can take advantage of all of the elements found in that section of Quicken.

Exploring the Spending Graph

When you click the Spending tab, a graph appears that displays the total amount (see Figure 5-1) you have spent from all of your banking accounts for the last 30 days. The top of the window shows the total in all categories. Next is a colorful pie chart with a legend to the right explaining the category associated with each of the "pie slices." The lower part of the window displays the transactions in register format.

If you choose to hide an account from the Transaction Entry List in the Display Options tab and its name in the account bar and account list, the account will not show on the Account Bar, but will show in the Spending tab list of accounts. (Accounts you have designated as Keep Separate will not show in the Spending tab list of accounts, but you can choose them using the Custom entry in the Accounts drop-down list.)

Figure 5-1 • Use the Spending tab information to generate a number of graphs and reports.

Account Filter

The Accounts drop-down list lets you decide which accounts to display in the Spending graph. You can choose from the following:

- **All Accounts**, which includes all of the accounts that appear in the Banking section of the Account Bar.

If you pay from a brokerage account, you must use the Custom account setting from the drop-down list and select the account from that list.

- **All Checking/Savings/Cash/Credit Cards** includes the accounts you have so named in Quicken.
- At the bottom of the drop-down list, all of your banking accounts are listed so that you can choose to use just one in your Spending graph.
- Choose Custom to open the Customize dialog, which allows you to choose more than one account to display in your graph. You can choose to display all of your accounts, even your hidden ones by selecting Show (Hidden Accounts) and Select All, shown next. The Customize dialog lists all of your accounts, not just your banking accounts.

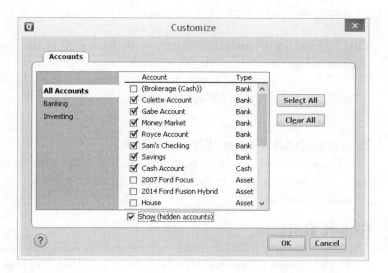

If you don't see the accounts you expected, use the Manage Hidden Accounts dialog to change your account settings. From the menu bar, select Tools | Manage Hidden Accounts.

Date Filter

While the default for your Spending graph is the last 30 days, you can use this drop-down list to choose any time period you wish. The pre-set options are:

- **All Dates**, which includes every date for which you have entered a transaction into Quicken.
- **This Month**, which displays just the spending you've done since the first of the current month and includes future-dated transactions that occur in the selected month.
- **Last Month** includes your expenditures in the last calendar month.
- **Last 30/60/90 Days** options are self-explanatory.
- **Last 12 Months** includes all of your expenditures for the last 365 days (or 366 days in leap years).
- **This Quarter** includes the information from the first day of this calendar quarter through the end of the calendar quarter.
- **Last Quarter** presents your spending for the most recent calendar quarter before this quarter.
- **This Year** presents all of your spending through the end of the current year, starting with January 1.
- **Last Year** displays all of last year's spending.
- **Custom** lets you set the date range for your graph.

This Month, This Quarter, and This Year display all of the spending for those respective time periods, even future dated transactions. For example, if today is 11/9/2014 and you have a transaction entered for 11/20/2014, the 11/20/2014 transaction will show in the spending for This Month, This Quarter, and This Year.

Transaction Types Filter

The Income/Spending drop-down list has only two options. You can choose to show how much you have spent (Spending) or how much has been added to your accounts (Income).

Reset Button

The Reset button, located to the right of the Spending/Income drop-down list, resets your graph to the default of All Accounts, Last 30 Days, and Spending.

Search Field

Enter a category or payee name in the Search field at the far right of the Spending tab view. After you

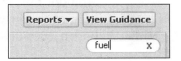

have typed in the name, the register displays the category, payee, or account name that you have entered. The register will show all of the transactions with that name for the time period and accounts you have selected. Click the red X to clear the field.

You can also enter an amount or memo text in the Search field. If the amount is greater than 1,000, you'll need to include the comma: 1,000.

Using the Spending Register

The register shown at the bottom of the Spending tab's Transaction view displays all of the transactions from the accounts you have chosen in the Accounts drop-down list at the top of the Spending graph. You may choose to include an Account column, in which Quicken displays the account into which the transaction was entered. To show this column, click the Register Columns gear icon and select Account.

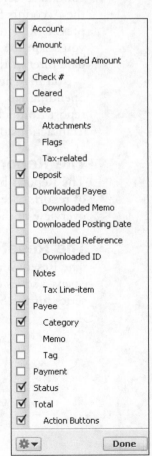

By default, this register is sorted by date, with the earliest date first. If you have chosen more than one account, the amounts shown in the Total column may not be useful. However, if you want to know how much you've spent at a particular store, use the Search field and set the Account Filter to All Accounts. After you type in the name of that specific store, the total you have spent for the time period you have set will display at the bottom of the register in the Total column.

You can tell Quicken which columns to display and which columns to hide. To access the list of Register Columns, click the small gear icon at the upper-right corner of the register. When you click the icon, the Register Columns list will appear as shown here. Click the check box for each column you want the register to display. Clear each check box for columns you don't want to use. When you have finished your selections, click Done. If you find you do not like the way your selections look, click the gear icon once more and, at the bottom left corner of the column list, click the gear icon drop-down arrow and click Reset To Default Columns. Once again, click Done to close the list.

Your Register Columns list may not look the same as the one in the illustration. Listed items and order vary by the type of account and the services you have activated on each account.

You can adjust the width of each of the register columns by placing your cursor on the line between two columns and dragging to the left or right. The default one-line display shows the Date, Payee, Category, and Amount columns. You can display additional columns by selecting from the Register Columns list. Click the gear icon at the right of the register to display the list.

The Spending Tab's Register

The register you see in the Spending tab is different from the individual registers you see for each banking and credit card account. The register you see here may contain information from more than one account, depending on your settings in the Accounts filter's drop-down list. To print from the Spending tab register, press CTRL-P to open the Print Register dialog. The date range will be the range you set in the Date Filter's drop-down list. To change the date range, adjust the date filter in the Spending tab.

You may not see your split transactions in the report you print from the Spending tab. To see the report with splits properly displayed, run the same report from a banking account register. Click the Actions gear icon | Print Transactions or press CTRL-P from the register.

The Reports Button

The Reports button in the Spending tab makes it easy for you to print a variety of reports. See "Creating Reports and Graphs" later in this chapter for an overview of the reports that Quicken can produce for you.

The Reset Guidance Button

The Reset Guidance button at the top right of the Spending tab's snapshots opens a series of tips and suggestions to help you. Shown next is the first of the series for the Spending tab. Click Next to read them all. As you cycle through

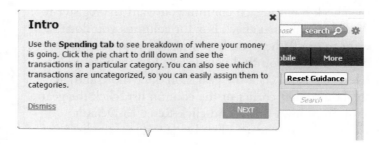

the tips, each tip will open in another part of the Spending tab's view with an explanation of that section. Click Dismiss (or Close) to close the box.

If you have converted from an earlier version of Quicken and turn the Reset Guidance messages off, you may not see them in Quicken 2014.

Quicken Reports Overview

Quicken offers a variety of reports and graphs, each of which can be customized to meet your needs. When you spend time entering data into Quicken, Quicken crunches the numbers for you, provides reports and graphs to analyze your spending habits, helps you find ways to save money, and formats your data to submit information to financial institutions when you apply for loans or credit cards.

While the Reports button in the Spending tab offers nine reports that you can create dealing with spending and income, there are many other reports available in Quicken. And not just in the Spending tab. You can access reports from the Reports button in the Planning tab, the Reports And Graphs window, and, if you use Classic menus, you can use the Spending and Planning menus as well. In this section, you'll learn about the various types of reports and graphs Quicken offers. Then you'll see how you can use a variety of techniques to quickly create reports and graphs based on the information in your Quicken data file, regardless of where it appears.

Reviewing Report and Graph Types

Within Quicken are two kinds of reports and graphs. Quicken creates a number of standard reports. By starting with any of the standard reports, you can create customized reports and save them as your own versions. Here's an overview of each one.

Standard Quicken Reports

When you click Reports on the menu bar, Quicken displays a number of standard reports and graphs, organized by topic: Banking, Comparison, Investing, Net Worth & Balances, Spending, Tax, EasyAnswer, and Graphs. If you do not see the Net Worth & Balances reports section, turn on the Property & Debt tab by clicking View | Tabs To Show | Property & Debt.

This section discusses standard reports found in the Deluxe edition of Quicken 2014. If you are using the Premier, Home & Business, or Rental Property Manager versions of Quicken, you have additional reports available.

IN MY EXPERIENCE

Many Quicken users have found that reports are their reward for taking the time to enter, download, and reconcile their accounts. You can quickly create a report of everything you've spent on automobile repair since the first of the year, for example, or summarize your total income from your second job.

Your tax preparer may appreciate you even more when you walk in the office next January with a complete list of all of your income, every expense, including your itemized charitable contributions, and property tax amounts. Those reports may even save you some money when that tax person sends your bill!

For example, the Banking report options include Banking Summary, Cash Flow, Cash Flow By Tag, Missing Checks, Reconciliation, and Transaction reports. These reports and graphs clearly show banking-related information. EasyAnswer reports and graphs, as seen at right, answer specific, predefined questions, such as, "Where did I spend my money during the period…?" and "How much did I spend on…?" You select a question and then provide optional information, such as a date range, payee, or account. Quicken gathers the information and generates the report or graph.

▼ **EasyAnswer**
🔲 ⬤ Where did I spend my money during the period…?
🔲 How much did I spend on …?
🔲 How much did I pay to …?
🔲 Am I saving more or less?
🔲 Has my spending changed in this category?
🔲 ⬤ What am I worth?
🔲 ⬤ Did I meet my budget?
🔲 What taxable events occurred?
🔲 ⬤ How are my investments performing?
🔲 ⬤ What are my investments worth?

Customized and Saved Reports

You can create custom reports and graphs based on standard reports and graphs. This multiplies your reporting capabilities, enabling you to create reports or

---

IN MY EXPERIENCE

Recently a client asked how he could find the beginning and ending balance on his transaction report from last month. When he looked at the report again, he saw that the beginning balance for the account (or accounts if you've included more than one bank account) is shown at the top of the report and the ending balance shows on the bottom line entitled "Balance." You may find as well that most of the Quicken reports do have the information you need—you just have to look a bit at the report you've created.

Another person asked why one of her checks showed up in the Income category of her report. When she double-clicked that transaction, she found she had entered that check into the register with an income category rather than an expense category. Once she found the error, it was easily corrected—she just had to change the category.

---

graphs that show exactly what you need to show. When you save your custom reports and graphs, they can be recalled, with just a few mouse clicks, to display current information.

Creating Reports and Graphs

With Quicken, creating a report or graph is as simple as clicking a few buttons. You can use several techniques: choosing a report or graph from the Reports menu, setting options in the Reports And Graphs window, using the Reports button, and choosing commands from contextual menus. In this section, you'll learn to use all of these techniques.

Reports & Graphs Center

The Reports And Graphs window (see Figure 5-2) offers one way to create reports and graphs. Open the Spending, Planning, or Investing tab, and from the Reports button, choose All Reports | Reports & Graphs Center to display it. You can also access the Reports & Graphs Center from the Quicken menu bar by clicking Reports | Reports & Graphs Center.

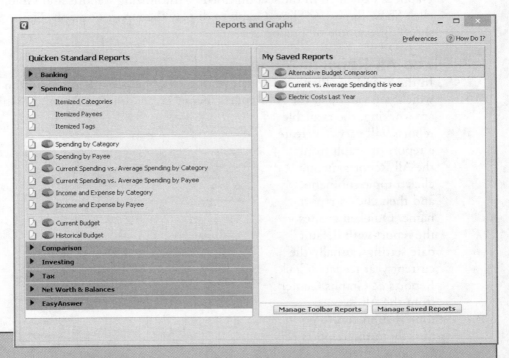

Figure 5-2 • **Use the Reports & Graphs Center to create reports to better understand your financial position.**

Consider adding the Reports & Graphs Center icon to your Quicken Toolbar to open the center without using menus.

Click one of the topics in any of the Quicken Standard Reports sections to display a list of the available reports and graphs. The icon that appears to the left of the report name indicates whether you are choosing a report or a graph. In the example shown here, we are creating a report, as indicated by the report icon. Those items that have both the graph and the report symbol to their left let you choose between the two when you create the report.

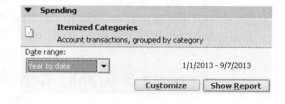

To create a report or graph, click its name. Set the Date Range option in the settings field. Click the Customize button to further customize the report or graph, as explained in the section titled "Customizing Reports and Graphs." Then click Show Report or Show Graph to display the report or graph. Figure 5-3 shows an example of a report.

The All Reports Menu

In the Spending, Planning, and Investing tabs, you see a Reports button from which you can open the All Reports menu. Depending on the tab in which you are working, the available reports will vary. To create a report or graph from the All Reports menu, click a topic submenu, and then click a report name. Quicken creates the report with default date settings, usually the current year to date. Click Reports & Graphs Center from the All Reports topical submenu to go directly to the Reports & Graphs Center.

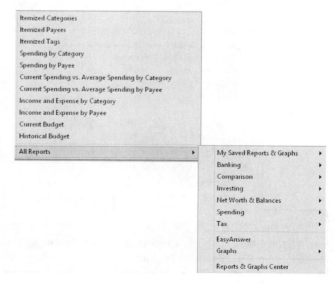

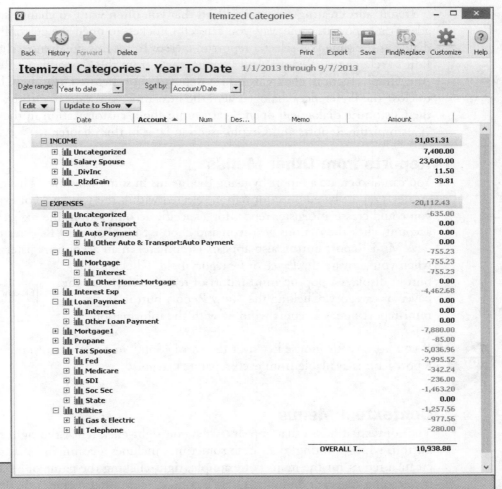

Figure 5-3 • **Quicken's standard reports make understanding your financial picture clear.**

If you have chosen to customize all of your reports and graphs before creating them in Quicken Preferences, a Customize dialog appears before the report is displayed.

You can sort from within reports using the Sort By drop-down lists or by clicking many of the headings.

If you start creating reports and find that you often want to change settings or adapt the report in some way, you can tell Quicken to open the customization dialog at the time you select a report to create. To set this preference, click Edit | Preferences | Reports And Graphs; then, from the Customizing Reports And Graphs section, click Customize Report/Graph Before Creating. Close OK to close the Preferences dialog. Then, the next time you want to create a report, the Customize dialog will open. Learn more about customization in the "Customizing Reports and Graphs" section later in this chapter.

Reports from Other Menus

You can also create a report by using the menus in some windows. This normally creates a report based on information selected within the window. For example, you could create a Register report for a specific account. From the register for that account, click the Actions gear icon and choose More Reports | Register Report.

A Mini-Report button also appears (seen here) in an account register window when you activate the Payee or Category field. Clicking this button displays a pop-up mini-report of recent activity for the payee or category. Clicking the Show Report button in the mini-report opens a report window with the information.

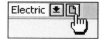

If you hover your mouse key over the word "Split" in a transaction, the mini-report icon is available from each separate category.

Contextual Menus

The contextual menu that appears when you right-click (click the right mouse button) while pointing to an item sometimes includes a command that will create a report for the item. For example, right-clicking the name of a payee in the account register window displays a context menu that includes the Payments Made To and Launch Mini-Report For Payee *nnnnn* at the bottom of that context menu. If you right-click a deposit's payee, the report will be Payments Received From.

Working with Reports and Graphs

Although Quicken's standard reports and graphs often provide just the information you need, you may want to do more with them. In this section, you will see how you can customize reports and graphs, save the reports and graphs you create so they're easy to recall, and print reports and graphs so you have hard copies when you need them.

Working with a Report Window

When you create a report or graph, it appears in a report window, as seen in Figure 5-3. Each report or graph has a number of features and options, discussed next and as seen below, with which you can customize the report to meet your specific needs.

Toolbar Icons

The report window includes a number of toolbar icons, seen above, that work with report contents:

- The **Back** arrow returns you to the Reports & Graphs Center when you have created your report from that center. The arrow does not appear if you have created your report from a Reports button within the Spending, Planning, or Investment tab. If you have created a subreport, you may see both forward and back arrows.
- The **History** icon displays a list of the parent report and all subreports you have created, as shown here. Click the History icon and select the name of a subreport to display it. Choose the Show Report List option to display the Report History navigation bar. This is a list of all of the subreports related to the current report. Click the Hide Report List to close the navigation bar.

- The **Forward** arrow is available only if you have clicked the Back button, and it allows you to move through subreports.

- The **Delete** icon deletes the report from the current Report History List. This button is gray if the report has not been added to the report list. See more about the report list in the section "Saving Reports and Graphs," later in this chapter.
- Click the **Print** icon to send the report or graph to the printer or a file.

- Click the **Export** icon to display a menu as shown at right. From this menu you can export the contents of the current report in several ways. See "Exporting Your Reports" later in this chapter.

Print	Export

Report to Excel compatible format

Copy report to Clipboard   Ctrl+C

Export to PDF format

- Select the **Save** icon to save the current report. See "Saving Reports and Graphs" later in this chapter for more information.
- The **Find/Replace** icon opens the Find And Replace dialog. See Chapter 3 for more information about using Find and Replace.
- Use the **Customize** icon, which looks like a small gear, to use the Customize dialog to tailor the currently displayed report.
- The last item on this toolbar is the familiar question mark **Help** icon.

Hiding or Displaying Report Detail

You can show or hide the details for some reports by clicking a plus (+) or minus (–) button beside a report line. Some reports include additional items that allow you to change what appears on the current report without using the Customize dialog. Shown next, these items appear under the report title and include:

> ### IN MY EXPERIENCE
>
> When you see Uncategorized as a category or payee on any report, double-click the amount to drill down to each transaction so that you can add a category or payee. Since many financial institutions download checks without your category, you may have quite a number of uncategorized transactions in one report. As explained in Chapter 4, ensure that you review each downloaded transaction and categorize it if necessary.

- The Expand All and Collapse All buttons do the same thing as the plus and minus signs by individual categories, but for all groups in that report.
- The Edit drop-down list, which displays in transactions reports, allows you to
  - Resolve a placeholder in an investment transaction report (if any exist)
  - Delete a selected transaction (or a group of transactions)
  - Recategorize the selected transaction (or group)

- Retag the selected transaction or group of transactions
- Rename selected payees
- Edit transaction memos

 When you double-click a transaction shown on a report, Quicken opens that transaction in the appropriate account register. You can return to the report by clicking the report's name at the bottom of the register.

- Date Range, Sort By, and Subtotal By fields allow you to change the focus of the current report.

Spending Trends

A very useful tool you will see in some Quicken Reports is the Spending Trend report. You see this symbol (shown here) in both the Spending by Payee and Spending by Category reports. Click the Spending Trend symbol to the left of a category or payee to see a small graph, shown next, that shows the trend for this category or payee over the last year. Click Done to close the graph and return to your report.

Category
▮▮ Birthday!
▮▮ BkChgs-Bank Charges

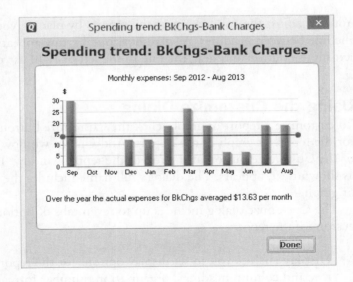

 To choose only one bank for a report, use the Accounts tab in the Customize dialog and clear the check marks from all the other accounts.

Customizing Reports and Graphs

You can customize just about any report or graph you create so it displays only the information you choose. Customization options vary from one type of report or graph to another, so it is impossible to cover all variables in this chapter. Here are the most common options so you know what to expect. When you can customize it, however, depends on how you create it:

- When you create a report or graph using the Reports And Graphs window (refer to Figure 5-2), you can customize it before or after you create it.
- When you create a report using other commands, you may be able to customize it only after you have created it, unless you have set your preferences to always display the Customize dialog.

 EasyAnswer reports do not display a Customize button when you create them from the Reports & Graphs Center; however, once the report is displayed on your screen, the Customize icon is available from the toolbar.

- Once your report appears on your screen, you can always customize that report with the Customize icon.

 You can adjust the columns on many reports by placing your mouse cursor on the line between headings. A small horizontal arrow appears. Hold down your left mouse button and drag the line to the left or right as you require.

Using the Customize Dialog

To customize a report or graph, click the Customize button in the options area for the report or graph in the Reports And Graphs window (refer to Figure 5-2) or the Customize button at the top of the report window. The Customize dialog, as shown next, appears. The dialog's full name includes the name of the report or graph.

The Customize dialog includes up to seven tabs of options that you can set to customize the report:

- **Display** enables you to set display options for the report, such as the title, row and column headings, organization, number formatting, and columns.
- **Accounts** lets you select the accounts that should be included in the report. Quicken will include transactions or balances in this report for only the accounts you specify.

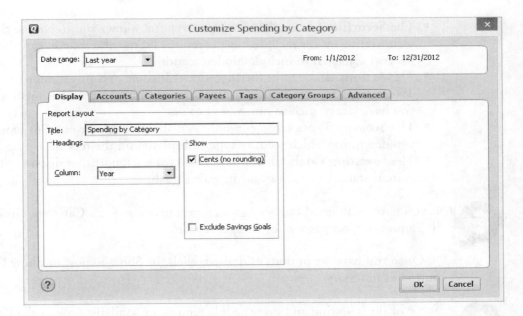

- From **Categories** you can select the categories to include in the report. If you choose, you can use this tab to include only transactions for which the payee, category, or memo contains certain text.

 Search Quicken Help for "match character," click the "How do I filter reports and graphs?" topic, and then expand "How do I enter match information?" in item 5. Use "match character" for sophisticated matching.

- The **Payees** tab shows options from which you can select the payees to include in the report. If desired, you can use this tab to include only transactions for which the category, payee, or memo contains certain text.
- The **Tags** tab lets you select the tags you want to show in your report.

 When working with split transactions where some items have tags and others do not, ensure you have cleared the Not Tagged check box in the Tags tab in the Customize dialog so that the non-tagged items are not included in your report.

- The **Advanced** tab offers different options, depending on the standard report with which you are working. For example, you can set additional criteria for transactions to be included in the report, such as amount, status, and transaction type. It is also from this Advanced tab that you can tell Quicken to exclude all transfers you make between your accounts.

- The **Securities** tab, available on some reports, allows you to choose the securities you want included in the report. From this tab, you can also instruct Quicken to include hidden securities.
- The **Actions** tab, seen in the Investment Income and Investment Transactions reports, lets you opt to display only certain investment actions you have taken, such as purchases or sales.
- The **Security Types** tab, again only available in some investment reports, lets you determine which security type is displayed on the report.
- The **Investing Goals** tab allows you to create a report that displays the current status of your various investing goals.

If you have established category groups, you may also see a Category Groups tab in Summary, Comparison, or Budget reports.

Once you have set options as desired, click the Show Report or Show Graph button as necessary.

Some of the investing and tax schedule reports are available only in the Premier or higher editions of Quicken.

If the custom report or graph isn't exactly what you want, that's okay. Just click the Customize button in the report or graph window and change settings in the Customize dialog to fine-tune the report or graph. When you click OK, Quicken creates a new report. You can repeat this process until the report or graph is exactly the way you want it.

Using QuickZoom
The QuickZoom feature enables you to create a report or graph on the fly. Simply double-click a report line item, graph bar, or legend item. Quicken generates and displays a *subreport* for the item you double-clicked. Click the Back arrow to return to your original report.

Working with Subreports
Each time you make changes to an existing report or graph, or create a QuickZoom report, Quicken creates a subreport. As you can imagine, it's easy to accumulate quite a few of these subreports when experimenting with Quicken's reporting features. This can be reduced somewhat by changing your preference settings. Select Edit | Preferences | Reports And Graphs | Customizing Reports And Graphs, and select Customizing Modifies Current Report Or Graph. Click OK to close the Preferences dialog.

To view a specific subreport, choose its name from the History menu in the report window's toolbar. The view changes to the report. You can also choose Show Report List from the History menu in the toolbar to display the Report History List. Click the name of the report you want to view to display it.

You can click the Back or Forward button at the top of the navigation bar to move among subreports you have already viewed.

To delete a subreport, display it and then click the Delete icon in the toolbar. You can also delete any subreport (other than the first one in the report list) by right-clicking the subreport name in the Report History List and selecting Delete This Report from the context menu.

Saving Reports and Graphs

You'll often create a predefined report and customize it to create a report you want to be able to see again and again. Rather than creating and customizing the report from scratch each time you want to see it, you can save the report's settings. Then, when you want to view the report again, just select it from a list and it appears. You can do the same for graphs.

Saving a Report or Graph

To save a report or graph, start by creating, customizing, and displaying it. When it looks just the way you want, click the Save icon in the report window's toolbar. The Save Report dialog appears.

Enter a name and description for the report or graph in the appropriate boxes. To save the report or graph in a specific folder, choose the folder name from the Save In drop-down list. You can create a new folder by clicking the Create New Report Folder option, which appears on the Save In drop-down list. Enter a name for the folder in the dialog that appears, and click OK. To save all versions of the report that you create, turn on the Save Report History check box. When you're finished setting options, click OK to save the report.

Viewing a Saved Report or Graph

When you save a report or graph, it appears in a number of places throughout Quicken, organized by folder if you have saved them into specific folders. Your saved reports and graphs appear in the My Saved Reports area of the Reports And Graphs window, as seen here. Click the name of the report or graph, change the date range if you choose, and click Show Report or Show Graph to display it.

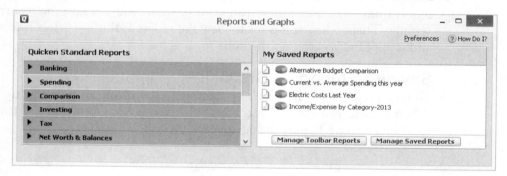

Saved reports and graphs also appear on the Reports menu as My Saved Reports & Graphs. (This submenu appears only if at least one report has been saved.) Choose a report name to display it. If you have a lot of saved reports, you will see an item, More Saved Reports & Graphs, which you can click to open the Reports And Graphs window.

Managing Saved Reports

Quicken offers two tools for managing saved reports: the Manage Saved Reports and Manage Toolbar Reports dialogs. When you choose the Reports & Graphs Center from the menu and look at the My Saved Reports pane, you may see one or two buttons at the bottom of the pane: Manage Toolbar Reports and Manage Saved Reports.

Manage Toolbar Reports   When you click the Manage Toolbar Reports button, its dialog appears. This dialog allows you to add saved reports to the Quicken

Toolbar for easy access. (This option appears only when you have chosen to show the Quicken Toolbar. Click View | Show Toolbar if you do not see this button on the My Saved Reports pane of the Reports And Graphs dialog.)

In the dialog, click the check box of each report you want to show as an icon in the Quicken Toolbar. Then, click OK to save your settings. You will see the icon on your toolbar. If the name is long, the entire name may not appear, as seen here. (If you do not see the text for your report's icon, right-click in the toolbar and choose Customize Toolbar | Show Icons And Text. Click Done to close the Customize Toolbar dialog.)

If you have created your own folders, as described next in "Managing Saved Reports," for your saved reports, you can choose to have one or more of those folders display on the Quicken Toolbar as well. When you click a saved report folder icon on the Toolbar, it will appear as a pop-up menu button that lists the reports within it. You can learn more about customizing the Quicken Toolbar in Appendix B.

Managing Saved Reports   The Manage Saved Reports dialog, shown next, enables you to organize saved reports by folder, edit report settings, or delete reports. Select the item you want to work with in the report list, and click a button:

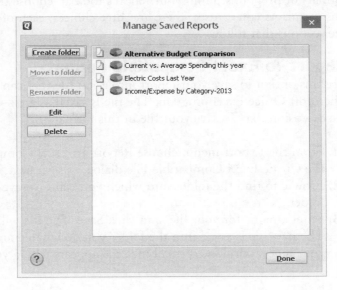

- **Create Folder** displays the Create New Report Folder dialog. Enter a name for the folder in the Name box, and click OK. The folder appears in the list.
- **Move To Folder** displays the Move To Report Folder dialog. When you select a report from the list, this button becomes available. Click the Move To Folder button to open the dialog, and select a different folder from the Name drop-down list. Click OK when you've made your choice, and the report is moved to that folder.
- Select a current folder, and the **Rename Folder** button becomes available. From the dialog that appears when you click this button, enter a new name for the folder in the Name box and click OK. The folder's name changes.
- When you have selected one of the saved reports, the **Edit** button is available for use. This button allows you to enter a new name and description for the report. Click OK to save your changes.
- **Delete** removes any selected item. When you click this button, a confirmation dialog appears. You must click OK to delete the item permanently. Remember, when you delete a folder you are deleting all the items in that folder. Should you want to save any of the items, move them before deleting the folder.
- **Done** closes the Manage Saved Reports dialog and returns you to the Reports And Graphs window.

Exporting Your Reports

Another method of working with your reports is to export them into other formats or programs. From your report's toolbar, choose the Export icon to view this menu. As you can see, there are three choices, each of which is explained in the sections that follow.

Report To Excel Compatible Format

Use this option to save your report into a .txt file that can be used with the Microsoft Office Excel program. The file is saved as a tab-delimited file with the file extension .txt. To save your file in this format:

1. From the Export menu, choose Report To Excel Compatible Format to open the Create Excel Compatible File dialog, as seen next.
2. Browse to find the folder into which you want to save this file, and click that folder.
3. Enter a name for your file, and click Save. The file will have a .txt extension. The new file is saved into the folder you designated and you are returned to your report window. A small message appears telling you the export was

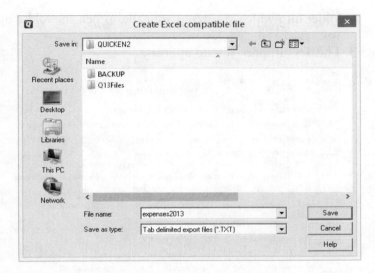

successful and notes the location of the Excel file. See "Work with Your Saved Excel File" next to see how to open the file in Excel.

Work with Your Saved Excel File

Once you have saved the file, you can work with it in Microsoft Excel. To do so:

1. Open Microsoft Excel. (The illustrations in this section refer to Microsoft Excel 2013, but the application works in similar ways with earlier versions of Excel.)
2. Click File | Open. Choose Text Files instead of All Excel Files as the type of file for which you want Excel to look. (See the next illustration.) Locate the

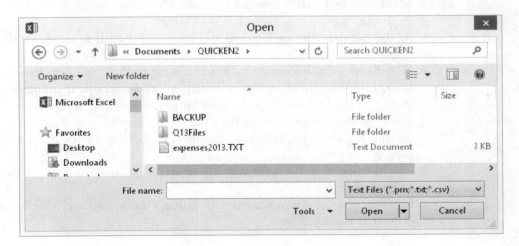

folder into which you saved your file. When the folder opens, select the file you saved and click Open.

3. The Text Import Wizard appears.

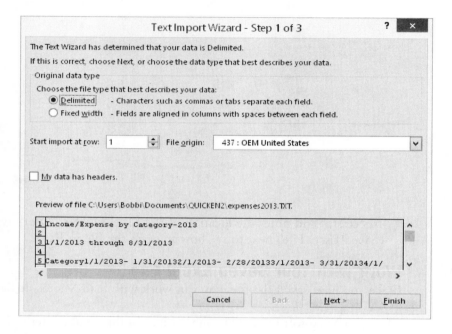

4. Ensure that Delimited is selected. Normally, this is the default option. Click Next.

5. Make sure that Tab is selected from the Delimiters column. Click Next to continue.

6. At the last step, choose General and then click Finish to complete the import.

7. Your Excel worksheet appears, as seen in Figure 5-4. You may have to make the columns wider to see the information on the report. If so, place your cursor on the line between the column letters and drag to the right.

8. You may also have to format the numbers to display as dollars and cents. To do this, highlight the cells with numbers in them and click the $ tool on the ribbon.

9. Save the file in an Excel format. To do so:
   a. Click File.
   b. Click Save As. From the Save As dialog, choose an Excel Workbook format and click Save.

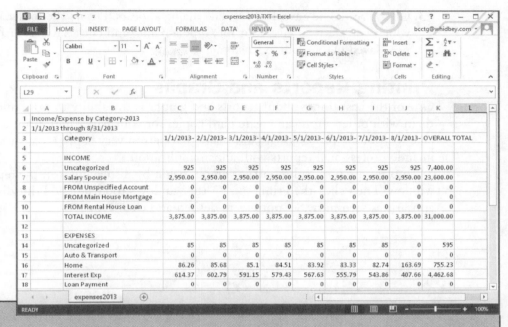

Figure 5-4 • Export your reports to Microsoft Excel to further customize your Quicken reports.

Copy Report to Clipboard

Use this option to copy the report into another Windows program. If you have set your keyboard shortcuts to the Windows Standard, you can also use the keyboard shortcut CTRL-C. To "paste" this report into another program, use the keyboard shortcut CTRL-V. You can even use this method to copy the report into Microsoft Excel, a much easier process than the one described earlier. To set the Windows Standard as your preference, click Edit | Preferences | Setup | Keyboard Mappings and choose Windows Standard.

Export to PDF Format

PDF stands for Portable Document Format. This format, patented by Adobe Systems, allows the reader to view and/or print a document from nearly any computer or word processor. This option is particularly useful if you are saving the report to e-mail it or sharing the file with someone who does not have either Quicken or Microsoft Office. To save as a .pdf file:

1. From the Export menu, click Export To PDF Format.
2. The Print dialog appears. In the Printer field you will see "Quicken PDF Printer on nnnn" rather than your regular printer.

3. Click Print. The Save To PDF File dialog appears. Locate the folder into which you want to save your file, type a name, and click Save. Your file is now saved with a .pdf extension.

Printing Reports and Graphs

One of the best things about reports and graphs is the ability to print and share them with others. You can create hard copies for your paper files, print a copy to take to your tax professional (and make that person very happy), or you can include professional reports with a loan application.

To print a report, subreport, or graph, begin by displaying it in the report window. Then click the Print icon on the window's toolbar. The Print dialog appears, as seen next. Set options as desired and click Print.

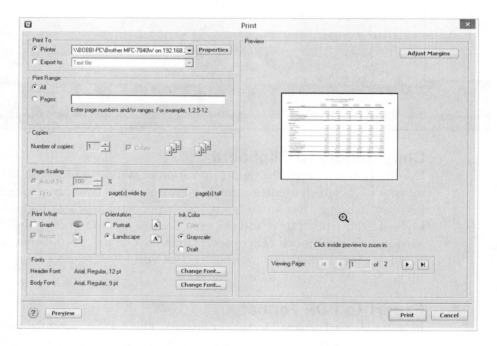

Here's a look at the available options.

- **Print To** options determine the destination of the printed report or graph. You have two choices:
  - **Printer** prints to the printer you choose from the drop-down list, which includes all printers, faxes, and related devices you have set up in Windows.

- **Export To** makes it possible to export the report information in one of three formats you choose from the drop-down list: Text File, Tab-Delimited (Excel-Compatible) Disk File, or PRN (123-Compatible) Disk File. This option is only available if you are printing a report.
- **Print Range** determines which pages will print. You can use this if the printed report is more than one page. The default setting is All, which prints all pages of the report. To print a range of pages, select Pages and then enter the page numbers for the page range you want to print.
- **Copies** determines how many copies of the report will print. If you enter a value greater than 1, you can select the Collate check box to collate the copies as they are printed.
- **Page Scaling** options enable you to resize a report or graph to a specific percentage or to fit on a certain number of pages. These options are only available for certain printers.
- **Print What** lets you toggle between two check boxes to determine whether to print a graph or report or both. The available options depend on what's in the report window.
- **Orientation** determines how the printed report will be viewed. The options are Portrait or Landscape. These are standard options offered by all programs. The icon beside each orientation option illustrates it.
- **Ink Color** allows you to choose between three options to determine the ink color and quality of the printout: Color (available only if a color printer is selected from the Printer drop-down list), Grayscale, or Draft.
- **Fonts** let you use the two Change Font buttons to change the header and body typefaces of the report or graph. Clicking the button displays the Font dialog, which you can use to set standard font options, such as font, size, and style.
- **Preview** shows a thumbnail preview of the document. You can click the buttons in the Viewing Page area to scroll through all pages of the report. To change the margins for the document, click the Adjust Margins button. The Preview area changes to offer boxes for entering margin values. To view a full-size preview, click the thumbnail in this area or click the Preview button at the bottom of the dialog.
- **Viewing Page** dialog allows you to scroll through the pages of your report to see how each page will look when printed.

Managing Your Investment Accounts

This part of the book explains how you can use Quicken Personal Finance Software to track your investments. It begins by explaining the basics of tracking investments in Quicken and then goes on to explain how you can use Quicken's online investment tracking features to download investment information from your brokerage firm and exchange information with Quicken.com. Along the way, it provides a wealth of information you can use to invest wisely and maximize your investment returns. Finally, it explains how you can use Quicken's Investing tab and reporting features to keep an eye on your portfolio and investment returns.

By the way, throughout these three chapters, the Investment Transaction list, which serves as a register for your investment accounts, will be referred to both as the transaction list and as the register.

This part has three chapters:

Entering Your Investment Transactions

Chapter 6

In This Chapter:

- *Understanding your portfolio*
- *Managing your portfolio*
- *Creating investing accounts*
- *Working with placeholder entries*
- *Understanding the Investment Transaction list*
- *Using the investment transaction dialog*
- *Entering common transactions*
- *Entering transactions in the Transaction List*
- *Editing transactions*
- *Adjusting balances*
- *Viewing the Security List*

Many people find that investing in stocks, bonds, mutual funds, or other types of assets are ways to save for future goals or retirements. Although more risky than deposits made to an FDIC-insured bank, certain types of investments have the potential to earn more, and make money grow faster. In this chapter, you will be introduced to investments and portfolio management and then you will learn how to use Quicken Personal Finance Software to keep track of the money you invest.

Quicken Investment Basics

An *investment* is a security or asset that you expect to increase in value and/or generate income. There are many types of investments—Table 6-1 lists some of them. This chapter concentrates on the investments you can track with the features in Quicken's Investing tab.

Before you learn how to use Quicken to track your investments, here's a review of Quicken's investment accounts and a more detailed explanation of why investment tracking is so important.

Type of Investment	Type of Account
CD	Savings account or standard brokerage account
Money market fund	Savings account or standard brokerage account
Stocks in your possession	Standard brokerage account
Brokerage account with one or more securities	Standard brokerage account, with or without an associated cash, checking, or interest-earning account
Employee stock options	Standard brokerage account
Employee Stock Purchase Plan (ESPP)	Standard brokerage account
Dividend Reinvestment Program (DRIP)	Standard brokerage account
Bonds, including U.S. Savings Bonds	Standard brokerage account
Treasury bills	Standard brokerage account
Single mutual fund with no cash balance	Single mutual fund account or a standard brokerage account
Variable or fixed annuities	Standard brokerage account
401(k) or 403(b) plan	401(k) or 403(b) account
529 Educational Savings Plan	529 plan account or Educational IRA (529) account (this account is sometimes known as a Coverdell ESA [IRA])
Traditional IRA, Roth IRA, or Education IRA	IRA account
Keogh Plan, SEP-IRA, or SIMPLE-IRA	Keogh plan or SEP-IRA account
Real estate	Asset account
Real estate investment trusts (REITs) account or partnerships	Standard brokerage account

Table 6-1 • Quicken Accounts for Various Investment Types

Understanding Your Portfolio

The term portfolio refers to the total of all of your investments. For example, if you have 50 shares of one company's stock, shares in a mutual fund, and a 401(k) plan account, these are the items that make up your portfolio.

Types of Investment Accounts

Your Quicken portfolio can include four types of investment accounts. You can have as many investment accounts as you need to properly represent the investments that make up your portfolio.

- A Quicken brokerage account is for tracking a wide variety of investments handled through a brokerage firm, including stocks, bonds, mutual funds, and annuities. Like the account at your brokerage firm, it can track income, capital gains, performance, market values, shares, and cash balances for multiple securities.
- A 401(k) or 403(b) account is for tracking 401(k), 403(b), or 457 plans, in which you make regularly scheduled, pretax contributions toward investments for your retirement. This type of account can track performance, market value, and distribution among investment choices. If you (and your spouse) have more than one plan, you should set up a separate account for each.
- An IRA or a Keogh account is for tracking a variety of retirement accounts, including standard IRA, Roth IRA, Coverdell Education Savings Account (formerly known as Education IRA), SEP-IRA, SIMPLE-IRA, and Keogh plans.
- A 529 plan account is for tracking 529 Educational Savings Plans. These plans enable multiple family members to make pretax contributions to invest money for a family member's college education. This type of account enables you to track cash, money market, and securities activity and balances.

There are two distinct account types in Quicken for 529s. One is a 529 plan you can find under Investing & Retirement in the first Add Account dialog. The second is under IRA or Keogh Plan on the same dialog. This second type is the account type referred to as Coverdell ESA in the IRA dialog and as Education IRA in the help.

Choosing the Right Type of Account

Since it is often not clear which kind of account is best for a specific type of investment, Table 6-1 offers some guidance. Keep in mind that you can also track many types of investments in asset accounts. But Quicken's investment accounts enable you to better track and report on the income, capital gains, and performance of your investments.

This chapter concentrates on investment accounts tracked in standard brokerage, IRA or Keogh, 401(k) or 403(b), and 529 plan accounts. Consider what type of account your financial institution requires for downloading transactions as you decide between a single mutual fund account and a standard brokerage account.

If you want to track the maturity dates of your CDs, you may need to use the brokerage account, as Quicken considers CDs to be investment instruments.

Managing Your Portfolio

You may be wondering why you should bother including investment information in your Quicken data file. After all, you get quarterly (or even monthly) statements from your broker or investment firm. Consider the benefits when you manage your portfolio with Quicken's tools.

Centralizing Your Investment Records

Unless you have only one brokerage account for all your investments, you receive multiple statements for the various investments in your portfolio. No single statement can provide a complete picture of your portfolio's worth—however, Quicken can. By entering the transactions and values on each statement within Quicken, you can see the details of your entire portfolio in one place.

Knowing the Value of Your Portfolio on Any Day

Brokerage statements tell you the value of your investments on the statement's ending date, but not what they're worth today—or what they were worth on July 20, 1994. Quicken, however, can tell you what your portfolio is worth on any day for which you have entered, or better yet, downloaded, security prices, and it can estimate values for dates without exact pricing information. You can even retrieve the latest security prices online to keep your portfolio's value up-to-date. Chapter 7 shows you how to take advantage of this feature.

Manually compiling a complete pricing and performance history for an investment is no small task, especially for periods spanning multiple statements. If you consistently enter (or download) investment information into your Quicken data file, however, preparing performance charts and reports is as easy as choosing a menu command or clicking a button.

Additional Enhancements in Quicken Premier

Those using Quicken Premier or higher can opt to update stock quotes every 15 minutes. Other features found in the Premier and higher versions are the ability to create snapshots of your portfolio value versus its cost basis, a "Growth of

10K" chart, and average annual return. In addition, these versions offer a buy/sell preview as well as mutual fund ratings from Morningstar.

Calculating Capital Gains Quickly and Easily

Calculating the gain on the sale of an investment isn't always easy. Considerations include not only the purchase and selling prices, but also commissions, fees, stock splits, and purchase lots. Quicken can take all the work out of calculating capital gains, even if you're just considering the sale and want to know what its impact will be. This is extremely helpful at tax time, as Chapter 13 explains.

A couple of other helpful things about keeping track of your investments in Quicken:

- Brokerages only keep records for so long, so if you have had dividend-paying stocks where you have reinvested the dividends for many years, Quicken will handily keep track of every lot even if your brokerage's history does not go back that far.
- If you change brokerages or your brokerage is acquired by another brokerage, often your cost basis information is not retained by the financial institution. If you have your investments in Quicken, you can easily transfer the cost basis information to the new account.
- If any of your securities have gone through an acquisition or merger, the tax treatment and associated changes to your cost basis are not always tracked, or tracked correctly, by your brokerage firm. You can use Quicken to accurately track these events.
- If you are keeping custodial accounts for a minor, when that minor is old enough to take over handling of the account, you can give them a complete buy/sell/cost basis history.
- When you use Quicken to track your investments, the data integrates seamlessly with the Lifetime Planner. This way, you can see the impact of investment value changes on your retirement plan at a glance.

Creating Investing Accounts

Before you can begin tracking your investments with Quicken, you must set up the investment accounts you'll need. Basic information about setting up accounts is contained in Chapter 1. This chapter provides the specifics for creating investing accounts. As you'll see on the following pages, when you create an investment account, Quicken not only prompts you for basic account information, but also gathers information about your security holdings. When you're finished creating an account, it's all ready to use for entering transactions and creating reports.

Choosing the Type of Investing Account

Begin by clicking Add An Account from the Account Bar or selecting Tools |
Add Account. In the Add Account dialog that appears, click the type of account
you want to create. You can refer to Table 6-1 if you need help deciding. The
option you select will determine certain settings for the account. For example, if
you choose an IRA or Keogh plan, Quicken will set tax-deferred options that are
not set if you select a brokerage account. After you choose a brokerage (or the
name of your 529 plan) from the list that appears, you may see a message that
Quicken is updating.

Using Simple Setup to Create an Investment Account

Quicken's extensive online account access features make it possible to automate
data entry for accounts held in participating financial institutions, including
many brokerage firms. To take advantage of these features, Quicken starts the
account creation process for standard brokerage, IRA or Keogh Plan, 401(k) or
403(b), or 529 Plan accounts by prompting you to enter the name of your
brokerage firm or choosing one from the provided list.

If you have chosen the default Simple Setup method of creating your account,
after you have typed or clicked the name of your broker, Quicken verifies the
connection to your broker using your Internet connection. You then see a window
that prompts you to enter the user ID and password given to you by your broker.
Quicken may display dialogs that prompt you for additional information about the
account. The dialogs that appear and the order in which they appear vary, depending
on your financial institution. Once you have entered your login information, click
Connect to proceed with the account setup. After you have proceeded through any
dialogs prompting for additional info, Quicken retrieves the account info and
transactions, creates the account, and displays an Account Added screen.

As explained in Chapter 1, it is not uncommon to set up accounts in Quicken
and decide later to activate online services for these accounts. The first time you
download transactions into a Quicken file with online access, Quicken prompts
you to create a new account for these downloaded transactions or to link them
to an existing account. If you are linking to an existing account, ensure it is the
correct one for these downloaded transactions. If you do not see an offer to link
to an existing account that has already been set up for downloading, you may
need to back out of the setup and deactivate downloading from the existing
account before Quicken offers to link to your account.

Using Advanced Setup   If your institution's name is not on the Simple Setup
list, has other connection methods, or you just prefer not to download, you can

set up your account manually. After you have chosen the type of investing account you want to set up, at the dialog where you are prompted for your institution's name, click Advanced Setup at the bottom of the window. From this dialog, as explained in Chapter 1, you have two options:

- **I Want To Select The Connection Method Used To Download My Transactions**   Select this option if your institution offers more than one online service or if you have been given specific instructions how to connect to their website.
- **I Want To Enter My Transactions Manually**   Select this option if your account is held by an entity that does not offer online services, or you just prefer to enter your transactions by hand. Also use this option if the account you are creating is not held at a financial institution—for example, an account to track the value of securities in your safe deposit box.

Account Name and Other Basic Information   Depending on your account, Quicken asks for other information. Quicken displays dialogs that prompt you for other basic information, including the account name, statement ending date, and cash and money market balances. Depending on the type of account, you may also be prompted for additional information as discussed next.

For IRAs and Keoghs
- Who owns the IRA.
- The type of IRA, such as traditional, Roth, Keogh, and so on.
- If you have not entered a cash value or more than one mutual fund, you may be asked whether this is a single mutual fund account.

For 401(k) or 403(b) Accounts
You will need to enter variations of this basic information for several types of accounts, most notably the 401(k)s:

- Statement ending date
- Employer name (either current or previous employer)
- Who owns the account
- Whether you have loans (and how many) against the account
- What securities you have in the account
- Whether you want to set up your paycheck information
- If the account tracks the number of shares, whether the statement lists the number of shares of each security
- For 401(k) or 403(b) accounts, Quicken displays a dialog that asks whether you want to track loans against the account. If you have any loans against the

account, be sure to indicate how many you have. Quicken will then display one or more dialogs prompting you for information about your loan(s).

Securities Held   A dialog like the one shown next prompts you to enter security ticker symbols and names. Enter one security per line, using the TAB key to move from one box to the next. If you don't know the ticker symbol for a security, you can click the Ticker Symbol Lookup button to look it up online. If you need to enter more than five securities in the dialog, click the Add More button to add more lines. Don't enter bonds in this dialog; you can add them later. You may see a prompt to connect to the Quicken Cloud Services.

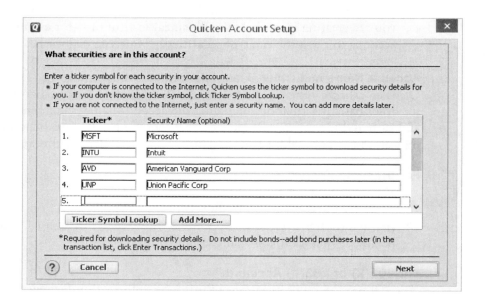

Current Holdings   After you have entered the ticker symbols for your securities, click Next. With your Internet connection, Quicken updates and verifies the symbols and displays a dialog like the one shown next. Enter the total number of shares for each security. For a 401(k) account, you may see a Total Market Value column. If the type of security—Stock, Mutual Fund, or Other—is incorrect, select the correct option.

When you click Next, Quicken displays a summary dialog confirming your entries and encouraging you to enter the complete transaction history for each of your holdings. To do so, click Done and then follow the directions on the window that appears.

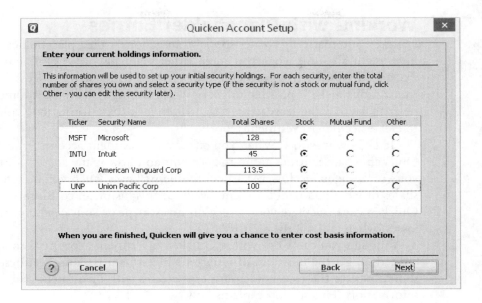

You may see a message asking if this is a single mutual fund account if you have not entered a cash balance and have entered only one mutual fund security. If you are creating this type of account, click Yes. Otherwise select No and click Next again. Quicken displays an Account Added window. Click Finish to close the window.

Paycheck Setup   When you create a 401(k) or 403(b) account, Quicken displays a dialog, asking whether you want to set up your paycheck. (If you have already set up a paycheck in Quicken, you will not see this message.) Quicken's Paycheck Setup feature is great for automatically entering 401(k) contributions and loan payments, as seen next. Learn about setting up your paycheck in Quicken in Chapter 4. Click Yes to set up your paycheck. Click No to continue, and then in the Account Added dialog, click Finish.

Working with Placeholder Entries

Quicken automatically creates special transactions, called placeholder entries, in investment accounts when you enter, either manually or via Online Account Access, currently held securities as part of the account setup process. These transactions make it possible to get up and running quickly with Quicken's investment tracking features, but they often lack the information Quicken needs to create accurate investment reports.

Here's how it works. When you create an investment account, you tell Quicken what securities are in the account and how many shares of each security you currently own. However, Quicken doesn't know when you bought those shares or what you paid for them. Without this historical cost information, Quicken can't calculate your return on investment or your capital gains (or losses) when you sell the security.

Although you can work with a Quicken investment account as soon as it's created, to get the most out of Quicken's investment tracking features, you should replace the placeholder entries it creates with investment cost information. This section explains how.

The placeholder "locks" the number of shares and cash balance for the given date to the number specified in the placeholder. If you enter transactions before the placeholder date, the cash balance will not be affected. This can be a good thing, as you don't have to account for where the cash came from for securities purchased long before you started tracking in Quicken, but it can also be a bad thing if you don't understand how the placeholder works. Many Quicken users wonder why cash is not subtracted from the account when they enter a "buy" transaction. Thus, many users don't use placeholders to avoid these sorts of complications.

Viewing Placeholder Entries for an Account

You can find an account's placeholder entries with the rest of the transactions for that account. Choose the account from the Account Bar to open its Transaction List (register). You can also click the Portfolio button after clicking the Investing tab and click the name of the account you want. You will see the placeholder transactions on the Transaction List. Figure 6-1 shows an example of an investment account that includes several placeholder entries.

You may see a little calculator icon in the Clr column for each placeholder transaction. You may also notice another calculator icon at the bottom left of the transaction list just above the Download Transactions tab, as well as a legend explaining what the placeholder transactions are and how to work with them.

Figure 6-1 • **Quicken uses placeholder entries to show current balances, not investment costs.**

If placeholder entries are not visible, you may need to set the preference for viewing hidden investment transactions. Select Edit | Preferences. Click Investment Transactions, and then select the Show Hidden Transactions check box. Click OK to save the preference and close the dialog.

Entering Cost Information for Placeholder Entries

To enter security cost information, begin by selecting the placeholder entry you want to work with. Click the Enter Cost link to display the Enter Missing Transactions dialog, which may take several seconds. See the next illustration for an example.

Transactions entered in the investment account before the date of the placeholder entry will not affect the cash balance of the investment account. It is often better to delete the placeholder and then enter all the historical transactions.

Two buttons at the bottom of the dialog offer methods for entering historical cost information for a security: Enter Missing Transaction and Estimate Average Cost.

Enter Missing Transaction   Click the Enter Missing Transaction button to open the Buy-Shares Bought dialog. From here you can enter the individual transactions that make up the total number of shares you hold. In many cases, these transactions include purchases, stock dividends, and stock splits. This option gives you the most accurate records, but if you have many transactions, entering them all can be time-consuming. (If the account is a 401(k) account, you may see an extra button labeled Cash Source.) See how to enter new transactions, such as purchases and stock dividends, later in this chapter, in the section titled "Investment Transactions."

For this dialog, complete the transaction information by moving through the fields with your TAB key. The transaction date should already be filled in. If you need to change the date, enter the correct date.

If you need to change a date for a placeholder transaction, it must be before the date you have entered for the placeholder when you set up the account.

1. The Account and Security Name fields are prefilled, and you cannot change the information.
2. Enter the number of shares you purchased on the date of the placeholder transaction. If this placeholder contains more than one lot, enter the oldest

lot first. You will have to enter each lot separately to ensure your investment account is correct.

3. Enter the price you paid for each share in the Price Paid field.
4. Enter the amount of any commission you paid for this transaction. Quicken calculates your total cost.
5. If you have made any errors, click the Clear button. If you want to start over, click the Cancel button. Otherwise, click Enter/Done.

A warning message appears telling you that you are attempting to record a transaction on the same date as a placeholder transaction, that your share balance will not be affected, and are you sure you want to do this. Click Yes to close the message and return to the Enter Missing Transactions dialog. If you have entered all the transactions to account for all the shares in the placeholder, you will have the option to click Done to close the Enter Missing Transactions dialog. Otherwise, you will see a button labeled Finish Later.

Estimate Average Cost   This option enables you to enter an average estimated cost for all of the shares you hold. Although this method is less accurate than entering individual transactions, it's a lot quicker and may be sufficient if you don't need detailed records of stock costs. You can always go back later and use the Enter Missing Transaction button to record more accurate acquisition details. If needed, click the Enter Cost link in the placeholder transaction, and then click Estimate Average Cost to open the Enter Missing Transactions dialog, as seen here.

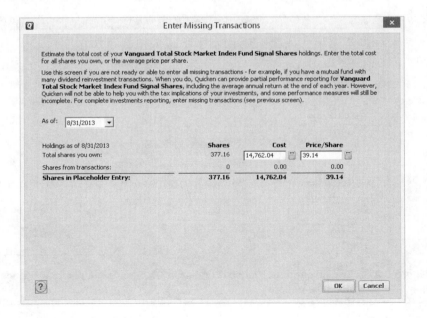

When you click the Estimate Average Cost button, the dialog shown above appears. Enter either the total cost of the shares in the Cost box or the average price per share in the Price/Share box. Quicken makes any necessary calculations. Click OK to save the entry and return to the register. The item then shows as a placeholder entry in the Investment Transaction list. If you enter the Cost first, then decide to enter Price/Share, once you have entered your desired Price/Share you will need to click in the Cost field to see the updated Cost value.

Working with Investment Accounts

To view an account's information, select the account name from the Account Bar. This opens the register for this account, as seen in Figure 6-2. From this Transaction List you can enter transactions and perform other activities.

The most important part of properly tracking investments is recording all investment transactions. This includes purchases, sales, dividends, and other activity affecting your portfolio's cost basis and value. This will make life much easier when you are ready to sell the security.

Before you enter a transaction, you must have all of its details. In most cases, you can find the information you need on the monthly statement, confirmation

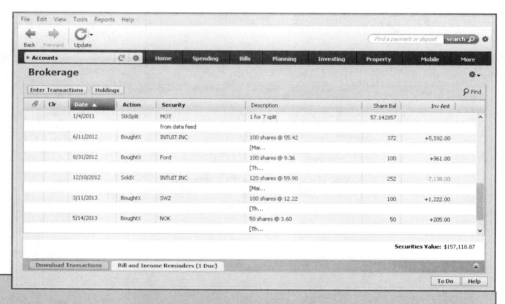

Figure 6-2 • The Investment Transaction list in Quicken is similar to a spending account's account register.

form, or receipt you receive from your broker or investment firm. The information varies, depending on the transaction, but it generally should include the security name, transaction date, number of shares, price per share, and any commissions or fees.

 For income tax purposes, it is better to record total cost rather than price per share, as that is the value you enter on Schedule D of your federal income tax return. Quicken will then calculate the price per share for you.

This section provides some information and advice for understanding the Investment Transaction list and entering the most common transactions into investment accounts.

Understanding the Investment Transaction List

The Investment Transaction list looks very much like the check registers. However, instead of the familiar Date, Check Number, and Payee fields, the Investment Transaction list has fields that pertain to your investing activities. See Figure 6-2 for an example.

The Investment Transaction list includes the following:

- **Attachment Icon** (the small paper clip)   When you attach a receipt or other item to this transaction, this icon appears in this column. See Chapter 3 for more information on attachments.
- **Clr**   When you reconcile your investment account, this column shows the cleared status of transactions.
- **Date**   The date of the transaction. Click the small arrow to sort transactions by date.
- **Action**   What this transaction represents. See "Investment Actions" later in this chapter for more information. Click the column to display the small arrow that allows you to sort by this column. It sorts in alphabetical order by action.
- **Security**   This column shows the name of the security. Since a single investment account can contain a wide variety of securities, each security is named.

 The five columns that appear with a bold font in the Investment Transaction list are sort fields. Click in the column name you want to use to sort by that column.

- **Description**   What action is represented. For example, if the Action column says "Bought," the number of shares of the named security and the price paid show in this column.
- **Share Bal**   This is the balance of the cumulative number of shares for all the transactions pertaining to that security in the account. This is not the amount of shares for the individual transaction unless the transaction is the first or only transaction in the account for that security.
- **Inv Amt**   Shows the amount of the investment in dollars. For example, if you purchased 50 shares of stock at $10.00 per share with a $35.00 commission/fee, this amount would be $535.00.
- **Cash Amt**   This column displays cash transactions for this account.
- **Cash Bal**   This column displays any cash balance in the account after the transaction on this line of the register.

Share Balance is the cumulative total of shares for that security on the date of the transaction. If you have three transactions for a security, each buying 10 shares, the Share Balance will show 10, 20, and 30 for the corresponding three "buy" transactions. You need to select the transaction to see how many shares were involved in that particular transaction. The number of shares involved in a transaction also appears in the Description column.

If your account has a linked checking account, the Cash Amt and Cash Bal columns do not appear in the Investment Transaction list.

Working with the Buttons

In addition to the register lines, at the top of the Transaction List are the Enter Transactions and Holding buttons, each with several options.

- **Enter Transactions**   Clicking the Enter Transactions button opens the investment transaction dialog as described later in this chapter.
- **Holdings**   Click the Holdings button to open an Account Overview window for this account. Similar to the Portfolio view in the Investing tab, you can see the current value, recent and historical performances, and the tax implications of the transactions in this account, as seen in Figure 6-3. See Chapter 7 for a complete review of the Account Overview window.

Account Actions   Click the Actions gear icon at the right of the Investment Transaction list to open the menu. This menu gives you access to several

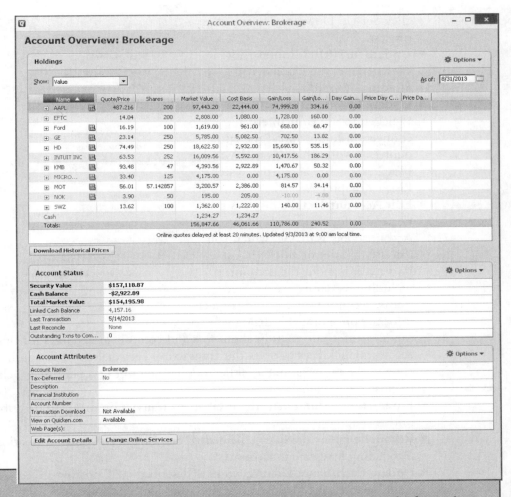

Figure 6-3 • **The Holdings button in the Investment Transaction list opens the Account Overview window.**

investment-related activities. The menu is divided into three sections: Transactions, Reporting, and Register Views And Preferences. Each is described next.

- **Update Transactions** (not shown) opens the One Step Update Settings dialog. Enter your password and click Update Now to update your accounts.
- **Set Up Download** appears when you have not yet activated this investing account for online services. If your financial institution offers online services,

click Set Up Download to start the process.

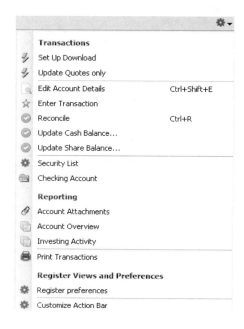

- **Update 401(k) Holdings** (not shown) starts the Update 401(k) Holdings Wizard.
- **Update Quotes Only** prompts Quicken to use your Internet connection to download the latest quotes on your holdings and Watch List. Learn more about the Watch List in Chapter 7.
- **Edit Account Details** displays the General Information tab of the Account Details dialog, which you can use to enter or edit basic information about the account, including its name, tax-deferred status, account number, and contact information. From this dialog you can also enter information about fees and commission charges for this account. Click Fees to open the Transaction Fees dialog. After you have entered the information, as either a dollar amount or a percentage, click OK to close the dialog.
- **Enter Transaction** opens the investment transaction dialog as described later in this chapter.
- **Reconcile** opens the Reconcile dialog. See Chapter 10 for information on reconciling investment accounts.
- **Update Cash/Share Balance** works as described in "Updating an Account's Cash Balance" and "Updating an Account's Share Balance" later in this chapter.
- **Security List** opens the Security List. See "Viewing the Security List" later in this chapter.

You will see a Checking Account entry here only if the investment account has a linked checking account.

- **Account Attachments** opens the Account Attachment dialog. See Chapter 3 to learn how to work with attachments.
- **Account Overview** opens the Account Overview window. See "Using the Account Overview Window" later in this chapter and Chapter 7 for more detailed information.

- **Investing Activity** opens a report about your investing activity for time ranges you can set.
- **Print Transactions** gives you the opportunity to print your Transaction List.
- **Register Preferences** opens the Preferences dialog to the Investment Transactions section. See Appendix B for more information about preferences.
- **Customize Action Bar** opens the Customize Action Bar dialog, as seen next. From this dialog, you can select additional actions to display on this investment account's Action Bar, seen at right, which shows the icons for the items we selected in the Customize Action Bar illustration. This customization affects only this investment account.

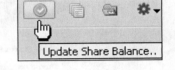

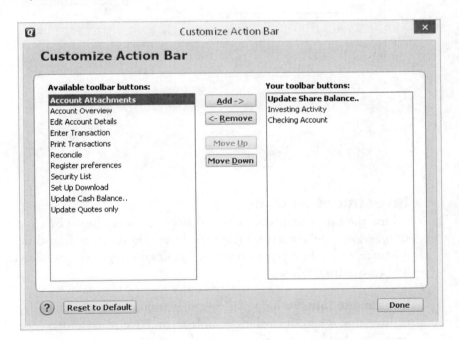

Using the Investment Transaction Dialog

You enter transactions into an investment account with the investment transaction dialog. This dialog, which is named for the type of transaction you are entering, is a fill-in form with all of the fields you need to enter transaction details.

To open the investment transaction dialog, click the Enter Transactions button in the transaction list for the account in which you want to enter the transaction (refer to Figure 6-3). It looks like the dialog shown next. (If the account is a 401(k) account, you may see a Cash Source button in the dialog.)

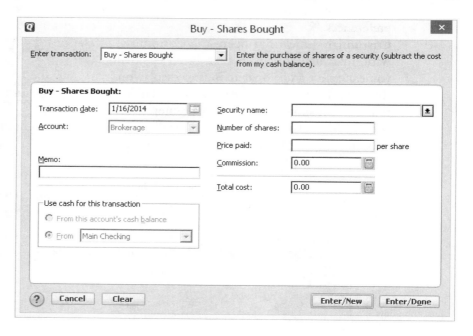

Investment Actions

To use the investment transaction dialog, you must begin by choosing a transaction type (or action) from the Enter Transaction drop-down list. There are dozens of action types organized into two categories: investment transactions and cash transactions.

Investment Transactions   Investment transactions directly affect your security or investment account balances, unless you have placeholders. See "Working with Placeholder Entries" earlier in this chapter.

- **Buy – Shares Bought** (shown earlier) enables you to add shares to an investment account. The cost of the shares (plus any commissions) is deducted from the account's cash balance (or another account's cash balance).

- **Sell – Shares Sold** enables you to remove shares from an investment account. The proceeds from the sale (net of any commissions) are added to the account's cash balance (or another account's cash balance).
- **Div – Stock Dividend (Non-Cash)** enables you to add shares of a security paid as a dividend.
- **Reinvest – Income Reinvested** enables you to account for investment income (such as dividends) that is reinvested in the security. This is common with dividend reinvestment plans and mutual funds.
- **Inc – Income (Div, Int, Etc.)** enables you to record income from interest, dividends, and capital gain distributions. It also enables you to record miscellaneous income that you can categorize as you wish.
- **Add – Shares Added** enables you to add shares to an investment account without an exchange of cash. You might use this option to add shares received as a gift.
- **Remove – Shares Removed** enables you to remove shares from an investment account without an exchange of cash. You might use this option to remove shares you have given to someone else as a gift.
- **Adjust Share Balance** enables you to create a placeholder entry transaction to make your share balance agree with your brokerage statement. You can enter cost information later, as discussed earlier in this chapter, in the section titled "Working with Placeholder Entries."
- **Stock Split** enables you to record additional shares received as a result of a stock split.
- **Return Of Capital** enables you to record the return of part of your investment capital.
- **Miscellaneous Expense** enables you to record investment expenses other than commissions. Unlike most other actions, you can assign a category to miscellaneous expense transactions.
- **Margin Interest Expense** enables you to record the amount of interest paid as a result of purchasing securities on margin.
- **Bonds Bought** enables you to record the purchase of bonds.
- **Grant Employee Stock Option** enables you to record the receipt of an employee stock option.
- **Exercise Employee Stock Option** enables you to use an employee stock option to buy stock.
- **Reprice Employee Stock Option** enables you to change pricing information for stock options.
- **Bought ESPP Shares** enables you to buy shares in an Employee Stock Purchase Plan.

- **Sold ESPP Shares** enables you to sell shares purchased through an Employee Stock Purchase Plan.
- **Short Sale** enables you to record a short sale of a security.
- **Cover Short Sale** enables you to record the purchase of stock to cover a short sale.
- **Corporate Name Change** enables you to record the change of the name of a company for which you own stock. This preserves the old name information; simply editing the security name in the Edit Security dialog does not.
- **Corporate Securities Spin-Off** enables you to record securities obtained through a spin-off of a smaller company from one of the companies in which you own securities.
- **Corporate Acquisition (Stock For Stock)** enables you to record securities obtained in exchange for other securities you own, normally as a result of a corporate acquisition.
- **Mutual Fund Conversion** lets you record the information for a mutual fund that you currently hold that is being replaced by another fund. Here you record the price per share after the conversion is complete.
- **Shares Transferred Between Accounts** enables you to move shares from one Quicken investment account to another.
- **Cash Transferred Into Account** enables you to record the transfer of cash into the investment account.
- **Cash Transferred Out Of Account** enables you to record the transfer of cash out of the investment account.

 If the investment account has a linked checking account, you will not see the Cash Transferred options.

- **Reminder Transaction** enables you to enter an investment reminder. If the Reminder Transaction has a future date, the reminder will not appear in the alert list until that future date. This reminder will appear as text in your Quicken investment alerts the next time you open Quicken.

Cash Transactions   Cash transactions affect the cash balance in an investment account. These actions make it possible to track an investment account's cash balance without using a linked cash account.

- **Write Check** enables you to record a check written from an investment account.
- **Deposit** enables you to record a cash deposit to an investment account.

- **Withdraw** enables you to record the withdrawal of cash from an investment account.
- **Online Payment** enables you to record an online payment from the investment account's cash balance. To use this feature, the account must be enabled for Online Payment or Online Bill Pay. Chapter 5 discusses Online Payment.
- **Other Cash Transaction** enables you to record any type of transaction that affects the investment account's cash balance.

Completing the Transaction

Investment transaction dialogs and forms are generally self-explanatory and easy to use. Simply fill out the fields in the form, and click one of the Enter buttons. Enter/New enters the current transaction and redisplays the investment transaction dialog so you can enter another transaction. Enter/Done enters the current transaction and dismisses the investment transaction dialog.

Entering Common Transactions

Although page-count limitations make it impossible to review every kind of investment transaction in this book, here's a look at a few common transactions. They should give you a solid understanding of how the investment transaction dialogs work so you can enter your transactions.

Buying Shares

A security purchase normally involves the exchange of cash for security shares. In some cases, you may already own shares of the security or have it listed on your Watch List. In other cases, the security may not already exist in your Quicken data file, so you'll need to set up the security when you make the purchase.

Start by selecting the investing account with which you want to work. Click Enter Transactions to display the Buy – Shares Bought dialog shown earlier. Enter information about the shares you have purchased:

- **Transaction Date** is the date of the transaction.
- **Account** is the name of the account you selected. You cannot change the option chosen from this drop-down list. If the account name is incorrect, click Cancel, open the correct investing account, and start over.
- **Security Name** is the name of the security. If you enter the name of a security that doesn't already exist in Quicken, the Add Security To Quicken dialog, which is discussed later in the section titled "Adding a New Security," appears so you can add the security to Quicken.

- **Number Of Shares** is the number of shares purchased.
- **Price Paid** is the per-share price.
- **Commission** is the amount of commissions you paid to your brokerage or investment firm.
- **Total Cost** is calculated by Quicken. Enter the total cost and number of shares, and let Quicken calculate the price paid. The total cost and number of shares is what gets reported on IRS Schedule D when you sell the shares. The total cost and number of shares should match exactly what your brokerage reports and the price per share can be off by a few pennies. Better to record the info so you can correctly report your transactions at tax time and be confident if you are audited.
- **Memo** lets you enter any comments about this transaction.
- **Use Cash For This Transaction** enables you to specify an account from which the total cost should be deducted. By default, this option is set to use cash from the same investment account. If the brokerage account has a linked checking account, the cash source will default to the linked checking account; this cannot be changed.

When you're finished entering information about the transaction, click one of the Enter buttons. The transaction appears in the Transactions list for the account.

If you want to add security shares to an account without an exchange of cash, use the Add – Shares Added action. Its form asks for most of the same information but does not affect any cash balances. In addition to not affecting the cash balance, Add Shares lets you specify a different acquisition date from the transaction date. This can be helpful if you received the shares as a gift or inheritance so you can track both the date you received the shares and the date the shares were originally acquired.

One odd thing about the acquisition date when entering transactions is you can enter an acquisition date as far into the past as you wish, but you can only enter a future acquisition date up to ten days into the future.

Selling Shares

A security sale also involves the exchange of cash for security shares. Normally, you dispose of shares you already own, but in some instances, you may sell shares you don't own. This is called selling short, and it is a risky investment technique sometimes used by experienced investors. (To record short sale transactions, use the Short Sale or Cover Short Sale action.)

IN MY EXPERIENCE

When working in your investing accounts, always ensure you are in the correct investment account and double-check the security name to be sure the security you wish to sell is in that account. Even experienced Quicken users report issues when they try to sell a security that is not in the account or the security name is similar. This is also where entering the correct number of shares, including all necessary decimal places for transactions, becomes critical. If you rounded the numbers or entered any incorrect numbers, you may not be able to record the sale of the number of shares you wish. The Share Balance column can be useful in troubleshooting this issue, as it shows the exact number of shares you have for each security.

To sell shares, choose Sell – Shares Sold in the investment transaction dialog to display the Sell – Shares Sold dialog. Enter information about the shares you have sold.

- **Transaction Date** is the date of the transaction.
- **Account** is the name of the account in which the transaction should be recorded. You cannot change the option chosen from this drop-down list if you are entering a transaction from within the account's Transaction window; if it's wrong, click Cancel, open the correct account register, and start over.
- **Security Name** is the name of the security. You can choose an option from the drop-down list, or if you have many securities, start typing the security name in the field and Quicken will show securities that begin with those letters.
- **Sell All Shares In This Account** tells Quicken to automatically enter the total number of shares you own in the Number Of Shares box.
- **Number Of Shares** is the number of shares sold.
- **Price Received** is the per-share price.
- **Commission** is the amount of commissions you paid to your brokerage or investment firm.
- **Specify Lots** enables you to specify which shares you are selling when you have multiple purchase lots.

You need to be able to instruct your brokerage which lots you are selling. Not all brokerages allow tax lot–specific transactions. The Specify Lots button will be grayed out if you do not have any shares of the selected security in the account where you are entering the sell data. It will also be grayed out if the security uses average cost, like a mutual fund.

- **Total Sale** is determined by multiplying the per-share price by the number of shares and deducting the commission. These are the proceeds from the sale. You can enter any three of the four fields (shares, price per share, commission, and total) and Quicken will calculate the fourth field. The technique Quicken uses is determined by the data you enter. However, your broker reports the total sale amount on the 1099B form he or she sends at the end of each year. This is the number you report on Schedule D of your annual income tax report. Therefore, total sale amount is more critical than the price per share.
- **Memo** lets you enter any comments about this transaction.
- **Record Proceeds?** enables you to specify an account to which the net proceeds should be added. If the investment account has a linked checking account, all proceeds go to the linked checking account. From that linked checking account, you can transfer proceeds to any account in Quicken.

When you click one of the Enter buttons, Quicken records the transaction.

Dividend Payments and Other Income

Many investments pay dividends, interest, or other income in cash. (That's why they're so attractive to an investor!) Recording this activity in the appropriate Transaction List enables Quicken to calculate performance accurately while keeping account balances up-to-date, as well as helping you at tax time.

Keep in mind that many mutual funds are set up to reinvest income rather than pay it in cash. Do not use the steps in this section to record a reinvestment of income. Instead, use the Reinvest Income action to enter transaction information.

IN MY EXPERIENCE

Use the Specify Lots option when selling your shares for additional control over capital gains. For example, if you want to take advantage of long-term capital gains tax breaks, you could sell shares that have been in your possession for more than 12 months. If you want to record a loss, you could sell shares that cost more than the selling price. Obviously, your options will vary, depending on the lots, their acquisition prices, and your selling price. If you select this option, click the Specify Lots button to display a dialog. (This dialog may include an Enter Missing Transactions button if placeholder entries exist for the security.) Use the dialog to enter shares in each lot you are selling, or select one of the Auto Select options and click OK. If you don't use the Specify Lots button to select lots, Quicken automatically sells the oldest shares (First In, First Out, or FIFO, method). As always, consult your tax professional if you want to select lots other than FIFO to determine what the IRS limitations might be.

To record dividend or interest income, choose Inc – Income (Div, Int, Etc.) from the drop-down list in the investment transaction dialog to display the Income dialog, shown next. Enter information about a cash payment on an investment:

- **Transaction Date** is the date of the transaction.
- **Account** is the name of the account in which the transaction is to be recorded. You cannot change the option chosen from this drop-down list if you are entering a transaction; if it's wrong, click Cancel, open the correct Transaction List, and start over.

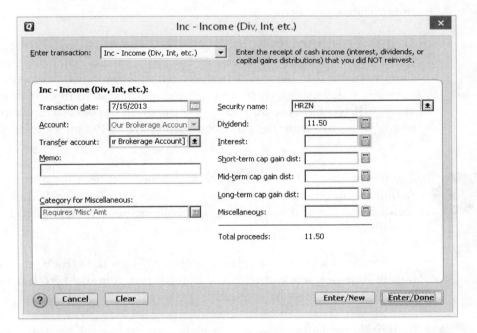

- **Transfer Account** enables you to specify an account into which the income is deposited. Leave this blank if the cash is deposited directly into the investment account. If the investment account has a linked checking account, the linked checking account will be designated as the transfer account and cannot be changed.
- **Memo** enables you to enter a brief note about the transaction.
- **Security Name** is the name of the security. You can choose an option from the drop-down list. If the transaction isn't related to a specific security—for example, interest paid on a cash balance in a brokerage account—you can leave this field blank.

- **Dividend**, **Interest**, **Short-Term Cap Gain Dist**, **Mid-Term Cap Gain Dist**, **Long-Term Cap Gain Dist**, and **Miscellaneous** are fields for entering various types of income. In most cases, you'll use only one or two of these boxes.
- **Total Proceeds** is the total of all income amounts calculated by Quicken.
- **Category For Miscellaneous** is the category you want to use to record miscellaneous income. This field is available only if you enter a value in the Miscellaneous field.

When you click one of the Enter buttons to record the transaction, it appears in the Transaction List.

Other Transactions

Other transactions are just as easy to enter as purchases, sales, and income. Simply choose the appropriate option from the drop-down list in the investment transaction dialog, and enter the transaction information in the form that appears. If you have the transaction confirmation or brokerage statement in front of you when you enter the transaction, you have all the information you need to record it.

You may wonder what the BoughtX and XIn/XOut items in your register's Action column mean. The X simply indicates that the action had no impact on the cash balance of the account and the transaction was transferred between accounts.

If you need additional guidance while entering a transaction, click the Help button (question mark icon) in the Enter Transaction dialog to learn more about the options that must be entered.

To quickly recalculate transactions in an account, use the keyboard shortcut CTRL-Z.

Entering Transactions in the Transaction List

You can also enter investment transactions directly into the Transaction List window. This feature makes entering transactions quicker for experienced Quicken users.

To begin, scroll down to the blank line at the bottom of the register. Click the line to activate it, and enter the transaction date in the Date column. Then choose an action from the pop-up menu in the Action column and press TAB. The two lines for the transactions fill in with italicized reminders of the information you should enter into each field. Fill in the fields with transaction details, and click Enter. Be aware that not all transaction types can be entered directly in the investment transaction list. If the form is required, it will pop up automatically.

Editing Transactions

You can quickly edit transactions from your account's register. In the register for the account (refer to Figure 6-3), select the transaction you want to edit. Click in the field you want to modify, and make the desired change. When you're finished, click Enter.

You can also select the transaction and select the Edit action button. The Edit dialog appears, as shown next. You can also double-click the transaction you wish to edit. Change any of the fields and click Enter/Done.

Edit Buy - Shares Bought

Enter transaction: Buy - Shares Bought ▼   Enter the purchase of shares of a security (subtract the cost from my cash balance).

Buy - Shares Bought:

Transaction date: 5/31/2013	Security name: Union Pacific Corp
Account: Our Brokerage Accoun ▼	Number of shares: 50
	Price paid: 154.10 per share
Memo:	Commission: 30.00
	Total cost: 7,735.00

Use cash for this transaction
○ From this account's cash balance
● From Thomasina's 401K ▼

? Cancel   Clear   Enter/Done

You can also right-click the transaction to open the context menu. Choose Edit to open the Edit dialog.

A few transaction types cannot be edited: Exercise Employee Stock Option and Sold ESPP Shares. These transactions must be deleted and re-entered if a change is needed.

Adjusting Balances

Occasionally, you may need to adjust the cash balance or number of shares in an investment account or update the balance in a 401(k) account. Here's how.

Updating an Account's Cash Balance

You can adjust the balance in an investment account with a cash balance. In the Account Bar, click the name of the account you want to adjust. From the register that opens, choose Action gear icon | Update Cash Balance. The Update Cash Balance dialog appears. (Note that this dialog does not display downloaded cash balance information if you have not enabled online access for the account.) Enter the date and the correct balance in the text boxes, and click Done. Quicken creates an adjusting entry.

Updating an Account's Share Balance

You can adjust the number of shares in an investment account. In the Account Bar, click the name of the account you want to adjust. From the Transaction List, choose Action gear icon | Update Share Balance to display the Adjust Share Balance dialog. (This is the same as choosing the Adjust Share Balance action in the investment transaction dialog.) Enter the adjustment date, security, and correct number of shares in the dialog. When you click Enter/Done, Quicken creates a placeholder entry that adjusts the share balance. Learn more about placeholder entries in the section titled "Working with Placeholder Entries," earlier in this chapter.

Updating 401(k) or 403(b) Balances

401(k) or 403(b) account balances change every time you contribute through your paycheck. To adjust the balance, click the name of the 401(k) or 403(b) account in the Account Bar to open its register. Click the Action gear icon, and from the resulting menu choose Update 401(k) Holdings. Then follow the prompts in the Update 401(k)/403(b) Account dialog that appears to update the information. Click Next to display the next page. When you're finished, click Enter/Done to record the adjustment.

You will only see the Update 401(k) Holdings item in the Action gear icon menu if the 401(k) account is manual. You will not see the item if the 401(k) account is enabled for transaction download.

Remember, if you set up your paycheck as discussed in Chapter 4, Quicken will automatically record contributions to your 401(k) or 403(b) account every payday.

Working with Securities

This chapter talks a lot about securities. But what, exactly, are *securities*? In Quicken, a security is a single investment that has a share price. Examples of securities include stock shares for a specific company, bonds for a specific company, and mutual funds offered by investment firms. Normally, when you own a security, you own a certain number of shares. To calculate the total value of the security, you multiply the number of shares you own by the most recent per-share price.

This part of the chapter explains how you can use the Security List to add a new security, choose market indexes, download quotes, edit security details, and more.

Viewing the Security List

The Security List window (see Figure 6-4) simply lists the securities in Quicken's data file. You can use this window to add, edit, delete, or hide securities, including *Watch List securities*—securities you don't own but want to monitor. To open this window, press CTRL-Y. You can also access the list from the Action

Security ▲	Symbol	Type	Asset Class	Download Quotes	Watch List	Hide	
AAPL	AAPL	Stock	Large Cap Stocks	☑	☑	☐	Edit Report Delete
Agilent	A	Stock	Large Cap Stocks	☑	☐	☐	
AMERICAN FUNDS PORTFOLIO S...	GAITX	Mutual Fund	Other	☑	☐	☐	
AMERICAN FUNDS PORTFOLIO S...	GWPCX	Mutual Fund	Other	☑	☐	☐	
American Vanguard Corp	AVD	Stock	Small Cap Stocks	☑	☐	☐	
Barnes Group	B	Stock	Small Cap Stocks	☑	☐	☐	
Dow Jones Industrials	DJI	Market Index	Unclassified	☑	☐	☐	
EFTC	ETFC	Stock	Large Cap Stocks	☑	☑	☐	
Ford	F	Stock	Large Cap Stocks	☑	☑	☐	
GE	GE	Stock	Large Cap Stocks	☑	☑	☐	
HD	HD	Stock	Large Cap Stocks	☑	☑	☐	
HRZN	HRZN	Stock	Small Cap Stocks	☑	☑	☐	
INTUIT INC	INTU	Stock	Large Cap Stocks	☑	☐	☐	
Kellogg Co	K	Stock	Large Cap Stocks	☑	☐	☐	
KMB	KMB	Stock	Large Cap Stocks	☑	☑	☐	
Macy's Inc	M	Stock	Large Cap Stocks	☑	☐	☐	
MICROSOFT CORP	MSFT	Stock	Large Cap Stocks	☑	☑	☐	
MOT	MOT	Stock	Large Cap Stocks	☑	☑	☐	
NASDAQ Composite	COMPX	Market Index	Unclassified	☑	☐	☐	
NOK	NOK	Stock	International Stocks	☑	☑	☐	
PIONEER HIGH YIELD FUND CL C	PYICX	Mutual Fund	Unclassified	☑	☐	☐	
Russell 2000	IUX	Market Index	Unclassified	☑	☐	☐	
S&P 500 Index	INX	Market Index	Unclassified	☑	☐	☐	
SWZ	SWZ	Mutual Fund	Asset Mixture	☑	☑	☐	
TIAA-CREF Lifecycle 2010 Fund Ins...	TCTIX	Mutual Fund	Asset Mixture	☑	☐	☐	
Union Pacific Corp	UNP	Stock	Large Cap Stocks	☑	☐	☐	

Figure 6-4 • **The Security List window offers many ways with which you can work with your investments.**

gear icon menu in an Investment Transaction list or from the Investing tab's Tools menu.

Adding a New Security

To add a new security to your Quicken data file as either a holding or a Watch List item, click the New Security button at the bottom of the Security List window (refer to Figure 6-4). The Add Security To Quicken dialog appears, displaying screens that prompt you for information about a security.

Quicken starts by prompting you for the security's ticker symbol and name. Entering the correct ticker symbol when you have an Internet connection can automate much of the security setup process. If you don't know the ticker symbol and have an Internet connection, you can click the Look Up button to connect to the Internet and look up the symbol.

This screen also offers a check box labeled Include This Security On My Watch List. Selecting this check box tells Quicken to track the security, even if you don't own any shares.

When you click Next, you are prompted to enter or create an Intuit ID. You may not see this prompt if you have previously created your Intuit ID and have selected to store the Inuit ID's login information in your Password Vault. Quicken connects to the Internet to obtain information about the security based on its ticker symbol. If it finds the ticker symbol, it displays the information it has downloaded in the Add Security To Quicken dialog, as seen next. Click Done to add the security to the Security List.

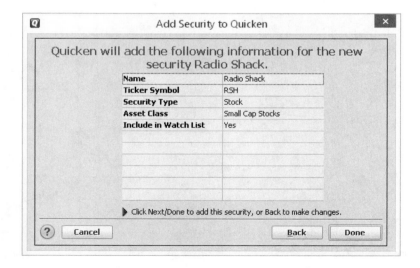

If Quicken can't find information about the security on the Internet, it displays a dialog enabling you to correct the ticker symbol or add the security manually. If you made an error when entering the ticker symbol, you can enter the correct symbol in the Ticker Symbol text box and click Next to try looking it up on the Internet again.

If you select the Add Manually option, select a security type; Bond, CD, Emp. Stock Option, ESPP, Market Index, Mutual Fund, Other, Stock, or U.S. Savings Bond, and click Next. Another dialog appears, prompting you for additional information about the security, such as its asset class (for a stock), asset class mixture (for a mutual fund), and bond type and maturity and call dates (for a bond). Enter whatever information you have for the security, and click Done to add the security to the Security List.

IN MY EXPERIENCE

Several students have asked the definition of "asset class." Strictly speaking, an asset class is a group of similar securities, such as equity instruments or stocks, income instruments such as bonds, and cash equivalents such as money market accounts. Within each asset class are categories. Quicken uses the shorthand name of "asset classes" to define types or categories of securities. When you enter "asset class" information in Quicken, you are categorizing the asset as one of several different asset "types":

- **Domestic Bonds**   These bonds are issued and traded in the currency of the country in which they are traded. That means they are not subject to fluctuations in currency exchange rates.
- **Global Bonds**   These bonds are traded in any international market, either foreign or domestic. The same bond issue may be offered in several countries at the same time.
- **Large Cap Stocks**   These securities are offered by large, publicly traded companies with a "market capitalization" of at least $10 billion. (Market capitalization is simply a generally accepted value of a company.)
- **Small Cap Stocks**   Securities offered by a publicly traded firm with a market capitalization of between $200 to 300 million and $2 to 3 billion.
- **International Stock**   These are securities sold by a company outside of the United States.
- **Cash/Other/Unclassified**   Assets that do not fit one of the other classifications.

If you select Employee Stock Option or ESPP, you start the wizards for those security types.

The security type market index is not the same as an index fund. Market index is only intended for true indexes like the Dow Jones Industrials index. Selecting market index for an index fund will prevent you from using the security as you normally would. For example, if you try to sell a security you have retyped to market index, the security will not show in the security drop-down list in the sell – shares sold form, even if you are in the correct account.

Choosing a Market Index

Within the Security List, you will see a Choose Market Indexes button. This option enables you to add common market indexes, such as the Dow Jones Industrial Average and the S&P 500 Index, to the Security List. This lets you download quotes for these indexes at the same time you download security prices, as discussed in Chapter 7.

- **Show Hidden Securities** This option will display any securities you've hidden on the Security List.
- **Mark All** The Mark All button selects Download Quotes for each security and index in the Security List.

To the chagrin of some Quicken users, there is no corresponding Clear All button available.

Working with Individual Securities

When you select a security on the list, three action buttons appear, as seen next. It is with these buttons that you can edit or delete a security as well as run a report. You can also access these actions by right-clicking the security name.

| RadioShack Corp | RSH | Stock | Small Cap Stocks | ☑ | ☑ | ☐ | Edit Report Delete |

Editing a Security You can edit a security to correct or clarify information you previously entered for it. Select the security's name in the Security List window (refer to Figure 6-4), and click the Edit button as shown above. The Edit Security Details dialog appears. The illustration shown next shows what it looks like for a stock. Enter or edit information in the dialog, and click OK to save your changes.

Quicken gets its asset information from Value Line. As shown in the Asset Allocation Guide, Value Line uses $4.0 billion as the market capitalization value to delineate between large-cap and small-cap domestic stocks. If you download the asset class for a mid-cap stock, it will be assigned Large Cap or Small Cap as its asset class, depending on whether its market cap is above or below $4.0 billion. To access the Asset Allocation Guide, click Investing | Tools | Asset Allocation Guide. To see the information about Value Line, click How Do I Update Asset Classes on the left of the Asset Allocation Guide. Select Common Questions About Downloading Asset Classes | What Asset Classes Are Assigned And Where Does the Information Come From.

Deleting a Security   Delete removes the currently selected security from your Quicken data file. You cannot delete a security that has been used in a transaction.

Creating a Report   When you select a security and click the Report button at the right of the selected row, you will see a Security Report, which summarizes all activity for the security. From the report window, you can print, export, save, customize, find, or replace information in the report, as seen below. See more about working with reports in Chapter 5.

Security Type List   Each security in the Security List must be assigned a security type. To see the Security Type List, open your Security List and select any security. Choose the Edit action button to open the Edit Security Details dialog. Click the Edit Types button to open the Security Type List, as shown next, to display a list of security types.

You can use buttons to modify the list:

- **New** enables you to create a new security type. Clicking this button displays the Set Up Security Type dialog, which you can use to enter a name for the security type.
- **Edit** enables you to change the name of the currently selected security type.
- **Delete** enables you to remove the currently selected security type from the list, although you cannot delete predefined security types assigned to an existing security.

Be cautious about editing or deleting security types. You can cause yourself some serious headaches by doing so.

- The **Help** icon displays the Quicken Personal Finances Help window with instructions for working with the Security Types. If another help topic appears, type **Security Types** in the search field to open that Help section.
- **Print** prints the Security Type List.
- Click **Done** to return to the Edit Security Details dialog, and OK to return to the Security List.

Investing Goal List   Many Quicken users invest for specific goals, such as a college fund or retirement. Quicken provides a list of investment goals you can customize for your own investing needs. You may find investment goals useful for organizing your investments based on what you expect them to do for you. To see the Investing Goal List, open your Security List and select any security.

1. Choose the Edit action button to open the Edit Security Details dialog.
2. Click the Other Info button in the Edit Security Details dialog.
3. The Additional Security Information dialog appears. Click Edit Goals to open the Investing Goal List, as seen next.

- **New** enables you to create a new investment goal. Click this button to open the Set Up Investing Goal dialog in which you can enter a name for the goal. Make the goal name short, as you have only 15 characters.
- **Edit** enables you to change the name of the currently selected investment goal.
- **Delete** enables you to remove the currently selected investment goal from the list.

If the goal is assigned to any securities, you'll see a prompt asking if you're sure. If you answer yes, your goal is deleted. The securities using that goal will be assigned the first goal in the Investing Goal List.

- The **Help** icon displays the Quicken Personal Finances Help window with instructions for working with the Investing Goal List.
- **Print** prints the Investing Goal List.

Click Done to close the Investing Goal List, then click OK to close the Additional Security Information dialog, then OK to close the Edit Security Details dialog and return to the Security List.

Using the Account Overview Window

The Account Overview window displays the holdings and status of an investment account. To access this window, select an account from the Account Bar, and from the Action gear icon menu, choose Account Overview or the Holdings button. This window is organized into snapshots of information about the currently selected account. See Chapter 7 for more detailed information.

If you commonly refer to the Account Overview, you may wish to add the action to your action bar using the Customize Action Bar dialog.

Using Transaction Download and Research Tools

In This Chapter:

- *Reviewing your investing accounts*
- *Setting up transaction downloads*
- *Using the Online Center window*
- *Exploring the Account Overview window*
- *Setting up the download*
- *Creating a Watch List*
- *Viewing downloaded quotes*
- *Exporting your portfolio*
- *Utilizing Quote Lookup*
- *Using online research*

Quicken offers three separate features for tracking investments online:

- **Downloading Transactions** enables you to download transactions and balances for your investment accounts to help automate the entry of investment transactions and keep your Quicken records in sync with your brokerage firm's records.
- **Quotes Download** allows you to obtain current and historical quotes; asset allocation information; and news headlines about individual stocks, mutual funds, and other investments. The feature automates the tracking of market values and provides

valuable information you can use to make better investment decisions. This feature can also alert you to important information about securities you own or watch.

- **Quicken.com Update** enables you to put a copy of your investment portfolio on the Quicken.com website, where you can track its value from any computer connected to the Internet—even without Quicken.

This chapter tells you about each of these features and explains how they can help you save time and stay informed about your investments. It also tells you about some of the features on Quicken.com that can help you research investments.

The instructions in this chapter assume that you have already configured your computer for an Internet connection. If you have not done so, do it now. This chapter also assumes that you understand the topics and procedures discussed in Chapters 1 and 4, and it builds on many of the basic concepts discussed in those chapters.

Transaction Download

You can download transactions, balance details, and holdings information directly from the financial institutions with which you maintain investment accounts. Each transaction can then be entered into your Quicken investment account with the click of a mouse button. You can also review downloaded account balance details and compare downloaded holdings information to the information recorded in your portfolio.

Reviewing Your Investing Accounts

When you click the Investing tab for the first time, you are taken to the Portfolio view of your investing accounts. This allows you to view information about your investment portfolio. Learn more about the individual views of the Investing tab in Chapter 8.

Click an account name, either in the Portfolio view or from the Account Bar, to open the account's Investment Transactions List. See "Reviewing and Accepting Transactions" later in this chapter for more information about investing account transactions.

From the Portfolio View

When you are in the Investing tab's Portfolio view, you can see the securities held in each investing account by clicking the small right-facing arrow to the left of each account, as seen next. The arrow turns into a downward-facing arrow, and the name of each security within that account displays. Click the small plus sign to the left of a security to see all the lots of that security you have entered in Quicken, listed from oldest purchase to newest purchase.

Portfolio	Performance	Allocations		

Show:	Value		Group by:	Accounts	

	Name ▲		Quote/Price	Shares
▶	Brokerage			
▶	IRA			
▶	IRA #1			
▶	KEOGH			
▼	Watch List (add) (edit)			
	AAPL	📇	494.04	
	Ford	📇	16.35	
	HRZN		13.25	
	NOK	📇	5.13	
	RadioShack Corp	📇	3.35	
	SWZ		13.6236	
	Zumiez Inc		26.03	

⊞ Ford	📇	16.35	100	1,635.00	961.00	674.00	70.14	16.00 ⬆
⊟ INTUIT INC	📇	64.35	252	16,216.20	5,592.00	10,624.20	189.99	206.64 ⬆
Lot 1/1/2010			152	9,781.20	0.00	9,781.20	N/A	124.64
Lot 6/11/2012		55.42	100	6,435.00	5,592.00	843.00	15.08	82.00
⊞ NOK	📇	5.13	50	256.50	205.00	51.50	25.12	61.50 ⬆

Click a security's name to open the Security Detail View. As seen in Figure 7-1, the Security Detail View displays extensive information about your security in one location. Click Close to return to the main Quicken window.

From the Account Bar

Click an account's name to open the Transaction List. Each transaction displays on a separate line. Unlike banking and asset registers, the gear icon Actions menu does not have a built-in option to change this view to a two-line display. To show your list as two lines,

1. From the Actions menu, select Register Preferences, which opens the Quicken Preferences dialog to the Investment Transactions Preferences.
2. From the List Display drop-down list, choose Two Line.
3. Click OK to close the Preferences dialog.

Figure 7-1 • Use the Security Detail View to see a wide variety of information about each security in your portfolio.

You may sort your transactions in an investment account's Transaction List by clicking the Date arrow. If the arrow is pointing up, the transactions sort with the oldest date on the first line of the Transaction List. If the arrow points down, the transactions sort with the most recent transaction listed first. You can also sort by any heading with a bold font, including the Attachments, Clr, Action, and Security columns.

You may also change the default date display in the Investment Transactions Preferences by choosing either Oldest First or Most Recent First.

Setting Up Transaction Downloads

As with any account, to download transactions for an account, you must first configure the account for online services. If you told Quicken you would enter an account's information manually, you will need to enter additional information as well. To download from any institution, you need your user ID for that institution, the password for the account, and in some cases, the account number.

Applying for Transaction Downloads

Before you can download transactions, you may need to apply for download access as you learned in Chapter 1. Normally, all it takes is a phone call, although many brokerage and investment firms allow you to apply online through the company website. To access your account with Quicken, you'll likely use the same user ID and password in Quicken as you use to access your account via the Web; however, this is not true in all cases. Check your brokerage firm's website to see if these instructions apply to you.

If you do need to apply for Quicken access to your account, it may take up to a week for the application to be processed. You'll know that you're ready to go online when you get a letter with setup information. The setup information may consist of the following.

- **Customer ID**   This may be your Social Security number or some other ID the brokerage firm provides.
- **Account Number**   This is the number for your account at the brokerage firm.
- **Password or PIN**   You'll have to enter your password or PIN into Quicken when you download transactions. Some firms send this information separately for additional security.

Setting Up the Account and Downloading Transactions

Once you have your identification numbers, it is easy to begin downloading your transactions. When the information is correctly set up, the process happens quickly.

1. From the Account Bar, right-click the account name you want to set up, and from the context menu, click Edit/Delete Account. The Account Details dialog appears. Click the Online Services tab.
2. Click Set Up Now. The Activate One Step Update dialog appears. Select or type the name of the financial institution, and click Next. Depending on your Internet connection speed, you may see a spinning circle while Quicken gathers the information.
3. Enter the user name and password you received, and click Connect. Quicken lists all the accounts it finds at the institution. Quicken may prompt you asking if you wish to add, link, or ignore accounts found at the financial institution, as shown here.

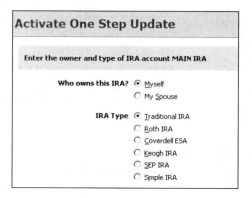

4. If you choose Add, you can enter a nickname for the account. Type the name you want to use, and click Next. Quicken connects to the Internet to download transactions and balances for your account.
5. If one of your accounts is an IRA, Quicken asks you to identify the owner of the account and the IRA account type, as seen here. Indicate your answers and click Next.
6. When the download has completed, you see the Account Added dialog with the name of your account, as well as the number of days for which transactions were downloaded. Click Finish to close the dialog.

As you enter your password, you see the Save This Password check box. If you check the box, the Password Vault dialog appears as explained in Chapter 4.

Activate Web Connect

If your institution does not yet offer Direct Connect services, you may be able to use Web Connect services or Express Web Connect if that connection method is available. You may recall from Chapter 4 that Web Connect services enable you to download information from your institution's website. To do this, you must log in to your financial institution's website using the information your financial institution supplies, navigate to a download page, and indicate what data you want to download. Once the Web Connect file has been downloaded, Quicken reads it and knows exactly to which Quicken account it applies. Read more about connection methods in Chapter 4.

While each institution is slightly different, at some point you will be prompted to enter your user ID and/or password. Depending on your institution, you may be asked for additional information, such as your security question, before you have access to your account.

You may tell Quicken to save your Web Connect downloads to a specific filename and location of your choosing. To do so, click Edit | Preferences | Web Connect | Web Connect Preferences, and click the Give Me The Option Of Saving To A File Whenever I Download Web Connect Data check box. Click OK to close the Preferences dialog.

Reviewing and Accepting Transactions

After you download, the One Step Update Summary appears showing that the account has been updated successfully. A small red flag to the left of your account in the Account Bar indicates that there are transactions to review. Click the account to review the transactions.

Depending on your preference settings, you may not see the One Step Update Summary unless there is an error.

Automatic Transaction Entry

Quicken has the ability to accept and enter your downloaded transactions automatically. To enable this action, click Edit | Preferences | Register | Downloaded Transactions | Downloaded Transaction Preferences | After Downloading Transactions, and click the Automatically Add To Investment Transaction Lists check box.

Many Quicken users do not enable the automatic transaction entry. Instead, they review the downloaded transactions and accept the individual transactions one by one, or they click Accept All after they have reviewed the download.

1. You can also tell Quicken which accounts to use for this automatic entry.
2. Right-click the account's name in the Account Bar, and choose Edit/Delete Account to open the Account Details dialog for that account.
3. Click the Online Services tab.
4. Click the Automatic Entry Is: On (or Off) link. The Automatic Transaction Entry dialog appears.

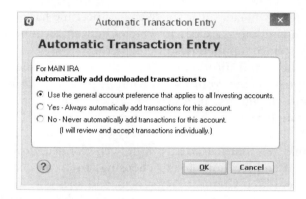

5. Choose one of the three choices:
   - Use The General Account Preference That Applies To All Investing Accounts if you want to have the option you chose in Preferences apply to this account.
   - Yes – Always Automatically Add Transactions For This Account if you want Quicken to enter all downloaded transactions without your acceptance.
   - No – Never Automatically Add Transactions For This Account. (I Will Review And Accept Transactions Individually.) This is your choice if you want to review each transaction before it is entered into the account's Transaction List.
6. Click OK to close the Automatic Transaction Entry dialog.
7. After clicking OK, you may see a warning dialog explaining more about your selection. Click OK or Cancel to dismiss this warning, and then click OK to close the Account Details dialog.

When you are in the account's Transaction List, click Downloaded Transactions to review and accept the items that have been downloaded. You may handle your downloaded transactions in two different ways:

- **Review Each Transaction**   Use this method if your account information is currently up to date. It allows you to look at each of the downloaded transactions before deciding to accept them into your "official" Transaction List. Usually, you'll simply select a new or matched transaction and click the Accept button to accept it. Once you have accepted the transaction, it appears in your Transaction List (register) with a small "c" in the Clr column, indicating that the transaction has been processed by your financial institution.

- **Accept All**   This choice may be best the first time you download transactions because it is the fastest, but not necessarily the safest or most accurate. When you click this, all of the transactions are transferred to the Transaction List and the Cash Amt and Cash Bal fields are updated. The Downloaded Transactions pane disappears. You can use a hybrid approach by reviewing each downloaded transaction and changing any transaction that needs special handling. Then, click Accept All to accept the rest.

Remember that unaccepted downloaded transactions are not entered in your Investment Transaction List. Thus, your Transaction List and portfolio balances may be misstated until you accept all downloaded transactions.

IN MY EXPERIENCE

Many Quicken users seldom, if ever, use Accept All for any type of downloaded transactions. If they do, they will often perform a backup first from which they can restore their original data. At a minimum, users have recommended that after doing a backup, you take the time to review all of the downloaded transactions thoroughly before you click that Accept All button.

When you click Accept All, if there are sold or removed transactions in the download, you may need to follow prompts so you can enter additional required information. However, after the first time you download, be sure to back up before you accept all the transactions. If you have been entering transactions manually, the download may be slightly different, causing duplication and incorrect balances.

If your account balance as downloaded does not match your Quicken balance, Quicken adds an adjusting transaction.

Renaming Transactions

Renaming rules are not very helpful in investment accounts. The rules only affect payee names, and only cash transactions have payees. However, you may want to rename some transactions in order to make them consistent with your naming conventions, or to avoid cluttering your Transaction List with a variety of names that don't give you the information needed. In this case, you can create rules telling Quicken how to change the names of downloaded transactions. You can "rename" securities in downloaded transactions by matching the downloaded security to a security in your Security List. Once the Matched With Online Security link is established, the security will be renamed to the name from the Security List. For example, TD Ameritrade downloads GE as GENERAL ELECTRIC CO COM, but you may prefer your Security List to use "General Electric," so transactions for GE are renamed to General Electric.

Quicken generally matches to an online security automatically, but if you find the wrong security is matched, you can edit the security and clear the Matched With Online Security option. Then, at the next download, Quicken should prompt you to match the security. Editing the security and changing the name changes the security name displayed in the Transaction List. This process is useful after your first download to change the security names to the name you want displayed.

To rename transactions, click the Renaming Rules button in the Downloaded Transactions tab, or choose Tools | Renaming Rules. The Renaming Rules dialog displays. It shows the list of existing rules. If you have not yet established any Renaming Rules for downloaded transactions, there will be text in light gray font stating that no rules have been defined.

Using the Online Center Window

You can use the Online Center to download account information and compare it to data in your Quicken file. From the menu bar, choose Tools | Online Center. If necessary, choose the name of your brokerage firm from the Financial Institution drop-down list near the top of the window.

IN MY EXPERIENCE

As our world becomes smaller, some investors are finding they need to use multiple currencies with their transactions. Quicken supports this need in several ways.

To set up multicurrency usage, click Edit | Preferences | Calendar And Currency, and click the Multicurrency Support check box. The Portfolio view in the Investing tab will now include a field for the currency to be used. While the default is the U.S. dollar, you do have a number of other choices. Click OK to save the Preferences change.

When you have enabled multicurrency usage, your One Step Update downloads will automatically include currency exchange rates. If you do not want to include the exchange rates, clear the Get Currency Exchange Rates check box in the One Step Update Settings dialog.

The buttons offer a number of options you can use for working with the Online Center window:

- **Delete** deletes a selected item.
- **Contact Info** displays the Contact Information dialog for the currently selected financial institution. You can use the information in the dialog to contact the brokerage by phone, website, or e-mail if this service is offered by your financial institution.
- **Password Vault** gives you access to Quicken's Password Vault feature, as explained in Chapter 4. (This option only appears if you have enabled Online Account Services for accounts at more than one financial institution and have not yet set up the Password Vault feature.)
- **Trade**, if offered by your financial institution, connects to the Internet and displays your brokerage firm's home page in an Internet window. You can then log in to make online trades.
- **Print** prints the transactions listed in the Transaction List window.
- **Options** displays a menu of commands for working with the current window.

Unusual in Quicken, there is no Help button or icon in the Online Center. However, you can always press the F1 key from within Quicken to open Quicken Help.

Downloading Transactions

To download transactions, make sure the brokerage firm is selected in the Online Center window, and then click the Update/Send button. Depending on the type of connection that is offered by your financial institution, you may see the One Step Update Setting dialog or be connected directly to your financial institution's webpage.

Enter any user names and/or passwords as required. If you are using One Step Update Settings, click Update Now. Wait while Quicken connects to your financial institution. If you want to see what you are typing when entering a password, check the Show Password Characters check box.

When Quicken is finished exchanging information, a One Step Update Summary window appears to summarize the activity that took place while you waited. (Depending on your preference settings, you may not see the One Step Update Summary dialog unless there is an error.) Click Close. If you have downloaded the information from a Web Connect website, sign off, if required, and close the connection to your institution's website.

If you display the Online Center window again, any transactions you downloaded show in the bottom half of the window's Transactions subtab for the selected financial institution.

Adjusting the Cash Balance

If the cash balance in your Quicken account doesn't match the cash balance at your brokerage firm, you can adjust the cash balance with the Update Cash Balance dialog. From the Account Bar, click the account you want to adjust. The account's Transaction List appears. From the account's Transaction List, click the Action gear icon | Update Cash Balance. Enter the correct cash balance and the date, and click Done. Quicken adjusts the account accordingly.

In the same way, use the Update Share Balance option to make any corrections to the number of shares in an account.

Reconciling Your Account

To keep your electronic investing accounts reconciled to your statement, you can perform a periodic reconciliation. If your account does not match your statement, you can adjust it with the Reconcile dialog. Select the account in the Account Bar to open the Transaction List. From the Action gear icon's menu, select Reconcile. The Reconcile dialog appears. Enter the starting and ending cash balance amounts and the statement ending date, and click OK.

If the brokerage account has a linked checking account, you will see a warning message telling you the account can only be reconciled from the linked checking account. Click OK to dismiss the warning. For the accounts with linked checking accounts, you'll need to perform the reconcile in the linked cash account instead. In this case, Quicken will not display the list of transactions in your brokerage account.

A list of the transactions displays. On the left are those transactions that decrease the cash balance, and on the right are those that increase it. As you click each transaction, the difference in the lower-right area of the dialog reflects the increase or decrease. Your account is successfully reconciled when the difference is equal to zero. If you want to start by marking all of the transactions, click

Mark All. This is particularly helpful when you have many transactions. When you have marked all and are finished, click Done. If you want to return to this later, click Finish Later.

When you have reconciled your account, a message will be displayed offering you the opportunity to create a reconciliation report. Click Yes or No.

- If you choose Yes, the Reconciliation Report Setup dialog appears. Enter a title name.
- Enter a date in the Show To Bank Balance As Of field.
- Choose to create a report including All Transactions or Summary And Uncleared, which shows only the uncleared transactions and a summary of the cleared items.
- Select Show Savings Goal Transactions if you choose to include them.
- Click OK to open the Print dialog. You may choose to print the report to a paper printer or to the Quicken PDF printer. You can also print to a file using the Export To option.
- If you choose No, you are returned to your account's Transaction List.

 If you click the Don't Show Me This Screen Again check box in the Reconciliation Complete dialog and want to be prompted to print a reconciliation report when completing future reconciliations, you will have to reset the warning in Preferences. From the Quicken Toolbar, click Edit | Preferences | Alerts | Warnings | Reset Quicken Warnings. Click OK to close the Preferences dialog.

IN MY EXPERIENCE

As with banking and credit card statements, Quicken does not keep prior period reconciliation reports. The only way to save them is to print them. If you do not want to keep paper copies, use the Quicken PDF printer to create a "digitally" printed file that you can view with the free Adobe Reader program.

1. In the Print dialog, click the Printer drop-down list and choose Quicken PDF Printer.
2. Click Print. A Save To PDF File dialog box appears.
3. In the Save In field, enter the name of the folder into which the report should be saved, or choose one using the drop-down arrow.
4. Name your file. Use a name that will mean something, perhaps something like Retirement Acct Reconciliation 3-31-2014.
5. Click Save. Your report is "printed" and saved to your selected folder and you are returned to the account's register or Transaction List.

Adjusting Holdings

If the holdings amounts in Quicken don't match what you've downloaded, the Enter Transactions dialog can be used to adjust your holdings. Select the account you want to adjust from the Account Bar to open the account's Transaction List. Click the Enter Transactions button located under the name of the account.

From the Enter Transaction drop-down list, select the type of transaction you want. Fill in the information needed, and when you are finished, click Enter/Done. For additional information on using the Enter Transaction dialog, see Chapter 6.

If you enter a transaction to correct an account that has a date more than one year from today's date, you may see a warning message. If you are sure the information you are entering is correct, click Yes.

Exploring the Account Overview Window

When you download transactions from your financial institution, you also receive detailed account balance information. To review this information, select the account in the Account Bar to open the Transaction List. From the Action gear icon's menu, select Account Overview. The Account Overview window for this account appears as seen in Figure 7-2. Or, you can click the Holdings button next to the Enter Transactions button. You can also add the Account Overview icon to the account's action bar for quick access each time you use the account's Transaction List.

Viewing Holdings

Your financial institution sends you information about your individual holdings. You can review this information in the Account Overview window and compare it to the information in your account statement. You can choose several ways of viewing your holdings. Click the Show menu to see the options.

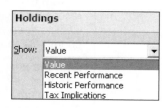

Some Quicken users prefer using the Portfolio view of the Investing tab to review their holdings.

- **Value** displays the following:
  - **Currency** displays if you have enabled multiple currencies.
  - **Quote/Price** as of the last time you downloaded.
  - **Shares** shows the number of shares you currently hold.

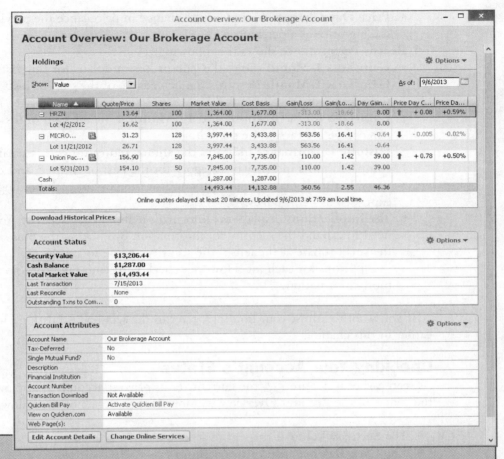

Account Overview: Our Brokerage Account										

Account Overview: Our Brokerage Account

Holdings ⚙ Options ▾

Show: Value ▾   As of: 9/6/2013

Name ▲	Quote/Price	Shares	Market Value	Cost Basis	Gain/Loss	Gain/Lo...	Day Gain...		Price Day C...	Price Da...
⊟ HRZN	13.64	100	1,364.00	1,677.00	-313.00	-18.66	8.00	⬆	+ 0.08	+0.59%
Lot 4/2/2012	16.62	100	1,364.00	1,677.00	-313.00	-18.66	8.00			
⊟ MICRO... 📄	31.23	128	3,997.44	3,433.88	563.56	16.41	-0.64	⬇	- 0.005	-0.02%
Lot 11/21/2012	26.71	128	3,997.44	3,433.88	563.56	16.41	-0.64			
⊟ Union Pac... 📄	156.90	50	7,845.00	7,735.00	110.00	1.42	39.00	⬆	+ 0.78	+0.50%
Lot 5/31/2013	154.10	50	7,845.00	7,735.00	110.00	1.42	39.00			
Cash			1,287.00	1,287.00						
Totals:			14,493.44	14,132.88	360.56	2.55	46.36			

Online quotes delayed at least 20 minutes. Updated 9/6/2013 at 7:59 am local time.

Download Historical Prices

Account Status ⚙ Options ▾

Security Value	**$13,206.44**
Cash Balance	**$1,287.00**
Total Market Value	**$14,493.44**
Last Transaction	7/15/2013
Last Reconcile	None
Outstanding Txns to Com...	0

Account Attributes ⚙ Options ▾

Account Name	Our Brokerage Account
Tax-Deferred	No
Single Mutual Fund?	No
Description	
Financial Institution	
Account Number	
Transaction Download	Not Available
Quicken Bill Pay	Activate Quicken Bill Pay
View on Quicken.com	Available
Web Page(s):	

Edit Account Details   **Change Online Services**

Figure 7-2 • Open the Account Overview window to see detailed information about an investment account.

- **Market Value** displays today's value of these shares.
- **Cost Basis** shows what you paid for these shares when you bought them, plus or minus any cost-basis–related adjustments, like dividend reinvestments, sales, or corporate actions.
- **Gain/Loss & Gain/Loss %** display your unrealized gain or loss as of the last time you downloaded in both dollars and percentages.
- **Day Gain/Loss** indicates the overall gain or loss based on the latest download prices in dollars.
- **Price Day Change** shows the trend for today for each security and the dollar amount of the change.

- **Price Day Change %** displays the change in price since the previous day's closing price as a percentage.
- **Recent Performance** shows the following:
  - **Gain/Loss 1-Month** shows the gain or loss in dollars for the past month.
  - **Gain/Loss 1-Month %** shows the percentage of the gain or loss percentage for the past month.
  - **Gain/Loss for % 3-Month and 12-Month** show the gain or loss percentage for these time periods.
- **Historic Performance** indicates the annual return for each security compared to its industry or category for the past one, three, and five years. It also displays the industry and/or category of each holding, expressed as percentages.
- **Tax Implications** displays tax information about each security. You may need to expand the security lot information by clicking the plus sign in the small square at the left of the security's name to see the tax implications for each lot. However, check with your tax professional for more information.

If you want to adjust your holdings, refer to the section "Adjusting Holdings" earlier in this chapter.

Checking Your Account's Status

As seen earlier in Figure 7-2, the current status of your account is displayed in the center of the Account Overview window. It includes all of the following:

- The **Security Value** of this entire account
- The **Cash Balance** held in this account
- The **Total Market Value**

You will also see the Linked Cash Balance if the account has a linked checking account.

This snapshot also includes the Last Transaction, Last Reconcile, and Last Statement Download dates. You can also see any transactions that need to be compared, as well as any e-mails to the account's financial institution that you need to send or read from the Online Center. Click the blue date shown to the right of Last Statement Download to go to the Online Center for this account.

Seeing the Options

In the Holdings snapshot of the Account Overview, the Options menu allows you to do the following:

- **Preferences** opens the Portfolio View Options dialog. See Chapter 8 for further information about this dialog.
- **Show Closed Lots** is also discussed in Chapter 8.
- **Get Online Quotes** uses your Internet connection to update your holdings.
- **Go To Full Portfolio** takes you to the Investing tab's Portfolio view.

If you are using Quicken Premier or higher edition, and have chosen to update your quotes every 15 minutes, your holdings are automatically updated while Quicken is the active application. To turn on this useful feature, select Edit | Preferences | Investment Transactions, and select the Automatically Update Quotes Every 15 Minutes check box. Click OK or Close to close the Preferences dialog.

The Options menu in the Account Status snapshot offers the following:

- **Reconcile This Account** opens the Account Reconciliation dialog.
- **View All My Accounts** opens the Account List.

Reviewing the Account's Attributes

The bottom snapshot of the Account Overview window displays the account name, its tax-deferment status, and other information about your account. This includes your account number and user name, so be careful if you view this information in a public setting.

From this section's Option menu, you can do the following:

- **Create a New Account**   Click this to open the Add Account dialog.
- **View/Edit Comments**   This option opens a dialog box in which you can add or edit comments about this account.
- **Set Tax Attributes**   This option opens the Tax Schedule Information dialog.
- **Set Web Pages**   You can enter the Home Page, Activity Page, and one additional webpage address for this account in this dialog.
- **Browse Web Pages**   After you have entered webpage addresses for this account, the option displays a link to those pages.
- **Transaction Fee**   This dialog allows you to enter any fees associated with this account. You may enter both fixed costs as well as percentages.

The Edit Account Details button at the bottom of the Account Overview screen opens the Account Details dialog at the General tab. The Change Online Services button opens the Account Details dialog at the Online Services tab.

Click Close to close the Account Overview screen.

Downloading Quotes and Investment Information

Quicken enables you to download up-to-date stock quotes, news headlines, and alerts for the securities in your portfolio and on your Watch List. You set up this feature once and then update the information as often as desired. You can even download historical price information so you can review price trends for a security that recently caught your attention.

Because the quote and investment information feature is built into Quicken, it doesn't rely on your brokerage firm for information. That means you can download quotes, headlines, and alerts even if your brokerage firm doesn't offer the downloading of transactions. All you need is an Internet connection and a willingness to sign up for an Intuit ID to link all your Intuit programs and website logins.

Setting Up the Download

Before you can get quotes online, you must tell Quicken to download the information. Click the One Step Update symbol (the blue right-curling arrow) on either the Account Bar or the Toolbar to open the One Step Update Settings dialog. Click the Download Quotes And Investment Information check box. Click the Select Quotes link to open the Security List, as seen in Figure 7-3. You can also open the Security List using the keyboard shortcut CTRL-Y.

Making Selections on the Security List

Using check boxes on the Security List, you may select the information you want to download for each of your securities. You may choose to

- Download quotes for each security.
- Include the security on your Watch List.
- Hide the security. However, even if you hide the security, Quicken does not uncheck the Download Quotes or Watch List check boxes.

The New Security button opens an Add Security To Quicken dialog with which you can enter a new security to the list. Review Chapter 6 for how to add a new security.

Creating a Watch List

To set up a group of securities you don't own but want to track, create a Watch List. Click the Investing tab and Portfolio. Look in the Name column for the

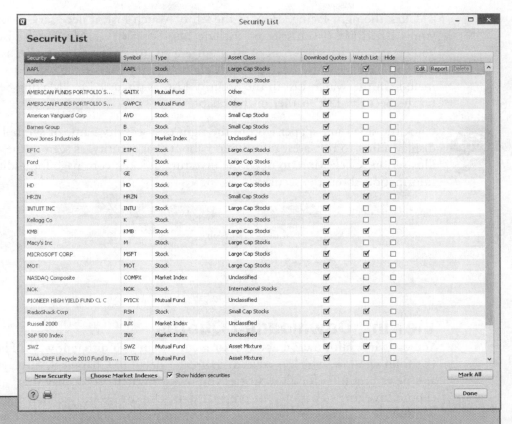

Figure 7-3 • **Use the Security List to tell Quicken the items for which you want quotes when doing a One Step Update.**

Watch List area, as shown here. If you do not see a Watch List in the Portfolio view you are using, you can click Customize, select the Accounts tab, and select Watch List in the list of accounts. Click OK to save the change and return to the Portfolio view.

Watch List (add) (edit)		
Ford	📇	17.08
HRZN		13.64
NOK	📇	5.41
RadioShack Corp	📇	3.53
SWZ		13.6525
Zumiez Inc		28.54

You can designate which securities in your Security List you want to watch by checking the Watch List check box. From any of the Portfolio views that you chose to display a Watch List, you can click the Add or Edit link to change the securities you are watching. You can also select one or more Portfolio views in which you want to display your Watch List.

Click the right-facing arrow to the left of Watch List, if necessary, to open your current list. If you selected Include This Security On My Watch List when you created each security, all of your current securities show on the list as well as any you have previously chosen to display. You may change the securities to include in the Watch List in the Security List, as discussed in "Making Selections on the Security List" earlier in this chapter.

Click the small newspaper icon to the right of a security name or symbol to display a link to the latest information about that security, as seen in the illustration. Click More to open the investing.quicken.com page for additional information about the security.

Viewing Downloaded Quotes

You can view information about your securities in two different ways. The Portfolio window, which is covered in greater detail in Chapter 8, displays quotes and news headlines for all securities you own or watch. To display this window, choose Investing | Portfolio, or press CTRL-U. Use the Security Detail View window, seen earlier in Figure 7-1, to see information about individual securities or market indexes. See "Using the Security Detail View" next in this chapter.

To open the Security Detail View:

- From the Investing tab, click Portfolio.
- Click the name of the security or index you want to view from the list that displays. If the name does not show, click the right-facing arrow to open the account, Watch List, or Indexes and click the name of the item you want to see. You can also access the Security Detail View window from the Security List, which sorts the securities by name.
- You can also access the Security Detail View from an investment account. Click any transaction, and then look for a tiny greenish chart icon to the right of the security name in that transaction. Click that icon to open the Security Detail View for that security.

You can open the Security Detail View from the Security List by clicking the name of the security or the index.

Using the Security Detail View

The Security Detail View window (see Figure 7-1) offers the most detailed quote information. If you have been faithfully downloading quotes for your securities (or you have downloaded historical quotes, as discussed in the section titled "Downloading Historical Quote Information" later in this chapter), a chart of the price history appears in the body of the window. You can use the drop-down list in the top-left corner of the window to switch from one security to another. The left side of the window discusses the details about the security, your holdings, and the latest quotes. From this window you can edit the details of your security, download quotes, create additional charts, and do online research. (See "Using Online Research" later in this chapter for more information about online research.)

Working with the Security View Detail Menu Bar   The Security View Detail menu bar has five items from which you can learn more about the selected security:

- **Edit Security Details** opens the Edit Security Details dialog, as seen here. Use this dialog to make any changes in the security, including its ticker symbol, asset class, and security type. See "Downloading Asset Class Information" later in this chapter for additional information about that topic. You can tell Quicken if this is a tax-free security. Click Other Info to open the Additional Security Information dialog in which you can indicate how much income you expect from this security, your goal for this security, your broker's name and phone number, its rating, and any other comments.

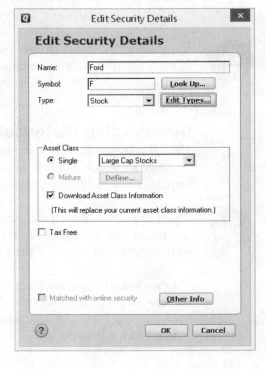

 Be cautious about editing the security's security type or investment goal. These changes can have unintended consequences.

Click OK to close the Additional Security Information dialog; then click OK to close the Edit Security Details dialog and return to the Security Detail View. There are several options at the top of the Security Detail View screen with which you can find additional information.

- **Update** opens a menu from which you can download quotes, send information to Investing.Quicken.com, download both asset classes and historical prices, and if necessary, edit the price history of this security.
- **Online Research** offers several tools, as discussed in "Using Online Research" later in this chapter.
- **Report** creates a security report that you can customize to fit your needs.
- **How Do I?** opens the Quicken Help window that discusses securities and security prices.

Viewing Price History   In the Investing tab's Portfolio view, downloaded quotes appear beside the security name or ticker symbol. Stock quotes are delayed 20 minutes or more during the trading day. Quotes for mutual funds are updated once a day by around 6:00 p.m. Eastern Standard Time. Prior to that, you'll see the previous day's prices with a small clock symbol icon beside the price, indicating that the price has not been updated since the previous trading day.

Click Close to dismiss the Price History window.

It's quicker to right-click the security in the Portfolio view and select Price History from the context menu. If you do go from the Portfolio view to the Security Detail View window, you only need to single-click the security.

Downloading Historical Quote Information

Use Quicken to download up to five years of historical quotes for any security you own or watch. Choose Investing | Update | Historical Prices. Quicken displays the Get Historical Prices dialog, shown in the next illustration.

If you happen to own a security that is not publicly traded, you won't be able to download historical quote info for it. If you have a source of price data for the security, you can import a price history file.

Choose a time period from the drop-down list at the top of the dialog. Your choices are Five Days, Month, Year, Two Years, and Five Years. Make sure check marks appear beside all securities for which you want to get historical quotes. (Click Mark All to get prices for all securities on the list.)

 Some Quicken users have reported trouble when selecting five years of prices for many securities at the same time. Several have suggested that you request data for five years for a single security or one month for several securities.

Then click the Update Now button. With your Internet connection, Quicken retrieves the information you requested. When it's done, it displays the One Step Update Summary window. Click Close to dismiss the window. Depending on your preference setting, you may not see the One Step Update Summary window unless there is an error.

Downloading Asset Class Information

For each publicly traded security you own or watch, you can include asset class information. This enables you to create accurate asset allocation reports and graphs. Chapter 6 explains how to enter asset class information manually; Chapter 8 explains how you can use this information to diversify your portfolio to meet your investment goals.

The trouble is that most mutual funds consist of many investments in a variety of asset classes. Manually looking up and entering this information is time-consuming and tedious. Fortunately, Quicken automatically downloads this information for you, including your mutual funds.

However, you can change the information at any time. To do so, choose the Investing tab and click Tools | Security List. Click the security you want, and then click the Edit action button. This opens the Edit Security Details dialog seen earlier in this chapter. Make sure the Download Asset Class Information check box is selected, close the dialog, and click OK. The next time you update, asset classes are automatically updated.

Using Investing.Quicken.com for Updates

Using Investing.Quicken.com enables you to track your portfolio's value on the Web. Although you can do this without Quicken by manually customizing and updating the default portfolio webpage at Investing.Quicken.com, it's a lot easier to have Quicken automatically send updated portfolio information to the page for you.

During the registration process when you installed Quicken, you created a member ID and password. The registration process set up a private Investing.Quicken.com account for you to store your portfolio data.

Exporting Your Portfolio

In Quicken, choose Investing | Update | Update Portfolio On Investing.Quicken.com. The Preferences dialog is shown next.

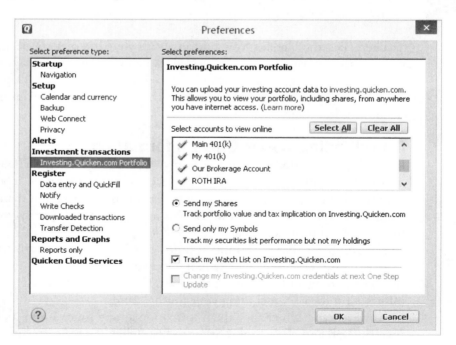

Click to place green check marks beside each account that you want to track on the Web. If you also want to track Watch List items on the Web, select the Track My Watch List On Investing.Quicken.com check box. Finally, select one of the following upload options:

- **Send My Shares** exports the ticker symbols and the number of shares of each security you own for your portfolio. This enables you to track both prices and portfolio values.
- **Send Only My Symbols** exports just the ticker symbols for your portfolio. This enables you to track prices but not portfolio values.

When you've completed your selections, click OK. The next time you run One Step Update, your account will be updated.

To access your Investing.Quicken.com account, go to the Internet from any location. In the address bar of your browser, type **http://investing.quicken.com**. You are prompted for your Quicken.com registration member ID and password. Type the information and click Sign In and your Investing Home page appears.

Utilizing Quote Lookup

Use the Quote Lookup feature in the Investing Home tab at Investing.Quicken.com, as shown here, to look up stock ticker symbols. These symbols are required to use Quicken's Online Research feature for getting quotes and obtaining information about securities on the Web.

In the Quote field, type the ticker symbol for your security. If you don't know the symbol, or it does not appear on the pop-up list, click Lookup. Quicken displays the Symbol Lookup dialog in a Quicken browser window. Type all or part of the security name in the text box, and click Search. Quicken organizes the results by security type: Stocks, Mutual Funds, ETFs, and Indices. Click the tab of the security type you want, and examine the securities it found that matched the criteria you entered.

Since the Lookup feature opens another browser window, once you are done looking up symbols, close the new browser window to return to the browser window displaying your Investing.Quicken.com information. You can also click the security name that matches the symbol you entered. This will close the second browser window and display the quote information for the security you selected.

Using Online Research

The Investing.Quicken.com site has a number of useful research tools. You can use these tools to find and learn about securities before you invest. This part of the chapter tells you a little about Quicken's online research tools so you can explore them. Most Quicken users find them valuable resources for making wise investment decisions. You can access online research information for a specific security from the Security Detail View window. Press CTRL-Y to open the Security List. Select a security, and from the Security Detail View menu bar, select Online Research to open a menu.

- **Get Full Quote and Quotes and Research** Both of these menu choices take you to the Investing.Quicken.com sign-in site. Sign in to see a wide variety of information about your security.
- **News** This option opens to the latest news about the security you selected. It can be information ranging from the company's board of directors announcement about a dividend or the latest press release from the company's media department.
- **One-Click Scorecard** This option displays reports to help you evaluate your security before you invest, using a variety of well-known analysis techniques and strategies.
- **Set Up Alerts** When you export your portfolio to Investing.Quicken.com you can set online alerts for price changes, volume movement, and any other news that might impact your portfolio.
- **Stock Evaluator** The Stock Evaluator command opens Investing.Quicken.com to the Evaluator section. From this section, both growth trends and the financial health of your chosen security are graphed and explained. Another useful section of the Evaluator is the Management Performance assessment. This section includes price to earnings, price to sales, and price to earnings growth ratios.
- **Multiple Security Charting** Use this option to chart the closing prices of up to five securities and include up to three indexes in your chart. To do so:

  1. Click Multiple Security Charting to open the Multiple Security Charting dialog, shown in the following illustration.
  2. Select the period of time you want to cover from the For What Period? drop-down list. The default is three months, but you can choose from seven more options.

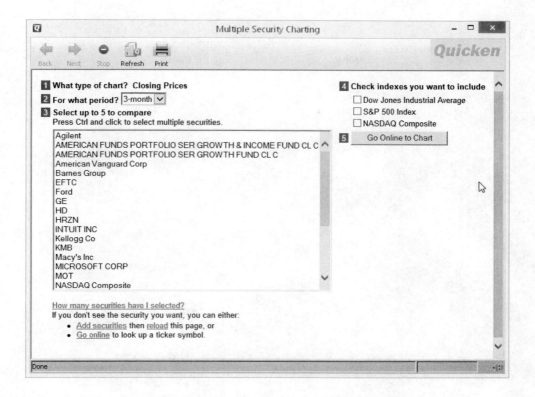

3. Choose the securities you want to chart. To do so, click the name of the first security and hold down your CTRL key while choosing up to four more.

4. Select any indexes you want to include. However, you may choose no more than a total of five selections, including both securities and indexes.

5. Click Go Online To Chart to complete your chart. Using your Internet connection and the Yahoo! Finance page, the chart displays information using the first security name (alphabetically) as its base.

You can access these tools as well from the Classic menu. Click View | Classic Menus to display the extended menu list. Choose Investing | Online Portfolio to open the Investing.Quicken.com login page. Sign in to open the site.

Evaluating Your Position

In This Chapter:

- *Understanding the Portfolio view*
- *Studying your performance*
- *Exploring asset allocation*
- *Updating your investments*
- *Working with reports*
- *Utilizing Investing tab tools*
- *Using asset allocation*
- *Analyzing your portfolio*
- *Previewing your buy/sell decisions*
- *Estimating capital gains*
- *Setting investment alerts*

As you enter transactions into Quicken—whether manually or automatically via Transaction Download—Quicken builds a portrait of your investment portfolio and performance. If you're serious about investing, you can use this information to evaluate your investing position and fine-tune your portfolio to diversify and maximize returns.

Quicken's Investing tab offers a wide range of tools—including reports, graphs, alerts, analysis tools, and reference materials—that you can use to evaluate and strengthen your investment positions. This chapter takes a closer look at the features that can make you a better investor.

Using the Investing Tab

The Investing tab should be your first stop for evaluating your investment position. Each of its views includes snapshots with calculated information and links to more information within Quicken and on the Quicken.com Investing page. Because the Investing tab always displays the most recent information it has, its windows are most useful immediately after downloading quotes, news, and research information, as discussed in Chapter 7. If you are using Quicken Premier or a higher version, you can tell Quicken to download quotes for you every 15 minutes. To do so, select Edit | Preferences | Investment Transactions | Automatically Update Quotes Every 15 Minutes.

Quicken must be the active window for this to work. If you are using another program or have minimized Quicken, Quicken will not update quotes until you make it the active window.

Click the Investing tab to open the Investing tab window. If you do not see the Investing tab, select View | Tabs To Show and click Investing. By default, the first time you open the Investing tab, the Portfolio view appears. Additional information is available in the views found by clicking the Performance or Allocations button as discussed later in this chapter.

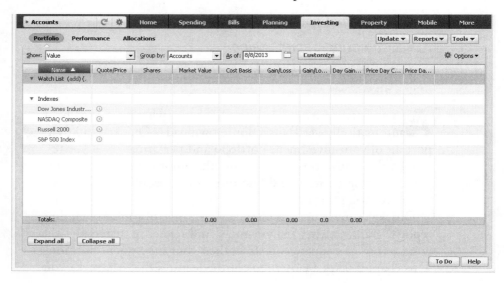

If you have visited the Investing tab before, you may need to select the Portfolio view, as Quicken remembers the last view on the Investment tab you visited.

This part of the chapter takes you on a guided tour of Quicken's Investing tab so you know exactly how you can use it to monitor your investments.

Understanding the Portfolio View

The Portfolio view of the Investing tab displays all of your investments in one place. You can view your information in a wide variety of ways to show exactly what you need to see to understand the performance, value, or components of your portfolio.

Open the Portfolio window by clicking the Portfolio button in the Investing tab or by pressing CTRL-U from any location in Quicken.

Using Portfolio View Options

You can quickly customize the Portfolio window's view by using the Show, Group By, and As Of drop-down lists right beneath the Portfolio, Performance, and Allocations buttons, seen next. You can further customize the view by clicking the Customize button. There are many view combinations—far too many to illustrate in this book. Here's a brief overview so you can explore these options on your own.

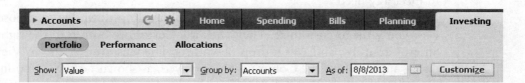

Using Show Options   The Show drop-down list enables you to specify the view by which you want the information displayed. You can customize each of the nine predefined views, shown here, with the Customize Current View dialog, discussed later in this section. You can also create nine "custom" views to see data in ways most useful to you.

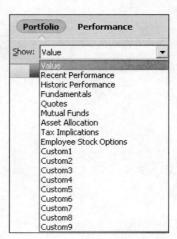

Using Group By Options   The Group By options enable you to select the order in which securities appear. The drop-down list offers six options: Accounts, Industry, Security, Security Type, Investing Goal, and Asset Class. These options correspond to information entered as part of a security's definition, either manually when you add the security to Quicken or automatically when you download asset class information. Learn how to add securities to Quicken in Chapter 6 and how to download security information in Chapter 7.

Using Portfolio Date Use the As Of drop-down list to set the date for which you want to view the portfolio. For example, suppose you want to see what your portfolio looked like a month ago, before a particularly volatile market period. You can either enter that date in the text box or click the calendar button beside the text box to display a calendar of dates, and then click the date you want to display. The view changes to show your portfolio as of the date you specified.

You can use several date keyboard shortcuts in the date field. Position your mouse key in the As Of date field and a small calendar appears. Press M for the beginning of the month and H for the end of the month.

Customizing a View

Quicken offers an incredible amount of flexibility when it comes to displaying information in the Portfolio window. In addition to the nine preconfigured views found in the Show drop-down list, you can quickly create additional views to meet any need.

To customize a view, begin by using the Show drop-down list to choose the view you want to customize. Then click the Customize button to the right of the Show, Group By, and As Of drop-down lists. The Customize Current View dialog appears with the Columns tab displayed, as shown next. Set options as desired in the dialog, and click OK to change the view.

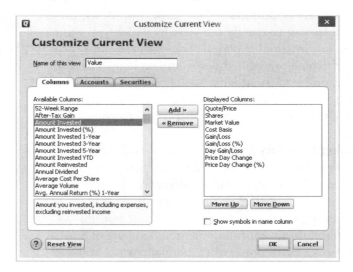

Selecting Columns to Show   To display a column of information, select it in the Available Columns list and click the Add button beside it. To hide a column of information, select it in the Displayed Columns list and click the Remove button. You're not removing the information, just choosing not to display it. You can change the order in which columns appear by selecting a column name in the Displayed Columns list and using the Move Up or Move Down button to change its order in the list.

A short explanation of the column's data displays with a yellow highlight at the bottom of the Available Columns list for the column you currently have selected. This feature is handy when you are trying to decide which columns will be most useful to you.

Displaying Symbols Rather Than Names   To display a security's ticker symbol rather than its name, select the Show Symbols In Name Column check box.

Return to Default   Click the Reset View button at the lower left of the Customize Current View dialog to return this view to the default settings.

Selecting Accounts to Include   As you are customizing your view, you can specific which accounts you want to appear. Click the Accounts tab, shown next, and toggle the check marks to the left of the account names in the Accounts To Include In This View list. Only those accounts with a check mark will appear. You can specify which accounts appear by selecting an account name in the Accounts To Include In This View list and clicking the Move Up or Move Down button.

Click Select All to include all of your accounts, or click Clear All to clear all of the check marks and start over. To include hidden accounts in the Accounts To Include In This View list, select the Show (Hidden Accounts) check box, as seen in the illustration here. To reset the view to the default settings, click the Reset View button.

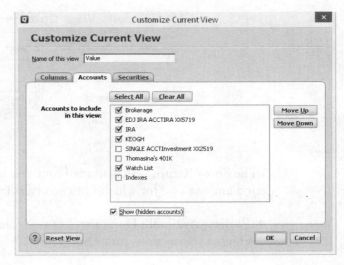

Selecting Securities to Include   Click the Securities tab to specify which securities should appear. Toggle the check marks to the left of the security names in the Securities To Include In This View list. Only those securities that are selected will appear. To include hidden securities in the Securities To Include In This View list, select the Show (Hidden Securities) check box.

Click Select All to include all of your securities, or click Clear All to clear all of the check marks and start over. To reset the view to the default settings, click the Reset View button at the bottom left of the Securities tab dialog.

When you have finished creating your new view, click OK to return to the Investing tab's Portfolio view.

Setting Portfolio View Options

Click either the Options Action icon (the small gear icon) or the word Options at the far right of the Portfolio view to customize the current view, as explained earlier, as well as to perform two additional tasks, as shown here.

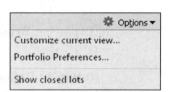

Portfolio Preferences   From the Investing tab Portfolio view, click Options | Portfolio Preferences to open the Portfolio View Options dialog.

This option enables you to specify the period for return calculations and the tax rate used in the Portfolio window, as shown here. Setting these options enables you to fine-tune the way Quicken makes Portfolio window calculations.

The Show Return Calculations From area offers options for determining the period and tax rate for which Quicken calculates the return on investment:

* **Earliest Available Date**, the default, includes all periods for which you have entered transactions into Quicken.

- A blank field allows you to enter a starting date for calculations. All transactions between the starting date you enter and the current date are included in the calculations. Alternatively, you can use the calendar icon to set the date.
- **Tax Rate Used In Portfolio View** allows you to choose tax rates that should be used in tax calculations for capital gains. If you are utilizing Quicken's Tax Planner, as covered in Chapter 13, keep the default, Use Tax Planner Rate, selected. Otherwise, choose the rates that are appropriate for your financial situation. Check with your tax professional for further information about your specific situation. Click OK to save your changes and return to the Portfolio view.

Show Closed Lots   This option tells Quicken that you want to display lots that have been closed.

Studying Your Performance

If you are using Quicken's Premier (or higher) edition, the Performance button's view in the Investing tab displays graphs, such as the one seen next, and tables of information about your investment performance. You can customize many of the snapshots that appear in the Performance view using commands on each snapshot's Options menu. You can further customize the Performance view window by using the drop-down list options at the top of the Performance view window. All of the snapshots on Performance and Allocations views are controlled by the drop-down list selections.

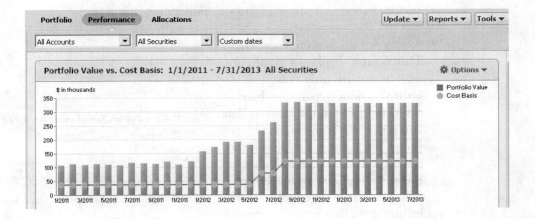

Portfolio Value vs. Cost Basis

The Portfolio Value vs. Cost Basis graph uses a line graph and a bar graph to illustrate your portfolio's cost basis—which may or may not be the amount you've invested—and its market value. Ideally, you want the tops of the bars to appear above the line, indicating that your account is worth more than you spent to buy the securities.

IN MY EXPERIENCE

The Investment Performance reports the average annual return (AAR) for each investment. One of my clients thought this report presented the return on investment (ROI), which is a different calculation.

- To compute ROI, you subtract the total cost of an investment from the total gain and divide that result by the total cost.
- To calculate the AAR, you add the annual return percentage rates and divide that result by the number of years.

To see ROI information, from the Investing tab, click Portfolio | Customize. From the Customize Current View dialog, choose any of the five ROI calculations from the Available Columns list and add your choice(s) to the Displayed Columns list on the right side of the dialog. Click OK to display the information, which is shown in percentages.

Be aware the investment amount is over the lifetime you have owned the security, so if you have bought, sold, and then bought some more, you may not get the results you expect.

The Options menu offers additional choices for this graph:

- **Go To A Full Screen View Of This Graph** displays a graph, as seen here, with only your portfolio value versus cost basis information as of the custom date you set in the Performance Date Range drop-down list. If you did not set a date, it uses today's date.
- **Show Value/Cost Basis Report** tells Quicken to show the information in a report format. You can hide the report and

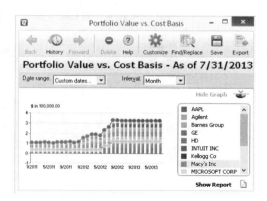

see only the graph, or hide the graph and see only the
report with one click on either the Hide Report or Hide
Graph icon.

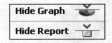

- **Go To Full Portfolio** returns you to the Investing tab's
Portfolio view.

Growth Of $10,000

The Growth Of $10,000 chart illustrates how an investment of $10,000 in your
portfolio has grown over the period you choose. You can select check boxes
beside popular investment indexes to compare your investment performance to
one or more indexes, as shown here.

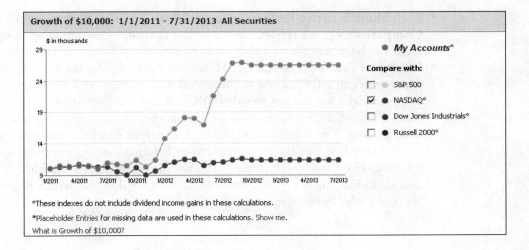

If you have not updated recently and chosen an index to compare to the
performance of your securities, you may see a message prompting you to do an
additional download.

Average Annual Return

The Average Annual Return chart displays the one-year, three-year, and five-year
return on each of your investment accounts. If the account has one or more
securities in the one-, three-, or five-year period, there will be an average annual
return reported for the account. If the account did not exist or no lots of the
account's securities existed during the one-, three-, or five-year period, the
average annual return will show as N/A.

Your account settings in Quicken 2014 impact the accounts displayed here. You will not be able to see any accounts you have marked as Keep This Account Separate. If you do not see the accounts you expect to see, check the Tools | Manage Hidden Accounts screen to see if the account is marked as Keep This Account Separate. Also, the drop-down list for selecting the accounts to show in the Performance view lists the accounts in alphabetical order, while the Average Annual Return graph shows the accounts in the order listed in the Account List. This may be different from alphabetical order if you have ever moved accounts around in the Account List. This also applies for the Allocations view.

The options for this section let you change the information's display.

- Both **Show Security Performance** and **Show Security Performance Comparison** open a report, similar to the Portfolio view, showing how your securities have done as of a date you choose.
- **Historical Prices** opens the Get Historical Prices dialog, shown next, from which you can tell Quicken to download historical prices for one or more of your securities for the last five days, the last month, year, two years, or five years. Place check marks in front of the name of each security for which you want pricing. The Mark All and Clear All buttons can help you make your selections. Click Update Now to use your Internet connection to download the data. The One Step Update Summary dialog displays when the download is complete. Click Close to close the dialog and return to the Investing tab's Performance view.

If you have selected the Show This Dialog Only If There Is An Error check box at the lower-left corner of the One Step Update window, you may not see the One Step Update Summary.

Exploring Asset Allocation

The Allocations view of the Investing tab displays a number of customizable snapshots of your investment data in both graphical and tabular formats. Each snapshot has links to other features. Each of the graphs that appear in the Allocations view can be customized using commands on the graph's Options menu. Buttons beneath each chart enable you to go to a full-sized graph in a report window or view a related report. You can further customize the Allocations view window by selecting one of the drop-down list options: All Accounts, Investing Only, Retirement Only, or one of your accounts. You can also select Custom to select specific accounts you want to display.

Reviewing Your Asset Allocation

Asset allocation, which is covered in detail later in this chapter, refers to the way in which your investment dollars are distributed among different types of investments. It's a measure of how well your portfolio is diversified.

The Asset Allocation graph displays two pie charts: Actual allocation and Target allocation. Actual allocation indicates your portfolio's current diversification, as seen next. The illustration shows that the majority of the

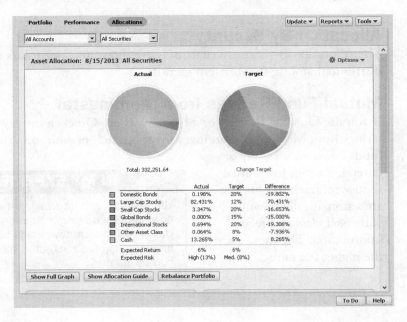

securities in this account are invested in large-cap stocks. Target allocation is the allocation you set up with Quicken's Portfolio Rebalancer, seen later in this chapter, in the section titled "Using the Portfolio Rebalancer." If you have not yet used the Portfolio Rebalancer, the Target allocation pie won't have any slices.

Allocation By Account

Also in the Allocations view of the Investing tab are two additional charts, shown next. The Allocation By Account chart indicates how your portfolio's market value is distributed among the investing accounts you have entered into Quicken.

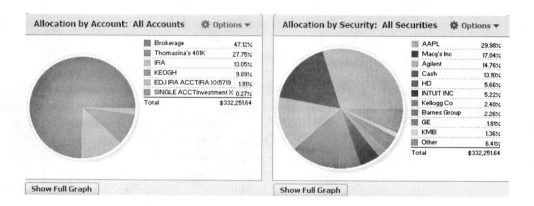

Allocation By Security

The Allocation By Security chart indicates how your portfolio's market value is distributed among the different securities.

Mutual Fund Ratings from Morningstar

If you use Quicken Premier or a higher version, Quicken displays up-to-date ratings from Morningstar, an investment research organization that rates mutual funds based on a variety of criteria. Ratings for mutual funds you track in Quicken are automatically downloaded with asset class and related information. The more stars, the higher the rating.

IN MY EXPERIENCE

You may notice that running the Quotes download takes longer than earlier versions of Quicken. Quicken downloads both current and historical quotes each time you download the current quotes.

Updating Your Investments

The Update button at the right of all three views in the Investing tab works with your Internet connection to keep your portfolio up to date:

- **Quotes** downloads the current quotations for either your entire portfolio or the securities you have selected.

 If it seems your portfolio values are not updating when you run the Quotes download, check your Download Quotes and Watch List selections in the Security List. Press CTRL-Y to open the Security List.

- **Historical Prices** opens the Get Historical Prices dialog discussed earlier in this chapter.
- **Update Portfolio On Investing.Quicken.com** opens the Preferences dialog for Investing.Quicken.com. Learn more about Investing.Quicken.com in Chapter 7, and learn more about Preferences in Appendix B.
- **One Step Update** opens the One Step Update Settings dialog from which you can tell Quicken which accounts you want to update.

Working with Reports

The Reports button's menu, shown here, offers a wide variety of reports, you can customize to meet your needs.

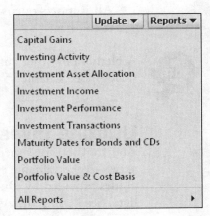

- **Capital Gains** reports can be for any date range you choose and can be subtotaled by Short- vs. Long-Term, Month, Quarter, Year, Account, Security, Security Type, Investing Goal, and Asset Class.
- **Investing Activity** reports display the activity, income (or loss), and capital gains for your accounts, based on the date range you set. This report is only available in Quicken Premier and higher versions.
- **Investment Asset Allocation** reports can be displayed both as graphs and reports. Use the Date Range drop-down list to tell Quicken the date range you want to display.
- **Investment Income** reports display the income and expenses related to your investments. These can be customized by date range, subtotals, or organization, such as Income & Expense or Cash Flow Basis.

- **Investment Performance** reports show the return and average annual return on your accounts based on the date range and subtotal options you choose.

When you customize the Investment Performance report, you may choose to display the cash flow detail as well as displaying the cents as in other reports. To do so, ensure the check box by Cash Flow Detail is checked in the Show area of the Customize Investment Performance dialog. This is the only report that allows you to display that information.

- **Investment Transactions** reports show complete data about your transactions for time periods you designate. You can subtotal in several different ways as well as customize the date range of the report to meet your needs.
- **Maturity Dates For Bonds And CDs** creates a detailed report of when your instruments will mature.
- **Portfolio Value** displays the total value of your holdings in both a graph and a report. This report can be customized by date range and subtotal intervals to show your information in the way you want to see it.
- **Portfolio Value & Cost Basis** reports show the cost and value of each of your securities as of the date and subtotal interval you specify.
- **All Reports** opens the same menu you see when clicking Reports on the menu bar.

A plethora of other customization options is available in the Customize Report dialogs. See Chapter 5 for a discussion of many of the options.

Utilizing Investing Tab Tools

The Tools button's menu gives you access to the valuable estimators and guides provided by Quicken, as seen here. See "Using the Asset Allocation Guide," "Previewing Your Buy/Sell Decisions," and "Estimating Capital Gains" later in this chapter.

Using Investment Analysis Tools

In addition to the Quicken.com-based investment research tools discussed in Chapter 7, Quicken offers a number of built-in tools that can help you learn more about investing and analyze your investment portfolio.

This part of the chapter introduces these analysis tools so you can explore them more fully on your own.

Using Asset Allocation

Many investment gurus say that an investor's goals should determine his or her asset allocation. If you're not sure what your asset allocation should be, Quicken includes a wealth of information about asset allocation, including sample portfolios with their corresponding allocations. You can use this feature to learn what your target asset allocation should be to meet your investing goals. Then you can monitor your asset allocation and, if necessary, rebalance your portfolio to keep it in line with what it should be.

Using the Asset Allocation Guide

The Asset Allocation Guide explains what asset allocation is, why it's important, and how Quicken can help monitor it in your portfolio. Choose Investing | Tools | Asset Allocation Guide. The Asset Allocation Guide window appears as seen next.

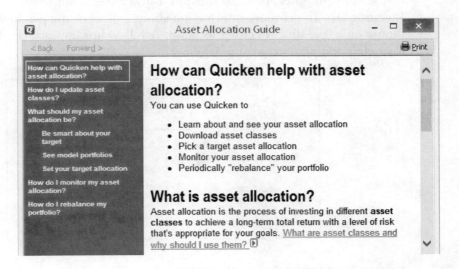

To take full advantage of this feature, read the information on the main part of the window. You can click links within the text or in the left column to learn more about specific topics. If you're new to asset allocation, you may find the See Model Portfolios link especially useful. It shows suggested asset allocations based on risk and returns for a number of portfolios. Click Close to return to the Investing tab.

Monitoring Your Asset Allocation

To monitor the asset allocation of your portfolio, you must enter asset class information for each of your investments. You can do this in two ways:

- **Manually enter asset class information** Although this isn't difficult for stocks, it can be time-consuming for investments that have an asset class mixture, such as mutual funds.
- **Download asset class information** If you have a connection to the Internet, this is the best way to enter this information. With a few clicks, Quicken does all of the work in seconds. The information is complete and accurate. Learn how to download asset class information in Chapter 7.

Viewing Your Asset Allocation

If you have chosen to display all of your accounts and all of your securities in the Asset Allocation graph in the Allocations view's Asset Allocation snapshot, the pie chart that appears in the Asset Allocation Guide window is the same chart you see in your Asset Allocation snapshot in the Allocations view of your Investing tab. To get more information about a piece of the pie, hover your mouse on a "pie slice" in either location. A yellow box appears, displaying the asset class and percentage of portfolio value.

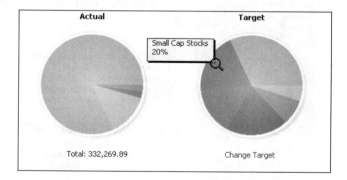

Setting Your Target Asset Allocation If you know what you want your asset allocation to be, you can set up a target asset allocation. Quicken then displays your target in the pie chart beside the current asset allocation chart on the Investing tab's Allocations button's Asset Allocation snapshot so you can monitor how close you are to your target.

Display the Allocations view of the Investing tab window. Then choose Change Target Allocations from the Options menu at the right of the Asset Allocation snapshot. The Target Allocation dialog appears:

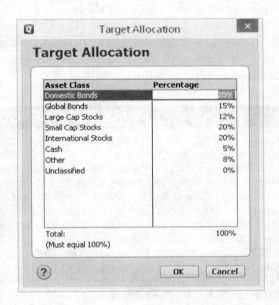

Enter the desired percentages for each asset class. When the total of all percentages equals 100, click OK to save your settings. The Target chart in the Asset Allocation snapshot of the Investing tab window reflects your new allocation settings. If your percentages do not add up to 100%, the difference appears as Unclassified.

You can also change your allocation percentages by clicking the Change Target link under the Target graph.

Using the Portfolio Rebalancer

If your current asset allocation deviates from your target asset allocation, you may want to rebalance your portfolio. This means buying and selling investments to bring you closer to your target asset allocation.

Keep in mind that brokerage fees and capital gains impacts are often involved when you buy and sell securities. For this reason, you should carefully evaluate your investment situation to determine how you can minimize costs and capital gains while rebalancing your portfolio. If small adjustments are necessary to bring you to your target asset allocation, you may not find it worth the cost to make the changes. Use this information as a guideline only! As always, consult your tax professional for additional information about your specific situation.

Quicken can tell you exactly how you must change your current asset allocation to meet your target asset allocation. In the Asset Allocation snapshot of the Investing tab's Allocations view, click Options | Rebalance Portfolio. The Portfolio Rebalancer window appears. It provides instructions and shows you how much you must adjust each asset class to meet your targeted goals.

Click Close to return to the Investing tab.

IN MY EXPERIENCE

The Quicken Portfolio Rebalancer does more than help you balance your current investments. At the top of the Portfolio Rebalancer dialog are two tools that can help you find new investments as well as evaluate them. Go to What Is Rebalancing? and click Search. A two-tab dialog opens that, with your Internet connection, connects to both stock and mutual fund sites to help you make educated investment decisions. In the Search tab you are offered links to both stock and mutual fund sites. The Evaluate tab opens another dialog from which you can find additional information and several views for both stocks and mutual funds. Click Close to close the Search/Evaluate screen and return to the Portfolio Rebalancer.

Click Evaluate to open the Quicken Investing website to the Quotes and Research tab. From this website, you can obtain a quote on any currently traded investment by entering the ticker symbol. You can also use the Lookup link to find out the ticker symbol for a specific stock or mutual fund.

Click Close to return to the Investing tab Allocations view.

Analyzing Your Portfolio

Quicken's Portfolio Analyzer enables you to look at your portfolio in a number of ways. To display it, first turn on Classic menus by clicking View | Classic Menus. From the Classic menu, click Investing | Investing Tools | Portfolio Analyzer. You'll find these options on the left sidebar, as shown in the following illustration.

- **Performance** shows your portfolio's average annual rate of return. It also shows your five best and worst performers, so you can see how individual securities are doing.

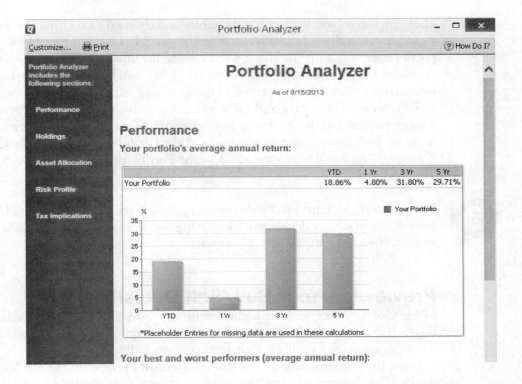

- **Holdings** lists your investment accounts and then shows a pie chart of your top ten holdings. Because most experts recommend that no single security take up more than 10 percent of your portfolio, you may find the percentage distribution helpful when considering diversification.
- **Asset Allocation** displays your current actual and target asset allocation so you can see how close you are to your target. How to set up a target allocation was explained earlier in this chapter.
- **Risk Profile** shows how "risky" your portfolio is when compared to the risk associated with specific classes of investments.
- **Tax Implications** summarizes your realized and unrealized year-to-date (YTD) capital gains or losses. Capital gains and losses are broken down into two categories: short term and long term. For additional information about tax implications, consult your tax professional.

What's great about the Portfolio Analyzer is that it provides tables and charts to show information about your portfolio, and then it explains everything in plain English so you know what the tables and charts mean. Using this feature regularly can really help you learn about the world of investing and how your portfolio measures up. To give it a try, choose Investing | Investing Tools | Portfolio Analyzer from the Classic menu. When you have finished reviewing the information, click Close to return to the Investing tab.

You can have your cake and eat it too. If you want to refer to the Portfolio Analyzer often, but don't want to have to switch from Standard to Classic menus to do so, with Classic menus selected, add the Portfolio Analyzer to the Quicken Toolbar. Then you'll have easy access to the Portfolio Analyzer from both Standard and Classic views.

You may want to return to the Standard menus. If so, click View | Standard Menus. Or, you may decide you like having menu access to every Quicken feature. If so, keep the Classic Menu selection.

Previewing Your Buy/Sell Decisions

In the Quicken Premier (and higher) editions, you will find a feature called Buy/Sell Preview, which offers a quick and easy way to see the impact of a securities purchase or sale on your finances—including your taxes.

From the Investing tab, choose Tools | Buy/Sell Preview. In the top half of the Buy/Sell Preview window that appears, enter information about the proposed purchase or sale. Quicken automatically enters the most recent price information for a security you own or watch, but you can override that amount if necessary.

If you choose to model a sell, ensure you select an account with an open position for that security first; otherwise, you will see an error message when you click Calculate.

When you're finished setting options, click Calculate. Quicken displays its results in the bottom half of the window, as seen in the next illustration.

The Buy/Sell Preview feature works with Quicken's Tax Planner, as discussed in Chapter 13, to calculate the net effect of a sale on your expected tax bill or refund. Check with your tax professional for additional information. Click Done to close the Buy/Sell Preview window and return to the Investing tab.

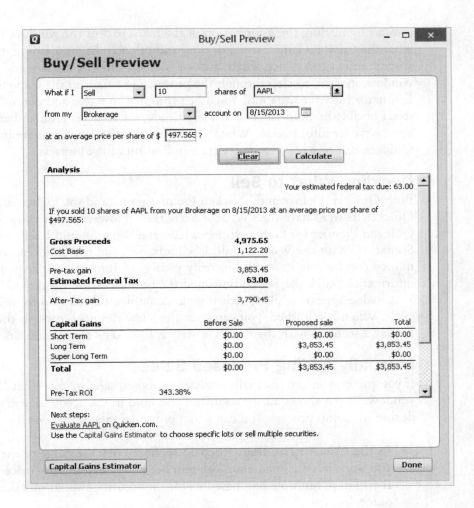

Estimating Capital Gains

Quicken's Capital Gains Estimator enables you to estimate capital gains or losses and their related tax implications before you sell a security. The information it provides can help you make an informed decision about which security to sell.

Getting Started

Choose the Investing tab and click Tools | Capital Gains Estimator. The Capital Gains Estimator's welcome window appears. If you have used the tool before, you may see an info message about previous proposed sales holdings changes.

Start by reading the information in the main part of the window. It explains what the Capital Gains Estimator does and offers links for learning more about specific terms and topics. Then click each of the links in the left side of the window, in turn, to step through the process of setting up the Capital Gains Estimator for your situation. You'll be prompted to name and choose a scenario, select taxable investment accounts to include, set your tax rate, and enter capital loss carryover information. When you enter complete and accurate information, Quicken can provide a more accurate indication of tax impacts.

Deciding What to Sell

Both Quicken Deluxe and Quicken Premier users (and the higher editions of Quicken as well) have the "What If Scenarios." However, only those who use Quicken Premier (or higher editions) have the What Should I Sell and What If Scenarios. With the What Should I Sell link, you can tell Quicken both the money you want to make and identify your goals for a sale. After you enter this information, click the Search button at the bottom of the window.

A dialog appears while Quicken makes complex calculations to meet your goals. When it's finished, you can click the View Results button in the dialog to display a scenario with the results as well as Quicken's recommendation.

Manually Adding Proposed Sales

If you prefer, you can manually indicate proposed sales in the What If Scenario window. Step 1 shows all the securities you hold in the accounts you selected during the setup process. You can add a proposed sale in two ways:

- **In the Current Holdings (Step 1) section**, click the name of the security you want to sell. Then enter the number of shares and sales price in Step 2. If you have multiple purchase lots for the security, this automatically sells the oldest lots first.
- **In the Current Holdings (Step 1) section**, if necessary, click the plus sign (+) to the left of the security that you want to sell to display the purchase lots. Then click the lot you want to sell. This enables you to specify exactly which lots are to be sold in the Proposed Sales area.

No matter which method you use, the sale is added to the Step 2 area of the window, which lists all of the proposed sales.

To adjust the number of shares to be sold, click in the Shares To Sell field for the proposed sale (in the Step 2 area), and enter a new value. The value you enter must be less than or equal to the number of shares purchased in that lot.

You can set up proposed sales for up to three scenarios—just click the Scenario link on the left side of the window to see and set that scenario's options. You can mix and match any sales you like to reach your goal.

Reading the Results

When all the information has been entered, you can see the true power of the Capital Gains Estimator. It tells you about the proceeds from the sales, as well as the gain or loss. If you scroll down in the What If Scenarios screen, you'll find more information about the proposed sale and its tax implications in the Step 3 area, including the gross profit and net proceeds from proposed sales. You can click links to view the results of additional calculations, such as the tax situation before and after executing the proposed sales and gain or loss on the proposed sales. Do the same for each scenario to see how they compare—then make your selling decision. Click Close to return to the Investing tab.

Setting Investment Alerts

Investment alerts are downloaded automatically with quotes and news headlines, as discussed in Chapter 7. To open the Alerts Center from the Quicken menu bar, click Tools | Alerts Center. When you select a specific alert, or a group of alerts, the Show All tab shows the alerts you have selected to track. To see the available alert selections, click the Setup tab of the Alerts Center. Ten investment alerts are available for your use:

- **Price And Volume** consists of two alerts. Price and Volume alerts notify you when a security's price rises above or falls below values you specify, as well as when the sales volume of a security exceeds a value you specify. News alerts give you the latest information about your securities, such as earnings announcements or analyst actions. The options for these are set in the Quicken.com Investing site. Once on the Quicken site, you will see that you can also add Portfolio alerts with which you can set alerts for your current portfolio or set up a watch list.

You may be prompted for your Quicken user name and password to connect to Quicken.com.

- **Reminders** has two options:
  - **Download Quotes**, which reminds you to download information so that your portfolio is up to date.
  - **Maturity Date**, which reminds you when a CD or bond reaches its maturity date.
- **Ratings And Analysis** lets you set two notifications:
  - When information becomes available for stocks you track
  - When information becomes available for mutual funds you track
- **Capital Gains/Losses** lets you set alerts for the following:
  - **Tax Implications On Sale** notifies you of your tax implications when you sell a security.
  - **Cap. Gains For The Year** notifies you if you exceed your capital gains limit for the year.
- **Tax Efficient Investments** provides you with information about investments that are more tax-efficient than those you already have.
- **Mutual Fund Distributions** provides you with information about mutual fund distributions.
- **Securities Holding Period** provides you with information about holding periods for securities you own.

Many Quicken users report the most useful alerts are Price And Volume, Maturity Date Reminder, Stocks Ratings And Analysis, and Cap. Gains For The Year. These alerts give timely information without information overload.

Setting Up Alerts   To set up investment alerts, click Tools | Alerts Center | Setup. Quicken displays the Setup tab of the Alerts Center window. (See Chapter 4 for more detail on setting alerts.) On the left side of the window, click the name of an alert you want to set, and then set options for the alert in the right side of the window. (You must set some alerts, such as the Price And Volume alert, on Quicken.com.) You can disable an alert by removing the check mark beside its name. When you are finished making changes, click OK to save them.

Deleting Alerts   To remove an alert, select Tools | Alerts Center, and click the Show All tab. Then check the alerts you wish to delete and click Delete. A warning message appears telling you the alert will be deleted. Click OK to confirm your deletion. If you want the alert to continue, click Cancel. Either choice returns you to the Show All tab of the Alerts Center.

Understanding Your Financial Position

This part of the book explains how you can use Quicken Personal Finance Software's Property & Debt features to keep track of your property and loans. It starts by covering assets, such as your home and vehicles, and any loans that you may have used to finance them. Then it moves on to tell you how you can use the Property & Debt tab and other Quicken features to monitor expenses related to your assets and debts. This part of the book has two chapters:

Part Four

Monitoring Assets and Loans

Chapter 9

In This Chapter:

- *Understanding assets and debts*
- *Reviewing loans*
- *Creating asset and debt accounts*
- *Creating a loan*
- *Viewing loan information*
- *Making loan payments*
- *Modifying loan information*
- *Adding and disposing of assets*
- *Updating asset values*

Assets and debts (or liabilities) make up your net worth. Bank and investment accounts, as discussed in Chapters 3 and 6, are examples of assets. Credit card accounts, also covered in Chapter 3, are examples of debts. However, you may want to use Quicken Personal Finance Software to track other assets and debts, including your house or family car, as well as any loans related to those assets. By including these items in your Quicken data file, you can quickly and accurately calculate your net worth and financial fitness.

This chapter explains how to set up asset and debt accounts to track your possessions and any outstanding loans you used to purchase them.

The Basics

Before you begin, it's a good idea to have a clear understanding of what assets, debts, and loans are, and how they work together in your Quicken data file.

Understanding Assets and Debts

An asset is something you own. Common examples are your house, car, computer, smart phone, television set, and furniture. Most assets have value—you can sell them for cash or trade them for another asset.

Although you can use Quicken to track every single asset you own in its own asset account, doing so would be cumbersome. Instead, many Quicken users monitor high-value assets in individual accounts and lower-value assets in a group asset account. For example, you may create separate asset accounts for your home and your car, but group personal possessions, such as your electronic devices, home theater components, and sporting equipment, in a single group asset account. This makes it easy to track all your assets, so you have accurate records for insurance and other purposes.

A debt is something you owe—often to buy one of your assets! For example, if you buy a house, chances are you'll use a mortgage to finance it. The mortgage, which is a loan that is secured by your home, is a debt. You can use Quicken to track all of your debts so you know exactly how much you owe at any given time.

Reviewing Loans

A loan is a promise to pay money. Loans are commonly used to buy assets, although some folks often turn to debt consolidation loans to pay off other debts—this is discussed further in Chapter 12.

While most people think of a loan as something you owe (a debt), a loan can also be something you own (an asset). For example, say you borrow money from your brother to buy a car. In your Quicken data file, the loan is related to a debt—money that you owe your brother. In your brother's Quicken data file, the loan is related to an asset—money that is due to him from you.

There are several types of loans, some of which are designed for specific purposes.

- **Mortgage** is a long-term loan secured by real estate. In today's volatile climate, many mortgages require a down payment on the property of 10 to 20 percent or higher.
- **Balloon mortgage** is a special type of short-term mortgage. Rather than make monthly payments over the full typical mortgage term, you pay the balance of the mortgage in one big "balloon" payment.

- A **home equity loan or second mortgage** is a line of credit secured by the equity in your home—the difference between the home's market value and the amount of outstanding debt.
- **Reverse equity loan** (sometimes called a *reverse mortgage*) provides people who own their homes with a regular monthly income. The loan is due when the home is sold—often after the death of the homeowner.
- **Auto loans** are loans secured by a vehicle, such as a car, truck, or motor home.
- **Personal loans** are unsecured loans—a loan that requires no collateral. Monthly payments are based on the term of the loan and the interest rate applied to the principal.

 "Payable" is an accounting term that means you have an obligation to pay the amount in this account to someone.

   When applying for a loan, a number of variables have a direct impact on what the loan costs you, now and in the future. Ask about all of these things before applying for any loan.

Interest Rate

The rate of interest you pay for borrowing someone else's money is the annual percentage applied to the loan principal. Several factors affect the interest rate you may be offered:

- **Your credit record** affects the interest rate offered.
- **The type of loan** affects the interest rate offered, because, generally speaking, personal loans have the highest interest rates, whereas mortgages have the lowest.
- **The loan term** affects the interest rate offered. For example, a 15-year mortgage usually has a lower interest rate than a 30-year mortgage.
- **The amount of the down payment** affects the interest rate offered, because the more money you put down on the purchase, the lower the rate may be.
- **Your location** affects the interest rate offered, because rates vary from one area of the country to another.
- **The lender** affects the interest rate offered, because rates also vary from one lender to another. Certain types of lenders have lower rates than others. Two kinds of interest rates can apply to a loan:
  - **Fixed rate** applies the same rate to the principal throughout the loan term.
  - **Variable rate** applies a different rate to the loan throughout the loan term.

Term

A loan's *term* is the period of time between the loan date and when the date payment is due in full. Loan terms vary depending on the type of loan:

- Mortgage loan and home equity reserve loan terms are typically 10, 15, 20, or 30 years.
- Balloon mortgage loan terms are typically 5, 7, or 10 years.
- Vehicle loan terms vary from 3 to 7 years.

Tips for Minimizing Loan Expenses

Borrowing money costs money. It's as simple as that. However, you can do some things to minimize the cost of a loan.

- Shop for the lowest rate
- Minimize the length of the loan
- Maximize the down payment
- Make extra loan payments
- Ensure your credit history is cleaned up

You can check your credit score with a link provided by Quicken. Click the Tips & Tutorials tab | Quicken Services and select Credit Score at the bottom of the page as seen here. You are entitled to a free credit report from each of the three major credit reporting providers once per year. Use the Annual Credit Report site located at www.annualcreditreport.com/cra/index.jsp. Don't pay for something you can get for free.

Credit Score

Get your free credit score in seconds

Get started ⊙

When evaluating the dollar impact of different loan deals, use Quicken's financial calculators. Chapter 11 explains how to use these tools, including the Loan Calculator and Refinance Calculator. To access these calculators, click the Planning tab and then the Planning Tools button.

Creating Property and Debt Accounts

To track an asset or debt with Quicken, you must set up an appropriate account. All transactions related to the asset or debt are recorded in the account's register.

In this section, you'll learn about the types of accounts you can use to track your assets and debts, and how to set up each type of account. Quicken offers the following Property & Debt account types for tracking assets and debts:

Property & Debt
For tracking your net worth

 **Property & Assets**
House
Vehicle
Other Asset

 **Loans & Debt**
Loan
Home Equity Line (HELOC)
Other Liability

- **House**   A house account is used for recording the value of a house, condominium, or other real estate. When you create a house account, Quicken asks whether there is a mortgage on the property. If so, you can have Quicken create a related debt account for you or associate the house account with an existing debt account. This makes it possible to set up both your house asset account and mortgage debt account at the same time.
- **Vehicle**   A vehicle account is similar to a house account, but is designed for vehicles, including cars, trucks, and recreational vehicles. Quicken asks if there is a loan on the vehicle; if so, it can create a related debt account or link to an existing debt account.
- **Other Asset**   An asset account is for recording the value of other assets, such as personal property. For example, a Quicken data file might include asset accounts for your workshop and its related equipment, your antique china collection, or other personal possessions.
- **Loan**   A loan account is for recording money you owe to others. As mentioned earlier, when you create a house or vehicle account, Quicken can automatically create a corresponding loan account for you. You may also create a loan account for money you lend to others. See "Creating a Lender Loan" later in this chapter.
- **Home Equity Line of Credit (HELOC)**   This type of loan uses the borrower's real property as collateral.
- **Other Liability (not a credit card)**   You can create a debt account to record other debts that are not related to the purchase of a specific asset. Debt accounts show in the Account List as liabilities.

Related Mortgage or Loan

As mentioned earlier, when creating a house or vehicle account, Quicken asks whether there is a related mortgage or loan. You have four options:

- **Yes. I'd Like To Track This Mortgage/Loan In Quicken. Set Up A New Account For This**   This option tells Quicken that there is a related loan and that Quicken should create a debt account.
- **Yes. I'm Already Tracking The Mortgage/Loan In Quicken**   This option enables you to select an existing debt account to link to the asset.

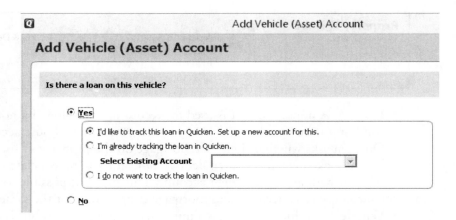

- **Yes. I Do Not Want To Track the Mortgage/Loan In Quicken** This option tells Quicken that there is a loan but you don't want to include it in your Quicken data file.
- **No** This option tells Quicken that there is no loan, so no debt account is necessary. (Lucky you!)

As you've probably guessed or noticed, the use of the word "mortgage" or "loan" in this dialog depends on whether you're creating a house or vehicle asset account. To select any of the Yes options, you must click Yes and then choose one of the options beneath it. Otherwise, choose the No option. If you selected No and clicked Next, a message appears that an account has been added, as discussed next in "Creating Asset and Debt Accounts." Click Finish to close the dialog.

Creating Asset and Debt Accounts

You create asset and debt accounts with the same Add Account dialog you used to set up your banking accounts. Quicken offers a number of ways to open this dialog for an asset or debt account, as well as several types of assets, loans, and debts. In the following example, we are adding a new vehicle asset. The specific steps are as follows:

1. From the Account Bar, click Add An Account.
2. From the Add Account dialog, choose Property & Assets | Vehicle.
3. The Add Vehicle (Asset) Account dialog appears with the name field highlighted and ready for you to enter a new name. Type a descriptive name for the vehicle and click Next.

4. Enter the Vehicle Make/Manufacturer's name. Press TAB.

5. Enter the Vehicle Model name.

6. Press TAB to go to the Vehicle Year field and enter that information. Continue through the dialog, pressing the TAB key to move from field to field. When you have entered all of the information, click Next to continue. Note that the Make and Model fields are not required and, once you click Next, there is no Back button with which you can return to this screen. However, you can edit the account details after you have completed entering the information.

7. You are then prompted to tell Quicken about any loans or mortgages (if the asset is real property) on this asset. Learn how to set up or track an existing loan for this asset in "Related Mortgage or Loan" earlier in this chapter. If there is no loan associated with this asset, click that option. If there is no loan, or you do not want to track a loan through Quicken, click No. Or, if there is a loan but you do not want to track it in Quicken, click Yes and then choose the I Do Not Want To Track The Loan In Quicken option. Click Next to continue.

8. The Account Added dialog appears with the name of your new asset shown with a green check mark. Click Finish.

A loan is actually a debt account that has special Quicken features attached to it. Use this option to set up a debt associated with a compounding interest loan, like a mortgage or standard car loan, as explained later in this chapter.

Chapter 1 explains how to use the Quicken Add Account dialog to create new Quicken banking accounts. This section provides information about the kinds of data you need to enter to create asset and debt accounts. The following information explains the information required when adding a new asset or debt account.

- **Account Type**   The Add Account dialog displays a list of asset types: House, Vehicle, or Other Asset in the Property & Assets section.
- **Account Name**   Give the account a name that clearly identifies the asset or debt. Be descriptive. Ford Focus and Dodge pickup do a better job identifying the cars than Car 1 and Car 2.

When creating a debt account, you may want to include the word "mortgage," "loan," or "payable" in the account name so you don't confuse it with a related asset.

For house and vehicle accounts, Quicken prompts you to enter information about the asset's purchase, including the acquisition date and purchase price. You can find this information on your original purchase receipts. Quicken also asks for an estimate of the current value. For a house, this number will (hopefully) be higher than the purchase price; for a car, this number will probably be lower.

This amount appears as the asset account balance. For other assets and debts, Quicken prompts you for a statement date and balance. If you don't know how much to enter now, you can leave it set to zero and enter a value when you know what to enter. You will see how to adjust asset values later in this chapter.

You can use Quicken's Attachment feature (as covered in Chapter 3) and your scanner to save images of an asset's paperwork, such as the receipt, the warranty, or delivery verification to store as digital images with your Quicken data file.

Optional Tax Information

For asset and debt accounts, click the Tax Schedule button on the Account Details dialog to enter tax schedule information for transfers in and out of the account. While this information is optional, check with your tax professional to see if this information will benefit your tax position. Chapter 13 explains how to set up Quicken accounts and categories to simplify tax preparation.

You can get to the Account Details dialog by pressing CTRL-A and then clicking the Edit button for the account with which you wish to work.

Loan Information

If you indicated that Quicken should track a loan for a house or vehicle, it automatically displays the Add Mortgage/Loan Account dialog, which you can use to enter information about the loan. If you set up a debt account, Quicken asks if you want to set up an amortized loan to be associated with the debt. If you selected Yes and I'm Already Tracking The Loan In Quicken, select the debt account from the drop-down list and click Next. You'll then see the Account Added screen with the green check mark near the new account's name. Quicken links the asset and debt accounts for you. See how to set up a loan later in this chapter, in the section "Creating a Loan."

Be sure to select the appropriate type for your loan so the appropriate interest category is associated with it.

Viewing the Asset or Debt Account Register

When you're finished setting up an asset or debt account (and related loans and loan payments, if applicable), Quicken automatically displays the account's register. Figure 9-1 shows what a house account might look like. The first transaction, dated 1/1/2000, shows the opening balance, which was the amount paid for the house. The next transaction, dated 1/1/2007, shows an adjustment created when the homeowner received the property tax statement and entered the value shown on that statement as of 1/1/2007. The next adjustment was 5 years later, again after the property's worth was received in the property tax statement.

The register in Figure 9-1 shows with a two-line display. To change your display from the default one-line display, press CTRL-2, which is a toggle between Quicken's default one-line register display and the two-line display shown

After you have entered more than one asset account, you'll note that the new accounts are listed alphabetically. In earlier versions of Quicken, the new accounts went to the bottom of the appropriate section in the Account List. Many Quicken users prefer to see their accounts in alphabetical order in the Account List, and this is in response to those requests.

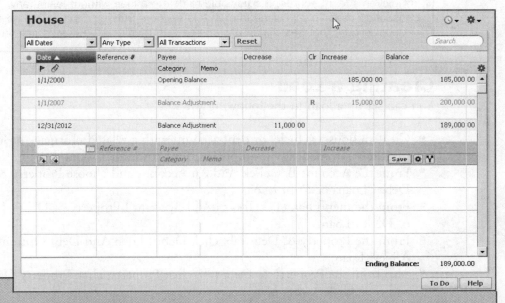

Figure 9-1 • **Like other accounts in Quicken, assets and debts have their own account registers.**

All transactions that affect an asset or debt account's balance appear in the account register. Learn more about using account registers for asset and debt accounts later in this chapter, in the section "Other Asset Transactions."

Loan Accounts in Quicken

Quicken makes it easy to track the principal, interest, and payments for a loan. Once you set up a loan and corresponding debt or asset accounts, you can make payments with Quicken using QuickFill, Scheduled Transactions (transaction reminders), or Online Payments (see Chapter 3). The Loan feature keeps track of all the details so you don't have to.

IN MY EXPERIENCE

Just so you know, a loan in Quicken is not the same as an asset or debt account. Quicken uses the loan information to calculate the amount of interest and principal due for each payment of an amortized loan, such as a mortgage or car loan. A loan must be associated with an asset account (if you are a lender) or a debt account (if you are a borrower), as well as an income or expense category to record either interest income or expense.

Loan transactions are recorded in the associated asset or debt account—not in Quicken's loan records. It's possible to delete a loan without losing any transaction data, as explained later in this section. But you can't delete an asset or debt account that has a loan associated with it unless the loan is deleted first.

Creating a Loan

You can set up a loan in the following ways:

- Create a house, vehicle, or debt account with a related mortgage or loan, Quicken automatically prompts you for loan information.
- From the Account Bar, click Add An Account and choose Property & Debt | Loans & Debt | Loan.
- From the menu bar, click Tools | Add Account | Property & Debt | Loans & Debt | Loan.
- From the Property & Debt tab, click Debt | Loan And Debt Options | Add A New Loan.
- Also from the Property & Debt tab, click Property, click Property Options, and then click Add A New Loan.

Quicken displays the Add Loan Account dialog. While the information is basically the same, the *type* of loan does matter so that you get the right interest category type. The interest category type cannot be changed after it is entered.

If you choose to create a loan account for which you will enter the information manually, click the Manual Loan Account link at the bottom of the dialog. The illustrations that follow are for a manual account.

Be aware! If you choose to download your loan transactions, your loan account register will be read-only and will not be accessible to review and make corrections. Don't do it! Downloading one possibly incorrect transaction per month that cannot be corrected is just not worth it. Set up your loan manually—you will be much happier!

Loan Details

The Loan Details dialog starts by prompting you for the name of the loan, as seen in Figure 9-2. The first choice is the type of loan for which you are creating an account. Click the downward arrow to choose from a list as shown here. Choose wisely—you cannot change the loan type or the associated loan interest type category later!

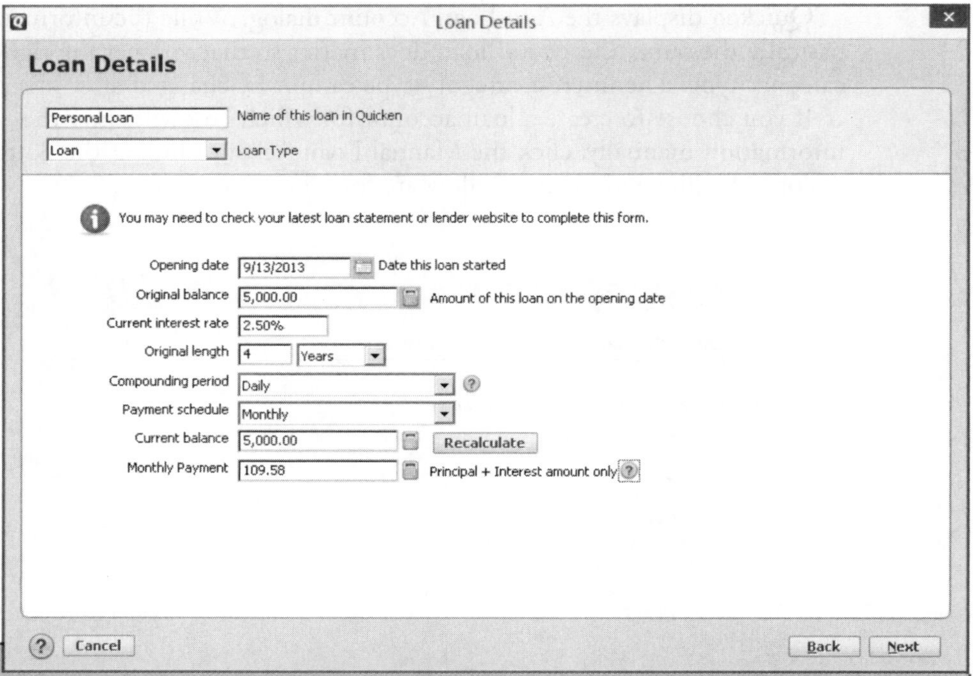

Figure 9-2 • When you create a loan account, Quicken asks for all of the details.

You have the following loan types from which to choose:

- **Mortgage** is a loan for some type of real property such as a house.
- **Loan** is for any type of loan not included in the other options. This loan type may be used for loans from individuals rather than financial institutions, such as borrowing $5,000 from your sister toward some vacation property you will both share.
- **Auto loan** is for vehicle loans, including trucks.
- **Consumer loans** are funds borrowed by a "person," rather than a business. Lenders for this type of loan are usually financial institutions.
- **Commercial loans** are normally loans to a business from a financial institution. Such loans are often for large purchases, working capital, or real property.
- **Student loans** are used for financing education.
- **Military loans** are designed specifically for those in the service of our country.

- **Business loans** are usually for the day-to-day operating costs of a business, rather than for large real property or equipment purchases.
- **Construction loans** are used when you build a house. These loans are often turned into mortgage loans when construction is completed.
- **Home equity loans** are loans against the equity you hold in your home. Many people use home equity loans to pay for major remodeling, although some home equity loans are taken to pay off other, higher cost debt.

You are asked for information about the opening date, the original balance, the current interest rate, the original contract length, payment schedule, and so on, as seen in Figure 9-2. It's important to be accurate; get the dates and numbers directly from your loan statement or agreement if possible. Quicken calculates the amount of payment and the interest based on the entries you make, as well as the extra principal, any balloon payment, and the number of remaining payments.

While Quicken's default compounding period is Monthly, most financial institutions compound interest daily and post it to your account every month. Use the Compounding Period drop-down list to choose Daily if your lender compounds interest daily.

Click Next to continue. The Loan Details dialog continues with the name of the loan at the top, as shown here. It displays the next payment due date for this loan, based on the opening date you entered in the first screen of the dialog. You may change this date if necessary. Enter any additional information.

Loan Details

Personal Loan

Monthly Payment

Next payment due 10/13/2013 (required)

Principal	$99.15
Interest	$10.43
Other	0.00
Extra principal paid Monthly	0.00

○ Extra principal determines total
○ Total determines extra principal

Total Payment: 109.58

- **Other** is used for additional payment on the loan such as escrow funds.
- **Extra Principal Paid Monthly** amounts are those additional principal payments you enter to reduce the total amount of the interest you will pay on the loan.

Select the Extra Principal Determines Total radio button if you want to determine the amount of the extra principal payment you make each month as seen below. When you enter an amount, the new monthly payment appears in the Total Payment field. In our example, because we want to pay exactly $110.00 per month, we will pay an additional $.42 to make the payment exactly $110.00.

Select the Total Determines Extra Principal if you want to set the total payment each month and let Quicken determine how much extra principal will be paid as seen in the following illustration.

Click Next to continue. The Loan Reminder dialog appears as discussed next.

Loan Reminder

When you set up a loan, Quicken creates a reminder. From this dialog, you can tell Quicken to enter the reminder into the register automatically and choose the number of days before the due date that you want the transaction entered. If you do not want Quicken to enter the transaction automatically, leave that check box clear and click Next.

The Loan Payment Reminder dialog appears. You may edit each field as explained here:

- The **Pay To** field shows the name of the loan if you have indicated that you will enter transactions manually to this loan account. Otherwise, it displays the name of the financial institution which loaned you the money.

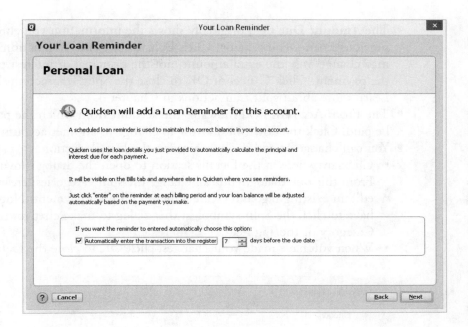

This field can be edited by highlighting what appears and typing over the highlighted area.

• The **Due Next On** date can be changed by typing in a new due date.

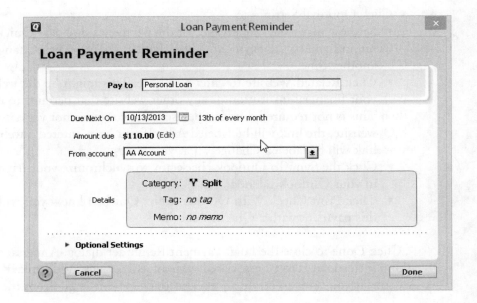

- The **Amount Due** field originally shows the information you entered in the previous Loan Details dialog. Click Edit to see a split transaction dialog. You may change only the extra amount, not the principal or interest portions of the payment. Click Cancel or OK to close the Split Transactions Dialog. Learn more about split transactions in Chapter 3.
- The **From Account** field indicates the account from which the payment will be paid. Click the downward arrow to change to another account.
- You can change or add to three areas in the Details section.
  - Click anywhere in the Details section to open the dialog shown here. From this one dialog, you can change the split categories, create a tag or edit an existing tag, and create a memo for each payment. Note that you have to click the Split symbol in this dialog to make changes to either the Category or the Tag field.
  - When you have made your changes, click OK to close the Details dialog.

- Click Optional Settings to
  - Set how many days in advance of the payment's due date Quicken should remind you of the payment. The default is 7 days. Click Change to set another time.
  - Click Related Website to enter a website. This might be the website of your financial institution or any other website that pertains to this loan. This is not required, but can be useful. If you have not yet entered a website, the link will be labeled Add. If you have entered a website, the link will be labeled Change.
  - Click the Sync To Outlook check box to synchronize your payment date in your Outlook calendar.
  - Click Print Check With Quicken to let Quicken know you will be paying this payment with a Quicken check.

Click Done to close the Loan Payment Reminder dialog. A message appears asking if this loan is to be associated with an asset. Click Add Linked Asset Account if you want to create an asset account for this loan. From the menu that

appears, you can choose from a Home, an Auto, Other, or click Existing
Account to link this loan to an existing asset.

If you choose to add a new asset account, the Add Account dialog appears. If
you choose an existing asset, you will see a small icon and the information that
this loan is linked to the asset you chose as seen here. The link icon depends on
the type of asset. For example, for an auto loan, the icon is a car. Click Done to
close the dialog.

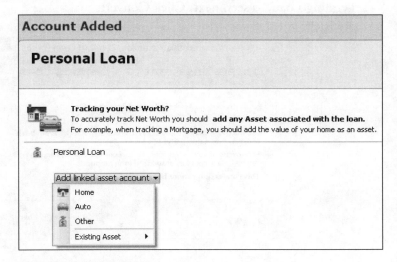

Creating a Lender Loan

From time to time, you may be in a position to lend money to someone else.
Quicken calls this type of loan a *Lender Loan.* You create this type of account in
a slightly different way.

Once you have completed all the necessary paperwork and everything is
signed and notarized, you are ready to set up the account. Quicken treats this
type of loan as an asset, with the value of the asset equal to the amount of
money you are lending.

1. Click Add An Account at the bottom of the Account Bar. Choose Property
   & Debt | Property & Assets | Other Assets to open the Add Asset Account
   dialog.
2. Enter a name for the account. Depending on the Quicken edition you use,
   you may have to choose the purpose for the account, such as Personal or
   Business. Click Next.
3. Enter the date on which you want Quicken to start tracking this loan, which
   is usually the starting date.

4. Enter the asset value, usually the total amount you are lending. Click Next to continue.
5. The Is There A Loan On This Account dialog appears. Select No and click Next and then in the final dialog, click Finish.
6. Your new loan account appears in the Account Bar. Open the account to the register.
7. Click the Account Actions gear icon and select Convert This Asset To A Lending Loan, as seen next. Click Convert.

8. The Loan Details dialog appears as discussed in the "Creating a Loan" section, earlier in this chapter. Complete the information, including the interest rate, loan length, and payment schedule. Click Next.
9. Make any additions or changes to the monthly payment in the dialog that appears and click Next again.
10. Make your choices in the Reminder dialog and click Next. At the final Reminder dialog, make any necessary changes and click Done. Your new asset account appears with loan information rather than a register.

Even if you are lending money to a relative, it is important that paperwork be created and signed by all parties, and in most cases, reviewed by a legal or accounting professional.

Viewing Loan Information

All loans are associated with asset and/or debt accounts. To view a loan, it must first be set up in Quicken. After you have set it up, you can access the loan information in two ways:

- Click on the loan name in the Account Bar.
- Click Tools | Account List and select the name of the account with which you want to work.

The loan information window appears as seen in Figure 9-3.

Making Loan Payments

When you first set up your loan, you told Quicken to create either a loan reminder or a memorized payee, or in some cases, both. Each time you make a payment on a loan, Quicken keeps track of the current loan balance in that loan account. If you have linked an asset to your loan, Quicken tracks your current equity as well. You can make a loan payment in several different ways, each of which is explained here:

- **Use A Loan Reminder**   If you instructed Quicken to set up a reminder for your loan payment each month (or other payment schedule), Quicken displays a message reminder. If you have asked Quicken to include the reminder in your register, the payment is already there.

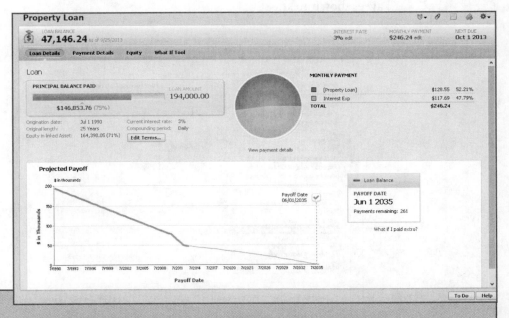

Figure 9-3 • Use the window for a loan account to view and edit information.

- **Enter the Loan Payment Directly**   You can quickly enter any loan payment into your register by simply typing the payee name, and the information from your memorized payee will appear. If you have not memorized the payee, complete the payment entry, and Quicken memorizes both the payee and the transaction so you can use that information each time you make a payment.

- **Use the Enter Loan Payment Option**   To enter a payment, click the loan account name in the Account Bar to open the loan. Select the Account Actions gear icon, and from the menu choose Enter Loan Payment, as shown here.

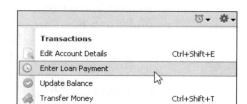

- **Create A Quicken Toolbar Button** Use a memorized payee to create a customized Quicken Toolbar button to make your payment.

  - Right-click the Quicken Toolbar and choose Customize Toolbar.
  - From the Customize Toolbar dialog, select the Show All Toolbar Choices check box.
  - In the Available Toolbar Buttons list, select Use A Specific Memorized Payee, shown next.

- Click Add to open the Assigned Memorized Payee To Action dialog.

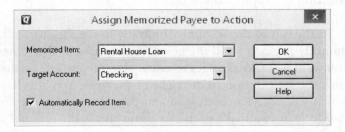

- Choose the appropriate payee from the Memorized Item drop-down list. Enter the account from which this payment will be made and select the Automatically Record Item check box if desired.
- Click OK to close the dialog and click Done to close the Customize Toolbar dialog. Your new button appears on the Quicken Toolbar.

When it's time to enter the payment, click your new toolbar button. The Confirm Principal And Interest dialog appears, shown here. Make any changes necessary and click OK. Your payment is posted into your register.

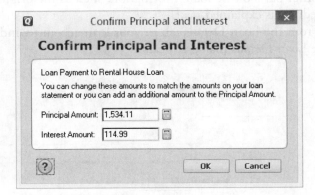

Modifying Loan Information

Once you've created a loan, you can modify it as necessary to record corrections, changes in the interest rate, or changes in payment methods. You can do all these things by clicking the account name in the Account Bar and choosing the Loan Details or Payment Details tab.

You can also open a loan account window by choosing Tools | Account List and selecting the appropriate account.

At the top of the account window, you see the current balance, interest rate, monthly payment, and the next due date as seen in the next illustration. Should you want to make changes to either the interest rate or the monthly payment, click the Edit button to the right of the item. You also have four tabs from which you can view both loan and payment details, the current equity, and a tool to help you make decisions about this loan.

Changing Loan Information

Should you need to make changes to other parts of the loan information, use the Loan Details window to compare the data with the information found on statements or loan agreement papers. You can then make any necessary changes to other parts of the loan information, such as the original balance or payment schedule, as explained next.

From the Loan Details tab in your loan account window, select Edit Terms. The Loan Details dialog appears.

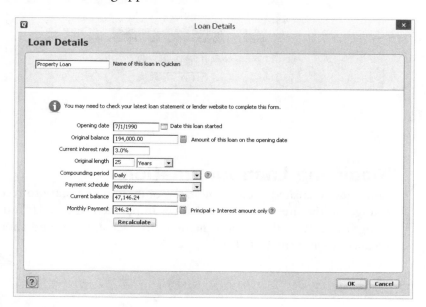

Modify values and select different options as desired.

- **Opening Date**   Usually this is the date the loan started.
- **Original Balance**   Use your loan statement papers to find this balance if you didn't enter it when you set up the account.
- **Current Interest Rate**   This can vary, depending on your loan.
- **Original Length**   See the original loan papers for the length of your loan.
- **Compounding Period**   While Quicken defaults to Monthly, normally banks and other lending institutions compound interest daily. Change this to Daily if that is true for this loan.
- **Payment Schedule**   This will often be monthly, although some loan terms have quarterly, semi-annual, or even annual payment schedules.
- **Current Balance**   Use the latest statement for this balance.
- **Recalculate**   This button may appear if you have changed any of the information.
- **Monthly Payment**   This is the total of principal and interest and does not include any other fees.
- **Recalculate**   You may see an additional recalculate button beneath the Monthly Payment, if you have made any changes.

Click OK to save your changes. If you have made any adjustments, you may see a message stating that Quicken has recalculated based on the information you entered, as seen next.

Viewing Payment Details

The second tab in the loan account window is Payment Details. To review or modify the payment details, you can either

- Click the Payment Details tab.
  –Or–
- Click View Payment Details under the pie graph in the top center of the loan account window.

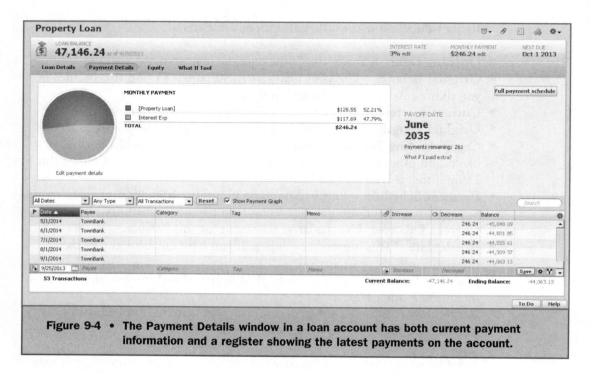

Figure 9-4 • The Payment Details window in a loan account has both current payment information and a register showing the latest payments on the account.

In either case, the Payment Details window appears as seen in Figure 9-4.

The snapshot at the top of the Payment Details tab is a graph that shows the current monthly payment for this loan, broken down by interest and principal. Click the Edit Payment Details button to make any changes to the monthly payment. Click OK or Cancel to close the Edit Payment Details dialog.

At the upper right of the Payment Details window is the current payoff date for the loan, as well as the number of payments remaining to be paid. Underneath the number of payments is a link to the What If Tool, entitled What If I Paid Extra. See "The What If Tool" later in this chapter for more information.

The Full Payment Schedule Click the Full Payment Schedule button at the top-right of the Payment Details window in a loan account to review or to print all of the payments, both past and future, for this loan, as seen next. This information is based on your current Loan Details and Loan Payment. There are links to both of these dialogs at the top of the dialog.

Click the printer icon to print the report to your default printer. Click Done to close the dialog.

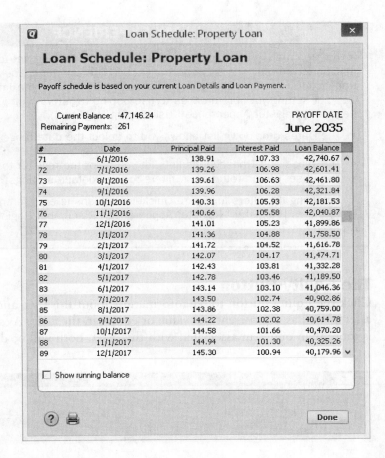

Payment Detail Register   The register at the bottom half of the Payment Details window shows each principal payment that was made on this account since the loan began. The payments that show on this register are only the principal amounts. To see the entire payment, go to the account register from which the payment was made. You can change what shows in this register by choosing the filter drop-down lists at the top of the register.

You can clear the graph to show more payments in the register. Click the check box to the left of Show Payment Graph to toggle the graph on and off.

IN MY EXPERIENCE

If you are on a laptop or just have your monitor resolution set to the Quicken minimum, you may see only one transaction line at a time. You can see more transaction lines by toggling to a one-line display (CTRL-2), maximizing the register (F11), or setting your preferences to use pop-up registers (Edit | Preferences | Register | Register Appearance | Use Pop-up Registers).

- The Dates drop-down list allows you to select the date range you want to see in the register.
- The Types and Transactions lists let you tailor the register to your needs.
- The Reset button returns the filters to their default settings.

Retaining the filters for future Quicken sessions is a preference. Click Edit | Preferences | Register | Register Appearance | Remember Register Filters After Quicken Closes.

The Equity Button

Click the Equity button to see information about this loan and its associated asset as well as the current net value or equity in the asset. As seen here, if there is more than one loan associated with this asset, both will be displayed.

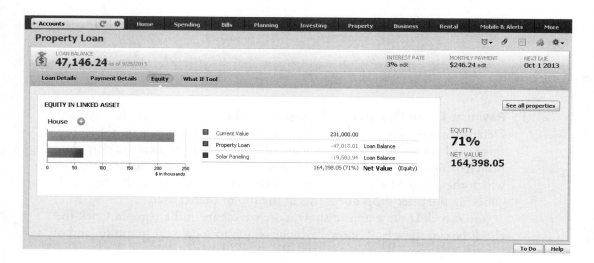

The amount of your equity in this asset is shown as both a percentage and a net value. If you click on the link to the left of Net Value, a small graph appears showing the change in your equity over the last year, as seen next.

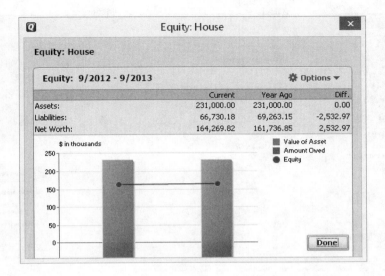

Click the Options gear icon at the right of the Equity graph to customize the graph. You can also click the Help Reduce My Debt link to be taken to the Debt Reduction dialogs. See Chapter 12 to learn about budgets and debt reduction in Quicken.

Click Done to close this equity dialog.

Click the See All Properties button to view a similar graph showing all of your assets and their corresponding liabilities.

The What If Tool

The What If Tool tab at the top of your loan account window opens a worksheet that allows you to see the effects if you made some different financial choices for this account. When the window opens, you see the Current Payoff Schedule at the right side of the window as seen here. This schedule, based on the current terms, shows the projected payoff date, total interest paid this year, total interest paid to today's date, and the projected total interest that will be paid using the current terms of the loan.

Within the tool itself, you can see projected changes if you make additional payments each month or a one-time payment. In the example shown in Figure 9-5, we have chosen to pay an extra $250.00 per month with our mortgage payment. After we click the See Results button, notice the change in both the

Current Payoff Schedule	
PAYOFF DATE:	Jun 2035
INTEREST THIS YEAR:	$3,016.44
INTEREST TO DATE:	$15,749.61
TOTAL INTEREST:	$32,871.41 (projected)

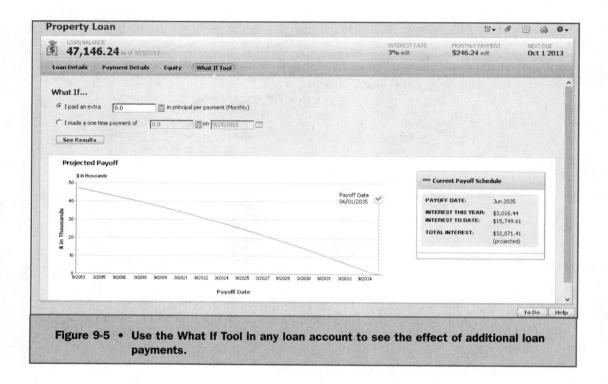

Figure 9-5 • **Use the What If Tool in any loan account to see the effect of additional loan payments.**

graph and the What If Payoff Schedule. By adding this $250.00, we will pay off this loan more than one year early and save about $763.99 in interest.

You can click Current Payoff Schedule to review that information once more. Then, to see the differences again, click What If Payoff Schedule.

When you have finished working with the What If Tool, click the Reset button at the lower right of the What If Tool window to return to the current information, or close and reopen Quicken. The changes are not saved.

Action Gear Options

At the upper right of the loan account window is the Action gear from which you can choose from the following options, most of which are links.

- **Edit Account Details**   Click this link to open the Account Details dialog you saw when setting up the account.
- **Enter Loan Payment**   This link opens the Enter Transaction dialog from which you can enter a payment into the appropriate banking (or credit union) register.

- **Update Balance**   This option opens the Update Balance dialog, which allows you to enter a new balance for the loan and the effective date of that change.
- **Transfer Money**   Select this option to open the Quicken Transfer Money dialog, which is discussed in Chapter 4.
- **Full Payment Schedule**   This report is the same report shown when you click the Full Payment Schedule button.
- **Account Attachments**   See Chapter 3 to learn more about adding attachments to register entries.
- **Account Overview**   This link opens a customizable graph showing the entire life of this loan from its inception.
- **Print Transactions**   With the dialog that opens when you select this option, you can print transactions in the register for time periods you choose.
- **Export to Excel Compatible File**   This option allows you to send the loan information to Microsoft Excel (or compatible programs).
- **Reminders To Show In Register**   This option is the same as the Reminders icon option shown earlier in this chapter.
- **Two-Line Display**   With this option selected, each transaction in the register shows in two lines. Clear the check box to have each transaction show on only one line.
- **Sorting Options**   This link lets you sort by 12 additional alternatives in addition to the default Date sort.
- **Register Columns**   Use this link to tell Quicken what columns you want to see in your register.
- **Register Preferences**   This option opens the Quicken Preference dialog to the Register Preferences section. See Appendix B for more information about setting Preferences.
- **Customize Action Bar**   From this dialog, you can set the icons you wish to see in the Action Bar, next to the Action gear icon. In the example shown next, we've selected Account Attachments, represented by the small paper clip; Two-Line Display represented by the check mark in the check box, and Transfer Money, represented by the dollar bill with the right-facing arrow. These icons are in addition to the Show Reminders icon, which is the Quicken 2014 default. Learn more about the Action Bar in Chapter 1.

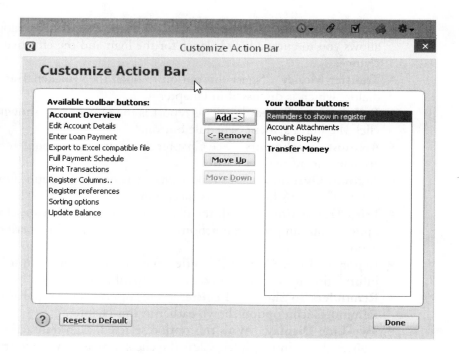

Other Asset Transactions

Part of tracking assets is keeping track of their current values and modifying account balances when necessary. Like bank or investment accounts, which are discussed in Chapters 3 and 6, activity for an asset account appears in its account register.

The best way to open an asset's register is to click the name of the account in the Account Bar. The asset account's register appears. If you do not see your account listed in the Account Bar, you may need to change the account's display. Press CTRL-A to open the Account List and check the Show Hidden Accounts check box to show all of your accounts.

In this section, you'll see how you can record changes in asset values due to acquisitions and disposals, improvements, market values, and depreciation.

Adding and Disposing of Assets

The most obvious change in an asset's value occurs when you add or remove all or part of the asset. For example, you may have a single asset account in which you record the value of all of your sports-related equipment. When you buy a set of golf clubs, it increases the value of the account. Similarly, if you sell your small outboard motor, it decreases the value of the account.

In many instances, when you add or dispose of an asset, money is exchanged. In that case, recording the transaction is easy: simply use the appropriate bank account register to record the purchase or sale, and use the asset account in the Category field. Enclose the category in square brackets [ ].

If the asset was acquired without an exchange of cash, you can enter the transaction directly into the asset account using the Gift Received category (or a similar category of your choice) to categorize the income. Similarly, if the asset was disposed of without an exchange of cash, you can enter the transaction into the asset account register using the Gifts Given or Charity category (or other category) to categorize the write-off.

You can also just record the transaction as an internal transfer in the asset account. If the asset account name is Sports Equipment, an internal transfer in the Sports Equipment account would use the category [Sports Equipment]. You may see a prompt warning you that you are recording a transfer back into the same account. Click Yes to save the transaction.

If you have completely disposed of the asset and no longer need the account, don't delete the account! Doing so will remove all income and expense category transactions and un-categorize all transfer transactions related to the account. Instead, consider hiding the account to get it off account lists, as explained in Chapter 1. In addition, while you are working with hiding your accounts, be very cautious about using the Close Account feature. Closing an account in Quicken 2014 is permanent.

Updating Asset Values

A variety of situations can change the value of a single asset. The type of situation will determine how the value is adjusted. Here are three common examples.

Recording Improvements

Certain home-related expenditures can be considered improvements that increase the value of your home. It's important that you keep track of improvements, because they raise the property's tax basis, thus reducing the amount of capital gains you may have to record (and pay tax on) when you sell the house. Your tax advisor can help you determine which expenditures can be capitalized as home improvements.

Since most home improvements involve expenditures, use the appropriate spending account register to record the transaction. Be sure to enter the

appropriate asset account
(House, Condo, Land, and
so on) in the Category field,
and enclose the account
name in square brackets [ ].

Adjusting for Market Value

Real estate, vehicles, and
other large-ticket-item assets
are also affected by market
values. Generally speaking,
real estate values go up,

vehicle values go down, and other item values can vary either way depending on
what they are.

To adjust for market value, click the Action gear icon | Account Overview | Asset
Status | Options | Update My Account Balance. The Update Account Balance
dialog appears. Use this dialog to enter the market value in the New Balance field
and then enter the date of this new value in the Date field. Be careful, as the default
date of the change is today's date. Click OK to close the dialog.

You can also click the Action gear icon and choose Update Balance.

When you click OK, the entry is added to the account register as a reconciled
transaction. The category for this transaction defaults to Misc. You may change
this category by clicking in the Category field and entering the category you
want to use.

If you don't want the adjustment to affect any category or account other than
the asset, choose the same asset account as a transfer account. When you click
OK, a dialog will warn you that you are trying to record a transfer into the same
account. Click OK again.

Recording Depreciation

Depreciation is a calculated reduction in the value of an asset. Depreciation
expense can be calculated using a variety of acceptable methods, including
straight line, sum of the year's digits, and declining balance. Normally, it reduces
the asset's value regularly, with monthly, quarterly, or annual adjustments.

Depreciation is commonly applied to property used for business purposes,
since depreciation expense on those assets may be tax-deductible. If you think
depreciation on an asset you own may be tax-deductible, use Quicken to track the

depreciation expense. Otherwise, depreciation probably isn't worth the extra effort it requires to track. As always, consult with your tax professional to be sure.

To record depreciation, create an entry in the asset account that reduces the value by the amount of the depreciation. Use a Depreciation Expense category to record the expense.

Keep in mind that you can set up monthly, quarterly, or annual depreciation transactions as scheduled reminders in the Bill & Income reminders. This automates the process of recording them when they are due. See more about scheduled transactions in Chapter 4.

Keeping Tabs on Your Net Worth

Chapter 10

In This Chapter:

- *Exploring the Net Worth view*
- *Using the Property view*
- *Opening the Debt view*
- *Accessing Property and Debt account registers*
- *Creating alerts for Property and Debt accounts*

Once you have entered your asset and debt account transactions into Quicken 2014, as discussed in the previous chapters, Quicken summarizes your entries and calculates their balances. The information displays in a number of places: the Account Bar, the Property & Debt tab, account registers, reports, and graphs. You can consult Quicken's calculated balances and totals at any time to learn about your equity and the expenses associated with your debts.

This chapter explains how to use Quicken's reporting features to keep tabs on your financial picture. As you'll learn in these pages, a wealth of information about your net worth is just a mouse click (or two) away.

The Property & Debt Tab

Asset and debt account information, as well as an overview of your financial standing (net worth), are part of Quicken's Property & Debt tab. Open the Property & Debt section by clicking its tab. Within the Property & Debt tab are three views with which you can view your financial standing in useful graphic format. You access these views with three buttons: Net Worth, Property, and Debt.

If you don't see the Property & Debt tab, click View | Tabs To Show, and select Property & Debt.

Each of these views displays graphs and report snapshots to help you understand your true financial position. An example is the two graphs you see when you click the Net Worth button, as shown in Figure 10-1. Click either the Net Worth Summary Report or the Account Balances Report buttons to display additional information about your net worth accounts. Together, these snapshots paint a picture of your overall financial situation.

In this part of the chapter, we'll take a closer look at the snapshots in the Property & Debt tab sections so you know both what you can find and how you can customize the information for your use.

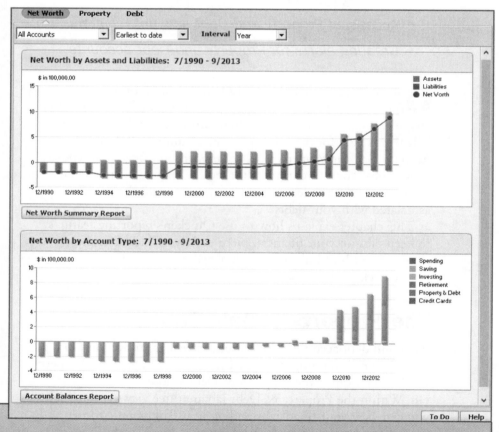

Figure 10-1 • The Net Worth by Assets and Liabilities is an example of the graphs available in the Net Worth view of the Property & Debt tab.

Exploring the Net Worth View

As you click the button to open the Net Worth view, you'll see both the Net Worth by Assets and Liabilities graph and the Net Worth by Account Type graphs, as shown in Figure 10-1. You can customize the information shown in this view, but you cannot customize the information for each graph separately.

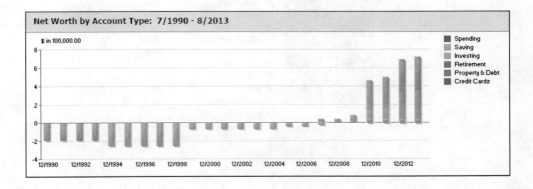

There is much more information available within the Net Worth view than first meets the eye. At the top of the section are three drop-down lists with which you can customize information to meet your requirements, as seen here.

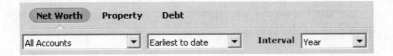

Accounts Drop-Down List   The first drop-down list displays the accounts you want to use for your graphs. The default, as shown, is All Accounts. Click the downward arrow and choose Custom to open the Customize dialog as seen next. From this dialog you may

- Click the Select All button to include all of your accounts in the graph.
- Click the Clear All button to deselect all of your accounts.
- Select or clear the check box displayed by each account name to include it in the graph.
- Click the Show (Hidden Accounts) check box to display the accounts you have chosen to hide so you can opt to include them as well. If you do not see the check box, you have not hidden any accounts.

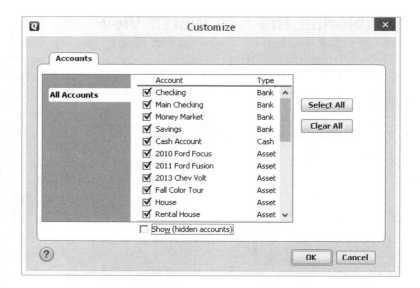

When you have completed your selections, click OK to close the dialog.

Time Period Drop-Down List   The second drop-down list in the Net Worth button's view allows you to set the time period for your graphs. You can choose from the Last 12 Months, the Last Year, the Last 3 Years, the Last 5 Years, the Last 10 Years, or the default time period, which is the Earliest to Date.

Use the Custom Date option to set the time period to show the information displayed in the graph.

Set the Interval to Display   The three choices on the Interval drop-down list are Months, Quarter, and Year. For example, if you want to see what your financial position has been for the last three years, you might choose to display the information by quarter instead of months to see the general trend.

Net Worth by Assets and Liabilities

The first snapshot in the Net Worth view is the Net Worth by Assets and Liabilities, as shown earlier in Figure 10-1. This graph uses a stacked column to indicate your net worth for the period you choose. In our example, we have chosen to display all of the accounts since we first started using Quicken. We chose annual intervals to get an idea of how our savings and investment plan has worked for the last 23 years. The period covered by the graph shows above the display. We can change the information displayed on the graph by changing the options in any of the drop-down lists.

The green bar represents your assets, the muted red bar represents your debt, and the red circle represents your net worth. Ideally, the green bars should get taller while the muted red bars get shorter. The net effect is a rise in the net worth line, as seen in Figure 10-1. In our example, the base line of the graph shows that since 1990, this family's assets did not substantially exceed their debt until 2010. If the net worth line is below the baseline of the graph, you're in some serious financial trouble because your debts exceed your assets.

How you perceive the colors may depend on your monitor's settings.

When you position your mouse over a specific area on the net worth line of this graph, you see your net worth as of that date, as shown next. When you position your mouse on a green area, a similar report appears showing exactly what your assets were worth as of that date. Similarly, put your mouse in the debt area to see how much you owed at that date. Click any bar location to open another chart that displays your assets and liabilities in a pie chart as seen on the following page. Click Done to close the chart.

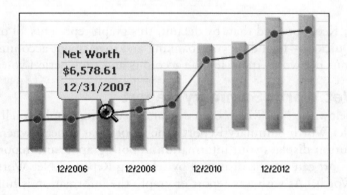

The size of the "pie" in the pie chart may vary depending on the number of accounts you have chosen to display. The pie charts are sized by the number of account-type legend entries. Therefore, if you have more account types for assets, the assets chart may be smaller than the liabilities chart. This can be a bit disconcerting to see your assets looking smaller than your debts. If you have chosen only one or two asset and liability accounts, the "pies" in the chart may appear to be the same size.

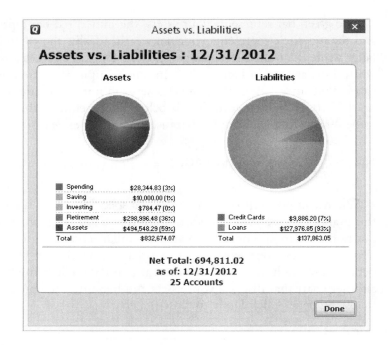

Keep in mind that, by default, this graph represents all of your accounts in Quicken—including your banking and investment accounts. It's a true view of your net worth trend for the accounts and time period you choose.

Net Worth Summary Report

Below the Net Worth by Assets and Liabilities graph, you'll see a button labeled Net Worth Summary Report. The report that appears when you click this button displays your information in both graphic and report format. (This report can also be displayed by selecting Reports | Net Worth & Balances | Net Worth.) As with any report or graph, the information is fully customizable. Click the red X to close the report and return to the Net Worth view. See Chapter 5 to review your many options when customizing reports.

Any accounts you have hidden in Quicken are not included in your Net Worth reports unless you choose to include them by customizing the report.

Net Worth by Account Type

By default, the Net Worth by Account Type graph appears in the lower portion of the screen when you select the Net Worth button in the Property & Debt tab.

This graph shows the percentage of your net worth represented by each of your account types. This is also a stacked bar graph with each account type represented by a different color. The legend to the right of the graph shows what color indicates which type of accounts, as seen here.

Account Balances Report

The Account Balances Report button, at the bottom of the Net Worth by Account Type graph, opens the Account Balances report with the date range settings you have entered at the top of the Net Worth views. This report can also be opened by choosing Reports | Account Balances. However, the default settings for the report you see using that method show your balances from the earliest date entered in your Quicken account with no interval (such as monthly, weekly, and so on) set. Click the red X to close the report and return to the Net Worth view.

Using the Property View

To open the Property view, click the Property button in the Property & Debt tab. Each of your assets and any associated liability show in a horizontal bar graph, as seen in Figure 10-2. If you have two current liabilities associated with one asset, as shown in the House account, each liability is displayed with a different color. At the right of each asset, the total equity you currently hold in this asset displays. The equity that shows is the current value of the asset less the current loan balance.

Depending on your screen or monitor, you may not see the different colors because the color differences are subtle.

If you have refinanced an asset, such as your house, zeroed-out mortgages may be included in the total equity value with a zero balance.

The drop-down list box at the top of the screen lets you select which of your accounts you want displayed in this graph. While All Accounts is the default choice, you may choose from several options:

- Personal Accounts Only
- One specific account (each shows by the account name)
- Custom (which opens a list of all of your asset accounts so you may choose two or more)

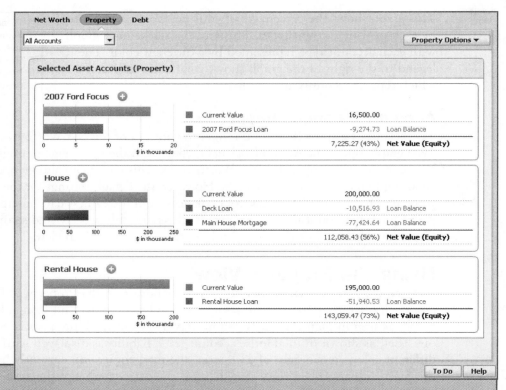

Figure 10-2 • Bar graphs in the Property view display both assets and any associated debt.

Click the Property Options button at the right side of the screen to open a menu from which you can choose among the following:

- Add A House Asset Account
- Add A Vehicle Asset Account
- Add Other Asset Account
- Add A New Loan

Each item on the Property Options menu has a small white plus sign in a green circle to its left. You open the appropriate Add Account screen when you click that green circle icon or click the adjacent text.

Creating a new account from the Property Options menu saves a step or two when adding a new account, as the Add Account dialog opens directly to the type of account you are creating.

Within the graph itself are similar icons to the right of each asset, as seen here. Use these green circle icons to open a menu with which you can perform the following actions:

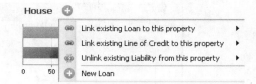

Link Existing Loan To This Property   This option opens a list of existing loans from which you can choose the loan to link to this property (asset).

Link Existing Line Of Credit To This Property   Choosing this option opens another list menu that displays all your current credit accounts from which you can choose.

Unlink Existing Liability From This Property   When you choose this option from the list, any current loans that have been associated with this asset are displayed. Click the one you want to unlink from this asset.

New Loan   Selecting this option opens the Add Loan Account dialog. Chapter 9 explains how to set up loans. If you have not downloaded yet today, when you select New Loan, Quicken will connect to the Internet and download an updated list of financial institutions.

> **IN MY EXPERIENCE**
>
> The ability to link credit accounts with assets can be valuable. However, unless you have set up a line of credit as a "credit" account instead of a loan, Quicken does not make this information available as an "existing line of credit." Since you cannot change the account "type" after you have entered it, be cautious when creating your new accounts.

Opening the Debt View

Clicking the Debt button opens the Debt view, which by default, displays two graphs that show your current debt position, as seen in Figure 10-3. Each graph portrays your liability information in a slightly different format. At the top of the graphs are several drop-down lists that let you select the accounts with which you want to work, the time period to cover, and the intervals to be displayed. A legend appears at the right telling you what color the graph uses for each debt listed.

The first drop-down list lets you choose which accounts you want to use in the graphs. You have your choice of the following:

- **All Debt Accounts** sets the graph to display all of your debts. This is the default setting.

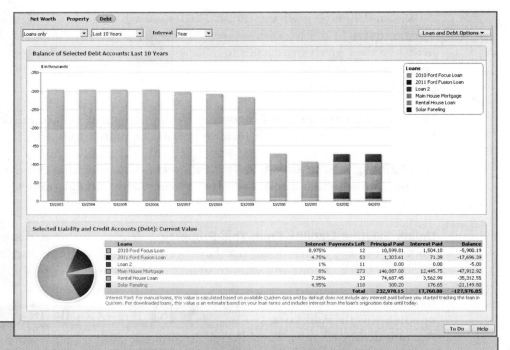

Figure 10-3 • **Click the Debt button in the Property & Debt tab to view your financial obligations in several ways.**

- **Credit Cards Only** displays just the amounts you owe to credit card companies.
- **Loans Only** shows all of your current loans, including any mortgages. If you move your mouse cursor over any section of the stacked bar graph, a small message appears that displays the balance of that loan at that point in time.

If you have designated a liability as "Other Liability" in the Add Account dialog, you may see an option for "Other Liabilities Only," which displays all items of this account type.

- **Custom** opens a Customize dialog that lets you choose which accounts to display. Click Select All to display all of your debts. Click Clear All and choose only the debts you want to display in your graph. Clicking the Show (Hidden Accounts) check box will enable you to include those debts that you have hidden in Quicken for selection in the graphs. Click OK to close the dialog and return to your graph.

- Specific debt account names let you create a graph that shows only one of your debt accounts.

The second drop-down list offers a variety of dates for which you can set your graphs. Most of the options are self-explanatory; however, when you click Custom Date, a dialog appears that you can use to set the period for which you want each graph to display. Be aware that in this dialog, unlike most dialog boxes in Quicken, you have to click in the To field to change the date instead of using the TAB key to move to it. In this dialog, pressing the TAB key when you enter a date in the From field moves your cursor to the OK button.

The third drop-down list lets you choose between three interval options for your graph's display: Months, Quarter, and Year.

Loan and Debt Options

At the top right of the Debt view is a drop-down list offering additional options as shown here:

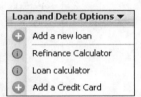

- Add A New Loan
- Add A Credit Card

Both of these choices open the Add Loan/Credit Card Account dialog with which you can quickly create a new account of the type you selected. Again, if this is the first time you have done any online activity for the day, Quicken will retrieve the list of financial institutions when you click the Add A New Loan or Add A Credit Card drop-down item.

The small "i" inside the blue circle icon opens several different dialogs as described in the sections that follow.

Refinance and Loan Calculators   As you might guess, these menu options open a special dialog with which you can quickly calculate a refinancing plan or a new loan. Financial calculators are useful items, and you can learn about their many benefits in Chapter 11.

Balance of Selected Debt Accounts Graph

As seen in Figure 10-3, the first graph you see in the Debt view of the Property & Debt tab is a stacked bar graph that shows your total debt by year for a period you designate. This graph includes a legend explaining the color used for each debt item account included in the graph.

Using the drop-down lists at the top of the screen, you can tell Quicken to show a wide variety of accounts, dates, and intervals to make the information meaningful to you.

Current Value Graph

The second graph in the Debt view of the Property & Debt tab displays the current value of the debts you selected in the first drop-down list at the top of the page. Each drop-down list selection you make displays the information in a slightly different way and includes somewhat different information, as shown next.

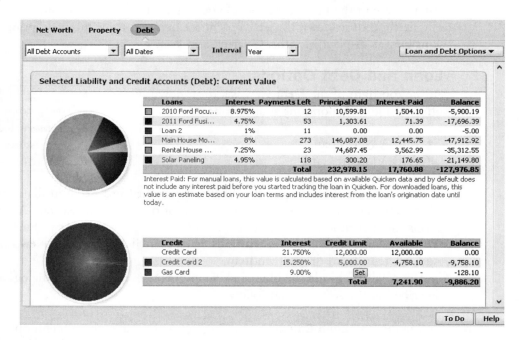

As you can see, the Selected Liability and Credit Accounts (Debt): Current Value graph displays information in both a pie chart and with columns of information. How you have chosen to display your debt accounts in the Debt view's first drop-down box will affect what shows on the Current Value graph. Depending on your choices, the information about the (non-hidden) debt accounts is shown in two sections: Loans and Credit. If you have other debt accounts that are not credit or loan, you will see a third debt type: Other Liabilities.

Loans   If you have selected All Debt Accounts or Loans Only in the first drop-down list, you will see the following:

- **Interest** displays the rate of interest for each loan.
- **Payments Left** shows you how many more payments you have through the life of the loan or debt.
- **Principal Paid** shows the amount of principal you have paid on this loan since its inception.
- **Interest Paid** totals the interest you have paid to date. Remember, interest is the amount you pay to rent someone else's money.
- **Balance** shows what you still owe on this debt. It shows as a minus because it subtracts from your net worth.

Credit   This section displays the credit cards you have entered into Quicken. If, by chance, you do not have any credit card accounts set up in Quicken, you will not see this section in the Debt view. The information displays in pie chart form for the options you chose in the drop-down boxes. You see the following:

- **Interest** displays the interest rate being charged on each card. If it does not show, click the Set button to open the Interest Rate dialog. Enter the interest rate for the card as shown on your monthly statement, and click OK to close the dialog. You may also use this dialog to change the interest rate for the credit card. Click the current rate to open the Interest Rate dialog and enter the new rate.
- **Credit Limit** displays the credit limit of the card. The amount does not show if you have not entered the limit. Click the Set button to open the Credit Limit dialog. Type the amount of this card's credit limit, and click OK to return to the graph.

You can also change the credit limit by clicking the existing value and entering a new amount.

- **Available** displays the amount you can still charge on this card. It is your credit limit minus the current balance.
- **Balance** displays the amount you owe on this card to the credit card company as of the date you set.

If you have not set the interest rate or the credit card limit on any of your credit accounts, two Set buttons appear. If you have set the interest rate but not the card limit, only one Set button appears, as seen here. You may adjust the interest rate and credit limits with either of the Set buttons.

9.00%   Set

1. Locate the account you wish to adjust and, in the proper column, click the Set button.
2. From the dialog that appears, you may set an interest rate or a credit limit. Type in the appropriate information and click OK.

You may also adjust any number that appears in blue in the graph. For example, when our credit card company complies with our request to lower our credit limit, we do the following:

1. Click the amount shown in blue in the credit limit column for the appropriate account.
2. In the Credit Limit dialog that appears, as seen here, type the new amount.
3. Click OK to close the dialog and return to the Debt snapshots in the Property & Debt tab.

Accessing Property and Debt Account Registers

To learn more about the transactions and balances for a specific account, you can view the account's register.

- Click the name of an account in the Property view in the Property & Debt tab's screen.
- Click the name of the account from the Account Bar.
- Click the account's name from the Current Value graph in the Debt view of the Property & Debt tab.

With any of the three methods, the account's register will open. The register lists all transactions entered into that account, as well as the ending balance. As with all of the Quicken registers, you can enter transactions directly into the register. Quicken automatically calculates and enters other transactions such as principal payments for a mortgage or other loans.

Viewing the transactions and entering or editing the transactions will work in all loan registers, except online loan registers. You cannot edit those registers.

Creating Alerts for Property and Debt Accounts

While Chapter 4 introduced you to Quicken Alerts, there are some special alerts that relate directly to your property.

Setting Up Property and Debt Alerts

To set up an alert, begin by opening the Tools menu and clicking Alerts Center. Click the Setup tab and choose General. Click the name of the alert you want to set from the two options on the left side of the window to display its options on the right where three alerts appear. Of the three, two alerts apply specifically to your property as shown next. The Reminders alerts are discussed at length in Chapter 4.

- **Insurance Reappraisal** notifies you before an insurance policy expires so you can either reevaluate coverage or shop for a new policy.
- **Mortgage Reappraisal** notifies you before a mortgage changes from variable to fixed (or fixed to variable) so you can consider refinancing. Even if your mortgage doesn't convert, you can use this alert to remind you periodically to check for better mortgage deals.

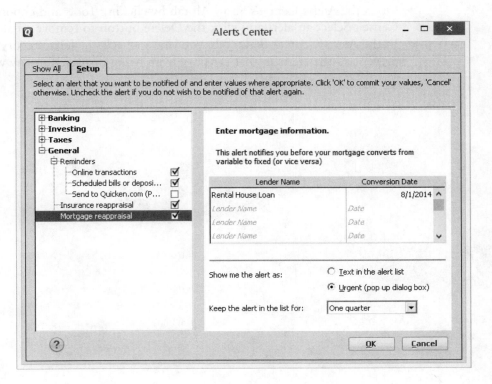

Both alerts work in much the same way. For each alert, enter a name and date in the right side of the window. For example, to set insurance policy expiration dates, click in the Policy Name field that contains the name of the policy holder with which you want to work. You can change the name or add a new policy holder (the insurance company). You'll see that your text appears on the right side of the box. Use your TAB key to move to the Expiration Date field. Enter the expiration date.

Select one of the options at the bottom of the window to indicate how you want the alert to appear: as text in the alert list or as a pop-up dialog that appears when you start Quicken. Finally, use the drop-down list to specify the length of time the alert should remain in the list and click OK.

Repeat this process for each alert you want to set. When you're finished, click OK.

Working with Property and Debt Alerts

Once you have established property and debt alerts, you can manage them in several ways:

- Open the Alerts Center's Show All tab by clicking Tools and choosing Alerts Center. Select an alert and click the Delete button to remove an alert.
- In the Alerts Center's Setup tab, you can uncheck an alert category to prevent all the alerts in that category from being displayed in any way.

Designing Your Financial Future

This part of the book tells you about Quicken Personal Finance Software's planning features, which you can use to plan for your retirement, major purchases, and other life events. It covers Quicken's built-in financial calculators, as well as features that can help you save money to make your dreams come true. You are introduced to the many tax tools that are available in Quicken to help you prepare for tax time. The three chapters are

Part Five

Planning Your Future with Financial Calculators

Chapter 11

In This Chapter:

- *Planning your steps*
- *Setting plan assumptions*
- *Viewing plan results*
- *Setting and using "What If" options*
- *Finding more planning tools*
- *Learning about financial calculators*
- *Accessing the financial calculators*
- *Working with the calculators*

You can use Quicken to help you with all of your financial decisions and to give you ideas of how much to save for the future. To most of us, the future is an unknown, a mystery. After all, who can say what will happen tomorrow, next year, or ten years from now? However, if you think about your future, you can usually come up with a few events that you can plan for: marriage, the purchase of a new home, the birth of your children (and their education years later), and a comfortable retirement. (These are just examples—everyone's life runs a different course.) These events, as well as many unforeseen events, all have one thing in common: they affect your finances. In this chapter, you'll learn how Quicken's tools can help you plan for many of life's milestones.

Planning for Retirement

It may seem strange to start planning with what may happen 20 or 30 years from now. Throughout your life, you work and earn money to pay your bills, buy the things you and your family need or want, and help your kids get started with their own lives. However, there comes a day you may choose to retire from going to work every day. Those regular paychecks stop coming, and you find yourself relying on the money you've been saving for those 20 or 30 years (or more!).

Retirement planning may be one of the most important financial planning jobs facing individuals and couples. Since this "job" requires long-term planning and, in many cases, sacrificing something today to create a secure tomorrow, we start with some planning steps and suggestions.

Retired people live on fixed incomes. That's not a problem, as long as the income is fixed high enough to support a comfortable lifestyle. You can help ensure that there is enough money to finance your retirement years by planning and saving now.

Planning is even more important these days as longevity increases. People are living longer than ever. Your retirement dollars may need to support you for 20 years or more, at a time when the cost of living will likely be even higher than it is today.

With proper planning, it's possible to finance your retirement years without putting a strain on your working years. By closely monitoring the status of your retirement funds, periodically adjusting your plan, and acting accordingly, your retirement years can be the golden years they're supposed to be.

Planning Your Steps

Retirement planning is much more than deciding to put $2,000 in an IRA every year. It requires careful consideration of what you have, what you'll need, and how you can make those two numbers the same.

Assess What You Have

Take a good look at your current financial situation. What tax-deferred retirement savings do you already have? A 401(k)? An IRA? Something else? What regular savings do you have? What taxable investments do you have? The numbers you come up with will form the basis of your final retirement funds.

Be sure to consider property that can be liquidated to contribute to retirement savings. For example, if you currently live in a large home to accommodate your family, you may eventually want to live in a smaller home. The proceeds from the sale of your current home may exceed the cost of your retirement home.

Consider any income-generating property that may continue to generate income in your retirement years or that can be liquidated to contribute to retirement savings.

Determine What You'll Need

What you'll need depends on many things. One calculation suggests you'll need 80 percent of your current gross income to maintain your current lifestyle in your retirement years.

Time is an important factor in calculating the total amount you should have saved by retirement day. Ask yourself two questions:

- *How long do you have to save?* Take your current age and subtract it from the age at which you hope to retire. That's the number of years you have left to save.
- *How long will you be in retirement?* Take the age at which you plan to retire and subtract it from the current life expectancy for someone of your age and gender. That's the number of years you have to save for.

Develop an Action Plan and Stay with It

Once you know how much you need, it's time to think seriously about how you can save it. This requires putting money away in one or more savings or investment accounts. Use the Lifetime Planner in Quicken to get you started. See "Getting Started with the Quicken Lifetime Planner" next in this chapter. After you have created the plan, stick to the plan!

The most important part of any long-term plan is consistency. For example, if you plan to save $5,000 a year, don't think you can just save $2,000 this year and make up the $3,000 next year. There are two reasons: first, you can't "make up" the interest lost on the $3,000 you didn't save this year, and second, you're kidding yourself if you think you'll manage to put away $8,000 next year. If you consider deviating from your plan, just think about the alternative: making ends meet with a job bagging groceries or waiting tables when you're 73 years old.

Getting Started with the Quicken Lifetime Planner

To help you prepare for many of life's financial goals, Quicken 2014 includes several comprehensive planning tools. From the Planning tab, you have access to all of Quicken's built-in planning features, including the Quicken Lifetime Planner's main plan assumptions and individual financial planners (refer to

Figure 11-1). Once you have set up your plan, simply view the Lifetime Planner to see an up-to-date view of how well your plan is working.

If you do not see the Planning tab, click View | Show Tabs | Tabs To Show and select Planning.

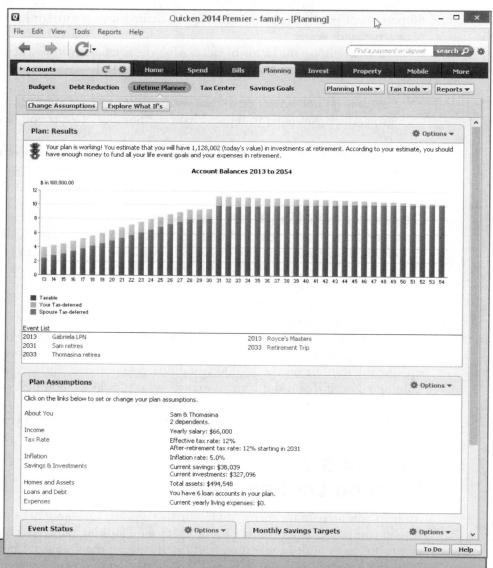

Figure 11-1 • The Lifetime Planner view displays the details and results for your plan.

Here's how it works. You start by entering plan assumptions, which include information about you, your current finances, and your tax rate. Quicken makes calculations based on what you entered to display plan results. As you continue working with Quicken, entering transactions that affect your finances, Quicken updates the result of the plan.

Setting up Quicken Lifetime Planner assumptions can take some time at first. However, the benefits of using this feature far outweigh the cost (in time) of setting it up. If you don't have the time to set up the Quicken Lifetime Planner today, schedule time in the near future. This can even be a family project on a rainy Saturday afternoon. If you are raising a family, helping them see how to plan and save can be a very valuable lesson.

You can enter information into the Lifetime Planner all at once or over time. Once you have entered information into the planner, Quicken retains the information for you and you can continue where you last were working.

This section explains how to set assumptions for the planners within the Quicken Lifetime Planner and how to view the results of your plan in the Planning tab.

Setting Plan Assumptions

The easiest way to see what plan assumptions you will need to make is to view the Plan Assumptions area of the Lifetime Planner. Click Planning | Lifetime Planner. When you first see the planner, the Plan: Results area is blank, waiting for your input, as shown next.

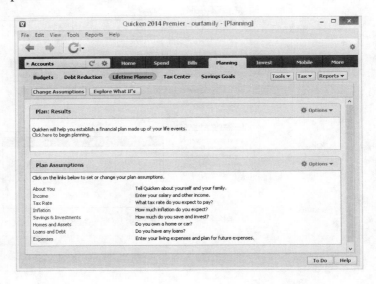

To begin, start by entering information in the Plan Assumptions snapshot. To set details for an assumption category, click its link. Each link opens a dialog you can use to enter information. Here's a look at each category.

About You

Clicking the About You link displays the About You dialog, as shown next. Its fields are pretty self-explanatory: your name and date of birth. When you're finished entering information in the dialog, click Done to save it.

IN MY EXPERIENCE

As you begin working with the Lifetime Planner, you may see slightly different wording from that shown in "Setting Plan Assumptions" elsewhere in this chapter. For example, if you have not entered information in a specific area to allow Quicken to perform the required calculations, Quicken reminds you with the message "You have not entered enough information for Quicken to analyze your life plan. Check to see the information you still need to provide." If you see this message, click the word Check, as it is a link to another Planning Assumptions screen showing a listing of planning assumption topics. Each topic with a check mark beside it indicates you have completed that topic.

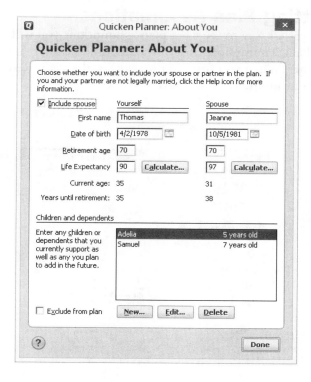

Here are some other items to consider when entering data into the About You dialog.

Include Spouse   If you select the Include Spouse check box, you can enter information into the Spouse column of the dialog. If you don't wish to include anyone else in your plan, leave that check box blank.

Life Expectancy   You can either enter what you think might be your life expectancy or click the Calculate button to display the Calculate Life Expectancy dialog. Set options in the dialog, and Quicken tells you how long you may live. Of course, this is an estimate based on current research into life expectancy; you may or may not live to reach the age Quicken suggests, or you may live even longer. Click OK or Close to dismiss the Calculate Life Expectancy dialog.

Many Quicken users set a life expectancy as 95 or longer to ensure their savings will last throughout their lives.

Children and Dependents   To enter information about children or other dependents, click the New button at the bottom of the dialog. This displays the Add Child/Dependent dialog, in which you can enter the name and date of birth for a dependent. Once you click OK, the person's name and age are added to the list. Repeat this process for each child or dependent you need to add. Once a child or dependent has been added, you can select his or her name and click the Edit button to change information about him or her, or click the Delete button to remove him or her permanently from the plan, or turn on the Exclude From Plan check box so Quicken doesn't use him or her in its calculations. When you have finished making entries, click Done to close the About You dialog.

The focus, or location, of your cursor may not automatically go to the first name field, so you may have to click in the field to begin entering information.

Income

Clicking the Income link displays the Income dialog. This section has three separate tabs of information. Select the appropriate tab to enter salary, retirement benefits, and other income information for you (and your spouse or partner, if you choose).

Salary   The Salary tab enables you to record information about current and future salary and self-employment income.

To add an income item into your Plan Assumptions section, click Income to open the Quicken Planner: Income dialog. In the Salary tab, click the New button to display the Add Salary dialog, as seen next. Then set options to enter information about the income item. As you can see in this illustration, the Add Salary dialog is extremely flexible, enabling you to enter start and end dates for a salary—which is useful for income from seasonal employment. If you don't need to enter specific dates, choose Already Started from the When Does This Salary Start? drop-down list and one of the retirement options from the When Does This Salary End? drop-down list. When you click OK, the salary item is added to your income list.

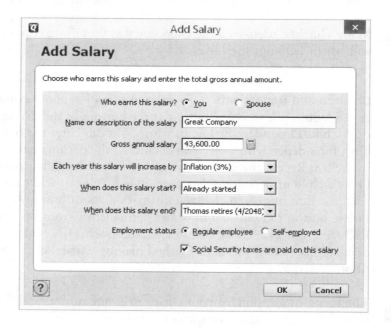

For each item you add, Quicken automatically includes adjustments that specify when the item begins and ends. You can add other adjustments if you know about changes that will occur in the future. Select the item in the top half of the dialog, and then click the New button at the bottom of the dialog. Enter information in the Add Salary Adjustment dialog as shown next. Click OK. The information is added to the bottom half of the Salary tab of the Income dialog.

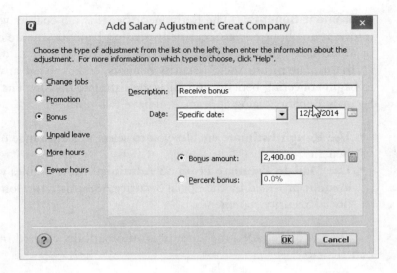

After you have completed the entries in the Salary tab, you can select any of the salary or adjustment items and click the Edit or Delete button, seen next, to change or remove them. You can also select an item and select the Exclude From Plan check box to exclude its information from the Quicken Planner.

Retirement Benefits   The Retirement Benefits tab enables you to enter information about Social Security or pension benefits you are currently receiving or to estimate future benefits.

To estimate future Social Security benefits, enter the age at which you expect to begin collecting benefits and click the Estimate button. The Estimate Social Security Benefits dialog appears. You have two options:

- **Use Rough Estimate** enables you to select a salary range option to estimate benefits.
- **Use Mail-In Estimate From SS Administration** enables you to enter the amount provided by the Social Security Administration on your annual Social Security statement.

When you click OK, the amount is automatically entered in the Retirement Benefits tab.

Currently the Social Security retirement age for those born between 1943 and 1959 is 66 while those born in 1960 or later may receive full Social Security benefits at age 67. There has been some talk about raising the retirement age for those born after 1978 to 70, although as of the date of this manuscript, that has not been enacted.

To add a pension, click the New button at the bottom of the Retirement Benefits tab of the Income dialog. This displays the Add Pension dialog. Enter information about the pension, and click OK to add it to the Retirement Benefits tab. In that tab, you can select the pension and click Edit or Delete to change or remove it, or select the Exclude From Plan check box to exclude it from the Quicken Planner's calculations.

Other Income   The Other Income tab of the Quicken Planner: Income dialog enables you to enter income from other sources, such as gifts, child support, and inheritances. Don't use this tab to enter income from investments or rental properties; the Quicken Lifetime Planner provides specific locations for that data.

Click the New button in the Other Income tab to enter an income item. An interesting option in this dialog is the ability to specify how the money will be used: either saved and invested or used to pay expenses. The option you select determines how this income is used in the plan. If you're not sure what to select, leave it set to the default option. When you click OK, the item is added to the Other Income tab's list. You can edit, delete, or exclude the item from the plan as desired.

When you have entered all the income items, click Done to close the Quicken Planner: Income dialog.

Tax Rate

Clicking the Tax Rate link in the Plan Assumptions snapshot displays the Average Tax Rate dialog shown next. You have two options:

- **Demographic Average** enables you to estimate your tax rate based on where you live and what your income is.
- **Tax Returns** enables you to estimate your tax rate based on the total income, total federal taxes, and total state taxes from your most recent tax returns.

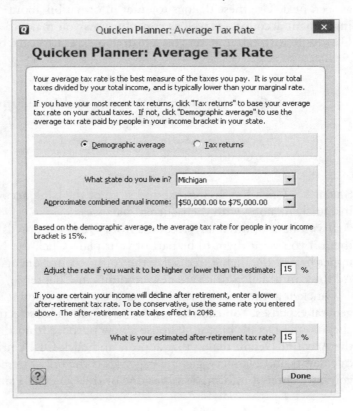

You can also enter an estimate of your post-retirement tax rate, which may be lower. Click Done to close the Quicken Planner: Average Tax Rate dialog.

Inflation

Clicking the Inflation link displays the Estimated Inflation dialog, which includes a field you can use to enter the inflation rate you want to use for your plan. Quicken suggests an inflation rate of 3 percent, which is the average inflation rate since 1927, but you can enter any rate you think is correct in the text box. Click OK to save your estimate.

Many Quicken users enter a higher inflation rate to reflect what they think will happen in the future.

Savings & Investments

Clicking the Savings & Investments link in the Plan Assumptions snapshot displays the Savings And Investments dialog, which is organized into three tabs, as seen next. Use these dialogs to enter information about current bank and investment accounts, as well as contributions you make to investment accounts. Use the Return tab to enter the return you expect to earn on your investments.

Savings Click the Savings tab to list all of the bank accounts you have set up in Quicken, along with their current balances.

If you have omitted any accounts from Quicken, now is a good time to add them if you want them to be part of your plan. Click the New button at the upper half of the dialog to display the Add Account dialog. Learn how to use the Add Account dialog to create new accounts in Chapter 1.

Quicken automatically assumes that each bank account will be used for general expenses. You can change this assumption by selecting an account and clicking the Details button. Choose a new purpose from the drop-down list in the Account Details dialog that appears and click OK. Until you use Quicken's calculators and planners, general expenses is the only offered option. However, if you have entered information into one of the Quicken Planners, such as college expenses in the Expenses Planner, an option for that expense appears in the drop-down list.

If you or your spouse makes regular contributions to one of your bank accounts, you can enter information about that contribution in the Savings dialog. In the top half of the dialog, select the account that receives the contribution. Then click the New button at the bottom of the dialog. Use the Add Contribution dialog that appears to indicate how much you contribute. The dialog walks you through the process of entering information based on whether the contribution is a percentage of a salary or a base amount that increases each year. Click Done to close the Add Contribution dialog.

Investments   The Investments tab lists all of the investment accounts you have set up in Quicken, along with their current market values. Remember, since market value is determined by security prices, the market value is only as up-to-date as the security price information in Quicken that you have most recently entered or downloaded.

This tab works just like the Savings tab. You can click the New button in the top half of the dialog to open the Add Account dialog to enter a new investment account. Choose an existing account, and click the New button in the bottom half of the dialog to enter regular contribution information for any selected investment account. You can also specify the intended use for any account by selecting the account name and clicking the Details button.

Return   The Return tab enables you to specify your expected rates of return for pre-retirement and post-retirement investments. If you turn on the check box near the top of the dialog, additional text boxes appear, enabling you to enter different rates of return for taxable and tax-deferred investments. At the bottom of the dialog, you can enter the percentage of the taxable return that is subject to taxes. This is normally 100 percent, but for your situation, the percentage may be different. Click Done to close the Quicken Planner: Savings And Investments dialog.

Homes And Assets

Clicking the Homes And Assets link displays the Homes And Assets dialog, which is organized into two tabs. This is where you can enter information about currently owned assets and assets you plan to purchase in the future.

Currently, Quicken's Lifetime Planner uses out-of-date limits, so if you enter the contributions to match the previously mentioned limits, the Planner uses the lesser, out-of-date limit amounts. You can work around this limitation by doing two or more contributions for each account, e.g., two 401(k) contributions of $17,500 divided by 2, or $8,750 each.

IN MY EXPERIENCE

Check with your tax professional for the current limits of contributions to any retirement plan such as a 401(k), a SEP IRA, or an IRA, whether Traditional or Roth. Current limits for the calendar year 2013 are

- 401(k) = $17,500
- 401(k) Catch-up for those 50 and older = $5,500
- IRA = $5,500
- IRA = Catch-up for those 50 and older = $1,000
- SEP = 25% of gross compensation not to exceed $51,000

2014 limits will be published in December of 2013.

Homes and Asset Accounts   The Asset Accounts tab, which is shown next, lists all of the asset accounts you have created in Quicken, including accounts for your home, vehicle, and other assets. If you have additional assets that have not yet been entered in Quicken and you want to include them in your plan, click the New button and use the Add Account dialog that appears to create the new account. See how to add a new asset account in Chapter 9.

If you plan to sell an asset, you can enter information for that sale. Select the asset in the top half of the dialog, and then click the Sale Info button. A series of dialogs prompts you for information about the asset's purchase and sale date and price, as well as other information that affects how much money you can expect to receive and pay taxes on. Quicken adds this information to your plan. Click Done to close the Sale Information dialog. If you change your mind about selling the asset, click Sale Info again and select I Do Not Plan To Sell This Asset in the second screen of the dialog.

Three buttons at the bottom of the dialog enable you to associate loans, expenses, and income with a selected asset. This is especially important when working with assets you plan to sell, since the sale of the asset should also end associated debt, expenses, and income.

- **Loans** enables you to link existing loans to the asset or add new loans, including home equity loans. It also enables you to enter information about planned loans—for example, if you plan to use a home equity loan to build an addition on your house sometime next year. You can also enter information about planned payoffs—perhaps you're settling an estate and will be getting an inheritance and plan to use it to pay down your house mortgage.

When you click New to add a loan, the dialog is titled Add Loan Account instead of just Add Account.

- **Expenses** enables you to enter property tax information as well as other expenses related to the asset. For a home, this might include association fees, homeowner's insurance, and estimated maintenance and utility costs. For a car, this might include registration, fuel, service, and insurance. For each expense you add, Quicken prompts you for information about the expense, including how you expect to pay for it—with money in a specific bank account or with a loan. It even enables you to set up a monthly savings target to pay for the item.

Ensure you do not duplicate expenses by adding them here as well as in the Home and Assets dialog.

- **Income** enables you to enter information about income you expect to earn from the asset. This is especially useful if you own rental property. The dialog that appears when you add an income item is almost the same as the Add Other Income dialog. It even allows you to specify how you plan to use the income: for investment or to pay expenses. Click Done to close the Loans, Asset Expenses, or Other Income dialogs.

Planned Assets   The Planned Assets tab lets you enter information about any assets you plan to purchase in the future. For example, suppose you indicated in the Asset Accounts tab that you plan to sell your home or car on a specific date. If you plan to replace it with another home or car, this is where you will enter information about the replacement. Quicken uses dialogs that walk you through the process of entering details about the future purchase. Once you've entered planned asset information, you can select the asset in the list and add loans, expenses, and income for it, as well as choose the accounts you plan to use to pay for it. Click Done to close the Quicken Planner: Homes And Assets dialog.

Loans And Debt

Clicking the Loans And Debt link in the Plan Assumptions snapshot displays the Loans And Debt dialog, which is organized into three tabs; Loan Accounts, Planned Loans, and after you have set up your debt reduction plan, Existing Debt Plan. Use these dialogs to enter information about current and planned loans, as well as information from your debt reduction plan.

If you have not yet set up your debt reduction plan, the Existing Debt Plan tab does not appear.

Loan Accounts   The Loan Accounts tab, which is shown here, displays information about current loans. This information comes from loans you have

set up within Quicken. To add another loan that isn't already recorded in Quicken, click the New button to display the Add Loan Account dialog, which is covered in Chapter 9. If you plan to pay off a loan before its last payment date, you can click the Payoff button to enter future payoff information.

Planned Loans　　The Planned Loans tab enables you to enter information about loans you plan to make in the future. This does not include any loans you may have already entered in the Homes And Assets dialog discussed earlier in this chapter. Instead, this is for loans that are not associated with any particular asset, such as a personal loan you plan to use for a second (or third!) honeymoon.

Existing Debt Plan　　The Existing Debt Plan tab includes information from the Debt Reduction Planner, which is covered in Chapter 12. If you have credit card and other debt, it's a good idea to create a debt reduction plan as part of your overall planning strategy.

　　You can choose whether or not to include your debt reduction plan information in your Lifetime plan. If you choose to include your debt reduction here, you will need to exclude debt reduction plan accounts in the Existing Debt Plan tab of the Loans And Debt planner, as shown next. Click Done to close the Quicken Planner: Loans And Debt dialog.

If you include your debt reduction plan here, you should exclude the included loan and credit accounts/expenses in the Loan Accounts tab/Expenses tab, as applicable, so as to not double-count the expenses.

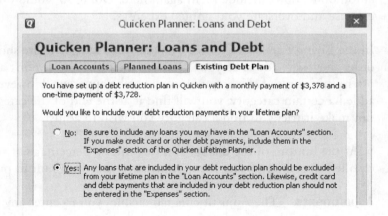

Expenses

Open the Expenses dialog by clicking the Expenses link. This section is organized into four tabs. Use these tabs to enter information about your living expenses, as well as any adjustments to expenses and the expenses for college or other special events.

Living Expenses   The Living Expenses tab uses two techniques to help you enter your estimated living expenses.

- **Rough Estimate** enables you to enter an estimate of your annual living expenses. Using this technique is quicker, but it may not be as accurate as using the Category Detail option.
- **Category Detail** enables you to have Quicken calculate an estimate of your annual living expenses based on transactions already entered in your Quicken data file. This technique is more accurate than Rough Estimate, especially if you have been using Quicken for a while and have a good history of transactions. If you select this method, you can click the Details button that appears in the middle of the dialog to display the Living Expenses Category Detail dialog. Toggle check marks in the list of categories to include or exclude specific categories and enter monthly amounts as desired. When you click OK, Quicken annualizes the amounts and enters them in the Living Expenses tab.

One thing to keep in mind here: don't include expenses that you may have already included for an asset. For example, if you included car insurance expenses in the Homes And Assets dialog as an expense associated with an automobile, don't include them again here. Doing so would duplicate the expense and overstate your annual expenses.

In the Living Expenses Category Detail view, categories are shown listed in the order they were added to your Quicken data file. If you don't add new categories often, this quirk of the list order may not be apparent. However, if you recently added a certain category, you will find it at the end of the category listing. This can make it tricky to find a category you wish to adjust.

At the bottom of the dialog, you can enter a percentage of surplus cash—any cash left over after paying living expenses—that you want to put into savings.

Adjustments   The Adjustments tab enables you to enter any adjustments to your expenses that are related to intended changes in your life. For example, perhaps you plan to hire a nanny to take care of your child while you go back to work. You can add this planned expense as an adjustment for a predefined period. When you click the New button in the Adjustments tab, the Add Living Expense Adjustment dialog appears. When you are done adding information, click OK to close the Add Living Expense Adjustment dialog.

College Expenses   The College Expenses tab, shown next, enables you to plan for the education of your children—or yourself! Clicking the New button in this tab displays the Add College Expenses dialog, which walks you through the process of entering expected college expenses for a plan member. You'll have to do a little homework to come up with realistic estimates of college costs, including tuition, room, board, books, and supplies. Remember, if you underestimate expenses, your plan won't be accurate. The dialog also prompts you for information about expected financial aid, student loans, and student contributions to cover all sources of financing. If you have a college fund—such as an educational IRA—already set up for the college expense, you can associate it with the expense to indicate how it will be paid for. Click Next to advance through the dialogs and click Done to close the Add College Expenses dialog.

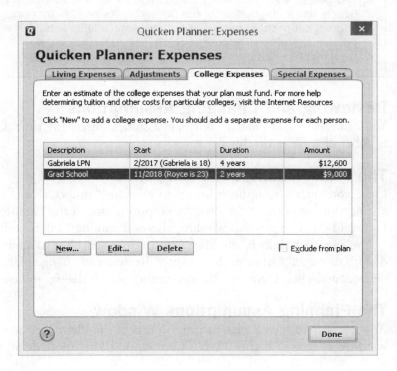

Be aware that some of the dialogs in the Add College Expenses dialog have a very small font.

Special Expenses   The Special Expenses tab includes any expenses you may have already added in the Homes And Assets dialog and enables you to enter other one-time or annual expenses you expect to incur. Use this for items like a vacation, wedding, or large purchase. When you click the New button, Quicken prompts you for information about the expense, including the amount and how you expect to finance it. Click Next to advance through the Add Special Expense dialogs. Click Done to close the Quicken Planner: Expenses dialog.

> ### IN MY EXPERIENCE
>
> Quicken even gives you help in finding outside funding for college expenses. Once you have created a plan that includes college expenses, follow these steps for some Internet links to help you or your student find college funding.
>
> **1.** From the Planning tab, click the Lifetime Planner button.
> **2.** In the Plan: Results | Event List, choose the appropriate college event.
> **3.** The College Event summary dialog appears for that event. Click Internet Resources at the bottom of the College Expense Plan that appears. With your Internet connection, open one of the resource links listed for additional discussions of funding college costs.
> **4.** Click the X to close the plan.

Reviewing and Changing Assumptions
You can review and modify your plan assumptions at any time. Quicken offers a number of ways to do this.

The Plan Assumptions Snapshot
Once you enter assumptions into the Quicken Planners, a brief summary of the assumptions appears in the Plan Assumptions area in the Planning tab (refer to Figure 11-1). To open this window, choose Planning | Lifetime Planner.

You can click links in the Plan Assumptions snapshot to open the same dialogs discussed earlier in this chapter. Review and change plan assumptions as desired, and click Done or OK, depending on the dialog, to save your changes.

The Planning Assumptions Window
Another way to review plan assumptions is in the Planning Assumptions window, as seen in Figure 11-2. This method shows more detail than the Plan

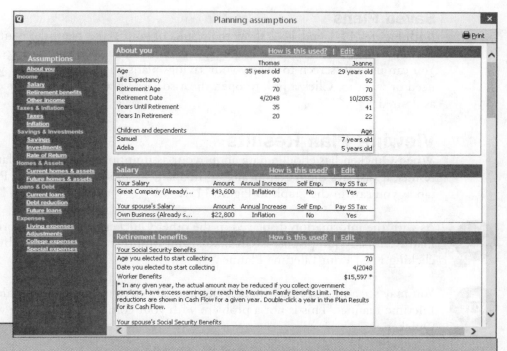

Figure 11-2 • Use the Planning Assumptions dialog to change information in your Lifetime Planner.

Assumptions snapshot. To open this window, choose Planning | Lifetime Planner. (You can access the Planning Assumptions window from the Options button in any of the four sections of the Lifetime Planner. Click Options | Review Or Change Plan Assumptions.)

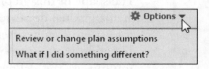

Use links on the left side of the Planning Assumptions window to navigate quickly from one category to another. The details appear in the main part of the window. Each assumption category offers two links:

- **How Is This Used?** explains how the information in that category of assumption is used in the plan.
- **Edit** enables you to edit the assumptions for that category, using the same dialogs discussed earlier in this chapter.

Saved Plans

Both Figures 11-1 and 11-2 show the results of your saved plan, the plan assumptions, the status of any planned events, and your monthly savings targets. You can use this screen to review your savings plans and change them if you need or want to. Click a link to open the associated planner and change data as desired.

Viewing Plan Results

When Quicken has enough data about your assumptions to calculate plan results, it displays them graphically in the Plan: Results snapshot of the Planning tab as you saw in the graph in Figure 11-1.

As with the information displayed in the other Quicken tabs, you can print the Plan Results, Assumptions, Event Status, and Monthly Savings Targets by clicking File | Print Lifetime Planner.

You may see a message that there is not enough space to draw the graphics in the Lifetime Planner. This is not a problem with your computer; it is a bug within Quicken.

The top of the Plan: Results area tells you whether your plan is working and how much you should have in investments at retirement. Amounts are in today's dollars; to view them in future dollars, choose Show Amounts In Future Value from the Options pop-up menu at the top-right corner of the Plan: Results snapshot.

The graph beneath this summary shows your taxable and tax-deferred savings. The shape of this graph often shows a steady increase until the year you retire and then a gradual decrease. Many of us would prefer to see a continuing increase or, at least, no change after retirement. Clicking a column opens a Plan Summary dialog for that year showing income and expenses, as seen in the next illustration. You can use the <<Prev Year>> and <<Next Year>> buttons in the dialog to scroll through the years in the graph. This enables you to see the detailed numbers that make up the graph columns—very helpful! Plan results change automatically based on a variety of changes within your Quicken data file:

- When the account balances referred to in the plan change, the plan changes accordingly.
- When you change plan assumptions, the plan changes accordingly.
- When you use Quicken's planners to plan for major purchases, college, retirement, and other events that affect your finances, the plan changes to include these events.

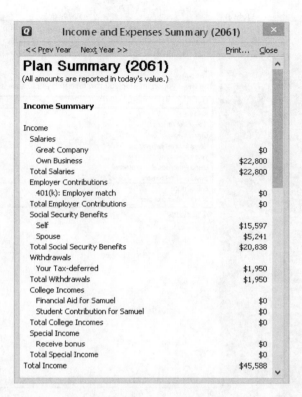

- When you play "what if " with assumptions and save the changes as your plan, the plan changes accordingly. You'll see how to enter "what ifs" a little later in this chapter, in the section "The 'What If 'Alternatives."

Viewing Event Status Items

Quicken also keeps track of your progress toward certain events and savings targets. It displays this information in the Planning tab of the Lifetime Planner. (Refer to Figure 11-1.)

The Event Status snapshot displays information about events in your plan that are funded with specific accounts. From this section, click Your Retirement Plan to open the My Retirement Plan window, seen in Figure 11-3, which looks a lot like the Plan Assumptions window. Click close to return to the Lifetime Planner.

Working with Your Future Expenses

The Monthly Savings Targets snapshot of your Lifetime Planner displays information about your savings toward events in your plan.

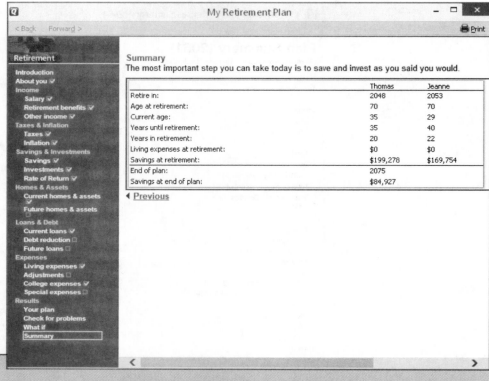

Figure 11-3 • **Use the Summary section of the My Retirement Plan window to view the information you entered about your retirement plan.**

Clicking any link for an expense displays the summary area for that expense in the Plan Assumptions window. You can review and modify event information in that window. When you are done reviewing the event, click Done or OK to return to the Lifetime Planner.

The "What If" Alternatives

Once you've entered assumptions, created plans for specific events, and viewed your plan results, you might wonder how a change in one or more assumptions would affect the plan. You can use the "What If" Event Scenarios feature to see how the changes would affect the plan without changing the plan itself.

Here's an example. Say you've been offered a job in another state. The job pays about the same salary that you make now, but you can move to a town where your living expenses would be greatly reduced. You can see how the job change would affect your financial plans for the future by playing "what if" to modify existing assumptions, and then see the old and new plan results side by side.

> ### IN MY EXPERIENCE
> When working with the Plan Comparison chart you may notice a slow response when applying the What If changes. Also, if you make a change that is too subtle, it may be hard to distinguish the lines.

Setting "What If" Options

Each of the snapshots of the Lifetime Planner in the Planning tab has an Options button from which you can play What If. Click Options | What If I Did Something Different? to open the What If window. The first time you use it, the window displays the account balances shown in your plan results.

Choose a goal option from the drop-down list at the top-left corner of the window. Then click appropriate links on the left side of the window to open dialogs to change assumptions.

Each time you make a change, the Plan Comparison chart changes. The original plan shows as an orange line and the change as a yellow line. (Depending on your monitor's settings, the colors may look slightly different.)

Using "What If" Results

When you've finished changing assumptions and viewing results, you can click one of the three buttons at the top of the What If window as seen next.

- **Reset What If** clears all of the assumptions you changed while playing "what if." This enables you to start over.
- **Save What If As Plan** saves the assumptions you changed while playing "what if" as your actual financial plan. When the window closes, you'll see the results in the Planning tab change accordingly.
- **Close Without Saving** simply closes the window so you can continue working with Quicken. Your settings are not saved.

What If

You can temporarily change any of your assumptions or goals (and even exclude goals) to see the effect. If you like the changes, you can save them.

[Reset What If]   [Save What If as Plan]   [Close Without Saving]

Finding More Planning Tools

Quicken offers additional tools found in the Planning tab: budgets, which are covered extensively in Chapter 12, and financial calculation tools, which are found in the Planning Tools drop-down list. These tools are discussed at length next in this chapter.

A Look at Quicken's Financial Calculators

Quicken includes five financial calculators you can use to make quick financial calculations: the Retirement Calculator, the College Calculator, the Refinance Calculator, the Savings Calculator, and the Loan Calculator. These calculators make complex calculations simple. Each calculator can help you enter more complete information into the Lifetime Planner and greatly assist you when looking at your financial options.

Learning About Financial Calculators

All five of the financial calculators share the same basic interface. Although they are similar in appearance, each has a specific purpose. It's important that you use the correct calculator to get the job done.

In most instances, you begin by telling the calculator what part of the formula you want to calculate. For example, when calculating a loan, you can calculate the loan amount or the periodic payment. Then you enter values and set other options in the calculator's dialog to give Quicken the information it needs to make its calculations. Clicking a Calculate button completes the process. Quicken is fast; the results appear as soon as you click Calculate—if not sooner.

Accessing the Financial Calculators

To view the financial calculators, click the Planning tab and choose the Planning Tools button. The five calculators appear at the bottom of the menu, as shown here.

If the tabs are not visible, click View | Show Tabs or View | Tabs To Show | Planning on the menu bar. (If the button says Tools instead of Planning Tools, maximize your window to see Planning Tools.)

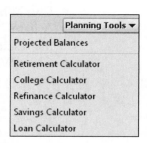

Projected Balances, the first item on the Planning Tools menu, is covered in Chapters 4 and 12.

Using the Financial Calculators

When you are ready to try Quicken's financial calculators, the rest of this chapter provides some detailed instructions for using each of them. All of the calculators open with one or more fields showing the text "CALCULATED" or "calculated." Click the Calculate button to change that text to the calculated number.

Working with the Retirement Calculator

The Retirement Calculator can help you calculate some of the numbers you need to plan for your retirement. To open it, choose Planning | Planning Tools | Retirement Calculator. The Retirement Calculator appears as seen in Figure 11-4.

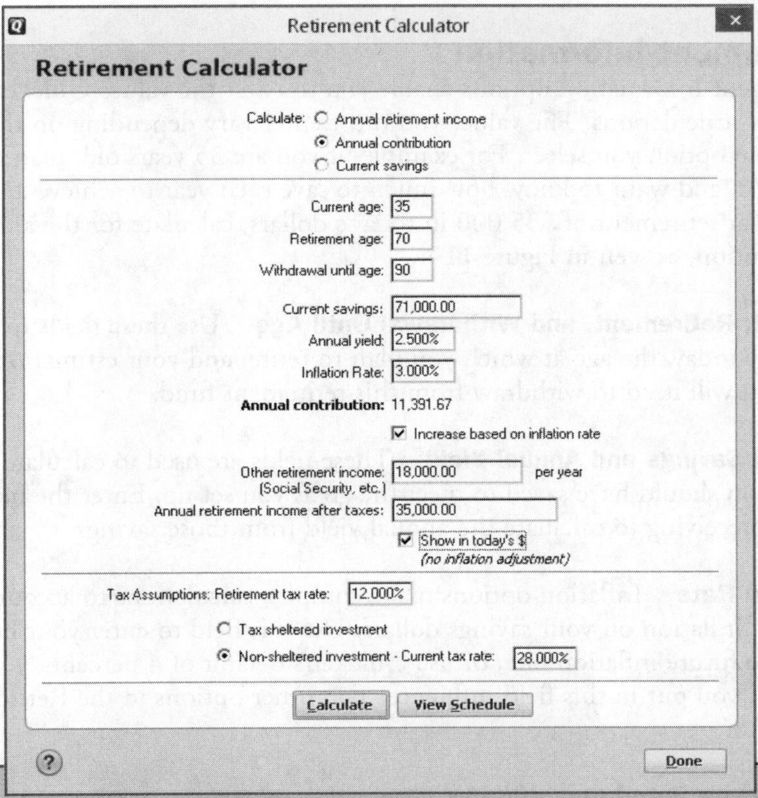

Figure 11-4 • Use the Retirement Calculator to see how much to save for your retirement.

As you will note at the top of the calculator, you may calculate for three different values:

- **Annual Retirement Income** calculates the annual amount of retirement income you'll have based on the values you enter.
- **Annual Contribution** calculates the minimum amount you should contribute to a retirement account to achieve the values you enter.
- **Current Savings** calculates the amount of money you should currently have saved to achieve the values you want when you retire.

Select an option, and then enter or select values and options throughout the dialog. Most options are pretty straightforward and easy to understand. When you're finished, click the Calculate button to see the results. Click Done when you're finished.

Here's a closer look at the options in the Retirement Calculator.

Retirement Information

Retirement Information options enable you to enter the values Quicken should use in its calculations. The values you must enter vary depending on the Calculate option you select. For example, if you are 35 years old, plan on retiring at age 70, and want to know how much to save each year to achieve an annual income at retirement of $35,000 in today's dollars, calculate for the annual contribution, as seen in Figure 11-4.

Current, Retirement, and Withdrawal Until Age   Use these fields to enter your age today, the age at which you plan to retire, and your estimation of how long you will need to withdraw from this retirement fund.

Current Savings and Annual Yield   These fields are used to calculate how much you should have saved to meet the goals you set up. Enter the interest rate you are receiving to calculate the annual yield from those savings.

Inflation Rate   Inflation options make complex calculations to account for the effect of inflation on your savings dollars. Use this field to enter your best guess as to the future inflation rate, or use Quicken's default of 4 percent.

What you put in this field influences two other options in the Retirement Calculator:

- **Increase Based On Inflation Rate** makes calculations assuming that the annual contributions will rise with the inflation rate.

- **Show In Today's $** makes calculations assuming that the Annual Retirement Income After Taxes entry is in today's dollars and not inflated.

Tax Assumptions   Tax Assumptions options enable you to indicate whether your retirement savings are in a tax-sheltered investment or a non-sheltered investment. If you select the Non-Sheltered Investment option, you can enter your current tax rate, and Quicken will automatically calculate the effect of taxes on your retirement income. By experimenting with this feature, you will see why it's a good idea to use tax-sheltered or tax-deferred investments whenever possible.

Calculate

Depending on the option you choose at the top of the Retirement Calculator, clicking the Calculate button does the computation for you. If you change any amounts, click Calculate a second time to see the results of your change.

View Schedule

Clicking the View Schedule button displays a printable list of deposits made and income withdrawn, with a running balance total. Use the vertical scroll bar to view the theoretical balance in the retirement account as our subject reaches each age.

1. Use the question mark to open Quicken's Help screen to answer questions about financial calculators.
2. Select the printer icon to print a complete schedule by year.
3. Click Done to close the Deposit Schedule window.

   Click Done to close the Retirement Calculator.

Running the College Calculator

The College Calculator enables you to calculate savings for the cost of a college education. Choose Planning | Planning Tools | College Calculator. The assumption in this calculator is that you will continue to save the entire time the student is in school.

   Select a Calculate option from these choices at the top of the Calculator:

- **Annual College Costs** calculates the annual tuition you'll be able to afford based on the values you enter.
- **Current College Savings** calculates the amount of money you should currently have saved based on the values you enter.

- **Annual Contribution** calculates the minimum amount you should contribute to college savings based on the values you enter.

Then enter values and options throughout the dialog. As with the other calculators, the available options are straightforward. When you click Calculate, Quicken calculates the results. When you are finished, click Done.

Annual College Costs   Use this field to enter your best guess at the cost of college per year when the person for whom you are saving enrolls in school.

Years   Both the Years Until Enrollment and Number Of Years Enrolled fields will influence the outcome of the calculations. If you have a 12-year-old who, you assume, will be attending college for only four years, enter that information.

Current College Savings   This field shows either what you have already saved for this person's education or, when used as the calculate field, what you should have saved to date to meet the other college goal requirements. Entering the yield you currently receive and your best guess at the inflation rate helps Quicken show you more realistic numbers.

While the calculator is named the "College Calculator," many Quicken users find that their students want to attend vocational training rather than a four-year school. Consider the current costs for specialized technical training, and use the College Calculator to determine how much you will need to save for that specialized training.

Calculate

The Calculate button computes the requested value.

Schedule

Clicking the Schedule button displays the College Savings Plan, a printable list of deposits made and money withdrawn for tuition, with a running balance total. The schedule will show the withdrawals for the period you defined in number of years enrolled, which may or may not be four years. The last four years of the schedule will show the withdrawals. Click Done to close the Schedule dialog, and click Done once again to close the Calculator.

Evaluating the Refinance Calculator

Today's volatile housing market makes many of us think about refinancing our home. Quicken 2014 provides a handy tool to help determine whether refinancing will really save money and, if so, how much. Choose Planning | Planning Tools | Refinance Calculator. The Refinance Calculator appears.

Enter values for your current mortgage and proposed mortgage in the various fields to calculate your monthly savings with the new mortgage. When you are finished, click Done.

Existing Mortgage

Existing Mortgage options enable you to enter your current total monthly mortgage payment and the amount of that payment that is applied to property taxes and other escrow items. Quicken automatically calculates the amount of principal and interest for each payment. If you already know the principal and interest amount, you can enter that in the Monthly Payment box and leave the Impound/Escrow Amount box empty. The result is the same.

Proposed Mortgage

Proposed Mortgage options enable you to enter information about the mortgage that you are considering to replace your current mortgage. The Principal Amount may be the balance on your current mortgage, but it could be more or less, depending on whether you want to refinance for more or less money. (Refinancing often offers a good opportunity to exchange equity for cash or to use cash to build equity.)

If you would have to pay closing costs or points to complete the refinancing, enter them in the appropriate fields. This will help Quicken compute a more accurate break-even point.

Break Even Analysis   Break Even Analysis options are optional. If you enter the closing costs and points for the proposed mortgage, Quicken will automatically calculate how long it will take to cover those costs based on your monthly savings. Click Done to close the Calculator.

Planning with the Savings Calculator

The Savings Calculator lets you calculate savings, that is, periodic payments to a savings account or an investment. Choose Planning | Planning Tools | Savings Calculator to open the Savings Calculator.

As with the other calculators, this calculator offers three options:

- **Ending Savings Balance** calculates the total amount saved at the end of the savings period based on the values you enter.
- **Regular Contribution** calculates the minimum amount you should regularly contribute to savings based on the values you enter.

- **Starting Savings Balance** calculates the amount of money you should currently have saved based on the values you enter.

Save For

The Save For drop-down box offers several options in which to enter values for Quicken to use in its calculations. Enter what you have today, the interest rate you are receiving, and the period of time you want to save. The drop-down list offers four options from which Quicken will calculate:

- Years
- Quarters
- Months
- Weeks

Inflation

Inflation options make complex calculations to account for the effect of inflation on your savings dollars. Enter your best estimate at the future inflation rate. Quicken will use this entry to determine the result of the option you chose at the top of the Savings Calculator screen.

When you have entered all of the information, click Calculate to show the outcome. As with other calculators, use the View Schedule button to see the result of the calculations.

Like the Retirement Calculator Schedule, this schedule can be printed. To print this schedule, click the printer icon at the lower-left corner of the schedule.

After you have completed your calculations, click Done to close the Deposit Schedule dialog, and click Done again to close the Savings Calculator.

Using the Loan Calculator

Perhaps the most used calculator is the Quicken Loan Calculator. With this tool you can quickly calculate the principal or periodic payment for a loan. Choose Planning | Planning Tools | Loan Calculator to open the Loan Calculator, as shown next.

This handy tool will calculate the total loan amount if you enter the payments, interest, and other requested information. Its most common use is to calculate the total payment per period—usually a monthly payment.

Select one of the options, enter information in the remainder of the dialog, and click Calculate. Getting the answer is a lot quicker and easier with the Loan Calculator than using one of those loan books or creating formulas in an Excel spreadsheet to do the job. When you're finished, click Done.

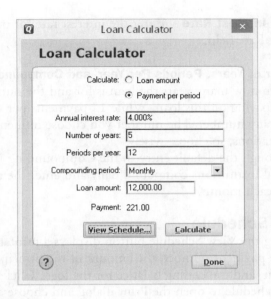

You may calculate for two different options:

- **Loan Amount** calculates the amount of the total loan, given the interest rate, number of years, how many payments per year, and the interest rate on the loan.
- **Payment Per Period** calculates how much your payment would be each month (or other period) to pay off the loan amount you enter, given the interest rate, number of years you would have to pay back the loan, and how many times a year you would make payments.

IN MY EXPERIENCE

If you have young people in your life, use the calculators as a teaching tool. Perhaps your teen wants a new mini-tablet. The device she wants costs $275.00, and she has saved $147.50 of her babysitting and birthday money, meaning she must earn or save an additional $127.50. Show her that by saving $10 each month from her $20 monthly allowance as well as half of her average $50.00 babysitting earnings (or $35.00 total from both sources per month), she can buy her new mini-tablet in only four months.

Loan Information

Loan Information options enable you to enter values for Quicken to use in its calculations. The information you must enter varies depending on the Calculate option you select.

Annual Interest Rate   Enter the interest rate for this loan in the Annual Interest Rate field.

Number of Years, Periods Per Year, and Compounding Period   This tells Quicken how many years the loan is for and the number of times per year you will be paying on this loan. While 12 payments per year is the norm, you may choose any number. The number you choose influences the calculator's computations, so choose wisely.

Although the default entry in the Compounding Period is Monthly, most financial institutions compound daily and enter the total to your account at the end of each month.

View Schedule

Clicking the View Schedule button displays a printable amortization table that lists the payment number, the amount of the principal and interest paid at each payment, and the ending balance for the loan. Click the Print button at the top of the schedule to open the Print dialog and choose a printer. Click Print from the Print dialog to create your paper copy. Click Close to close the dialog.

Until you click the Calculate button, the Approximate Future Payment Schedule will be blank.

Calculate

The Calculate button at the bottom of the calculator performs the calculation based on your choices and the information you have entered.

Reducing Debt and Saving Money

Chapter 12

In This Chapter:

- *Taking control*
- *Using the Debt Reduction Planner*
- *Understanding Quicken's automatic budget*
- *Working with your automatic budget*
- *Organizing categories into groups*
- *Forecasting for your future*
- *Understanding why we save*
- *Saving strategically*
- *Using Savings Goals*

O ne of the best things we, as a society, are learning from our parents, is the importance of saving money and reducing debt. Budgeting and saving to prepare for life events is an important part of financial management. Savings enable you to take vacations and make major purchases without increasing debt, help your kids through college, handle emergencies, and have a comfortable retirement.

This chapter tells you about tools within Quicken Personal Finance Software that can help. If you're in debt and can't even think about saving until you dig your way out, this chapter can help you, too. It starts by covering Quicken tools for reducing your debt.

Reducing Your Debt

Consumer credit is a huge industry. It's still easy to get credit cards—even with the new regulations. And it's a lot easier to pay for something with a piece of plastic than with cold, hard cash. The "buy now, pay later" attitude has become an acceptable way of life. It's no wonder that many Americans are deeply in debt.

Those credit card bills can add up, however. And making just the minimum payment on each one only helps the credit card company keep you in debt—and paying interest—as long as possible. If you're in debt, don't skip this part of the chapter. It'll help you dig yourself out so you can build a solid financial future.

Taking Control

It's difficult to save money if most of your income is spent paying credit card bills and loan payments. If you're heavily in debt, you might even be having trouble keeping up with all your payments. But don't despair. There is hope! Here are a few simple things you can do to dig yourself out of debt.

- **Break the Debt Pattern**   Your first step to reducing debt must be to break the pattern of spending that got you where you are. Eliminate all but one or two major credit cards for emergencies, such as car trouble or unexpected visits to the doctor. The cards that should go are the store and gas credit cards. They can increase your debt, but they can be used in only a few places.
- **Reduce Your Credit Limits**   High credit limits are a trap. The credit card company or bank flatters you by offering to lend you more money. What they're really doing is setting you up so you'll owe them more—and pay them more in monthly finance and interest fees.
- **Shop for Cards with Better Interest Rates**   If you do not pay off the balance of a credit card at the end of each billing period, you pay the interest on that balance. The balance and interest rate determine how much it costs you to have that special picture or name on a plastic card in your wallet. Low-interest credit cards are still widely available; try a web search. But before you apply for a new card, read the terms carefully. Many offer the low rates for a short, introductory period—often no longer than 6 or 12 months. Some offer the low rate only on new purchases, while others offer the low rate only on balance transfers or cash advances. Be sure to find out what the rate is after the introductory period.

Be sure that any fees involved in a balance transfer are not more than the savings you will receive with the new, lower interest rate!

- **Consolidate Your Debt**   Consolidating your debt may be one way to dig yourself out. By combining balances into one debt, whether through balance transfers to a single credit card or a debt consolidation loan, you're better able to pay off the balances without causing financial hardship. This is sometimes the only option when things have gotten completely out of control and you can't meet your debt obligations. However, make sure you have cut up the old cards so you don't add new debt to the older, consolidated amount.

 If you do choose to use a debt consolidation company, investigate them thoroughly before you give them any money.

- **Using Charge Cards, Not Credit Cards**   Understand the difference between a credit card and a charge card:
  - **Credit cards** enable you to buy things on credit. If each month you pay less than what you owe, you are charged interest on your account balance. Most major "credit cards," such as Visa and Discover, are true credit cards. Most store "charge cards" are also credit cards.
  - **Charge cards** enable you to buy things on credit, too. But when the bill comes, you're expected to pay the entire balance. You don't have to pay any interest, but if you don't pay the entire balance on time, you may have to pay late fees and finance charges.

 The benefit of charge cards is that they make it impossible to get into serious debt. Using these cards can prevent you from overspending. Or, you could use Quicken Mobile to check your available funds and budget before making any purchase.

- **If You Can't Stop Spending, Get Help**   Many people who are deeply in debt may have a spending problem. They can't resist buying that fifth pair of running shoes or that trendy new outdoor furniture. They don't need the things they buy, but they buy them anyway. There's nothing wrong with that if your income can support your spending habits, but if your net worth is less than $0, it's a real problem—one that might require counseling to resolve. The next time you make a purchase, stop for a moment and think about what you're buying. Is it something you need? Something you can use? Something you can justify spending the money on? If you can't answer yes to any of these questions, don't buy it. If you have to buy it anyway, it's time to seek professional help.

- **Live Debt-Free** It is possible to live debt-free—and you don't have to be rich to do it. Just stop relying on credit to make your purchases and spend only what you can afford. Imagine how great it would feel to be completely debt-free. It's worth a try, isn't it?

Using the Debt Reduction Planner

Quicken's Debt Reduction Planner is a great tool to help you reduce your debt. After you enter information about your financial situation, Quicken develops a debt reduction plan for you. The Debt Reduction Planner is thorough, easy to use, and an excellent tool for teaching people how they can get out of debt as quickly as possible, saving hundreds (if not thousands) of dollars in interest charges.

If you're in serious debt—actually having trouble making ends meet because you can't seem to get any of your debts paid down—a pair of scissors (for cutting up charge cards), a telephone (to call your credit card companies to get your interest rates reduced), and the Debt Reduction Planner (to come up with a solid plan for reducing your debt) are probably your three best tools for getting things under control.

Here's what the Debt Reduction Planner can help you do that you might not be able to do on your own. The Planner will

- Objectively look at your debts and organize them by interest rate. Use the Planner to see the debts with the highest interest rate (that cost you the most), and ensure they are the first to be paid, thus saving you money.
- Show you the benefit of using some of your savings to reduce the balances on your most costly debt.
- Create an itemized plan based on real numbers that you can follow to reduce your debt.
- Show you, with a nice graph, in dollars and cents, how much money you can save and how quickly you can become debt-free by following the plan.
- Help you to stop dreading the daily mail and its package of bills. Use the Debt Reduction Planner to get things under control.

While you can track and include all of your debt in the plan, Quicken suggests you begin with the debt that costs you the most (the debt with the highest interest rate). These debts are often one or more credit card accounts. That means setting up accounts for your credit cards rather than simply tracking monthly payments as bills paid. Chapters 1 and 3 discuss the two different ways to track credit cards in Quicken.

The wording on the first debt reduction plan you see is a little different depending on which accounts you have already set up. If you have not created any accounts, there is a line just above the Get Started button that says "Add your Accounts to get started." If you have created accounts other than credit cards and loans, the line will say "Add your Credit Card and Loans Accounts to get started."

Using the Debt Reduction Planner with Your Currently Entered Debt Accounts

To get started with the Debt Reduction Planner, from the Planning tab, choose the Debt Reduction button. The Debt Reduction Planner appears with its Get Started button. What you see next depends on whether you have entered information about your debt into Quicken.

If you have not yet entered any credit card or other debt into Quicken, you are prompted to do so after you click the Get Started button. The Add Account dialog appears so that you can enter any credit cards or other personal loans. (See Chapter 1 if you need to review how to enter a new account in Quicken.) See the section "Starting Debt Reduction Planner from Scratch" later in this chapter to work with new accounts in the Debt Reduction Planner. Click the Get Started button to start. This takes you to the Identify Your Debt screen.

- If you have already entered debt information, you will see a dialog that reflects the balances you have currently entered, as well as a debt reduction plan created by Quicken, as seen in Figure 12-1. The balance of this example assumes at least some of the information about what you owe is already entered into Quicken.
- If you have entered credit cards and other debt accounts but have not yet created a debt reduction plan, you will see the Get Started button without a tagline suggesting you add accounts. You can click the Get Started button to start, which will take you to the Identify Your Debts screen.

If you have an existing debt plan, click Plan Actions | Edit Your Plan to get to the Identify Your Debts screen.

What Do You Owe?   The first step in creating a plan is to recognize what you owe. By default, Quicken has designed the Debt Reduction Planner to help you decrease high-interest debt before long-term debt, which Quicken assumes to have lower interest. However, you may add any debt account to the plan.

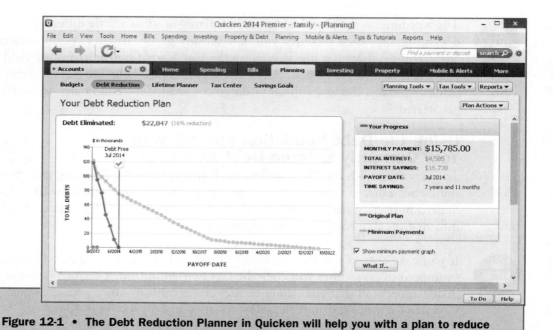

Figure 12-1 • The Debt Reduction Planner in Quicken will help you with a plan to reduce your current debt.

Figure 12-1 shows a completed Debt Reduction Plan that saves the planner more than $16,000 in interest.

1. To include an account in your Debt Reduction Plan, click the Plan Actions button at the right side of the window, as seen here. If you have not yet set up a plan, click the Get Started button to begin.

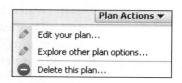

2. Click Edit Your Plan to open the Debt Reduction Planner dialog as seen in Figure 12-2. Note that your current credit cards appear on the left side of the Planner in the Accounts To Include In This Plan section. Other debt accounts, such as your mortgage, appear on the right side of the screen in the Other Debt Accounts section. If you have an existing plan and choose Edit Your Plan, your account selections will reflect your previous plan selection, which may or may not be with credit cards first. If you delete your existing plan or are setting up a brand-new one by clicking the Get Started button, Quicken selects the credit card accounts first.

A non-zero ending balance is the criteria for displaying debt accounts in the Identify Your Debts screen. If you have future-dated payments that pay your account balance down to zero, you will not see these debt accounts in the Identify Your Debts screen. Also, debt accounts with a positive balance (one on which you have paid more than you owe) will not be included.

3. Position your mouse cursor to the left of the account you want to add to the Planner. Click the Include link that appears. The account now appears as part of your plan in the column on the left side and is no longer included with the Other Debt Accounts column on the right side of the Planner.

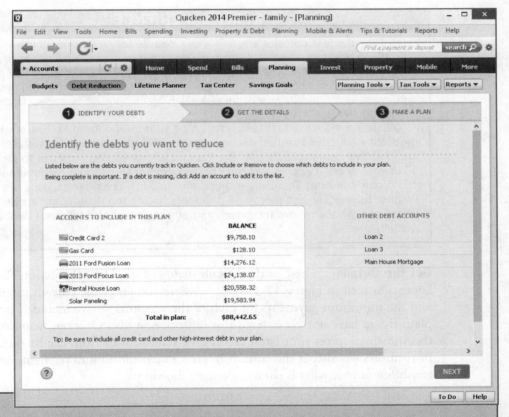

Figure 12-2 • Understanding how much you actually owe is your first step in reducing debt.

When you hover your mouse over any of the account names in the panel on the left, the Remove link appears. Conversely, when you hover your mouse over any of the text in the panel on the right, the Include link becomes available.

4. To remove an account from the plan, position your mouse cursor to the right of the account, and click Remove. The account is not included in the plan and appears in the Other Debt Accounts section of the Planner dialog as seen here.

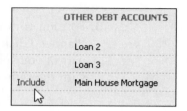

5. After you have selected all of the debts you want to include in your plan, click Next.

IN MY EXPERIENCE

One of the hardest parts of starting a new plan is facing how much you owe, both the grand total and the monthly payments. It is often so overwhelming that people stop right there. The thought of paying off thousands of dollars of debt as well as the feeling like the task is impossible often causes family arguments and, sometimes, avoidance techniques such as compulsive shopping or other non-productive activities.

Quicken makes the first task, identifying your total debt load, easier with the Debt Reduction Planner. I encourage you to just start working with the Planner. One of the beauties of the Planner is that you do not have to include all of your debt. Try using just the charge cards or the charge cards and the credit cards at first. Then, when those are paid off, consider applying the Planner to your car and mortgage payments. Using the Planner in "small bites" can greatly relieve the shock and stress of seeing how much debt you actually owe.

Get the Details   The Get the Details dialog of the Debt Reduction Planner appears as seen in Figure 12-3. Here is where you enter the current interest rates and the minimum payments for each of the accounts you've included in your plan. If you have not yet entered this information into Quicken, you can find this information on your latest credit card statement or from the financial institution's website. If the current interest rate or minimum payment amounts are different that what is shown, do the following:

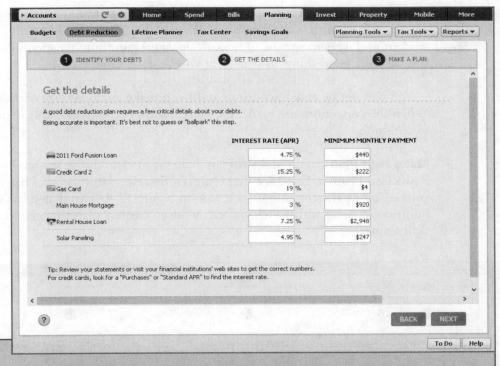

Figure 12-3 • **Use the Get the Details dialog to verify or update the current interest and minimum payment for all of your debt.**

1. Enter the actual interest rate in the Interest Rate field for each account. When you click in that field, the current information is highlighted. If the information is not correct, type in the correct rate.
2. Click in the minimum payment field for each account. If there is an existing amount, it will be highlighted and you can type in the proper amount. If you enter a minimum payment that does not meet the minimum based on the interest rate you entered, you'll see a warning message as shown here.

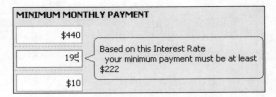

Some Quicken users have reported their financial institutions' minimum payments are less than the minimum calculated by Quicken. The only workaround is to accept the Quicken-calculated minimum payment. However, this can be a good thing, as your debt will be gone sooner.

You will not be able to continue until you make any necessary corrections. When the corrections are made, the Next button becomes available. Click Next to continue.

Make Your Plan   The Make A Plan dialog is the workhorse section of the Debt Reduction Planner. You'll see that Quicken first calculates the plan based on your current payment amounts, as seen in Figure 12-4. This dialog has several information areas with which you can work to create a plan that gets you out of debt sooner.

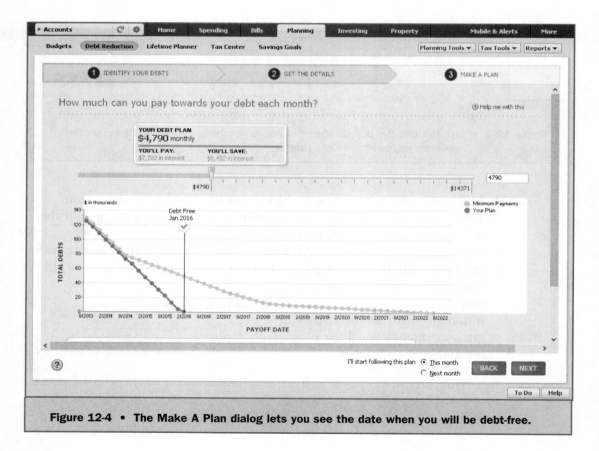

Figure 12-4 • The Make A Plan dialog lets you see the date when you will be debt-free.

1. Your Debt Plan is shown above the chart of the Make A Plan dialog. As you start your planning, the amount displayed shows how much interest you will be paying if you continue paying just the minimum monthly payments. Below the minimum payment information is a chart showing when you will be debt-free making just the minimum payment on each outstanding account. The Your Debt Plan summary may appear anywhere along the slider above the chart, depending on the accounts and minimums in your plan.
2. Move the slider or enter a new amount into the field to the right of the chart to see how much you will save by paying more than the minimum payment each month, as seen in Figure 12-4.

At the bottom of the Make A Plan dialog, Quicken displays another slider that lets you tell Quicken how much you could pay on debt if you choose to make a one-time payment from your savings and nonretirement investments. Shown at the right of the Kickstart Your Plan slider, as seen next, are the balances of accounts you have that might be used to pay down your debt.

The Help Me With This link at the upper-right side of the Make A Plan dialog offers several suggestions to help with your plan.

Once you have entered your plan amounts, finish your Debt Reduction Planner session by telling Quicken when you plan on starting the new payment schedule. See the option at the bottom right of the plan next to the word "Back" as shown here.

- Click This Month if you intend to pay more than minimum payments starting with this month's payments.
- Click Next Month if you've already paid the minimum for this month and want to start paying more than the minimum next month.

If you are satisfied with your plan, click Next to see your completed plan as seen in Figure 12-5.

In your Debt Reduction Plan dialog, use the Plan Actions button to explore other plan options or delete the current plan and start over. You can click the legends at the right of the graph to see summary info on either Your Plan or Minimum Payments. See "Modifying Your Plan" later in this chapter for more information. If you have had your plan for a few months, you may also see the Original Plan in gray in the legends.

You can opt to display the plan graph or include the minimum payment graph along with the graph for your plan. Click the Show Minimum Payment Graph check box to toggle between the two displays.

Use the What If button to experiment with other plan options, change the pay-off order, and update your plan.

- Click the downward arrow in the Payment Schedule section to hide the schedule of upcoming payments. You can also click the See Full Schedule link, as seen next, at the bottom right of the Payment Schedule section to see

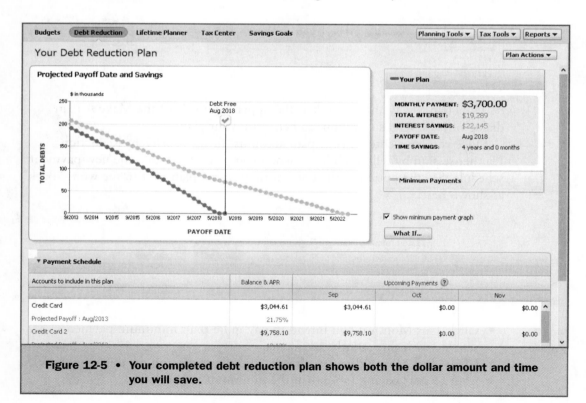

Figure 12-5 • **Your completed debt reduction plan shows both the dollar amount and time you will save.**

the schedule for this month and next month. This schedule also shows the projected balance for each account after the plan's payment schedule is met. You can also print a 6 Month or a 12 Month Plan from the My Payment Schedule dialog.

8 accounts, **$3,700.00 per month**	See full schedule

- Click Print 6 Month Plan in the My Payment Schedule dialog, as seen next, to open the Print dialog from which you can preview or print the payment schedule for the next six months. This schedule also shows the projected balance for each account after you meet the plan's payment schedule.

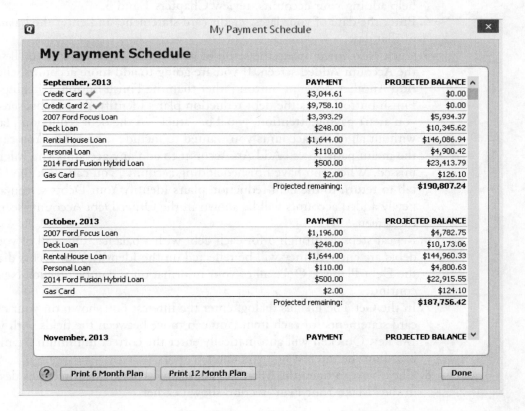

- Click Print 12 Month Plan to print or preview the scheduled payment plan for the next year.
- Click Done to close the schedule and return to your plan.

Starting Debt Reduction Planner from Scratch

If you have not entered any of your credit cards or other debt into Quicken, the Debt Reduction Planner will prompt you to do so. To get started, from the Planning tab, choose the Debt Reduction button. The Debt Reduction Planner appears with its Get Started button. (If your Planning tab is not currently displayed, choose View | Tabs To Show | Planning.)

1. Click the Get Started button. The Add Account dialog appears.
2. From the Add Account dialog, select Credit Card and click Next.
3. Enter your financial institution's name or select it from one of the lists. You can also use Advanced Setup, choosing I Want To Enter My Transactions Manually, to enter your information without downloading. If you need more help adding your accounts, review Chapters 1 and 3.
4. Enter the date of your latest credit card statement, and enter the balance as of that date.
5. Click Next to complete the setup of your debts. At this point, you'll see the Account Added screen. If you are going to add more accounts, click the Add Another Account button rather than the Finish button. Clicking the Finish button starts the debt reduction plan's Identify Your Debts screen. If you aren't paying attention, you'll be "stuck" in the debt reduction plan without all of the accounts you wanted to include in the plan. You can click the menu path Tools | Add An Account to add any accounts you might have missed. When you have finished adding accounts, you can click the Planning tab to return to the debt reduction plan's Identify Your Debts screen and the newly added accounts will be shown in the Other Debt Accounts section of the screen.
6. Repeat steps 1 through 5 for each debt with a balance. Once all of your debts are entered, they will be reflected on the Identify Your Debts dialog in the Debt Planner. Once all of your information is complete, click Next to continue.
7. In the Get The Details dialog, enter the interest rate shown on your credit card statements for each item. You can move between the fields with your TAB key. Quicken will automatically enter the correct minimum payment based on the interest rate you enter.
8. Click Next to open the Make A Plan dialog. Follow the directions described in the "Make Your Plan" section shown earlier.

Modifying Your Plan

Once you have created your plan to reduce debt, you can adjust it at any time. To review the plan, go to the Planning tab and choose the Debt Reduction button. Your current plan appears. Click the Plan Actions button and choose from one of the menu options:

- Click Explore Other Plan Options to open the Experiment With Other Plan Options dialog as described in "Use the What If Option" later in this chapter.
- Click Delete This Plan to delete your current plan and start over.
- Choose Edit Your Plan from the drop-down menu to work with your current plan.

Both the What If and Plan Actions buttons open the Experiment With Other Plan Options dialog.

Editing Your Plan   When you choose Edit Your Plan you are returned to the Identify Your Debts dialog, where you can remove or include any of your accounts. Once you have made changes, click Next to continue.

1. In the Get The Details dialog, make any necessary changes to interest rate and/or minimum payments. Click Next to open the Make A Plan dialog.
2. Make any changes in the Make A Plan dialog. Perhaps you've decided to pay an additional $50 per month to reduce debt faster. Or you've decided to take more money from savings. Whatever the choices, indicate as appropriate and click Next to complete your modifications. Once you have clicked Next in the Make A Plan dialog, the next screen does not include the Back button.
3. Position your mouse cursor and click any "tick" on the Projected Payoff Date and Savings graph lines to see how much you will owe at a specific date, as seen here. The yellow line shows your Minimum Payment plan, while the green line shows Your Plan lines in the Projected Payoff Date and Savings graph.

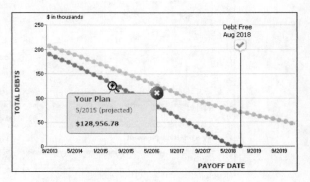

You can toggle between showing or hiding the Minimum Payment graph with the Show Minimum Payment Graph check box.

Your plan displays the monthly payment, total interest you will pay, the interest savings, the payoff date, and how much time you will save over paying just minimum payments. Click the green bar to show Your Plan; click the yellow bar to see the result of paying just the minimum payments.

Use the What If Option

You may be pleased with your debt reduction plan as it stands but curious about what would happen if you applied your income tax return to your debt, or increased or decreased the monthly payment amounts. The What If option allows you to see these changes without really changing the plan. To see your options, select the What If button to open the Experiment With Other Plan Options dialog, as seen in Figure 12-6.

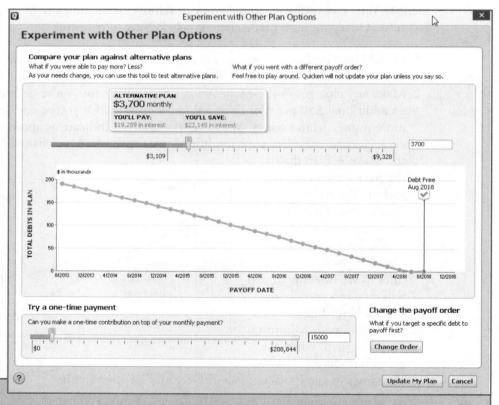

Figure 12-6 • **You can experiment with different payment schedules without changing your plan in the Experiment With Other Plan Options dialog.**

Change Your Monthly Payment   Either use the sliders or type a new amount directly in the payment field in the Experiment With Other Plan Options dialog. Position your mouse key on a tick on each graph line to see the total due at that point in time. Note that the second graph line in this dialog is blue, indicating your possible alternative plan.

Try a One-Time Payment   Considering selling that gas-guzzling second car? Did you win the sports pool at work? If you come into some extra cash, think about applying those funds directly to your debt load. Enter the amount in the payment field or use the slider to see how those extra funds would lessen your debt load.

Change Payoff Order   By default, Quicken maximizes your interest savings by selecting the order in which you pay off your credit card debt. You can use another method if you choose. Click the Change Order button to open the Change Payoff Order dialog as seen next. From this dialog you can

- See the default order, which maximizes your interest savings.
- Use the Debt Snowball method.
- Choose the order yourself.

IN MY EXPERIENCE

One of the suggested methods of paying off credit card debt is the snowball method. Using this method, people start by paying as much as possible on the card with the lowest balance while paying minimum payments on the rest of their credit cards. Then, when they have paid off the first card, they apply the same method to the card with the next lowest balance and so on. The main advantage to this system is a feeling of accomplishment; one debt is gone forever.

While this method may not save the debtor as much interest as when paying off the card with the highest interest rate first, people use this plan when they are faced with a very high debt load and feel overwhelmed.

You can decide what method, or combination of methods, works the best for your financial situation. The main goal is to get out of debt and then stay away from the credit card debt merry-go-round.

Select the Custom Order option to tell Quicken the order in which you plan to pay off your debts. When you select that option, small blue up and down arrows appear to the left of each card. Click the upward-pointing arrow to move a card up in the list and the downward-pointing arrow to move it down.

Click OK to save any changes to the Change Payoff Order dialog, or click Cancel to return to the Experiment With Other Plan Options dialog.

At the Experiment With Other Plan Options dialog, click Update My Plan if you have made changes you want to keep. If you are satisfied with your current plan, click Cancel to return to your Debt Reduction Plan screen.

Budgeting with Quicken

When money is tight and you're interested in meeting financial goals, it's time to create a budget and monitor your spending. However, if you're serious about managing your money, consider creating a budget before you need one. Although Quicken's categories give you a clear understanding of where money comes from and where it goes, budgets enable you to set up predefined amounts for each category, thus helping you to watch and control spending.

Budgets also make it easier to create forecasts of your future financial position, for example, to see how much cash will be available next summer for your vacation.

The idea behind a budget is to determine expected income amounts and specify maximum amounts for expenditures. This helps prevent you from spending more than you earn. It also enables you to control your spending in certain categories. For example, say you realize that you go out for dinner a lot more often than you can really afford. You can set a budget for the Dining category and track your spending to make sure you don't exceed the budget. You'll eat at home more often and save money.

If you don't like the word "budget," consider it as a "spending" or even a "making better use of our money" plan.

This section explains how Quicken works with budgets, and how you can use the budgeting tools to set up a budget and use it to keep track of your spending. Hopefully, you'll see that budgeting is a great way to keep spending under control.

Quicken's Automatic Budget

Quicken automatically generates a budget for you based on past transactions. You can edit the budget it creates to meet your needs, or you can create a budget from scratch.

The quickest and easiest way to create a budget is to let Quicken do it for you based on your income and expenditures. For Quicken to create an accurate budget, however, you must have several months' worth of transactions in your Quicken data file. Otherwise, the budget may not reflect all regular income and expenses.

To get started, choose the Planning tab and click the Budgets button. Click the Get Started button to open the Create A New Budget dialog. Quicken assigns the default name of Budget 1. If you wish to change the name, highlight

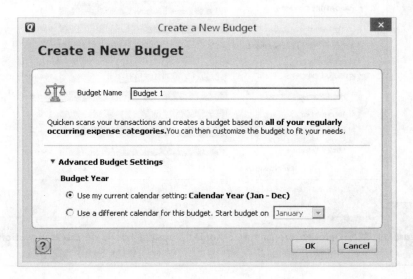

it and type in your own. Click Advanced Budget Settings to set a Budget Year.
The default is the calendar year (January through December), but you can use a
different calendar for your budget. For example, if you earn most of your income
during the school year, you might want to start your budget year in September.

Once you have named your budget and set any additional options, such as the
calendar year, click OK to create the new budget.

If you do not see the Get Started button, click the Budget Actions button and
select Create New Budget. If the Planning tab does not appear, click View | Tabs
To Show | Planning.

Your automatic budget appears as seen in Figure 12-7. As you can see, the
automatic budget graphs the top expenses and puts all of the other expenses into
the Everything Else category.

When creating a budget, Quicken can use as few as three months' worth of
expenses, but it is better to have more transactions.

Figure 12-7 • Quicken creates an automatic budget based on the transactions you have entered.

Understanding Quicken's Automatic Budget

Quicken creates its budget based on the amount you spent on each category and the total number of months in which you spent money in that category. In our example, we spend a total of $35 on our telephone bill for August, while we had budgeted only $33.

The average is for the full month of each of the prior months. Therefore, if you are creating the budget on June 24, 2014, and you have 12 months or more of transactions, the first full month included in the average is June, 2014. For a phone bill or other regular monthly bill, this may not make much difference. For an irregular expense like gas or groceries, knowing the first month in the average is a full month might make a big difference on the calculation.

Thus, $33 displays in the Budget column of our automatic budget. Since we spent $35 so far in September, we are $2 over the "budgeted" average amount computed by Quicken, as seen in Figure 12-7.

Quicken rounds all amounts to the nearest dollar in Budget dialogs.

If you want to adjust the "budgeted average" displayed by Quicken, click in the Budget column to highlight the current number. Type in the number you want to use as seen next.

Utilities: **Telephone**		35	2 over			33	
Everything Else		630					

Working with Your Automatic Budget

As seen in Figure 12-7, Quicken's automatic budget has a wealth of information. Since we are looking at our budget in the Monthly view, the total monthly summary is displayed for the current month. Each bar shows the total budgeted for the time period selected, the amount you have spent, and the amount you have left over or have overspent.

The Graph View

In the Graph View with which we are currently working, each category has a green, gray, or red bar:

- A green bar means you have spent what you budgeted or less.
- A red bar means you have spent more than you budgeted. In both cases, the actual amount you spent shows as a number on the bar.
- A gray bar means there are no transactions for the current period in that category.
- A light green or red portion within a bar means you have scheduled reminders for the future in that category. The sum of any reminder transactions shows as a number within the bar as well.

Graph View Filters The graph view has several filters from which you can choose. If you have more than one budget, the first filter toggles between them, as seen here. The next filter toggles between the graph view and the Annual View. See "The Annual View" later in this chapter.

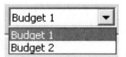

Use the date filter in the graph view to set the time period with which you want to work. Your choices are

- **Monthly** As we show in Figure 12-7, this is information for the current month. As seen here, you can use the arrows to the right and left of the current month to look at previous and future months.

- **Quarterly** This option shows your budget by quarters. The previous and future filters to the left and right of the selected quarter's name allow you to see all four quarters of the year.
- **Yearly** This filter option shows the current year's budget information. If you click the left or right arrows in the year shown at the right of the time period option, a dialog appears from which you can add a budget for that year, as seen next. In our example, we clicked the right arrow. We then saw the dialog prompting us to enter a budget for 2014.

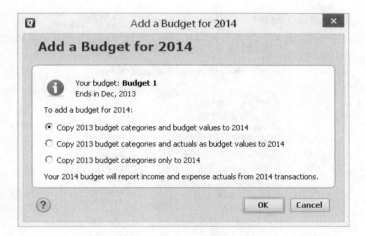

- **Quarter/Year To Date**   This option reflects the transactions and budgets for the current quarter (or year) through today's date.
- **Last Three/Six Months**   Choosing this filter displays transactions and budgeted amounts for the last three or the last six months, no matter when in a quarter you are viewing the information.
- **Last Year**   This filter displays an annual graph for all of the transactions you entered for the last year.

Click the small arrow to the left of Everything Else at the bottom of your expenses to see the items included in that figure, as seen here. If you use custom category groups, you may see more than one instance of Everything Else.

▼	**Everything Else**	1,578
	Clothing	109
	Dining Out	95
	Gifts	169

You can learn more detail about any category by hovering your mouse over or clicking the red, gray, or green line for that category.

Selecting Categories   To add a category to the budget, click Select Categories To Budget at the bottom left of the Budget window as seen in Figure 12-7. This displays the Select Categories To Budget dialog as seen next.

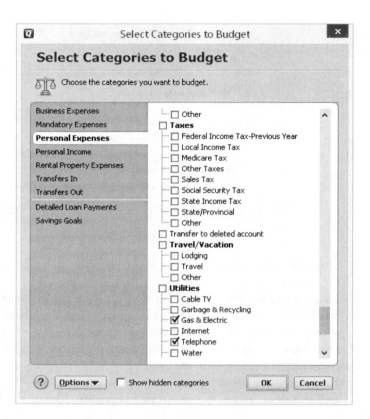

Select the categories you want to budget by clicking the check box to the left of each category name. To ensure all categories are listed, including any hidden categories, click the Show Hidden Categories check box at the lower left of the dialog. If you have created custom category groups, the custom category group name will appear on the left side of the dialog, along with the standard category groups such as Personal Income and Personal Expenses. To learn more about creating custom category groups, see "Organizing Categories into Groups" later in this chapter.

After you have marked all the categories you want to budget, click OK to close the dialog and return to your budget.

To use a specific category group in your budget, you must choose at least one of the categories within that group in the Select Categories To Budget dialog.

Budget Actions   The Budget Actions button at the right of your budget screen opens a menu, as seen in the following illustration. From this menu, you can

- **Select Categories To Budget**   This option opens the Select Categories To Budget dialog described earlier.

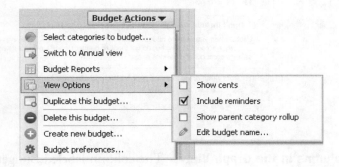

- **Switch To Annual View**   See "The Annual View" section later in this chapter to learn about the annual view of a Quicken Budget.
- **Budget Reports**   This option allows you to create both a current and a historical budget report.
- **View Options**   Use this menu item to tell Quicken how to display your budget items.
  - **Show Cents** includes the cents in each amount.
  - **Include Reminders** includes scheduled payments in your budget amounts.
  - **Show Parent Category Rollup** includes both subcategories and parent categories in your budget graph. For example, choosing this option would display both your principal and interest amount of your mortgage payment.
  - **Edit Budget Name** displays a dialog with which you can type a new name. Click OK to close the dialog,
- **Duplicate This Budget**   Click this option to open the Duplicate Budget dialog.
- **Delete This Budget**   This option opens the Delete Budget dialog.
- **Create New Budget**   This option opens the Create A New Budget dialog.
- **Budget Preferences**   Choose this option to tell Quicken which specific transfers to exclude or include in your budget, as seen next.

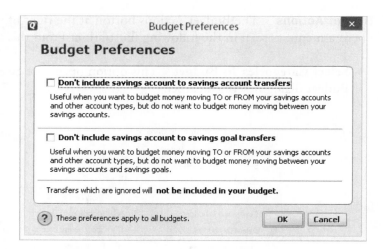

Columns in the Graph View   The column labeled Budget in the graph view indicates the budgeted amount for each category for the date range you selected in the date filter.

The amount in the (unlabeled) balance column is the difference between the amount you have budgeted for a specific time period and the amount you spent during that same time period.

There are three additional controls you see when you have a category selected. These are Rollover Options, Budget Amount Options, and Category History.

Everything Else   The Everything Else amount is the sum of all categories you have chosen not to include in your budget. You can

- Budget the "Everything Else" amount by assigning an amount to create a collective budget for all of the categories contained in this total. To do so, click the white cross within the green circle as shown here. A new line will appear in your graph showing the total spent in that collective "category" for the time period selected.

Once you have clicked the white cross within the green circle, there is no way to remove the Everything Else amount from the budget!

- Eliminate or reduce the "Everything Else" amount by adding those categories to your budget. To see the categories within the Everything Else amount, click the small right-pointing arrow to the left of the words "Everything Else." The individual categories that have been included in the Everything Else total appear. You may add them to your list by clicking the white cross within the green circle.
- Simply ignore the amount shown in Everything Else.

Other Budget Choices   As you are working in the default Monthly filter of the graph view of your budget and select a specific category, you'll see several additional tools, as shown next:

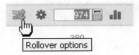

- The Rollover Options tool allows you to create or change rollover categories and amounts. See "Using Rollovers in Quicken Budgets" later in this chapter.
- Click the Budget Amount Options tool (small gear icon) to open a menu from which you can choose to
  - Apply the current (monthly) budget amount to the end of the current year.
  - Apply the current (monthly) amount to every month of the current year.
  - Edit the Yearly Budget.
  - Calculate the Average Budget.
  - Set the current month's budget amounts based on the average spending for this category.
  - Get help setting a budget amount. This choice opens the Quicken Help screen to the Budget Amount information.
- Set a different amount in the Budget column, as discussed earlier in this chapter.
- Click the Category History icon (small blue bar chart) to see the category's transaction history for the current year, as seen next. The History tab shows all of the transactions in columnar form, while the Transactions tab shows only the transactions for the time period you have selected to display in the graph view's date filter. Click the white X in the gray circle to close the history. You can also press ESC on your keyboard to close the Category History.

You can also open a category's history by clicking anywhere on that category's red or green bar in the graph view of your budget.

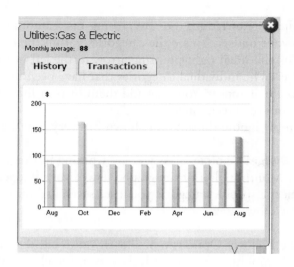

The Annual View

The annual view of your Quicken budget displays information in a columnar format, as shown in Figure 12-8. This view gives you the opportunity to assign budget amounts and scrutinize your spending.

After you have added more budgets, a new filter appears in both the Graph View and Annual View of your budget. See "Filters in Annual View" next for more information about this filter.

Filters in Annual View When you work in the annual view of your budget, there are several filters from which you can choose. If you have created more than one budget, you can choose the other budget. You can choose to see your budget at any time in Graph View.

The Year filter gives you the opportunity to apply your budget to both the last and next calendar years. Use the left arrow to open the Add A Budget for 20xx to work with the previous year's information. Click the right arrow to work with the next calendar year, or to set up next year's budget if you have not yet done so.

The Details filter, as seen in Figure 12-8, allows you to see the current year's budget information displayed in four ways:

- **Details** shows both the budgeted amount and the actual amount spent in each category for each month. In this view, click in any category, and in the Budget column you can enter a new budget amount. Click the Action gear

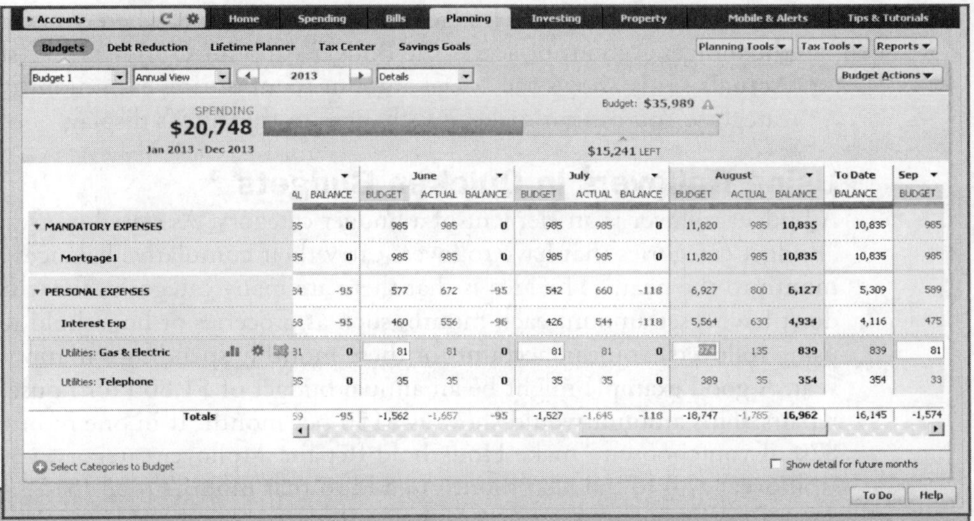

Figure 12-8 • Use your budget's Annual View to see more detail about your budget.

icon to open a menu that allows you to apply the budgeted amount forward or to all of the current year. You do not see the gear icon until a category is selected. You can also set the budget for the chosen month based on the average spending in this category for this current year or see help on setting the budget amount. You can see information for future months by clicking the Show Detail For Future Months check box at the lower right of the dialog.

- **Balance Only** shows the amount over or under budget for each category for each month. Click the Show Balance In Future Months check box to show the current budget balance in each of the months following the current month.

- **Budget Only** displays only the budgeted amount for each category for each month. Click in

---

IN MY EXPERIENCE

When working with Quicken budgets, occasionally there may be one-time items you do not want to include, such as a large down payment on a new car. Normally, Quicken would categorize this expense as an Auto & Transport expense, but the amount would certainly skew your budget if it were included. You might consider creating a subcategory under Auto & Transport entitled Down Payment and then excluding that item from your budget. See "Creating Your Own Budget" later in this chapter to understand how to exclude a category or subcategory from a budget.

any month to make the budget amount field active, where you can change the budget amount or access the Budget Amount Options icon (small gear).

- **Actuals Only** shows the actual amount spent during each month for each category. You cannot make any changes to this filter's display.

Using Rollovers in Quicken Budgets

A budget rollover is an element of a budget category. As stated in Quicken Help, "Budget categories that have rollovers carry their cumulative balances from one month to the next." The idea is that there are many categories for which you don't have a set amount each month, such as groceries or household repairs. By using rollovers, you can account for these monthly spending variations over the year. A good example might be an annual budget of $1,800 for household repairs. This amount would show as $150 per month. If in one month you spent $70, if you choose to make Household Repairs a rollover category, you could "roll over" $80 to the next month to add to that month's total ($150 – $70 = $80). Quicken gives you the option to roll over both negative (you've spent more than you budgeted for that month) and positive (you did not spend as much as you budgeted) amounts.

Budget categories do not automatically "roll over." You have to add this attribute to each budget category to which it applies. To do so:

1. Click the Planning tab. If the Planning tab does not show, from the Quicken menu choose View | Tabs To Show | Planning.
2. From the Planning tab, click the Budgets button.
3. In either Graph or Annual View, select a category in your budget and click the small criss-cross icon to open a list of options as seen next:

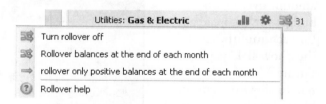

a. **Turn Rollover Off** turns off the rollover characteristic you've set before.
b. **Rollover Balances At The End Of Each Month** tells Quicken to include the amount you have left, whether positive or negative, in the next month's totals.
c. **Rollover Only Positive Balances At The End Of Each Month** tells Quicken to include only positive amounts in the next month's totals.

   d. Rollover Help is a shortcut to the What Is A Budget Rollover? section of Quicken Help.

Creating Your Own Budget   While Quicken's automatic budget is great, you might want to create an alternate budget to see "what if" scenarios and then compare both your original budget with the alternate one.

   To create another budget, from the currently displayed budget (either view), click Budget Actions | Create New Budget, or click the Get Started button. This opens the Create A New Budget dialog from which you can make changes. Enter a name for your customized budget and click OK.

   A new Quicken budget appears, based on the average spending for each category. If the time between your first budget and creating this budget is minimal, you probably don't have enough change in your spending, so the new budget appears the same as the original budget.

Working with More than One Budget   If you have created more than one budget, you can choose the budget with which to work. From the Planning tab, click Budgets. Click the Budget Name drop-down list to see your choices. Click the budget you want to use.

   To edit a budget's name, select the budget name and click the Budget Actions button at the upper-right corner of the budget window. Select View Options | Edit Budget Name from the drop-down list. Enter a name in the Edit Budget Name dialog that appears, and click OK. If you have only one budget, the Edit Budget Name dialog in the View Options menu is the only place to edit the budget name.

Deleting a Budget   If you have created more than one budget, you can delete one or more of the existing budgets. However, if you have only one budget, there is no need to delete it, nor will Quicken allow you to do so. To delete a budget, select the budget name. From the Budget Actions menu, choose Delete This Budget. The Delete Budget dialog appears. Click Delete to eliminate this budget or Cancel to close the dialog.

Showing a Budget in Your Home Tab   You can display your budget graph in either the Main View or a customized view of the Quicken Home tab's window. With this feature, you can keep an eye on the budget that interests you most. To choose which budget to display, in the Budget section of the Main View tab, click Options | Show Budget from the menu that appears. A list of the budgets you have created appears. Choose the budget you want to show in this view. It replaces the original budget.

You can add a budget to other views that you may have customized. Choose the view with which you want to work and click Customize. Use the Customize View dialog to choose Budget in the Available Items list, and click Add to move it to the Chosen Items list. Click OK to close the dialog.

Open the view, and in the budget section, click Options | Show Budget from the menu. A list of the budgets you have created appears. Choose the budget you want to show in this view.

You can see more information about creating customized Home tab views in Appendix B.

Organizing Categories into Groups

Budgets are based on transactions recorded for categories and subcategories. (That's why it's important to categorize all your transactions—and not to the Miscellaneous category!) Quicken also enables you to organize categories by customizable category groups. Although you don't have to use the Category Groups feature when creating your budget—it's entirely optional—grouping similar categories together can simplify your budget.

Some Quicken users see Category Groups as an annoyance when working with budgets, as each group displays the Everything Else total, which clutters the Budget display.

Choose Tools | Category List to display the window. (You can also open the Category List by pressing SHIFT-CTRL-C.) If the Group column does not appear in your list, choose the Category Action gear icon at the far right of your Category List, click the Group check box and then click Delete.

By default, Quicken assigns nearly every category to either the Personal Income or Personal Expense group. Your bank and investment accounts have no groups assigned. See "Assigning a Group to a Category," later in this chapter to learn how to assign a group.

The Default Groups   By default, Quicken includes two category groups that it assigns to the categories it creates when you first set up your Quicken data file:

- **Personal Income** is for earned income, such as your salary, and miscellaneous income items, such as interest, dividends, and gifts received.
- **Personal Expenses** are all of your personal expenses, items you pay for and record in your account registers.
- **Transfers** are for transfers between existing accounts. You may not see this available until you have added several accounts to your Quicken file.

Creating a New Custom Category Group   To create a new custom category group, open the Category List by clicking Tools | Category List. In the Category List window, click Options and choose Assign Category Groups. The Assign Category Groups dialog appears. As seen in Figure 12-9, if this is the first group you are creating, the Assign Category Groups dialog will display a message that you have not created any custom groups.

IN MY EXPERIENCE

If your Quicken data file includes business-related categories, Quicken includes Business Income and Business Expenses groups to track the income and expenses from your business.

To create a Business Income or Business Expense group, you must have created either an income or an expense category and assigned it to a business tax schedule in the Tax Reporting tab of the New Category setup.

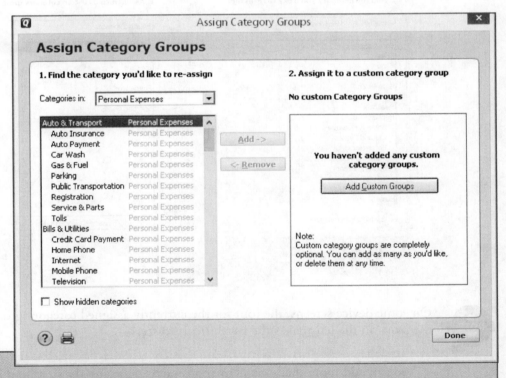

Figure 12-9 • You can assign category groups and create new groups to organize your categories.

Click the Add Custom Groups button (or if you have already added a custom group, click the Add/Rename Custom Groups button) to open the Custom Category Groups dialog. When it appears, click New to open the Create Custom Group dialog. Type the name of your custom group and click OK.

The new group appears in the Group Name list. Click Done to close the Custom Category Groups dialog and return to the Assign Category Groups dialog.

To add categories to your new group, select a category from the list on the left side of the dialog and click Add. The categories will appear on the right side of the dialog in the Assign It To A Custom Category Group column, as seen next. Continue through the list of categories until you have finished selecting the categories you want to include in this group.

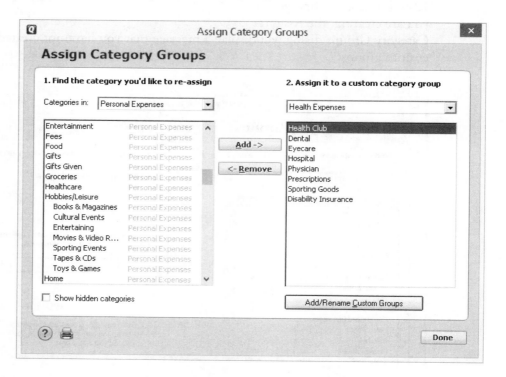

On some device screens, the font for the currently assigned category groups in the pane on the left makes the list difficult to see.

You can add more than one item at a time by choosing the first item in a group of categories in the left column, holding down your SHIFT key, and choosing several categories in a row. You can select categories from several locations in the list on the left side as well. To do this, hold down your CTRL key and while continuing to hold it down, click the items you want. If you have to scroll, keep holding down the CTRL key until you have selected (clicked) all the categories you want to include. Then, release the CTRL key and click the Add button. All of your selected items will appear in the right column.

Should you want to include categories you have hidden, click the Show Hidden Categories check box.

If you want to remove a category, select it from the list in the right column and click Remove. It will once again appear in the left column.

After you have completed your choices for this custom group, click Done to close the Assign Category Groups dialog and return to the Category List.

Assigning a Group to a Category   You can assign a new or existing category to a standard or a custom category group. To assign a custom group to a new category, in the Category List window, click Add Category to create a new category. The Set Up Category dialog appears. Enter the category name and whether it is an income or an expense item. Click the arrow next to the Group box to display the drop-down list and choose a group from the list. Click OK to save your new category and its category group assignment.

You can also assign a standard group to a category.

1. Right-click the category you want to assign. Select Edit. The Set Up Category dialog appears.
2. Select one of the three radio buttons: Income, Expense, or Subcategory.
3. Clear any information in the Group field by putting your cursor in the field and press DELETE on your keyboard.
4. Click OK to close the dialog and return to the Category List.
5. Click Done to close the Category List.

If you have not yet created any custom category groups, you will not see the Group field in the Set Up Category dialog. Return to the Category List, click Options | Assign Category Groups, and create at least one custom category group.

To add a group to an existing category, right-click the category, and click Edit to open the Set Up Category dialog. Click the arrow next to the Group box to display the Group drop-down list. If the category is one of the default Quicken categories, the Personal Expenses group may appear in the Group box, although it is not an option in the group list. Simply click the group to which you want this category assigned, and click OK. The custom group is now assigned to this existing category.

Modifying the Custom Category Group List   You can modify or delete custom category group names. From the Category List, click Options | Assign Category Groups, and click Add/Rename Custom Groups. The Custom Category Groups dialog appears. Select a group name, and click Rename to rename an existing group. To delete a custom category group, select the group name and click Delete.

After you have made your changes, click Done to return to the Assign Category Groups dialog. Click Done one more time to close the Assign Category Groups dialog and return to the Category List. Click Done once more to close the Category List.

Where Does Your Money Go?

Now that you have been working with the various planners and reports available in Quicken, you are probably getting more comfortable understanding just where your hard-earned dollars are going. If you've used the Debt Reduction Planner and created a budget, you may also be thinking about the future and how your financial situation will be improving. Quicken offers several tools that help you understand where you will be spending your funds. Using either Quicken's new reminders feature, which shows transaction reminders in your register, or the Projected Balances tool will help you to understand what expenditures are coming up in the near future. Then, in the second part of this section, we'll discuss saving your money.

Remember when you got your first piggy bank? It may not have looked like a pig, but it had a slot for slipping in coins and, if you were lucky, a removable rubber plug on the bottom that made it easy to get the coins out when you needed them. Whoever gave you the bank was trying to teach you your first financial management lesson: save money.

As an adult, things are a little more complex. See the later section entitled "Understanding Why We Save," which explains why you should save, provides some saving strategies, and tells you about the types of savings accounts that make your old piggy bank obsolete.

Forecasting for Your Future

Forecasting uses known and estimated transactions to provide a general overview of your future financial situation. This "crystal ball" can help you spot potential cash flow problems (or surpluses) so you can prepare for them. Quicken helps you to see your projected balances and can also help you create savings goals.

Projected Balances

Quicken helps you keep up with what your account balances will be in the future with the Projected Balances report. This report can be found in the Bills tab, or by choosing the Planning tab and then Planning Tools | Projected Balances. If you do not see the Planning tab, from the Quicken menu, click View | Tabs To Show | Planning.

You can set the range for the Projected Balances report for the next 7 days, next 14 days, next 30 or 90 days, or the next 12 months, or even customize a range that suits your requirements. See the next illustration for an example of the Projected Balances report for the next 30 days. See Chapter 4 for more information on Projected Balances.

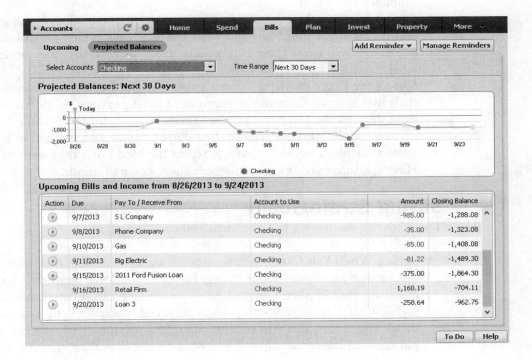

Reminders

A new feature in Quicken 2014 allows you to display a reminder about future bills in your register. The reminder appears with a small "bill due" icon at the left of the register entry. You can set the range for these bill reminders for the same periods as the Project Balances report. See Chapter 1 for more discussion of the new reminders options.

Understanding Why We Save

Most people save money so they have funds available when the funds are needed. Others save for a particular purpose. Still others save because they have so much they can't spend it all. Here's a closer look at why saving makes sense.

- **Saving for "Rainy Days"** When people say they are "saving for a rainy day," they probably aren't talking about the weather. They're talking about bad times or emergencies—situations when they'll need extra cash. If your paychecks stop coming, do you have enough savings to support yourself or your family until you can get another source of income? On the "rainy day" scale, this could be a torrential downpour. Your savings can be a good umbrella.
- **Saving for a Goal** Planning for your future often includes planning for events that affect your life—and your wallet. Saving money for specific events can help make these events memorable for what they are, rather than what they cost.
- **Saving for Peace of Mind** Some people save money because events in their lives showed them the importance of having savings. Children who lived through the Depression or bad financial times for their families grew up to be adults who understand the value of money and try hard to keep some available. They don't want to repeat the hard times they went through. Having healthy savings accounts gives them peace of mind.

Saving Strategically

There are two main ways to save: when you can or regularly.

- **Saving When You Can** When money is tight, saving can be difficult. People who are serious about saving, however, will force themselves to save as much as possible when they can. Saving when you can is better than not saving at all. One suggestion given by financial specialists is to "pay yourself first." This means that you consistently take a portion of any income and put it into a savings account. The amount really doesn't matter; it is the consistency that creates the habit.
- **Saving Regularly** A better way to save money is to save a set amount periodically. For example, consider putting away $25 every week or $200 every month. Timing this with your paycheck makes sense; you can make a split deposit for the check. A savings like this is called an annuity, and you'd be surprised at how quickly the money can accumulate.

There are different types of savings accounts, each with its own benefits and drawbacks. Check with your financial institution (or do an Internet search) to see what products might best meet your needs. A short list of possibilities shows here:

- Standard Savings Accounts
- Payroll Savings
- Certificates of Deposit
- Money Market Accounts
- Interest-Bearing Checking Accounts

As current interest rates are so low, none of these options is a very good choice for building savings. Try doing an Internet search for reputable financial institutions that offer better interest rates.

Using Savings Goals

Quicken's Savings Goals feature helps you save money by "hiding" funds in an account. You set up a savings goal and make contributions to it using the Savings Goals window. Although the money never leaves the source bank account, it is deducted in the account register, thus reducing the account balance in Quicken. If you can't see the money in your account, you're less likely to spend it.

IN MY EXPERIENCE

Kind of sounds silly, doesn't it? Using Quicken to transfer money from your checking account to another account that doesn't even exist?

But don't laugh—the Savings Goals feature really works. A small-business client used a similar technique. They simply deducted $50 or $100 from their personal checking account balance, thus giving the illusion that there was less money in the account than was really there. They were saving money by thinking twice about writing a check for something they really didn't need. The same method prevented any "bounced" checks as their new business was getting started and their personal account had a dangerously low balance. When they had the opportunity to buy some "nearly new" graphics equipment from a competitor that was retiring, there was enough money in this "secret" account to pay for the equipment and donate it to their fledgling company!

Give it a try and see for yourself!

Getting Started

Open the Savings Goals window by choosing Planning | Savings Goals. The Savings Goals startup screen appears. Click Get Started to open the Create New Savings Goal dialog as seen here. If you do not see the Planning tab, from the Quicken menu, choose View | Tabs To Show | Planning. If you do not see the Get Started button, click Goal Actions and select New Savings Goal from the drop-down list.

Enter your goal's name, the amount you want to save, and the date by which you want to have saved the money. The finish date should be shortly before you leave for your trip or before you've planned dad's 80th birthday party. Click OK to close the dialog. Your Savings Goals dialog appears as shown in the following illustration.

The name of the savings goal cannot be the same as any Quicken category or account.

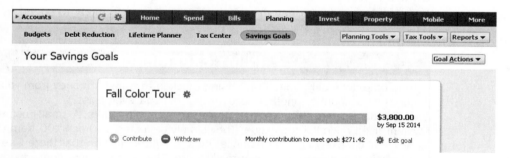

Contributing Funds to a Savings Goal

To contribute funds to a savings goal, select the Contribute icon (the white cross in a small green circle) or the Contribute text to open the Contribute To <goal name> dialog.

Select the account from which you want to transfer the money from the From Account drop-down list. The balance and name of that account appear in the bottom of the dialog. Then enter the amount of the transfer in the Amount box. By default, Quicken suggests the projected monthly contribution amount, but you can enter any amount you like. When you've finished, click OK.

If you make a contribution, Quicken will create an entry in the account register of the account from which the money was contributed. It also updates the progress bar and information in the Your Savings Goals dialog. To show this entry:

- Click the Goal Actions button in the Your Savings Goals dialog.
- Click Show Savings Goal Transactions In Register And Reports. Your entry appears in the register of the selected account.

When you create a savings goal, Quicken creates a Savings Goals account to record the goal's transactions and balance. This account is shown, with the total of your contributions, at the bottom of your Account Bar, as seen here.

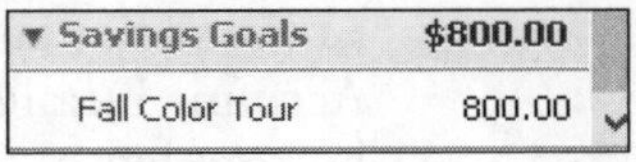

▾ Savings Goals	$800.00
Fall Color Tour	800.00

To automate contributions to the goal, you can create a scheduled transaction to transfer money periodically from one of your bank accounts to the savings goal asset account, but only in the maximum amount contributed to that savings goal. The Withdrawal From: <goal name> dialog will show the maximum amount you can withdraw from the savings goal for each contribution account. Scheduled transactions are covered in Chapter 4.

Meeting Your Goal

Once you have met your savings goal, you can either withdraw the funds from the savings goal so they appear in a Quicken account or delete the savings goal to put the money back where it came from.

Withdrawing Money   You can withdraw funds from your savings goals should you need to do so. Click the Planning tab and choose Savings Goals. All of your savings goals will appear. If you have more than one goal, select the one from which you want to withdraw money. Click the Withdraw icon (a small white minus sign in a red circle) or just the word Withdraw. The Withdrawal From <goal name> dialog, which works much like the Contribute To Goal dialog, appears. Use it to remove funds from the savings goal and put

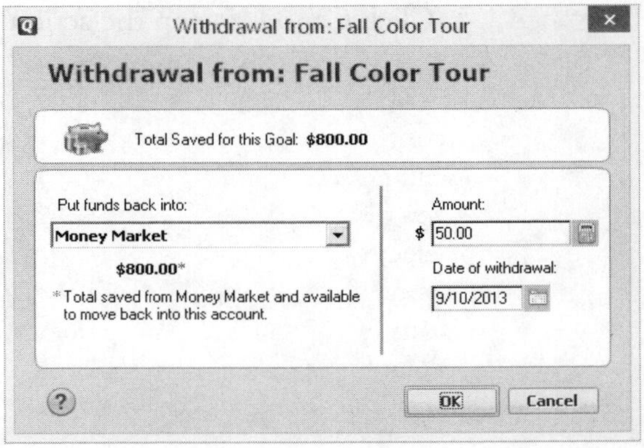

them back into the account from which they were contributed. Unlike the
Contribute To Goal dialog, your only choice is to put the funds back into the
account from which they were deducted. Enter the amount and the date of
withdrawal. Click OK to close the Withdraw From <goal name> dialog.

Editing a Savings Goal   To edit an existing savings goal, from the Planning
tab, click Savings Goals. Select the Edit Goal gear icon in the goal you want to
change. The Edit Savings Goal dialog appears. Enter the new goal amount
and/or finish date. Click OK or Cancel to close the dialog.

Deleting a Savings Goal   To delete a savings goal, right-click its name in the
Account Bar and, from the context menu, select Edit/Delete Account. From the
Account Details dialog that appears, select the Delete Account button at the
bottom left of the window. A message appears that the account will be
permanently removed and all transfers put back into the account from which the
transfers were made. You must type **Yes** to confirm the deletion and then click
OK to close the dialog. If you decide not to delete the account, click the Cancel
button. You can also delete a goal directly from the Savings Goals view.

1. Click the Planning tab and select Savings Goals.
2. Click the Action gear icon to the right of the goal's name. From the list that
   appears, choose Delete Goal. The Delete Savings Goal dialog appears. The
   dialog states that all funds will be returned to their source accounts and you
   are to determine what to do with the Savings Goal account.
3. Choose Remove It From Quicken Completely to remove all record of this
   goal.

   –Or–

   Choose Keep It As A Zero Balance Asset Account For My Records.
4. Click Cancel to stop the action or OK to close the dialog.

Planning for Tax Time

Chapter 13

In This Chapter:

- *Including tax information in accounts*
- *Connecting tax information with categories*
- *Using TurboTax*
- *Working with the Tax Planner*
- *Creating scenarios*
- *Minimizing taxes by maximizing deductions*
- *Utilizing the Itemized Deduction Estimator*
- *Exploring the Tax Withholding Estimator*
- *Understanding the Tax Center*

Tax time is no fun. It can force you to spend hours sifting through financial records and filling out complex forms. When you're done with the hard part, you may be rewarded with the knowledge that you can expect a refund. But it is more likely that your reward will be the privilege of writing a check to the federal, state, or local government—or worse yet, all three.

Fortunately, Quicken Personal Finance Software can help. The reporting features can save you time. By using the tax planning and monitoring tools that are available through Quicken's Tax Center, the next tax season may be a little less stressful. This chapter will show you how.

Tax Information in Accounts and Categories

As mentioned briefly in Chapter 1, Quicken accounts and categories can include information that will help you at tax time. This section explains how you include tax information in accounts and categories.

Including Tax Information in Accounts

You can include tax information in each account you establish in Quicken. Use the Tax Schedule dialog included with each account to enter the information.

- Choose Tools | Account List or press CTRL-A to display the Account List window.
- Select the name of the account, and click the Edit button that appears to the right of the account name or right-click the account name in the Account Bar and select Edit/Delete Account.

Hidden accounts appear in the More Accounts link in the Account Bar. Right-clicking the More Accounts list does not offer an edit or delete option on the resulting menu.

- In either case, the Account Details dialog appears. At the bottom of the Account Details dialog, click the Tax Schedule button. The Tax Schedule Information dialog, shown here, appears.

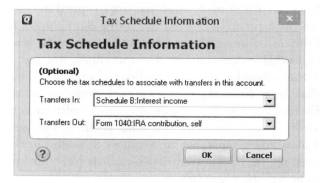

- Use the Transfers In and Transfers Out drop-down lists to map account activity to specific lines on tax return forms and schedules. In our example, all transfers into the account are interest income and track to Schedule B of the individual tax return, while all transfers out go into an IRA and will appear on that line of the tax return.

There are a few Tax Line Items set as default for various types of accounts, such as IRAs. Changing the default could cause a problem on your tax return. Be sure to check with your tax professional before changing any default item.

When you're finished, click OK. Repeat the process for all accounts for which you want to enter tax information.

 You may have to scroll either up or down to find the appropriate Tax Line Item on the list.

Keep in mind that if you use the Paycheck Setup feature to account for all payroll deductions, including any retirement plan contributions, you may not have to change the settings for many of your accounts. (That's another good reason to set up your regular paychecks in Quicken. Chapter 4 explains how to do this.) However, as with all things tax-related, check with your tax professional.

 Remember, when working with accounts and categories, and especially subcategories, you cannot use names that contain the characters : } / { | ^.

Connecting Tax Information with Categories

Quicken automatically sets tax information for many of the categories it creates. You can see which categories are tax-related and which have tax form lines assigned to them in the Category List window, as seen here.

Interest Exp	55	Expense	Personal Expenses	
Interest Inc	0	Income	Personal Income	✅ Schedule B:Interest income
Investment Income	0	Income	Personal Income	✅
IRA Contrib	0	Expense	Personal Expenses	✅ Form 1040:IRA contribution, self
Job Expense	0	Expense	Personal Expenses	
Non-Reimbursed	0	Expense	Personal Expenses	✅ Schedule A:Misc., subject to 2% AGI limit
Reimbursed	0	Expense	Personal Expenses	
Loan	0	Expense	Personal Expenses	
Loan Interest	0	Expense	Personal Expenses	
Mortgage Interest	0	Expense	Personal Expenses	✅ Schedule A:Home mortgage interest (1098)
Student Loan Interest	0	Expense	Personal Expenses	✅ Form 1040:Student loan interest

If this information does not appear, click the Actions gear icon at the far right of the Category List (under the Add Category button), and ensure Tax Line Item is checked, as seen here. Concentrate on the categories without tax assignments; some of these may require tax information, depending on your situation.

Use the Set Up Category dialog to enter or modify tax information for a category.

	Hide	Action	⚙
☑	Category		
☑	Usage		
☑	Type		
☐	Description		
☑	Group		
☑	Tax Line Item		
☑	Hide		
☑	Action		
⚙▼		Done	

- Open the Category List window by choosing Tools | Category List.
- Select the category for which you want to enter or edit tax information to highlight the category.
- Click the small arrow that appears in the Action column to display the Edit menu. When you position your mouse over the arrow, it shows a "Click" message, as seen next.

Auto	0	Expense	Personal Expenses	☐	
Fuel	54	Expense	Personal Expenses	☐	◉
Insurance	0	Expense	Personal Expenses	☐	
Loan	0	Expense	Personal Expenses	☐	Click

When you use the ALT-TAB keyboard shortcut to move between Quicken and another Windows application, when you come back to Quicken, the arrow in your selected category line disappears. This is also true when you come back to the selected category line after you have entered information in the Set Up Category dialog.

- Click Edit to open the Set Up Category dialog and choose the Tax Reporting tab. (If the category is a transfer category, Edit does not appear on the context menu.)

You can also open the Category List by pressing CTRL-SHIFT-C.

- If the category's transactions should be included on your tax return as either income or a deductible expense, select the Tax Related Category check box.
- Then use the Tax Line Item For This Category drop-down list to choose the form or schedule and line for the item. (You can expand this list by selecting the Extended Line Item List option.) A description of the tax-line item you

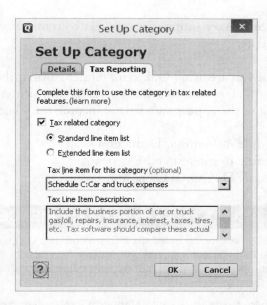

chose appears at the bottom of the dialog, as seen here. Keep scrolling to see all of the options.

- Click OK to return to the Category List. The tax-line item you chose appears on the same line as your category.
- Repeat this process for all categories that should be included on your tax return. Keep in mind that you can also enter tax information when you first create a category, as explained in Chapter 1.

Tax Reports

You can make tax time easier with several tax reports included in Quicken. Quicken creates all of these reports from the tax information settings for the accounts and categories in your Quicken data file. You can learn more about Quicken's reporting feature in Chapter 4.

To create a specific report, select Reports | Tax from the menu bar. Choose the name of the report from the menu:

- **Capital Gains** summarizes gains and losses on the sales of investments, organized by the term of the investment (short or long) and the investment account.
- **Tax Schedule** summarizes tax-related transactions, organized by tax form or schedule and line item.

- **Tax Summary** summarizes tax-related transactions, organized by category and date.

And, if you are using Quicken Premier edition, there are three additional options. All allow you to print reports from which you can enter information directly into the appropriate federal income tax schedules.

- Schedule A–Itemized Deductions
- Schedule B–Interest and Dividends
- Schedule D–Capital Gains and Losses

IN MY EXPERIENCE

By taking the time to enter tax information into Quicken, you can save hours of time and maybe even a bunch of money. You see, by including tax information in Quicken accounts and categories, you make it possible for Quicken to do several things for you:

- Prepare tax reports that summarize information by tax category or schedule. Take these tax reports to your tax preparer and make it a lot easier for him or her to do your taxes. This might even save you money in tax preparation fees!
- Display tax information in the Tax Center window, which shows an up-to-date summary of your tax situation. Knowing how you stand now helps to prevent surprises at tax time.
- Save time using the Tax Planner, a Quicken feature that uses information from your Quicken data file based on tax information you enter. If you do a little work here, you can save a lot of work later. See "Working with the Tax Planner" later in this chapter.
- Distinguish between taxable and non-taxable investments, so you can create accurate reports on capital gains, interest, and dividends. That way, tax-exempt income and taxable income are separated for preparing your tax returns!
- Use TurboTax to prepare your tax return based on information imported right from your Quicken data file.

So, by spending a few minutes setting up tax information for your accounts and categories, you can save time and money at tax time, and know your tax situation all year long.

Online Tax Tools

From both within Quicken and online, you have access to a number of tools for tax planning and preparation. From Quicken's menu bar, click the Planning tab, and then click Tax Tools button to open a menu. Click Online Tax Tools, as shown next. (The menu displayed in the following illustration shows the Itemized Deduction Estimator, the Capital Gains Estimator, and the Tax Withholding Estimator. These items are available only in Quicken Premier and higher editions.) The Online Tax Tools submenu offers several tax-related features and information sources from the TurboTax.com website to help you with your taxes. All you need to take advantage of these features is an Internet connection.

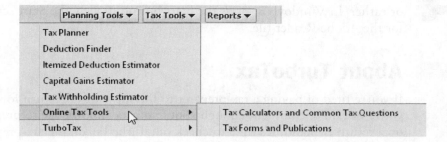

If you do not see the Planning tab, click the View tab. Ensure Show Tabs is checked and then click Tabs To Show | Planning.

Here's a quick look at the online tax tools. The next time you're thinking about taxes, be sure to check these out.

Tax Calculators and Common Tax Questions

With your Internet connection, the Tax Calculators option displays the TurboTax page, with links to various online tools for making tax and other financial calculations. You will see both video links and links that offer tax guides for specific categories. There are even links to a TurboTax blog, Facebook, and Twitter. This page states, "We make becoming tax savvy easy with our how-to-guides," and delivers the tools to fulfill that promise!

Tax Forms and Publications

With your Internet connection, choosing Tax Forms And Publications opens another TurboTax page from which you can link to both federal and state returns as well as other official IRS forms.

When you click the IRS Forms and Publications link, the Internal Revenue Service site appears from which you can download many federal forms. The forms are Acrobat PDF files that appear in either a web browser window or an Adobe Acrobat Reader window. (You must have the freely distributed Adobe Acrobat Reader software to open and use these forms.) You may fill out some of the forms online and print or save them on your computer. Others must be downloaded or printed, and then filled out by hand.

Click any state link to go to that state's website, from which you can download your forms. Most states offer additional information and publications on their sites as well as the tax forms. As with the federal forms that you download from the IRS page, most state forms download as Acrobat PDF files.

 Adobe Reader is often included with computers you purchase "off-the-shelf." Click Start I All Programs to see if it is already on your computer in Windows 7 or earlier. In Windows 8, press the Start button to view the Start screen and look for the Adobe Reader tile.

About TurboTax

If you're tired of paying a tax preparer to fill out your tax return for you, but you're not quite confident enough about your tax knowledge to prepare your own return by hand, it's time to check out TurboTax online tax-preparation software. It's a great way to simplify tax preparation.

TurboTax works almost seamlessly with Quicken to prepare your taxes. Just follow the instructions in this chapter to set up your accounts and categories with tax information. Purchase the TurboTax program online to be downloaded or the boxed program from your local store. Then, from within TurboTax, import your Quicken data. TurboTax takes you through an easy interview process to make sure you haven't left anything out—much like the interview you might go through with a paid tax preparer. TurboTax then calculates the bottom line and makes it possible for you to file the return electronically or print it on your printer.

Using TurboTax

Intuit offers several versions of TurboTax, each of which you can access online. You can learn more about them by opening the Planning tab in Quicken and selecting Tax Tools I TurboTax I File Your Taxes With TurboTax. With your Internet connection, the link takes you directly to the TurboTax Products and Pricing page.

You can choose from several options. With each option, you can start "for free" from this page. With options varying from the Basic through the Home & Business edition, TurboTax programs meet the tax filing requirements of nearly all of us.

All online editions featured on this page require no payment until you file the return. Of course, you can also purchase either a downloadable or a CD version of each program directly from this site.

- **TurboTax Basic Edition** is for taxpayers with basic tax preparation needs. It includes just the 1040EZ form.
- **TurboTax Deluxe** can perform tax calculations for taxpayers who own a home, make donations, or have childcare or medical expenses. In other words, most of us.
- **TurboTax Premier** offers all of the functionality of TurboTax Deluxe and adds tax calculations for taxpayers who own stocks, bonds, mutual funds, or rental properties.
- **TurboTax Home & Business** offers all of the functionality of TurboTax Premier and adds tax calculations for small businesses, such as sole proprietorships or single-owner LLCs.
- **TurboTax Business** (click the Small Business link at the right of the page) provides tax preparation for corporations, partnerships, and multimember LLCs while maximizing business tax deductions. It does not include the means to prepare your personal taxes.
- **TurboTax Military Edition** (click the Military link at the right of the page) is a customized edition of TurboTax designed for those who help protect our country in the military. The two versions in this special edition of TurboTax help service members find deductions and other tax breaks specific to their situation.

Import TurboTax File

From the Planning tab's Tax Tools menu, select TurboTax | Import TurboTax File to import last year's TurboTax information. Many Quicken and TurboTax users store a copy on an external device, such as an external hard drive or flash drive. This backup copy ensures the safety of the tax information. When it is time to prepare your current year's tax return, you can import the information from either a location on your computer or an external device.

For more information about backups and Quicken, see Appendix A.

Export TurboTax Reports

Use the last two links in the TurboTax submenu with TurboTax to quickly create and send both the Tax Schedule and Capital Gains reports into the TurboTax program. When you choose either of the menu items, a file is created with the .txf extension (i.e., transfer files) and that file can be quickly imported into the TurboTax program.

Planning to Avoid Surprises

One of the best reasons to think about taxes before tax time is to avoid surprises on April 15. Knowing what you will owe before you owe it can help ensure that you pay just the right amount of taxes up front—through proper deductions or estimated tax payments—so you don't get hit with a big tax bill or tax refund.

You may think of a big tax refund as a gift from Uncle Sam. Well, it isn't. The money that Uncle Sam has been using, interest-free, for months is actually *your* money. When you overpay your taxes, you're giving up money that you could be using to reduce interest-bearing debt, earn interest, or investment income. Making sure you don't overpay taxes throughout the year helps you keep your money where it'll do *you* the most good.

Quicken Personal Finance Software's tax planning features, like the Tax Planner and Tax Withholding Estimator, can help you avoid nasty surprises. Other built-in tax tools, like the Deduction Finder and Itemized Deduction Estimator, can save you money and help you make smarter financial decisions. From the Planning tab's Tax Tools menu, you will find all of these features. Each tool offers options to help you plan and monitor your tax situation.

Quicken offers built-in tax planning tools that you can use to keep track of your tax situation throughout the year. The Tax Planner helps you estimate your federal income tax bill for the 2013 and 2014 tax years. You can add up to three additional scenarios to your planner to help plan for possible changes in your life. In addition, Quicken provides several estimating tools to help you with your taxes. For example, the Tax Withholding Estimator helps you determine whether your withholding taxes are correctly calculated. Finally, the Tax Center in the Planning tab summarizes your tax situation with a number of useful snapshots. Here's a closer look at each of these features.

If it is still 2013 when you first open the Tax Planner and you try to project values for tax year 2014, you may see a message stating that Quicken cannot display projected tax values for a future year. When your computer's calendar changes to 2014, you will be able to use both years for the Projected Value scenario. This does not apply to other scenarios that you can create.

Working with the Tax Planner

Quicken's Tax Planner includes features from Intuit's TurboTax tax preparation software to help you estimate your federal income tax bill for the 2013 and 2014 tax years. While this can help you avoid surprises, it can also help you see how various changes to income and expenses can affect your estimated tax bill.

Opening the Quicken Tax Planner Window

To open the Tax Planner, open the Planning tab and choose Tax Center | Show
Tax Planner. You can also click Tax Tools | Tax Planner. (If you don't see Tax
Tools, expand your screen.) Read the introductory information to get a clear
understanding of what the Tax Planner can do for you and how it works.

If you find yourself using the Tax Planner regularly, consider adding a button for
it to your Quicken Toolbar. See Appendix B for more information about
customizing your Quicken Toolbar.

Viewing the Tax Planner Summary

To see what data is already entered in the Tax Planner, click the Tax Planner
Summary link in the navigation bar on the left side of the Tax Planner window.
A summary of income tax–related data, as well as the calculated tax implications,
appears as shown in Figure 13-1.

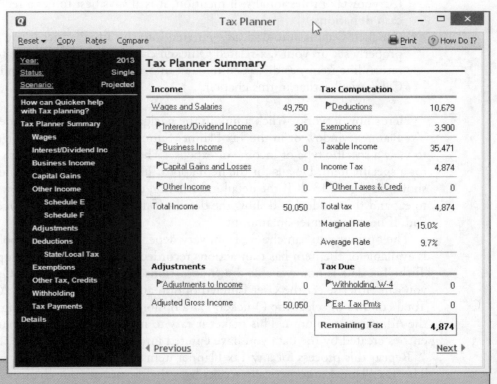

Figure 13-1 • **See a summary of your currently entered tax-related information on the Tax
Planner's Summary screen.**

Entering Tax Planner Data

Data can be entered into the Tax Planner from three different sources:

- TurboTax data can be imported into Quicken. In the main Quicken application window, from the Planning tab, choose Tax Tools | TurboTax | Import TurboTax File. Then use the dialog that appears to locate and import your TurboTax data. You can use this information to project current-year amounts in the Tax Planner.

You can also open the TurboTax import dialog by clicking File | File Import | TurboTax File.

- User Entered data can override any automatic entries. Use this to enter data that isn't entered any other way or that has not yet been entered into Quicken—such as the $100.00 cash you donated to your local food bank. (As your tax professional will mention, it is always best to get a receipt for cash donations.)
- Quicken Data is automatically entered into the Tax Planner if you have properly set up your tax-related Quicken categories with appropriate tax return line items, as discussed in "Tax Information in Accounts and Categories" earlier in this chapter.

Here's how it works. Click a link in the navigation bar on the left side of the Tax Planner window or in the Tax Planner Summary screen (refer to Figure 13-1) to view a specific type of income or expense. Then click a link within the window for a specific item. Details for the item appear in the bottom of the window, as shown in Figure 13-2. If the detail information doesn't show, click Show Details to expand the window and show the details. If desired, change the source option and, if necessary, enter an amount.

The options you can choose from vary depending on whether TurboTax data is available or the item has transactions recorded in Quicken. For example, if TurboTax data is not available, but transactions have been entered in Quicken, you can either select the User Entered option and enter a value in the Annual Total column or select the Quicken Data option and enter an adjusting value in the Adjustment column. This makes it easy to manually override any automatic entries created by the data you have entered into Quicken.

Repeat this process for any Tax Planner items you want to check or change. The Tax Planner automatically recalculates the impact of your changes.

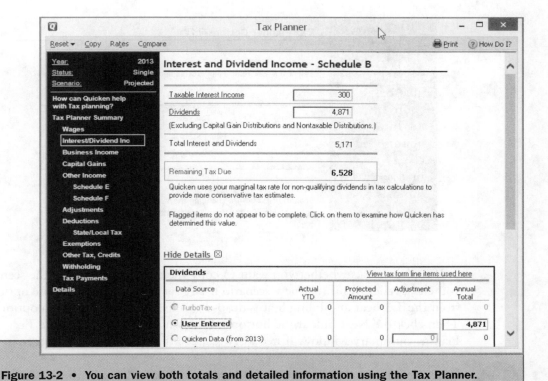

Figure 13-2 • You can view both totals and detailed information using the Tax Planner.

To reset values quickly to amounts automatically entered by Quicken, choose Reset on the Tax Planner's button bar and click Reset To Quicken Default Values.

Creating Scenarios

The Scenarios feature of the Tax Planner enables you to enter data for multiple scenarios—a "what if" capability that you can use to see tax impacts based on various changes in entry data. For example, suppose you're planning to get married and want to see the impact of the additional income and deductions related to your new spouse. You can use a scenario to see the tax impact without changing your Projected Value scenario.

To use this feature, click the Scenario link in the upper section of the navigation bar on the left side of the Tax Planner window (refer to Figure 13-1). The Tax Planner Options screen, shown next, appears. Click the Scenarios down arrow to choose a different scenario from the drop-down list.

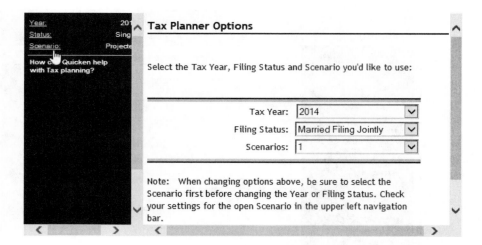

If Quicken asks whether you want to copy the current scenario to the scenario you chose, click Yes if that new scenario hasn't yet been created. Choose options from the Tax Year and Filing Status drop-down lists to set the scenario options. Then click the Next link at the bottom of the window to return to the Tax Planner Summary window. If necessary, change the values in the new scenario.

When creating or editing a scenario, you must choose the scenario first before you change the tax year or filing status.

To compare one scenario to another, click the Compare button in the Tax Planner window's button bar. A Tax Scenario Comparisons dialog appears, showing the results of each scenario's calculations. When you're finished viewing the comparative information, click OK to dismiss the dialog.

Finishing Up

When you're finished using the Tax Planner, click the Close button on the title bar. This saves the information you entered and updates the Projected Tax calculations in the Tax Center. (Learn about the Tax Center later in this chapter, in the section "Understanding the Tax Center.")

Meeting the Estimators

You can find some of the most useful tips to aid your tax planning under the Tax Tools button in the Planning tab. From helping you find and itemize your tax deductions to helping you determine your tax refund (or payment), each tool can help you make your tax situation clearer. The more you know about taxes that you must pay, the better you will be able to manage your money to ensure there are funds to pay them.

Minimizing Taxes by Maximizing Deductions

One way to minimize taxes is to maximize your deductions. While Quicken can't help you spend money on tax-deductible items—that's up to you—it can help you identify expenses that may be tax-deductible so you don't forget to include them on your tax returns.

Quicken offers two features to help maximize your deductions. The Deduction Finder asks you questions about expenditures to determine if they are tax-deductible. The Itemized Deduction Estimator helps make sure you don't forget about commonly overlooked itemized deductions.

Deduction Finder

The Deduction Finder uses another TurboTax feature to help you learn which expenses are deductible. Its question-and-answer interface gathers information from you and then provides information about the deductibility of items based on your answers.

Working with the Deduction Finder Window

To open the Deduction Finder, open the Planning tab and choose Tax Tools | Deduction Finder. An Introduction dialog may appear. Read its contents to learn more about Deduction Finder and then click OK.

If you do not want to see the introduction the next time you open the Deduction Finder, clear the Show Next Time Deduction Finder Is Started check box.

The next illustration shows what the Deductions tab of the Deduction Finder window says about the tax implications of paying mortgage interest on a first or second home.

Use the buttons to work with the Deduction Finder window:

- **See Introduction** displays the Introduction window so you can learn more about how Deduction Finder works.
- **Clear Checkmarks** removes the check marks from items for which you have already answered questions.
- **Print** prints a summary of deduction information about all the deductions for which you have answered questions.

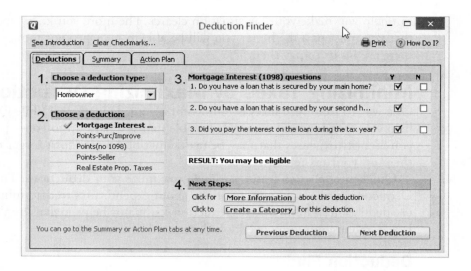

- **How Do I?** opens the Quicken Personal Finances Help window, where you can find additional information about using the Deduction Finder.

Finding Deductions

As you have seen, the Deductions tab of the Deduction Finder window uses clearly numbered steps to walk you through the process of selecting deduction types and deductions, and then answering questions.

It's easy to use. You need only choose the type of deduction from the drop-down list. As you see, Employee is the first option. Click the downward arrow to see your other options as shown here. You don't have to answer questions about all the deductions—only the deductions you think may apply to you. When you've finished answering questions about a deduction, the result appears near the bottom of the window. You can then move on to another deduction.

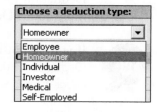

The Summary tab of the window summarizes the number of deductions available in each category, the number for which you answered questions, and the number for which you may be eligible to take deductions based on your answers to the questions.

When you've finished answering questions, you can click the Action Plan tab to get more information about the deductions and the things you may need to do to claim them. Although you can read the Action Plan information on-screen, if you answered many questions, you may want to use the Print button on the button bar to print the Action Plan information for reference.

When you have completed your entries and printed your Action Plan, click the Close button to close the Deduction Finder.

Utilizing the Itemized Deduction Estimator

The Itemized Deduction Estimator feature, which is available in the Quicken Premier and higher editions, helps make sure you don't overlook any itemized deductions, specifically the deductions on Schedule A of your tax return, for which you might qualify. It does this by guiding you through a review of deduction ideas and providing the information you need to know to determine whether you may qualify. To get started, open the Planning tab and choose Tax Tools | Itemized Deduction Estimator. The How Can I Maximize My Deductions? window appears. As shown in Figure 13-3, you can select a

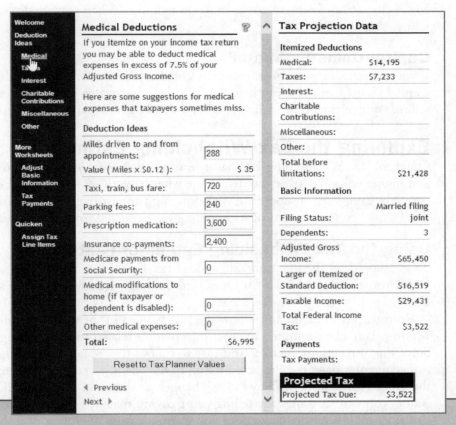

Figure 13-3 • In Quicken Premier, the Itemized Deduction Estimator will help you find Schedule A deductions.

deduction idea from the navigation bar at the left of the window and an additional dialog appears. In our example, we've chosen medical deduction ideas and entered our actual expenses.

Follow the instructions in the middle column of the Welcome window. You'll be prompted to enter information related to itemized deductions for medical expenses, as seen in Figure 13-3, taxes paid, interest paid, charitable contributions, and other items. The instructions are clear and easy to follow. Each time you enter information that can change your taxes, the Projected Refund Due or Projected Tax Due amount in the lower-right corner of the window changes. Your goal is to get a projected refund due amount as high as possible or a projected tax due amount as low as possible.

None of the entries you make in the Itemized Deduction Estimator feature will affect your Quicken data or any other tax-planning feature within Quicken. Make changes and experiment as much as you like. When you are done, click Close.

Capital Gains Estimator

If you are tracking your investments in Quicken Premier or a higher edition, the Capital Gains Estimator can help you calculate the taxable consequences of selling an investment. See Chapter 8 for a detailed explanation of this tool.

Exploring the Tax Withholding Estimator

Quicken's Tax Withholding Estimator feature, also available in Quicken Premier and higher editions, helps you determine whether your W-4 form has been correctly completed. It does this by comparing your estimated tax bill from the Tax Planner to the amount of withholding tax deducted from your paychecks.

Using the Tax Withholding Estimator Feature

To get started, in the Planning tab, choose Tax Tools | Tax Withholding Estimator. The Am I Under Or Over Withholding? window appears as seen in Figure 13-4.

Read the information and follow the instructions in the middle column of the window. You'll be prompted to enter information related to withholding taxes. Since the instructions are clear and easy to follow, they're not repeated here. Each time you enter data, the Projected Refund Due or Projected Tax Due amount in the lower-right corner of the window changes, as shown in the figure. If a refund is due, you will see a message telling you that you may be over-withholding. Consider increasing the deductions you claim on your W-4 at work if the refund number is sizeable.

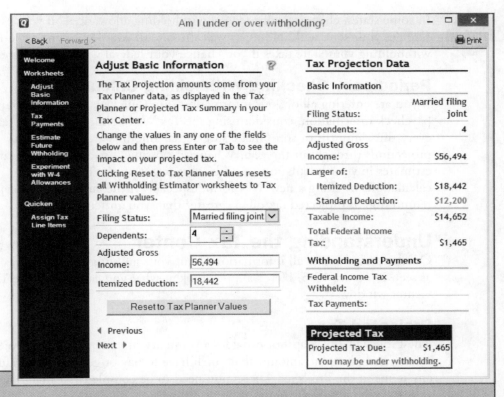

Figure 13-4 • **Use Quicken tools to help determine the deductions you claim on your W-4.**

None of the entries you make in the Tax Withholding Estimator feature will affect your Quicken data or any other tax planning feature within Quicken, so don't be afraid to experiment.

Acting on the Results of Tax Withholding Estimator Calculations

What do you do with this information once you have it? Well, suppose your work with the Tax Withholding Estimator feature tells you that you should change your W-4 allowances from 1 to 2 to avoid overpaying federal withholding taxes. You can act on this information by completing a new W-4 form at work. This will decrease the amount of withholding tax in each paycheck. The result is that you reduce your tax overpayment and potential refund.

In some states, changing your federal withholding allowances on your W-4 changes your state withholding as well. Be careful you do not end up under-withholding your state taxes if you change your federal withholding rate.

Periodically Checking Withholding Calculations

If you are entering all of your information into Quicken, including your paycheck information, consider using the Tax Withholding Estimator feature every three months or so to make sure actual amounts are in line with projections throughout the year. Whenever possible, use actual values rather than estimates in your calculations. And be sure to act on the results of the calculations by filing a new W-4 form, especially if the amount of your projected refund due or projected tax due is greater than you anticipated.

Understanding the Tax Center

Quicken summarizes all information about your tax situation in the Tax Center as seen in Figure 13-5. Here's a quick look at what you can find in the Tax Center window.

Projected Tax

The Projected Tax snapshot provides a summary of your upcoming projected tax return, including the amount that you'll have to pay or get back as a refund. If any items in the Projected Tax section need to be completed, a small flag will appear to the left of the item.

The information in this snapshot is based on the Tax Planner's Projected scenario, discussed earlier in this chapter. From the Options menu in the Projected Tax section of the Tax Center you can

- Open the Tax Planner.
- Create a Tax Summary Report. This report can also be created by clicking the Show Tax Summary Report button at the bottom of the Projected Tax section of the Tax Center.

Watch for small red flags that appear to the left of any item in the Projected Tax snapshot. Quicken is warning you that this item may not be complete.

Tax Calendar

The Tax Calendar section warns you of upcoming IRS tax deadlines. From here you can create Tax Alerts from either the Options menu or the Set Up Alerts button at the bottom of the section.

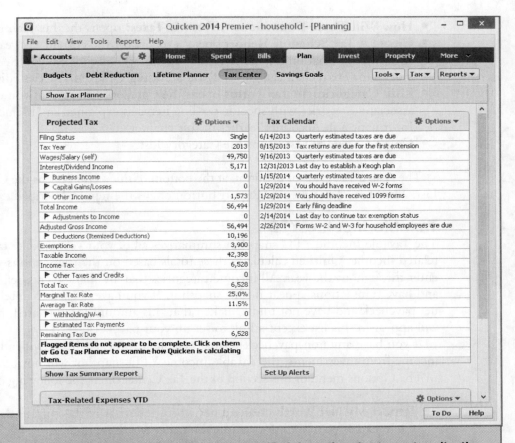

Figure 13-5 • The Tax Center window displays specific information about your tax situation.

While quarterly estimated taxes are due on January 15, April 15, June 15, and September 15, if those dates fall on a holiday or a weekend, the actual payment is due the next working day.

Tax-Related Expenses YTD

The Tax-Related Expenses YTD snapshot summarizes all of your year-to-date tax-related expenses. Quicken automatically calculates this information based on the transactions you enter throughout the year. All expense categories that are marked "tax-related" and have transactions appear in this list. The Options available from this section are as follows:

- **Find Other Deductions** opens the Deduction Finder, explained in the section "Deduction Finder" earlier in this chapter.

- **How Will These Deductions Affect My Taxes?** opens the Tax Planner.
- **Create A Tax Schedule Report** opens a report for the current tax year showing information for Form 1040. The report contains Schedule A and B entries for tax-related categories if you are using Quicken Premier edition.
- **Link Categories To Tax Forms** opens the Category List so that you can associate categories with specific tax-line items as explained in "Including Tax Information in Accounts" earlier in this chapter.
- **Go To Category List** opens the Category List.

The Assign Tax Categories button at the bottom of this section opens the Category List. The Show Tax Schedule Report button opens the report described earlier.

Taxable Income YTD

The Taxable Income YTD snapshot summarizes all of your year-to-date tax-related income. Quicken calculates these totals based on the transactions you enter throughout the year. All income categories that are marked "tax-related" and have transactions appear in this snapshot. If you have chosen to enter your net paycheck and have not told Quicken that this amount is tax related, nothing will appear in this list except a link to set up your paycheck.

If you have any non-paycheck-related taxable income, such as dividend income from investments, the Taxable Income YTD snapshot will not be blank.

The Options menu of this section of the Tax Center offers the following options:

- **Report My Net Worth** creates a net worth report as of the current date. See Chapter 13 for more information about net worth reports.
- **How Does This Income Affect My Taxes?** opens the Tax Planner.
- **Go To Category List** opens the Category List.

The Add Paycheck button at the bottom of the section opens the Paycheck Setup dialog. The process is explained in detail in Chapter 4.

Tax Alerts

Tax alerts are only visible in the Alerts Center, which is where you go to set alerts related to your tax situation. You can access the Tax Alerts feature through the Options menu in the Tax Calendar or from the menu bar by choosing Tools | Alerts Center | Setup. In the Setup dialog, you have three options related to taxes.

If necessary, click the plus sign to the left of the Taxes item in the Alerts Center's Setup tab to expand the tax-related alerts.

- **Withholding Threshold** enables you to set a value of dollars withheld from your paycheck to alert you if your payroll withholding is too much or not enough. However, this alert only works when you set up your paycheck in Quicken.
- **Schedule A – Personal Deductions (Schedule A Reminder)** displays information about the types of personal deductions you can claim on Schedule A of your tax return.
- **Important Tax Dates** notifies you in advance of tax calendar events, such as estimated tax due dates and extension deadlines.

Learn more about setting alerts in Chapter 5.

You can also see tax alerts in the Alerts snapshot that you can add to your Main View on the Home tab or into another view you create on the Home tab.

Appendixes

This part of the book provides some additional information you may find helpful when using Quicken Personal Finance Software. These two appendixes explain how to work with Quicken data files and how to customize Quicken.

Part Six

Managing Quicken Files

In This Appendix:

- *Creating a data file*
- *Opening, saving, and copying Quicken data files*
- *Setting backup preferences*
- *Backing up your data*
- *Restoring data files*
- *Protecting a data file*
- *Protecting existing transactions*
- *Working with passwords*
- *Importing files into Quicken*
- *Exporting Quicken files*
- *Working with additional file operations*
- *Using keyboard shortcuts*

All the information you enter in your Quicken Personal Finance Software is stored in a Quicken data file. This file includes all account and category setup information, transactions, and other records you enter into Quicken. Technically speaking, your Quicken data file consists of a single file with the QDF extension.

Commands under Quicken's File menu enable you to perform a number of file management tasks, such as creating, opening, backing up, restoring, password-protecting, importing and exporting, and copying portions and years of data files, as well as validating and repairing your data files. This appendix discusses all of these tasks.

Working with Multiple Data Files

Chances are, you won't need more than the Quicken data file you created as part of the Quicken Setup process, covered in Chapter 1. However, if you need to keep financial records for someone else, such as your local community group or an aging relative, you can easily create a new Quicken file.

Creating a Data File

Start by choosing File | New Quicken File. A dialog appears, asking whether you want to create a new Quicken file or a new Quicken account, as shown here. (Some users confuse the two and try to use the File menu's New command to create a new account. An account is a part of a Quicken *file*. A Quicken file can contain any number of accounts. You learn how to create an account in Chapter 1.) Select New Quicken File and click OK.

A Create Quicken File dialog, like the one shown next, appears. Use it to enter a name for the data file. Although you can also change the default directory location, it's easier to find the

data file if it's in the Quicken subdirectory of your Documents folder with other Quicken data files. It is also easier to find the Quicken file if it is renamed with no spaces or other special characters. Click OK.

Consider making your filename eight characters or less. While most modern programs can use longer filenames, there can be occasional issues if the filename is longer than eight characters.

Quicken's Setup appears next. Create your first account and continue setting up your new file as you did your first Quicken file. Refer to Chapter 1 for step-by-step instructions or just to refresh your memory.

Opening, Saving, and Copying Quicken Data Files

The first options on the File menu help you work with your Quicken files. Use these commands to create a new file, as discussed earlier, open an already existing Quicken file, determine the location, and save a copy of your current file.

Opening a Different Data File

If you have more than one Quicken data file, it's important that you enter transactions into the right one. You can see which data file is currently open by looking at the filename in the application window's title bar as shown here. Note that the title bar shows the version of Quicken that you are using, the file in which you are working, and the tab with which you are currently working. In our example, we are using the household file in Quicken 2014 Premier, and we are working in the Home tab.

To open a different data file, choose File | Open Quicken File, or press CTRL-O, and use the Open Quicken File dialog that appears to select and open a different file. Only one Quicken data file can be open at a time. To open the new file, click on the name of the file and press OK. Alternatively, simply double-click on the filename. In the example shown next, there are two files from which to choose.

In the same illustration, you may note a folder named "BACKUP." See "Backing Up Your Quicken Data File" later in this appendix to learn more about Quicken Backup files and folders.

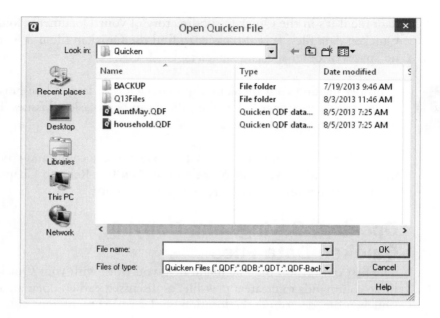

Save A Copy As

Use this menu command to open a dialog with which you can save an exact copy of your current file to another location. This other location can be a flash (sometimes called a "thumb") drive, another location on your network, or an external hard disk. If you have a CD or DVD burner on your computer, you can use your computer's CD or DVD writing software to copy the file to a CD or DVD.

 You can use the Save A Copy As dialog to rename your file as well.

Quicken makes it easy for you to copy your currently open file.

1. Click File | Save A Copy As, as seen in the next illustration. The Copy Quicken File dialog appears. (This dialog looks similar to the Create Quicken File and Open Quicken File dialogs shown earlier.)

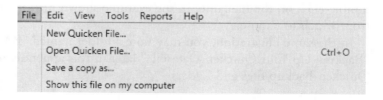

2. Choose the folder into which you want to save this Quicken file by clicking the drop-down list arrow in the Save In: field.

3. Select the location for your copied file, give it a new name such as "myfilecopy" to distinguish it from your original file, and click OK. Your file is now copied to the other location.

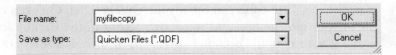

4. A message appears stating that your file has been copied successfully and showing the name you gave it. You are asked if you want to open the copied file. If you click Yes, you see an additional prompt asking if you want to close the current file. To return to your currently open Quicken file, click No.

Show This File On My Computer

You can immediately find where your current file is located by choosing File | Show This File On My Computer. When you click this command, Quicken opens a Windows Explorer window showing where the currently open file is located on your computer.

Backing Up Your Quicken Data File

Imagine this: You set up Quicken to track all of your finances, and you record or download transactions regularly so the Quicken data file is always up-to-date. Then one evening, when you start your computer to check your e-mail or enter a cash transaction into Quicken, you find that your hard drive has died. Not only have your plans for the evening been ruined, but your Quicken data file is also a casualty of your hard drive's untimely death.

Throughout this book, you've been encouraged to back up your data files. If you back up your Quicken data as regularly as you update its information, the loss of your Quicken data file will be a minor inconvenience, rather than a catastrophe. In this section, you'll learn how to back up your Quicken data file and how to restore it if (or when) the original data file is lost or damaged.

Setting Backup Preferences

By default, Quicken reminds you to run a manual backup every third time you leave your Quicken program. However, you can change this prompt in Quicken Preferences. The Backup Preferences dialog also allows you to tell Quicken how often to automatically save a copy of your files. Open the Backup Preferences dialog by clicking Edit | Preferences | Setup | Backup. The dialog appears as seen in Figure A-1.

About Automatic Backups

Quicken creates a Backup folder in the same location where your data files are stored. Every fifth time you open your Quicken file, Quicken creates a backup file of your information and stores that record in the Backup folder. While this is useful if your data file becomes corrupted or there is a software or hardware error, storing the file on your hard drive does not protect you against hard drive failures.

Each automatically backed up file is saved as QData-YYYY-MM-DD.aphh.mm .QDF-backup. (Data filename - four-digit year - two-digit month - two-digit day - AM or PM - two-digit hour - two-digit minute.QDF-backup.) Manual backups are formatted as QData.QDF-backup or QData-YYYY-MM-DD .QDF-backup, depending on whether you opted to include the date or not.

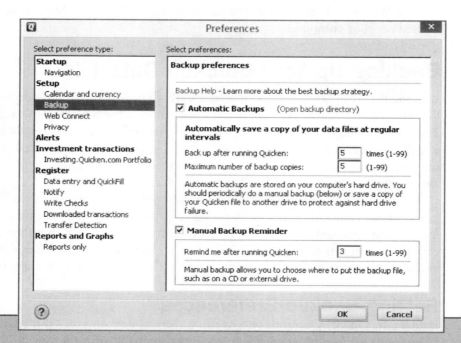

Figure A-1 • Use Quicken Backup Preferences to tell Quicken how you want to back up your Quicken files.

IN MY EXPERIENCE

One of the points I stress to clients and students alike is that eventually all hard drives will fail. The *only way* to protect yourself in the event of such a failure is by having a current backup of your data. By far, the most secure backup file is the one that resides somewhere *other* than near your computer. Otherwise, if your computer is stolen, damaged in a tornado, fire, or other disaster, your backup disks might also be lost.

For a small fee, Quicken Online Backup can help protect your data by making it easy to back up your data to a secure server far from your computer and other backup files. After you have signed up for Quicken's Online Backup you simply follow the same steps as a manual backup, but choose to save your data online rather than to a physical device at your location.

If your Quicken data is important to you, check out this feature. Click the Learn More link under Quicken Online Backup in the Quicken Backup window to get the details on this useful service. You can test it free for the first 30 days, and the service's interface is easy to use.

For more information about backing up, see "Backing Up Your Data" later in this appendix.

As seen in Figure A-1, you can change both the number of times Quicken saves your file to this folder and the number of copies maintained in that folder. Enter any number between 1 and 99 to change from the default of 5. Each file is saved with the word "backup," as seen in the following illustration, showing a manually backed up file. The date and time of the backup are recorded in the Backup folder for both automatic and manual backups.

| QDATA-2013-07-19.AM09.46.QDF-backup | 7/19/2013 9:46 AM | Quicken QDF bac... | 188,652 KB |

If you use the Quicken attachments feature discussed in Chapter 4, be aware that there must be enough room on the media to which you are backing up, or any attachments will not be backed up with the file.

Setting Manual Backup Reminders

The Preferences setting tells Quicken how often you want to be reminded to back up. A manual backup allows you to change the location for your backed up file.

Backing Up Your Data

While you are using Quicken, you begin the backup process by choosing File | Backup And Restore | Backup Quicken File or by pressing CTRL-B at any time.

This displays the Quicken Backup dialog for the currently open Quicken data file. As you see in Figure A-2, we are saving our file to a Backups folder on a flash drive named "E".

Select one of the following backup location options.

Back Up On My Computer Or Hard Drive (CD, Hard Drive, Thumb Drive)

This option enables you to back up to another disk, either on your computer or on one that's accessible via a network. If you select this option, you can use the Change button to locate and select a backup disk and directory. It's a good idea to alternate between two disks for backup purposes. This means you'll always have two versions backed up, in case one version is corrupt. Choosing a backup location other than your hard disk, such as a thumb drive (for small files) or an external hard disk, protects your data by placing it away from your regular hard drive. (Backing up to your computer's internal hard disk defeats the purpose of backing up!) If you want to automatically append the current date to the backup filename, select the Add Date To Backup File Name check box. (These instructions assume you have selected Back Up On My Computer.) Keep in mind that your computer may not be able to write directly to a CD-R or

Figure A-2 • The Quicken Backup dialog offers two ways of saving your data as well as giving you the opportunity of telling Quicken where to store the backed up file.

DVD-R. If you choose to back up to an optical disk such as a CD or DVD, you might have to back up to your hard disk and then burn the resulting file to disk.

1. Select Back Up On My Computer Or Hard Drive (CD, Hard Drive, Thumb Drive).
2. The folder into which your backed up file will be saved is displayed. To back up to another folder or location, click Change.
   a. Select the drive, folder, and location into which you want to save your backed up files.
   b. Click OK.
3. Click Back Up Now. Your Quicken data file briefly disappears and a small message appears telling you that Quicken is backing up your data.
4. When the backup is complete, the data file's windows reappear and a dialog informs you that the file was backed up successfully, as shown here. Click OK to dismiss the dialog.

 Quicken and the folks at Intuit do not recommend storing your Quicken file on a network drive and working with your file across your network. While backing up to a network drive can work effectively for many, it's a good idea to store your actual Quicken data file in the Quicken subfolder in your Documents folder on your computer.

Use Quicken Online Backup

Choose this option to back up to a server on the Internet, using Quicken's Online Backup service, which is available for a nominal fee. You can learn more about this service by selecting Learn More in the Use Quicken Online Backup section to connect to the Quicken Online Backup website.

   If you have an online backup account, click the I Am Already An Online Backup Customer link to enter your account ID and password.

IN MY EXPERIENCE

Students and clients have shared a common backup issue, whether it be to CDs, DVDs, or flash drives. The issue is "my Quicken data did not back up properly." In addition, there seem to be as many error messages as there are different CD/DVD burning programs available. Many of these errors are due to formatting issues. In most cases, one way to solve the question is as follows:

1. To back up to a CD or DVD, create a folder on your desktop.
   a. Right-click a blank area on your desktop.
   b. Click New | Folder. Name your folder and press ENTER.
2. Back up your file to that folder.
3. Burn the backed up file to your CD or DVD following the manufacturer's directions.
4. After you have verified that the backed up file is on your external device, find the backed up file icon on your desktop and delete it.
5. Remember that some CD/DVD programs will not accept filenames longer than 31 characters. This is another good reason to keep your filenames short!

Try following the same procedure if Quicken does not back up to your flash drive. Occasionally, flash drives are formatted by the manufacturer and can cause some of the same issues as CD or DVDs.

Do check the amount of space available on your CD or DVD. If, for some reason, your Quicken data file is too large to fit on the available space, the file will not back up. Since many CD and DVD programs determine the backed-up file size, if there is a question in your mind, you're better off to burn to a new, blank disk.

Remember that files burned to a CD or DVD may be "read-only," meaning you cannot work with files on that optical device directly. For this reason, it is a good idea to use external hard drives or similar devices for backup and store your active Quicken data file on your computer's hard drive.

- When working with online backup through Quicken, there have been issues with some firewall hardware and software. Refer to the documentation that came with your product to forestall any problems.
- Make sure you keep a record of your Quicken Online Backup account ID and password. If you forget it, you'll have to contact Quicken Support to complete your backup.
- Antivirus and non-Quicken backup programs can interfere with Quicken Online Backup.
- Quicken Online Backup cannot access files stored on CDs, DVDs, flash drives, or Zip drives.

Restoring Data Files

In the event of loss or damage to your data file, you can restore from a recent backup. You can restore from an external file or one on your hard drive. Each process works in a similar way.

Start the restoration process by opening Quicken and clicking File | Backup And Restore | Restore From Backup File. You may restore from one of Quicken's automatic backups, a backup file that you created, or from an online backup.

1. To restore from one of Quicken's automatic backups:

a. Click Restore From Automatic Backups.

b. If no backup files appear, click Open Backup Directory to locate the Quicken Backup folder.

c. Select the file you want to restore and click Restore Backup. If the file you want to restore is the currently opened file, you are prompted to write over the current file or to create a copy of the file.

2. To restore a backup file that you have created, ensure the device on which the file is stored is connected to your computer.

3. Click Restore From Your Backup | Browse to locate and select the appropriate backup file.

4. Click Restore Backup. If a file by the name of the file you are trying to restore exists, you'll see a message asking what you want to do. If you are restoring your backed up file over the current file, choose Overwrite The Open File With Restored File (This Cannot Be Undone). Overwriting a file means replacing all the information that is in the current file. This cannot be reversed, so make very sure that is what you want to do!

5. If you choose to create a copy of the backed up file, click Create A Copy. You see a message that the file was restored and are asked if you want to open the restored file.

6. To restore a file from your online backup, choose Restore From Online Backup to log into Quicken Backup. You see a list of the last 90 days of backups.

7. Select the file you want to restore. After Quicken has restored your files, click OK to close the confirmation message.

8. To open your restored file, click File | Open.

Moving a Quicken Data File Between Two Computers

Intuit's technical support staff is often asked how to move a Quicken data file from one computer to another. In fact, this question is so common that we are including it here.

The best way to move a data file from one computer to another is with the Backup and Restore Backup File commands. Begin by opening the file in Quicken on the computer on which it resides. Then follow the instructions in this appendix to back up the file to removable media, such as a thumb (or flash) drive, CD, DVD, external hard drive, or to a network drive (preferably one that is connected to the other computer). Then start Quicken on the other computer and follow the instructions in this appendix to restore the backup copy. When you're finished, the Quicken data file is ready to use on the new computer.

It's important to remember that once you begin making changes to the file on the new computer, the file on the old computer will no longer be up-to-date. This means that if you want to use the file on the old computer again, you need to complete the backup and restore process to move the file back to that computer. As you can imagine, if you often move the file from one computer to another and back, it can be difficult to keep track of which version of the file is the most up-to-date.

Although you can make your Quicken data file "portable" by keeping it on removable media so you can access it from any computer, this is not the recommended method. Flash drives, CDs, and DVDs are all more susceptible to

IN MY EXPERIENCE

As you can see, restoring your files from most locations is pretty straightforward. However, there may be some additional steps when restoring a file from a CD or DVD. The most common issue when restoring from your CD is a message that Quicken cannot find a file or access the disk in Drive "D" (where "D" is the name of your DVD or CD drive). The easiest way to solve this is as follows:

1. Create a new folder on your desktop and name it "Restored Files" or some similar name.
2. Use Windows Explorer to copy the file from your CD or DVD into the folder you just created.
3. Restore the file as described in "Restoring Data Files" earlier in this appendix.
4. For some files, you may have to change the properties of the file from its read-only state. To do this:
   a. Right-click the file you've just copied to the new folder on your desktop.
   b. Click Properties to open a dialog.
   c. Clear the Read-Only check box.
   d. Click Apply and OK to close the dialog.

   You can then proceed with the restoration as described in "Restoring Data Files."

IN MY EXPERIENCE

Many computer users are confused about the difference between backing up their files and copying their files. When should you back up and when should you copy? In today's computing world, that's a great question. When personal computers first came into general use, the storage devices, such as floppy disks, held much less information than today's spacious devices. Saving data was no less important in 1990, but the media held much less information. The 3½-inch floppy disks that were used most often held only 1.44MB of information. Today's flash (or thumb) drives (those small storage devices about 3 inches × 0.75 inches), measure their capacity in gigabytes. (When you remember that 1,024MB is 1GB, you get an idea of the storage capacity of a flash drive.) In order to save data efficiently and safely, earlier backup programs compressed the information to fit on the small media. One had to use the same program to restore the information back to the hard disk.

Today, all Quicken files, including the backups, are encrypted for security. When you run the Quicken Backup utility, Quicken appends the word "backup" to each file during the process. This tells Quicken that the file is not the current working file.

With today's large external hard disks, saving space may not be as important as easy retrieval of your data. If that is the case, consider using either of the two Copy commands offered by Quicken. These commands copy the information rather than save it as a backed up file. While Quicken recommends the Backup and Restore utility when moving data files from one place to another, the Copy options are available, and with them, you can easily retrieve your data and get back to work.

data loss and damage than an internal or external hard disk. Quicken users have reported numerous problems using this technique; don't add your own problems to the list. A networked drive may not be a good place to store your file either, at least if you are going to keep it networked while you work on it.

Password-Protecting Quicken Data

Quicken offers two types of password protection for your data: file passwords and transaction passwords. This section shows how these options work.

Protecting a Data File

When you password-protect a data file, the file cannot be opened without the password. This is the ultimate in protection—it prevents unauthorized users from even seeing the data on your computer.

Setting Up the Password

Choose File | Set Password For This Data File to display the Quicken File Password dialog, which is shown here. Enter the same password in each text box, and click OK.

Read the suggestions from Quicken about secure passwords. And one more thing: no password is secure if it is written on a sticky note and affixed to your monitor.

Opening a Password-Protected Data File

When you open a data file that is password-protected, the Enter Quicken Password dialog appears. You must enter your password correctly and then click OK to open the file. As mentioned in the dialog, passwords are "case-sensitive." That means if you've used capital letters when setting your password, you must enter your password with capital letters.

If you are updating to Quicken 2014 from Quicken 2011 or earlier, the allowable password length was changed in Quicken 2012. If the password you used in earlier versions was 15 or 16 characters, you may have a problem getting Quicken 2014 to accept your password. Try re-entering your password and leaving off the last one or two characters. You could also change the password in the older Quicken version before you update to Quicken 2014.

Changing or Removing a Password

Choose File | Set Password For This Data File to display the Quicken File Password dialog. Enter the current password in the Old Password box, and then enter the same new password in the two boxes beneath it. (To remove a password, leave the two bottom boxes empty.) Click OK.

Protecting Existing Transactions

When you password-protect existing transactions, the transactions cannot be modified unless the password is properly entered. This prevents unauthorized or accidental alterations to data.

Setting Up the Password

Choose File | Set Password To Modify Transactions to display the Password To Modify Existing Transactions dialog, shown here. Enter the same password in the top two text boxes. Then enter a date through which the transactions are to be protected, and click OK. This is an especially useful tool when you have completed entering all of your transactions for the year and are ready to run your reports for your income tax return. Protecting your transactions through the end of the year will ensure

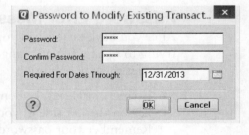

that you don't inadvertently change a number that might affect your return.

Transaction passwords may be up to 16 characters in length.

Modifying a Password-Protected Transaction

When you attempt to modify a transaction that is protected with a password, the Transaction Password dialog appears. You must enter your password correctly and then click OK to modify the transaction.

Changing or Removing a Password

Choose File | Set Password To Modify Transactions to display the Change Transaction Password dialog. Enter the current password in the Old Password box, and then enter the same new password in the two boxes beneath it. (To remove a password, leave the two bottom boxes empty.) Click OK.

Working with Passwords

Here are a few things to keep in mind when working with passwords:

- File passwords can be up to 15 characters, while transaction passwords can contain up to 16 characters. Both passwords can contain any character, including a space.
- Passwords are case-sensitive. That means, for example, that "PassWord" is not the same as "password."
- If you forget your password, you will not be able to access the data file. Write your password down and keep it in a safe place.
- Your data file is only as secure as *you* make it. Quicken's password protection can help prevent unauthorized access to your Quicken data files, but only if your password is effective.
- Consider including numbers, capital and lowercase letters, or symbols such as !, ?, or * in your password.
- Do not use personal birthdays, addresses, or other such information as your password.
- Do not use the password you use for your financial institutions as a Quicken file or transaction password.

Password Error Messages

After you have established your passwords, you may see error messages when trying to open a file or change a transaction. Before you call Quicken Support, consider these possibilities:

- Is your CAPS LOCK key on? If you have inadvertently pressed the CAPS LOCK key on the left side of your keyboard, you may be typing in all caps. Remember your passwords are case-sensitive.
- Is your NUM LOCK key off? When your password contains numbers and you enter those numbers from the ten-key pad at the right side of your keyboard, you may be entering symbols instead of numbers if you have turned off the NUM LOCK key.

- Are you in the right data file? If you have more than one data file on your computer, you may have opened the wrong one by mistake.
- Try another password. Many of us have several passwords that we use, and you may be entering the wrong password.
- If you have recently changed your password and have just restored from a backup copy, you may have restored a file with an old password. Try that old password.

Quicken's Password Removal Tool

If you should ever lose your password for your Quicken accounts, Quicken has created a downloadable Password Removal Tool. To access the tool and begin the process:

1. From any web browser, go to quicken.com
2. In the Search box type **Password Removal Tool**.
3. From the resulting dialog, click the Quicken Data File Password Removal Tool link under "Forgot Your Quicken Data File Password?"as seen in Figure A-3.
4. Follow the instructions on the screen.

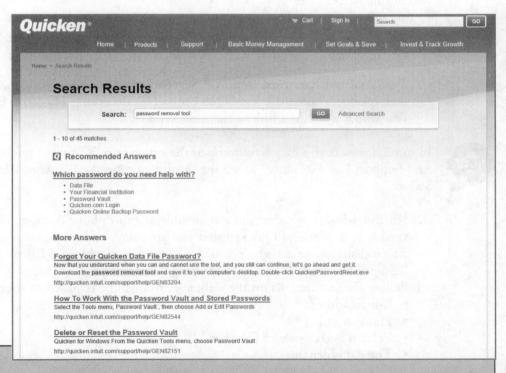

Figure A-3 • Use the Quicken Data File Password Removal Tool to retrieve data files with lost passwords.

Then, using the Removal Tool, you will be asked to upload your data to the secure Quicken server. You will be required to verify that the files for which you are trying to remove the password are, indeed, your files. Intuit takes customer privacy and security very seriously. After Quicken has removed the password from your file and verified that you are the owner, they download your file.

This tool is only available for data file passwords on currently supported versions of Quicken for Windows (Quicken 2012 and newer). Should you have password issues on earlier versions of Quicken, you must use the Password Removal Service.

Quicken's Assisted Password Removal Service

If you cannot use the Password Removal Tool, Quicken offers a service to remove the password from your file. While the service is currently free, support charges may apply and the service is available only for currently supported U.S. versions of Quicken including Quicken for Windows 2012 through 2014. According to current information, the process is usually completed within one to two business days.

You will need to send a copy of your file to Quicken. Their process is secure and confidential. Your first step is to contact Quicken Support via their website at Quicken.com.

1. Type **Assisted Password Removal Service** into the Search box. From the list that appears, choose the text "Quicken Is Not Accepting The Data File Password," which is a link to the next step.

 In some browsers you may have to open the subsection "Contact Quicken Help And Support For Assistance" to see the information on the Password Removal Service.

2. You'll need to give them your e-mail address, your phone number, the version and release of Quicken that you are using, and the name of your file. The website shows the versions of Quicken that the Assisted Password Removal Service is currently supporting.

3. Follow the instructions on the webpage. You will be required to submit your
   - E-mail address
   - Phone number
   - Version and release of Quicken
   - The data filename.

 Intuit is not able to return your file in an unsupported version of Quicken.

If neither the Password Removal Tool nor the Assisted Password Removal Service can help you, your options are to restore your data from a backup that either has no password or has a password that you know, or start a new data file.

Additional File Procedures

In addition to the processes discussed earlier, there are several other tasks you can perform from the File menu.

Importing Files into Quicken

Importing information into Quicken can make your financial life much easier. As discussed in Chapter 4, importing data such as downloading information from your financial institution saves you time.

From within Quicken, click File | File Import to open the submenu that shows your options, as shown here. As you can see, several types of files can be imported:

Web Connect File...
QIF File...
Quicken Transfer Format (.QXF) File...
Import Security Prices from CSV file...
TurboTax File...
Microsoft Money® file...

- **Web Connect Files** are those files created by financial institutions that do not have Direct Connect availability. You download these files onto your hard drive and then import them into your Quicken data file. See Chapter 4 for detailed information about Web Connect files.
- **QIF Files** are Quicken Interchange Format files that have been created in a third-party program for importing into Quicken. While not all programs support this format, many financial programs do.
- **Quicken Transfer Format (.QXF) Files** are files that permit the exchange of banking data with other Quicken data files, such as Quicken Essentials for Mac.
- **Import Security Prices From CSV File** allows you to utilize security price reports in this format.
- **TurboTax Files** can be imported into Quicken for tax planning.
- **Microsoft Money Files** can be quickly converted into Quicken data files.

Exporting Quicken Files

Several types of files appear on the File Export menu, as shown here. These file types are used to transfer information

QIF File...
Quicken Transfer Format (.QXF) File...
Export TurboTax tax schedule report
Export TurboTax capital gains report

between Intuit products, such as Quicken Essentials for Mac, as well as the Windows versions of Quicken:

- **QIF Files** are used to export Quicken data from one Quicken account to another Quicken account or to another Quicken file.
- **Quicken Transfer Format (.QXF) Files**, as explained earlier, are Quicken financial data files used to transfer data files from Quicken for Windows to Quicken Essentials for Mac. Click File | File Export | Quicken Transfer Format to open the Export To Quicken Transfer Format dialog. By default, the file with which you are working is the filename you will export. Click Save. You will see a message box when the export file is created successfully. You will then need to import this .qxf file into your Quicken Essentials file.
- **Export TurboTax Tax Schedule Report** and **Export TurboTax Capital Gains Report** allow you to transfer TurboTax files (.txf) into other programs.

Working with Additional File Operations

There are four options listed in the File Operations menu as shown here. Each option is discussed next.

| Copy... |
| Year-End Copy... |
| Validate and Repair... |
| Find Quicken Files... |

Copy

This copy command enables you to copy all or portions of the current data file to a different disk or save a copy with a different name. While similar to the Save A Copy As command discussed earlier in this appendix, this command gives you choices regarding what time period to include in the copied file, as well as a choice to include uncleared and investment transactions. It also may clear unused space in the Quicken file.

When you choose File | File Operations | Copy, the Copy File dialog, shown next, appears. Click Browse to choose a location for your file if you want the copied file stored in a location other than the current folder. The new filename will be the same as the current file, but will have "Cpy" at the end of the filename. You can change the name if you choose. Select the date range that is to be included in the copy, and clear the check box if you do not want to include earlier, uncleared transactions. While you may choose to clear the Include All Prior Investment Transactions, consider keeping them for a more complete record of your investment transactions. Click OK to make the copy.

 The Quicken Copy command may cause issues if you are using mobile sync or Express Web Connect.

If there is already a Quicken file with the same name in your Quicken folder, you will receive a prompt to give a new name to the file copy. Type a new name for this second file copy, and click OK.

When the copy is finished, a dialog asks if you want to continue working with the original data file or the new copy. Select the appropriate option, and click OK to continue working with Quicken.

The process does not change the original file in any way. Perhaps you want to copy categories, scheduled transactions, and memorized payees to a new file without the transactions. Or, perhaps there is a date range in which you had some major changes in your financial life and want to review those transactions.

Making a Year-End Copy of a Data File

The Year-End Copy command creates two special copies of your data file. Choose File | File Operations | Year-End Copy to display the Create A Year End Copy dialog, shown next, and set options for the two files.

Current Data File   The Current Data File section allows you to set options for the file you will continue working with in Quicken.

Do Nothing. My Current Data File Will Remain Unchanged   This option simply saves a copy of the current data file as-is.

I Only Want Transactions In My Current Data File Starting With This Date
This option enables you to enter a starting date for the files in the data file you will continue to use. For example, if you enter 1/1/2013, all reconciled transactions prior to that date will be removed from the data file.

Archive Data File   The Archive Data File section allows you to set options for creating an archive copy of the file. An archive is a copy of older transactions saved in a separate file. You can set two options:

- Enter a complete path (or use the Browse button to enter a path) for the archive file.

- Enter the date for the last transaction to be included in the file. For example, if you enter 12/31/2012, the archive file will include all transactions in the current file, up to and including those transactions dated 12/31/2012.

Creating the Files   When you click OK in the Create A Year End Copy dialog, Quicken creates the two files. It then displays a dialog that enables you to select the file you want to work with: the current file or the archive file. Select the appropriate option (normally Current File), and click OK to continue working with Quicken.

Checking the Integrity of a Data File

The Validate And Repair command facilitates checking the integrity of a Quicken data file. This command is particularly useful if you believe that a file has been damaged. It is a good idea to copy your file to an external device, such as a CD or external hard drive, before you perform the Validate And Repair function—in other words, perform a backup before working with this utility!

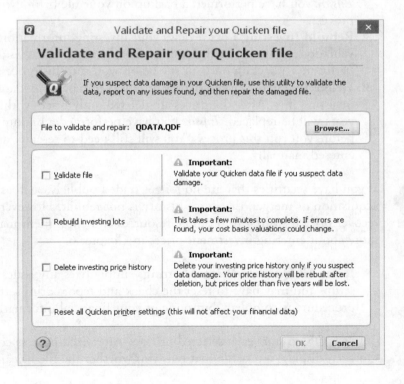

The Validate And Repair utility is one that many experienced Quicken users recommend as the first step when there are problems with your Quicken file. Of course, this is after you perform a backup!

When you choose File | File Operations | Validate And Repair, the Validate And Repair Your Quicken File dialog appears, as shown previously. By default, the current file is selected, but you may click Browse to select another file to check if you choose.

There are four specific operations that affect your data in different ways:

- **Validate File** should be run when you feel your data might be corrupted. *Ensure* you have performed a backup on your file before you run this process.
- **Rebuild Investing Lots** reviews your investing information. Current valuation amounts could change if this file has errors. *Ensure* you have performed a backup on your file before you run this process.
- **Delete Investing Price History** attempts to repair any data damage in your investing files. After the prices are deleted, only prices within the last five years will be replaced. *Ensure* you have performed a backup on your file before you run this process. You will still need to re-enter any prices you've entered manually.

If you have securities that are no longer traded publicly, such as with an acquisition or merger, that price history is not rebuilt. However, you can still recover price histories from online resources and enter them manually. Learn more about entering investment prices in Chapter 6.

- **Reset All Quicken Printer Settings** simply fixes any issues with your printer setup. You may have to reset the check and report print settings after this procedure is complete, but none of your financial information is affected.

Click OK to start each selected process. After each process completes, Quicken displays a text file that tells you whether the file has any problems.

Some Quicken users use this process and add one more step. If you hold down the CTRL and the SHIFT keys when clicking OK, you perform an additional validation step called a Super Validate. This additional step may find more errors in a damaged file. As always, before you perform any function that may impact your financial transactions, do a backup!

IN MY EXPERIENCE

One additional thought when working with files you suspect are damaged: try uninstalling and then reinstalling your Quicken program. Often, it is something that has been scrambled within the data and its interface with the program that can cause your files to appear damaged. Just remember to back up *before* you uninstall the program.

Using Keyboard Shortcuts

If you have been working with computers for a long time and are comfortable with your keyboard, Quicken has a number of keyboard shortcuts that can save time. When you see a keyboard combination to the side of a menu command, it means that you can press that combination of keys and achieve the same result as when you click that command on the menu. For example, by choosing Open Quicken File on the File menu, you see the keyboard shortcut CTRL-O. Hold down the CTRL key on your keyboard, press the O key, and release both keys to open an existing Quicken file. Note the CTRL-P keyboard shortcut by the Print Checks command on the File menu. Many views in Quicken are available for you to print.

Since printing is covered in each appropriate chapter of this book, we do not cover the print options in this appendix.

Quicken Keyboard Shortcuts

Quicken lets you access many of its features directly from the keyboard with one or a combination of keys. Table A-1 lists some of these shortcuts, which are also mentioned throughout the book.

Quicken Keyboard Command	Result
CTRL-A	Opens Account List
CTRL-B	Opens Quicken Backup dialog
CTRL-C	Opens the Category List if you have set your keyboard mapping to the Quicken standard. See CTRL-SHIFT-C if your keyboard mapping is set to the default Windows standard.
CTRL-H	Opens Find And Replace dialog
CTRL-J	Opens Bill And Income Reminders dialog
CTRL-K	Opens the Quicken Calendar
CTRL-L	Opens the Tag List
CTRL-M	Opens the Memorized dialog (from within a register transaction)
CTRL-N	Opens the Customize View dialog from the Home tab, from which you can create a new view. Opens a blank line at the bottom when you use it in an account register.
CTRL-O	Opens the Open Quicken File dialog
CTRL-S	Opens the Split dialog (from within a register transaction)
CTRL-T	Opens the Memorized Payee dialog
CTRL-U	Opens the Portfolio view of the Investing tab
CTRL-W	Opens the Write Checks dialog (from within a register transaction)
CTRL-Y	Opens the Security List
CTRL-SHIFT-A	Opens the Account Attachments dialog (from within a register transaction)
CTRL-SHIFT-C	Opens the Category List if you have your keyboard mapping preferences set to the default Windows standard instead of opting for the Quicken standard
CTRL-SHIFT-E	Opens the Account Details dialog (when an account is selected in the Account Bar or you are working in an account's register)
CTRL-SHIFT-H	Opens the View Loans dialog (if a loan exists)
CTRL-SHIFT-O	Opens the Account Overview window (when an account is selected in the Account Bar or you are working in an account's register)
ALT-E	Opens the Edit menu from the Quicken Toolbar
ALT-F or ALT-SHIFT-F	Opens the File menu from the Quicken Toolbar
ALT-H	Opens the Help menu from the Quicken Toolbar
ALT-R	Opens the Report menu from the Quicken Toolbar
ALT-T	Opens the Tools menu from the Quicken Toolbar
ALT-V	Opens the View menu from the Quicken Toolbar
F1	Opens Quicken Help

Table A-1 • Quicken Keyboard Shortcuts

Mapping Your Keyboard

By default, Quicken's shortcuts are the traditional Windows shortcuts, such as CTRL-C for copy and CTRL-V for paste. However, Quicken has its own set of shortcuts, which you can choose in Preferences. To change your preferences, click Edit | Preferences | Setup | Keyboard Mappings. Choose Quicken Standard and click OK.

For more information about the keyboard shortcuts available in Quicken 2014, press the F1 key (or from the Quicken menu bar, click Help | Quicken Help). Select Search Quicken Help and, in the search box, type **keyboard shortcuts**.

Customizing Quicken

In This Appendix:

- *Creating custom Home tab views*
- *Re-creating the Summary view*
- *Crafting an Analysis & Reports view*
- *Customizing the Toolbar*
- *Telling Quicken your preferences*
- *Converting your older Quicken files to a new computer*
- *Changing multiple transactions*
- *Using the Emergency Records Organizer*

Once you have become familiar with Quicken Personal Finance Software, you may want to fine-tune parts of the program to meet YOUR needs. While there are options for changing the look of Quicken throughout this book, other customization options, such as customizing the Toolbar, may be useful to you. This appendix explains many ways you can customize Quicken.

Customizing Quicken's Interface

Quicken offers many customization possibilities. Since the Home tab is often the opening point for many Quicken users, this part of the appendix explains how to customize both the Home tab and the Quicken Toolbar.

Creating Custom Home Tab Views

We mentioned in Chapter 1 that you could customize views in the Home tab to see specifics about your Quicken data. You can create multiple Home tab views, each of which shows the "snapshots" of summarized financial information that you want to display. Figure B-1 shows an example.

If you've upgraded to Quicken 2014 from an earlier version, you may already have custom views set up in your Quicken data file. You have access to these views on the Home tab, where you can switch from one to another, modify them, and delete them, as discussed in this section.

Displaying the Home Tab Views

To get started, click the Home tab near the top of the Quicken window. Quicken displays the Main View button. Before you customize this view, it displays three snapshots: See Where Your Money Goes, Stay On Top Of Monthly Bills, and Track Spending Goals To Save Money. Once you've customized the Home tab, it displays the snapshots you added to it (refer to Figure B-1).

Modifying the Current View

Click Customize to change the current view. The button opens the Customize View dialog, as shown next. Move items from the Available Items list on the left to the Chosen Items list on the right with the Add button. Make changes as desired, and click OK to save them.

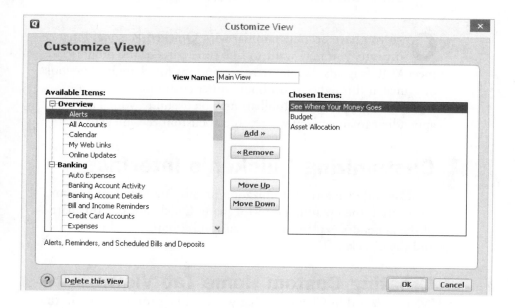

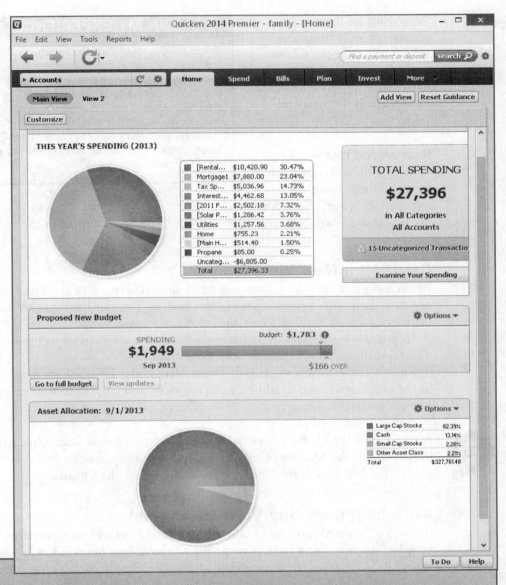

Figure B-1 • Use the Home tab to create snapshots of your financial data that are useful to you.

Removing an Item   To remove an item from the view, select it in the Chosen Items list and click Remove. This action simply moves the item back to the Available Items list.

Rearranging Items   To rearrange the order of items in the Chosen Items list, select an item and click Move Up or Move Down. Repeat this process until the items appear in the order you want.

Creating a New View

By creating multiple views, you can make several versions of the Home tab window, each with a specific set of information. You can then quickly switch from one view to another to see the information you want.

In the Home tab window, click the Add View button (refer to Figure B-1). The Customize View dialog, as seen earlier, appears.

Enter a name for the view in the View Name box. Then follow the instructions in the previous section to add items to the view, and click OK. Your new view appears on screen.

At the top of the Home tab view is a small button labeled Reset Guidance. This button opens the Quicken Qcards which give you suggestions and direction for many Quicken functions. Click the small X to close the Qcards.

Switching from One View to Another

If you have created more than one view for the Quicken Home window, each view has its own menu button at the top of the Home tab window, as seen in Figure B-1. To switch from one view to another, simply click its button.

Deleting a View

To delete a view, select the button for the view you want to delete. Click Customize to open the Customize View dialog. Then choose the Delete This View button. Click Yes in the confirmation dialog that appears. The view is deleted. You must have at least one view in the Home tab, meaning you cannot delete the "last" view.

Re-creating the Summary View

In earlier versions of Quicken, a Summary view displayed a number of snapshots with useful information about your banking accounts. If you liked this view, as many did, you can easily create it, as described next.

1. Open the Home tab, and click Add View. The Customize View dialog appears. In the View Name field, type **Summary View**. If any information appears in the Chosen Items list, click the first item, hold down your SHIFT key, and click the bottom item to select the entire list. Then, click Remove to remove these items. You are only removing them from the Chosen Items list in the current view. They are still available in the Available Items list on the left.

2. Start by selecting Alerts in the Available Items list, and click Add. You will note that all of the items are in this order within the six sections: Overview, Banking, Investing, Property & Debt, Planning, and Tax. Remember, you may not see all the sections if you have hidden one or more tabs.

3. Add the following from the Banking section of the Available Items list: Spending And Savings Accounts, Credit Card Accounts, and Bill And Income Reminders, in that order. When you click OK, you'll see a Summary View, similar to the one that was in previous Quicken versions, as shown next.

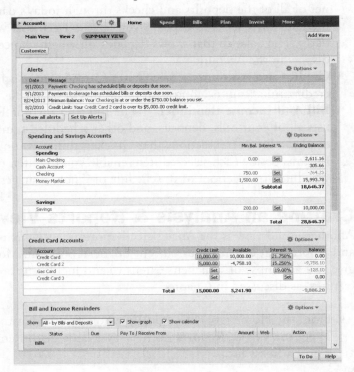

The layout depends on your screen width and the order in which you have placed the snapshots. To get the layout you want, change the width of your Quicken window and/or the order in which the snapshots display.

In your new Summary View, all snapshots include an Options menu and buttons that you can use to work with that snapshot. For example, the Alerts snapshot at the top of the view has both buttons and Options menu commands for showing, and setting up alerts. You can click links to view the account register, set up balance alerts, and set interest rates in any of the snapshots. You have seen many of these options throughout the book. Try exploring some of the others!

Here's a brief summary of each snapshot in your new Summary View:

- **Alerts**   The Alerts snapshot lists alerts you have set up. You can click blue links to go to the account or to other applicable alert items that you learned about in Chapter 4.
- **Spending And Savings Accounts**   The Spending And Savings Accounts snapshot lists all of your checking, savings, and cash accounts, along with their current or ending balances. Remember, the *current balance* shows the net of all of the deposits and checks through today's date. The *ending balance* includes any checks or deposits you have entered that will occur on future dates. The balance that shows depends on which choice you have made to display in the Account Bar.
- **Credit Card Accounts**   The Credit Card Accounts snapshot lists all of your credit card accounts along with their current balances.
- **Bill And Income Reminders**   The Bill And Income Reminders snapshot lists all of your bills, deposits, and other scheduled transactions. It may also display a list of transactions that Quicken thinks you may want to schedule. Buttons beside each selected item enable you to enter, edit, or skip a scheduled transaction, or to schedule or ignore a suggested transaction.

Crafting an Analysis & Reports View

Another useful view is the Analysis & Reports View, which includes both graphs and reports that explain your current financial position. Most of these snapshots give you a glimpse of Quicken's extensive and highly customizable reporting features, as discussed in Chapter 5.

1. From the Home tab, click Add View to open the Customize View dialog. Type **Analysis & Reports** in the View Name field. Remove any items in the Chosen Items list.

2. Add the following from the Available Items list: Expenses, Income vs. Expenses, and Budget, in that order. Click OK to see an Analysis & Reports View, as shown next.

If you have not yet created your budget, a placeholder view with the Get Started button appears.

If you have not yet set up a budget, you will see Budget Your Spending with the Get Started button. Clicking the Get Started button takes you to the Budgets view on the Planning tab so you can set up your budget.

Customizing the Toolbar

The Quicken Toolbar is an optional row of buttons along the top of the screen, just beneath the menu bar. These buttons offer quick access to Quicken features. If you do not see the Quicken Toolbar, display it by clicking View | Show Toolbar.

By default, the Quicken Toolbar shows both a left and right pointing arrow and the One Step Update button. You can customize the Toolbar by adding, removing, or rearranging buttons, or by changing how the buttons display. To do this, you use the Customize Toolbar dialog. To open the Customize Toolbar dialog, open the View menu and click Show Toolbar. With the Toolbar displayed, position your mouse anywhere on the Toolbar, right-click, and choose Customize Toolbar, as seen next. (You can click View | Customize Toolbar as well or click the small gear icon at the right of the Toolbar.)

 Quicken calls the Toolbar items "buttons," but other Quicken users call them *icons*. Either way, they are simply links to other Quicken items.

To customize the Toolbar, make changes in this dialog as discussed next, and click OK.

Adding Buttons

To add a button, select it in the Available Toolbar Buttons list and click Add. Its name appears in the Your Toolbar Buttons list. If you want more items to choose from, click the Show All Toolbar Choices check box to display all the possibilities. The list expands to show the various items for which you can create a toolbar button.

If you have chosen to hide the display of some of the tabs in the View | Show Tabs menu, you may not see all the available sections in your Available Toolbar Buttons list.

You can include as many buttons as you like on the Toolbar. If the Toolbar includes more buttons than can fit within the Quicken application window, a More button, with two right-pointing arrows, appears on the Toolbar. The More button may also appear on the Toolbar when you resize your Quicken window to make it smaller. Click this button to display a menu of buttons and select the button you want.

 If you have chosen to display only buttons rather than both buttons and text, you may not see the More button!

Adding Saved Reports to the Toolbar

To add a saved report to the Toolbar, click the Add Or Remove Saved Reports button in the Customize Toolbar dialog. Then select the In Toolbar check box beside each saved report you want to add to the Toolbar. Click OK to save your changes.

Removing or Rearranging Buttons

To remove a button, select it in the Your Toolbar Buttons list and click Remove. Its name is removed from the Your Toolbar Buttons list, but is still available on the Available Toolbar Buttons list should you want to include it at another time.

You can rearrange the order of buttons on the Toolbar by changing their order in the Your Toolbar Buttons list. Simply select a button that you want to move, and click Move Up or Move Down to change its position in the list

Moving More than One Button

Many Quicken users want to put more than one button on the toolbar at a time. This is easy to do.

To choose items that are listed in the Available Toolbar Buttons list in a row (one after the other):

1. Select the first button you want to use in the Available Toolbar Buttons list.
2. Hold down the SHIFT key on your keyboard.
3. Click the last item you want to use. Release the SHIFT key. You'll note that the items you chose are "bolded" as seen next.
4. Click the Add button (or the Remove button if you are taking them off the Quicken Toolbar). As before, the items are not removed from your Available Toolbar Buttons list, only the Toolbar itself.

To move items that are not in a row, use the CTRL key rather than the SHIFT key. Select each item that you want to move while you are still holding down the CTRL key. Release the CTRL key after selecting the items.

Changing the Appearance of Buttons

At the bottom of the Customize Toolbar dialog are two options that determine how Toolbar buttons are displayed:

- **Icons And Text** displays both the Toolbar button and its label, as shown here.

- **Icons Only** displays just the Toolbar button. When you hover over a button, its label appears.

The Global Search field does not appear on the Quicken Toolbar by default. You display it on the Toolbar by checking the Show Global Search check box in the Customize Toolbar dialog.

IN MY EXPERIENCE

A useful option in Quicken is the ability to create custom keyboard shortcuts for the buttons on your Toolbar. From the Customize Toolbar dialog:

1. Select the item you want to edit from the Your Toolbar Buttons on the right of the dialog.
2. Click Edit Shortcut Or Label to open the Edit Shortcut Or Label dialog, as shown here.
3. Change the label name, create a shortcut key combination, or both, and then click OK.

You can now open that item from your keyboard using the keystrokes shown in the Edit Shortcut Or Label dialog. However, if you remove the button from the Toolbar, the keystroke combination no longer works for that item. In addition, the label change does not appear in the Your Toolbar Buttons list, but it does appear on the Toolbar when you save your customized settings.

Changing a label name is effective only in the Toolbar display when you've chosen to show both buttons and text. It does not change the label that appears when you hover over the button with your mouse.

Restoring the Default Toolbar

To restore the Toolbar back to its "factory settings," click the Reset To Default button in the Customize Toolbar dialog. Then click OK in the confirmation dialog that appears. Click Done to close the dialog and return to the main Quicken window. The Toolbar buttons return to the way they display when you first installed Quicken.

Setting Preferences

Many Quicken users find the Preferences settings give them better control when using the program. While we discuss many of the settings throughout other chapters in this book, this section reviews all of the options you can change and tells you where you can learn more about the features they control.

Telling Quicken Your Preferences

As the name suggests, Preferences allow you to control Quicken's appearance and operations. To access these options, open the Edit menu and choose Preferences to open the Preferences dialog, as seen next. It lists a variety of categories as follows.

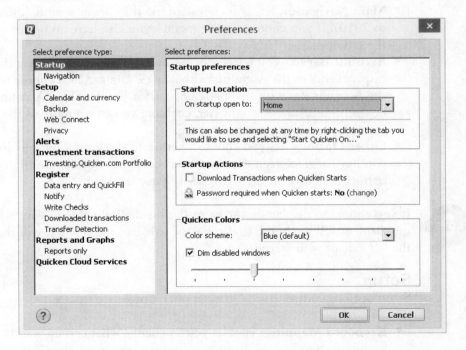

Startup

Startup preferences enable you to specify what should appear when you start Quicken. Use the drop-down list to select Home (the default setting), one of the tabs (Home, Bills, Planning, and so on), a specific account register, the Transaction List, or one of the views within the tabs.

You can choose what you want Quicken to do when it starts, such as download transactions or require a password, and choose one of the predefined color schemes for the Quicken program: blue (the default), green, purple, or tan. You can also choose to have non-active (disabled) windows dimmed. Use the slider to determine how much or how little "dimming" should occur.

 Depending on your monitor settings, sometimes changing the color scheme may make Quicken easier for you to read. Also, you can make the font easier to read by selecting View | Use Large Fonts. However, you may find that not all of your information appears in your Quicken window when you use large fonts.

Navigation   Startup Navigation allows you to choose how you want to get around Quicken:

- **Main Navigation** lets you choose to use the Classic menus (those used prior to 2010). If you choose Classic menus, you also have an option to turn off the tab display.
- **Account Bar** lets you select where to place the Account Bar and whether to display cents in the Account Bar balances. You can also choose to not show the Account Bar with this preference. Clearing the Show Account Bar check box minimizes the Account Bar, enabling you to see more of the Quicken screen with which you are working.
- **Other Options** lets you choose whether to show the Quicken Toolbar. If you have a widescreen monitor, from here you may choose to dock the side bar permanently on the right side of your monitor.

 If you choose to display the Account Bar on the right side of your widescreen monitor, as well as choose to display the side bar, the side bar will then dock on the left side of your screen.

Setup

Setup options control basic Quicken operations.

- **Keyboard Mappings** enables you to change what certain standard Windows keyboard shortcuts do. In most Windows programs, the CTRL-Z, CTRL-X,

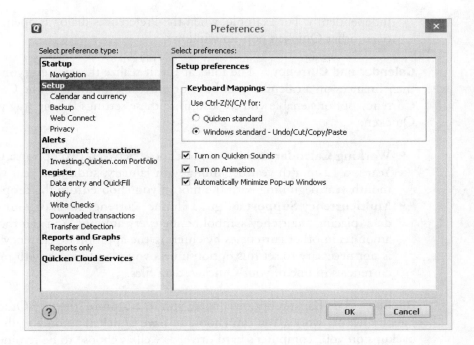

CTRL-C, and CTRL-V shortcut keys perform commands on the Edit menu. In Quicken 2014, these keyboard shortcuts are set to the Quicken standard. See Appendix A for more information about keyboard shortcuts.

If you are upgrading from a previous Quicken version, the preferences you set in that version may not be the same in Quicken 2014. To ensure the settings are what you want, choose Edit | Preferences | Setup | Keyboard Mappings to verify the settings on your machine.

- **Turn On Quicken Sounds** turns on Quicken sound effects. You may want to leave this check box off if you use Quicken in an environment where sounds might annoy the people around you.
- **Turn On Animation**, which is turned on by default, activates the Quicken animation effects that appear when you complete certain actions.
- **Automatically Minimize Pop-up Windows** automatically minimizes a Quicken window, such as a report window or the Category List window, to the Quicken task bar when you click outside that window. (This is the window behavior in some older versions of Quicken.) With this option turned off, you can have multiple Quicken windows open at once and can manually minimize each one. Note that not all Quicken windows open

independently. For example, when the Preferences dialog is open, you cannot open other Quicken pop-up windows.

Calendar and Currency The folks at Intuit realize that not everyone manages their finances on a calendar-year basis or only in U.S. dollars. The Calendar and Currency options enable you to customize these settings for the way you use Quicken:

- **Working Calendar** enables you to choose between two options: Calendar Year is a 12-month year beginning with January, and Fiscal Year is a 12-month year beginning with the month you choose from the drop-down list.
- **Multicurrency Support** assigns a "home" currency to all of your current data, placing a currency symbol beside every amount. You can then enter amounts in other currencies by entering the appropriate currency symbol. It is not necessary to set this option unless you plan to work with multiple currencies in one of your Quicken data files.

Backup The Backup options enable you to customize the way Quicken's Backup feature works. You can choose to have Quicken automatically do backups on your computer's hard drive, as well as choose to be reminded to do manual backups on any drive you want. See Appendix A for a complete discussion of how and when (DO IT OFTEN) to back up your data.

Web Connect The Web Connect options enable you to customize the way Quicken's Web Connect feature works. Web Connect, as discussed in Chapter 4, is a method for downloading transaction information from your financial institution into your Quicken data file.

- **Give Me The Option Of Saving To A File Whenever I Download Web Connect Data** displays a dialog after a Web Connect session that enables you to save the downloaded Web Connect information to a file.
- **Keep Quicken Open After Web Connect Completes** tells Quicken to keep running after Web Connect completes a download from the Web.

Privacy This option opens Privacy Preferences. Click Learn More to read about how Quicken uses your usage information to enhance their product. Use the two options to share how you use Quicken with the Intuit team.

- **Send Feature Usage Statistics** anonymously sends statistical data to Quicken citing the number of times you use a specific feature within the program.

- **Send Online Banking Connectivity Success Rates** tells Quicken the number of times you successfully connect to a financial institution from within Quicken.
- Click the **Read Our Privacy Statement** link to learn how Quicken collects information and uses what you share.

Alerts

Alerts preferences enable you to set the lead-time for calendar notes to appear in Alerts snapshots as well as the Alerts Center. Learn about alerts in Chapter 4. Chapter 4 also discusses the Billminder feature which displays your scheduled bills and deposits. You can select a lead-time period to display from the drop-down list; timing options range in time from Last Month to Next Month. The items you display in the Billminder have no effect on the lead-time you've set for alerts.

Warnings allow you to change all Quicken warnings back to their default. Click Reset Quicken Warnings, and a message appears that all warnings are reset. This can be helpful if you turned off a warning by checking the Don't Show Me This Again check box and now realize you really did want to see the warning.

Investment Transactions

The Investment Transactions options, seen next, let you customize the way the Investment Transaction lists look and work. Learn about the Investment Transaction lists in Chapter 6.

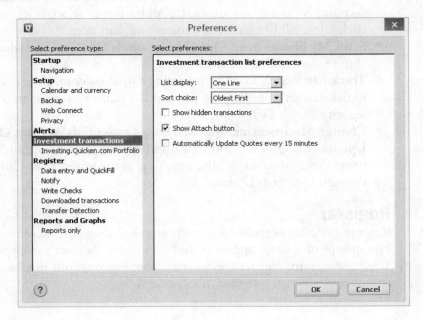

This option does not appear if you have turned off the Investing tab display.

- **List Display** determines whether transactions should appear with one or two lines in the list.
- **Sort Choice** determines whether transactions are sorted in ascending or descending order by date.
- **Show Hidden Transactions** displays hidden transactions in the list.
- **Show Attach Button** displays the Attach button beside the Edit and Delete buttons for the current transaction. You may want to turn off this check box if you do not use the Image Attachment feature. Chapter 3 explains how to attach images to transactions.
- **Automatically Update Quotes Every 15 Minutes** updates your stock portfolio with your Internet connection every 15 minutes. This feature comes with Quicken Premier and higher editions.

Investing.Quicken.com Portfolio   As explained in Chapter 7, http://investing .quicken.com is an online site where you register and can then track your investment information from any location with Internet access.

- **Select Accounts To View Online** tells Quicken what accounts to view online at Quicken.com and how to send information. You can choose which accounts to use, or use the Select All button to select all of your accounts, or click Clear All to clear your choices and start over.
- **Send My Shares/Send Only My Symbols** tells Quicken what information about your holdings to track.
- **Track My Watch List On Investing.Quicken.com**, if cleared, stops Quicken.com from keeping track of the items you've included in your security Watch List.
- **Change My Investing.Quicken.com Credentials At Next One Step Update** tells Quicken you want to update or amend your online credentials (your login information) the next time you connect with Quicken.com through One Step Update.

Register

Register preferences enable you to fine-tune the way the account register works. Five groups of settings appear in addition to the Register preferences themselves. You'll see account register windows discussed throughout this book, but complete details are provided in Chapter 3.

Register Preferences   Register options affect the way the transactions you enter appear in the account register window:

- **Show Date Before Check Number** is the default setting for your registers. Clear this check box to have the check number appear in the first column.
- **Show Memo Before Category** puts the Memo field before the Category field in your account register.

Transaction Entry

- **Automatically Enter Split Data** turns the OK button in the Split Transaction window into an Enter button for entering the transaction. See Chapter 3 for a complete explanation of split transactions.

IN MY EXPERIENCE

Quicken tries to assign a category to every transaction. If you see an uncategorized downloaded transaction, it is because Quicken does not recognize the vendor. Quicken assigns categories to downloaded transactions in this order:

1. A transaction in your Memorized Payee List with a matching payee name with the category shown for that payee.
2. Your financial institution has associated a standard industrial classification (SIC) code with this transaction.

You also have the option to edit the category from the Memorized Payee List. Click Tools | Memorized Payee List, edit the memorized payee, and choose the correct category. This will then memorize the payee name to the correct category for future downloads. See more discussion about memorized payees in Chapters 1 and 4.

- **Automatically Place Decimal Point** automatically enters a decimal point two places to the left when entering dollar figures in Quicken or using Quicken's built-in calculator. For example, if you enter 1543 in the calculator, Quicken enters 15.43.

Register Appearance

- **Gray Reconciled Transactions** displays all reconciled transactions with gray characters rather than black characters.
- **Remember Register Filters After Quicken Closes** remembers any register filter settings you may have made when you close Quicken so those settings are in place the next time you start the program.

- **Use Pop-Up Registers** opens registers in separate windows, allowing you to have several different windows with a variety of information open at the same time.

The Use Pop-Up Registers option is unavailable if you have chosen a bank, credit card, or an investing account as your Startup Location. See "Startup" earlier in this appendix.

- **Fonts/Colors** display dialogs with which you can select the font and font size as well as the colors for your register windows.

Data Entry and QuickFill   Data Entry and QuickFill options, seen next, allow you to fine-tune the way Quicken's QuickFill feature works.

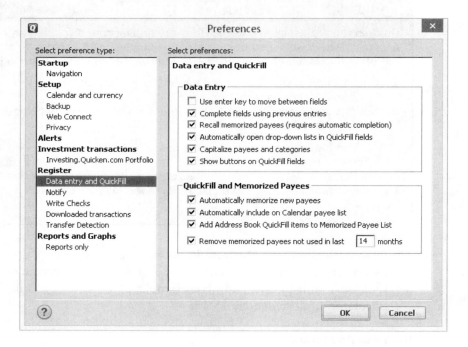

Data Entry
- **Use Enter Key To Move Between Fields** enables you to use either the ENTER or TAB key to move from field to field when entering data.
- **Complete Fields Using Previous Entries** enters transaction information using the information from previous entries.

- **Recall Memorized Payees** uses memorized payees to fill in QuickFill entries. This option is not available if the Complete Fields Using Previous Entries option is disabled.
- **Automatically Open Drop-Down Lists In QuickFill Fields** automatically displays the drop-down list when you advance to a field with a list.
- **Capitalize Payees And Categories** automatically makes the first letter of each word in a payee name or category uppercase.
- **Show Buttons On QuickFill Fields** displays drop-down list buttons on fields for which you can use QuickFill.

QuickFill and Memorized Payees

- **Automatically Memorize New Payees** tells Quicken to enter automatically all transactions for a new payee to the Memorized Payee List.
- **Automatically Include On Calendar Payee List** tells Quicken to add automatically memorized payees to the Calendar window. This option is turned on by default.
- **Add Address Book QuickFill Items To Memorized Payee List** tells Quicken to add entries from the Address Book to the Memorized Payee List so the address fields are filled in automatically when writing checks.
- **Remove Memorized Payees Not Used In Last *NN* Months** tells Quicken to remove memorized payees that have not been used within the number of months you specify. By default, this feature is turned on, with the number of months set at 14. By entering a value of 6 (for example), Quicken retains only the memorized payees for transactions you entered during the past six months, thus keeping the Memorized Payee List manageable. In this way, you can weed one-time transactions out of the Memorized Payee List. Changing this option does not affect already entered transactions. Chapter 4 discusses memorized transactions.

Notify   Notify options affect the way Quicken notifies you about problems when you enter transactions in the register:

- **When Entering Out-Of-Date Transactions** warns you when you try to record a transaction for a date more than a year from the current date.
- **Before Changing Existing Transactions** warns you when you try to modify a previously entered transaction.
- **When Entering Uncategorized Transactions** warns you when you try to record a transaction without assigning a category to it.

- **To Run A Reconcile Report After Reconcile** asks if you want to display a Reconcile Report when you complete an account reconciliation.
- **Warn If A Check Number Is Re-used** warns you if you assign a check number that was already assigned in another transaction.
- **When Changing The Account Of An Existing Transaction** notifies you when you change the account of a transaction you have already entered.
- **To Save A Transaction After Changing It** asks you if you want to save the changes you made to the last transaction you viewed.

Write Checks   Write Checks preferences affect the way the checks you create appear when printed using the Write Checks window:

- **Printed Date Style** enables you to select a four-digit or two-digit date style.
- **Spell Currency Units** tells Quicken to spell out the currency amount in the second Amount field.
- **Allow Entry Of Extra Message On Check** displays an additional text box for a message in the Write Checks window. The message you enter is printed on the check in a place where it cannot be seen if the check is mailed in a window envelope.
- **Print Categories On Voucher Checks** prints category information, including splits and tags, on the voucher part of voucher checks. This option affects only voucher-style checks.
- **Change Date Of Checks To Date When Printed** automatically prints the print date, rather than the transaction date, on each check.

After Downloaded Transactions   Downloaded Transactions preferences, which are shown next, control the way Quicken handles transactions downloaded into it from your financial institution. You learn more about downloading transactions into Quicken in Chapter 4.

- **Automatically Add To Banking Registers** saves manually reviewing and accepting each banking transaction, and possibly leaving an unaccepted transaction out of Quicken reports and graphs. Many Quicken users prefer not to use this option. This is especially true when using Cloud syncing.
- **Automatically Add To Investment Transaction Lists** saves you time by entering your downloaded transactions to your investment account "registers" rather than having to manually review and accept each transaction.

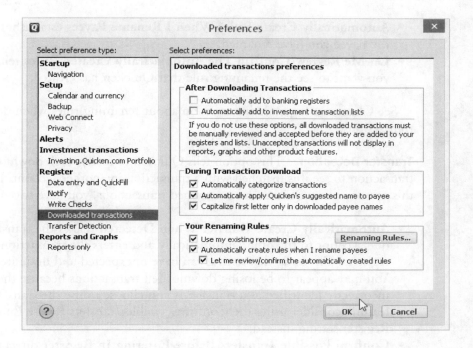

During Transaction Download

- **Automatically Categorize Transactions** sets the transaction's category based on what you have used before for that payee.
- **Automatically Apply Quicken's Suggested Name To Payee** uses Quicken's "best guess" name for the downloaded transaction. Selecting this option can, depending on your financial institution, cause some unexpected or strange payee names to appear in your downloaded payees.
- **Capitalize First Letter Only In Downloaded Payee Names** is self-explanatory.

Your Renaming Rules   The Renaming Rules options allow you control over how Quicken deals with the differences between the payee names in your records and those of the bank's.

- **Use My Existing Renaming Rules** tells Quicken to use the rules you have created to name the downloaded payee name.
- Click the **Renaming Rules** button to open the Renaming Rules dialog, which you can use to create, modify, and remove renaming rules.

- **Automatically Create Rules When I Rename Payees** establishes a rule for the payee you have renamed.
- **Let Me Review/Confirm The Automatically Created Rules** tells Quicken you want to see the renaming rule that Quicken has created.

See Chapter 4 for more information about renaming rules when downloading transactions.

Transfer Detection   This option tells Quicken to review each downloaded transaction to see if is matched with a transaction in another account. If you select this option, when Quicken finds matched transactions, you have two options:

- **Automatically Create Transfer When Detected** makes the transfer from the one account to the other automatically and enters the transaction in both registers. Choosing this setting can have unexpected and undesired results. You may appear to be losing downloaded transactions because they are incorrectly identified as a transfer. If you choose to use the transfer detection feature, consider using the Confirm Possible Transfers Before Entering In Register setting instead.
- **Confirm Possible Transfers Before Entering In Register** directs Quicken to ask you whether the transaction is, indeed, a transfer.

Reports and Graphs

Reports And Graphs preferences include two categories of options for creating reports and graphs. Chapter 5 discusses creating reports and graphs in detail.

Reports And Graphs Preferences   Reports And Graphs options enable you to set your own default options for creating reports and graphs:

- **Default Date Range** and **Default Comparison Date Range** enable you to specify a default range for regular and comparison reports. Choose an option from each drop-down list. If you choose Custom, you can always enter exact dates.
- **Report Toolbar** allows you to tell Quicken to show only icons or both icons and text.
- **Customizing Reports And Graphs** options determine how reports and graphs are customized and what happens when they are. Customizing Creates New Report Or Graph, which is the default setting, creates a subreport based on the report you customize. Customizing Modifies Current Report Or Graph changes the report you customize without creating a subreport.

- **Customize Report/Graph Before Creating** tells Quicken to offer to customize a report or graph when you choose one.

Reports Only   This group of options applies only to reports:

- **Account Display** and **Category Display** enable you to set what you want to display for each account or category listed in the report: Description, Name, or Both.
- **Use Color In Report** tells Quicken to use color when displaying report titles and negative numbers.
- **QuickZoom To Investment Forms** tells Quicken to display the investment form for a specific investment when you double-click it in an investment report. With this check box turned off, Quicken displays the investment register transaction entry instead.
- **Remind Me To Save Reports** tells Quicken to ask whether you want to save a customized report when you close the report window.
- **Decimal Places For Prices And Shares** enables you to specify the number of decimal places to display for per-share security prices and number of shares in investment reports.

Quicken Cloud Services

After you have set up your Intuit ID, you can set several preferences for your online (or Cloud) services, as seen in the following illustration:

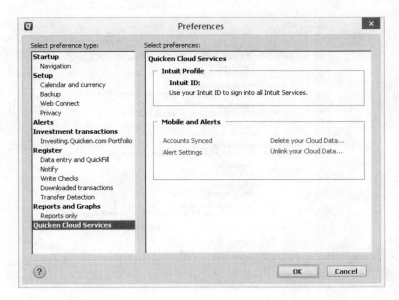

- **Intuit Profile** shows your current Intuit ID, which you use to sign in to all Intuit services.
- **Accounts Synced** opens the Edit Account Settings dialog, where you can select the accounts for which you enable access to your smart phone or tablet.
- **Delete Your Cloud Data** opens the Delete Quick Cloud Account dialog, where you can delete all online access to previously selected accounts. This does *not* delete the information from your desktop or laptop computer.
- **Unlink Your Cloud Data** simply stops synchronization between your accounts and your Quicken Cloud ID. It does not delete the Cloud ID or any of the data that has been previously synced.
- **Alert Settings** opens the Edit Alerts Settings dialog. The options in this dialog are covered in depth in Chapter 2.

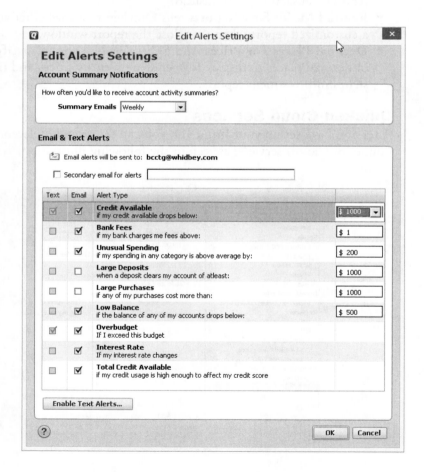

Useful Tips

While most Quicken users find the program exactly to their liking after they use some of the customization features mentioned earlier, others have questions about some specific how-tos.

Converting Your Older Quicken Files to a New Computer

After using the Quicken program for a number of years on a desktop computer, you may decide to get a new laptop and want to upgrade to Quicken 2014. Depending on the version you are running, the best way to do this is as follows:

Convert from Quicken 2004 and Newer

These steps apply to converting Quicken 2004 and newer files. If you are converting from Quicken 2003 or older, see "Use Intermediate Versions of Quicken to Convert Your Old Data Files."

1. Back up your old files before you start anything else.
2. On the "old" computer, choose File | Validate And Repair to ensure your old files are in the best shape possible. (See Appendix A for more information on Validate and Repair.)
3. Install Quicken 2014 on your "old" computer.
4. Open your Quicken data file, and let Quicken update all of your current files. Quicken will only convert the last used data file. If you have more than one data file, you will need to open each data file to convert it to Quicken 2014 format.
5. Install Quicken 2014 on your new computer. The Quicken license agreement allows you to install up to three copies of your Quicken program onto computers within your own household.
6. Copy the files from your "old" computer to your "new" computer, and you're ready to go.

Because the file format in Quicken versions prior to 2010 was different from the single file format today, it is best to convert your old data before transferring it to your new computer. That way, you will only have one data file on your new computer. That way, you won't miss a file from the pre-Quicken 2010 data file set and have a bad conversion.

When you are installing Quicken, you may see an option asking if you are a new Quicken user. If you inadvertently choose that option, you can still access your data files. Click File | Open Quicken File, and choose the data file you want to use. Your data will be converted to use with Quicken 2014.

Using Intermediate Versions of Quicken to Convert Your Old Data Files

For those users who are using Quicken 2003 or older versions, you may need to use an intermediate version of the program to convert your files to use with Quicken 2014.

Quicken 1 (through Quicken 5) for Windows users must install Quicken 6 and update their files to Quicken 6 for Windows. From there they can convert to Quicken 2004, the intermediate program for Quicken 2005 and later.

You can read more information about converting from older versions of Quicken from a website. With your Internet connection, type **http://quicken .intuit.com/support/help/GEN82211** into the address bar of your browser. From there you can even download the intermediate programs required to complete your conversion.

If you are unsure which version of Quicken you are using, click Help on the Quicken menu bar and select About Quicken.

Changing Multiple Transactions

As companies merge and life changes, you may have a recurring transaction that needs to be changed. While you can edit the payee, category, tag, or memo for current month and future transactions in the Bills tab, as explained in Chapter 4, you may want to change all of the previous transactions as well. It is not a difficult task to do so; however, as always when making any changes to your data, perform a backup before making those changes.

The process shown here assumes that the transactions are all from the same account.

1. Create a backup of your data file.
2. Open the account in which you posted the transactions.
3. Sort by the name of the item you want to change—in this example, it is the Payee.
4. Click the first item on the list and, holding your SHIFT key down, click the last item on the list. Each of the items is highlighted.

Depending on your monitor and the color preferences you have set for your register, the highlighting may be hard to distinguish.

5. Right-click one of the highlighted selections to open a context menu.
6. From the context menu choose Edit Transactions.
7. The Find And Replace dialog appears.
8. In the With field, enter the new name. Keep in mind that if you are changing something other than the payee, you will need to select the appropriate field in the Replace drop-down list.
9. Click Replace All to replace the payee name.

 If you do not want to create a renaming rule, click Cancel. You will find that you may have to choose Cancel for as many transactions as you have selected.

10. You are returned to the Find And Replace dialog. Click Done.
11. You are returned to the register where your new payee name is now showing. (Remember, you've sorted in alphabetical order, so if your new name starts with a different letter, you will have to scroll down the register to see it.)

 You can perform this same process using any register field, including Amount, Category, Memo, and Tag, as well as Check Number, Cleared Status, and Date. However, be sure to run a backup before starting the process just to ensure your data's safety.

Quicken Emergency Records Organizer

Earlier versions of Quicken included an organizational tool in which users could maintain important information about emergency contacts, personal and legal documents, mortgage and investment information, and so on. While the Attachment utility has taken over much of the necessity of using this tool, many Quicken users still rely on the data that can be kept.

You can still install the Emergency Records Organizer in Quicken 2014. To do so, first run a backup of your data file. Then, from the Quicken menu bar, click View | Classic Menus. In the Property & Debt menu, choose Emergency Records Organizer as seen here.

Depending on your computer's operating system, a message may appear asking if you want to allow the

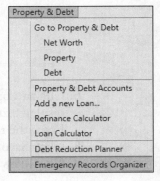

Intuit program to make changes to your computer. Click Yes and Quicken asks if you want to add the Emergency Records Organizer to Quicken. If you click Yes, the program is installed and you see a message telling you that the installation was successful.

Using the Emergency Records Organizer

After you have installed the Emergency Records Organizer, you must be using Classic menus to access it.

1. Click View | Classic Menus.
2. Click Property & Debt.
3. See the Emergency Records Organizer at the bottom of the menu. The Emergency Records Organizer window opens.
4. Click the Create/Update Records tab.
5. Click the Select An Area down arrow, and click one of the 11 areas in which to enter information.

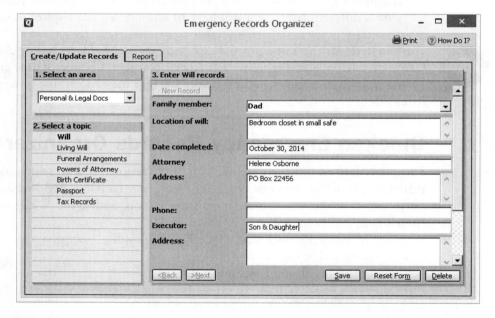

6. Click an option under Select A Topic. The records pane on the right will display text boxes to enter information pertaining to that topic.
7. Enter the relevant information in each field. Press TAB to move between fields.
8. Click Save to save the record when finished.
9. Click New Record to add another record in this topic.

Creating Reports in the Emergency Records Organizer

One of the best uses of the Emergency Records Organizer is to create reports for various professionals in case of an emergency.

With the Emergency Records Organizer displayed, click the Report tab, click the Report Type down arrow, and choose which report you want.

1. Click Sort By Family Members to include all information about each family member separately. Otherwise, it displays by topic area.
2. Click Print Topics With No Data Entered to show that data has not been entered about this topic as yet.
3. Click Print to print the report. The report goes directly to the printer. If you need more than one copy, you must click Print for each copy.
4. Click Close to exit the Emergency Records Organizer.

Index